THE CHRISTIAN WRITERS MARKET GUIDE 2018

THE CHRISTIAN WRITERS MARKET GUIDE 2018

Your Comprehensive Resource for Getting Published

STEVE LAUBE

CHRISTIAN WRITERS INSTITUTE

THE CHRISTIAN WRITERS MARKET GUIDE 2018

ISBN – 978-162-184-0862 (paperback)
ISBN – 978-162-184-0879 (ebook)

Cover design and typesetting by Five J's Design (*fivejsdesign.com*)
Edited by Lin Johnson

Printed in the United States of America.

Visit The Christian Writers Institute at *www.ChristianWritersInstitute.com*.

E-mail: *admin@christianwritersmarketguide.com*

Disclaimer: The information in this guide is provided by the individuals or companies through online questionnaires and email inquiries, as well as their websites and writers guidelines. The individuals or companies do not pay to be listed in the *Guide*. The entries in the *Guide* are not necessarily endorsed by Steve Laube or The Christian Writers Institute. Steve Laube and The Christian Writers Institute make every attempt to verify the accuracy of the information provided. The entries in the *Guide* are for information only. Any transaction(s) between a user of the information and the individuals or companies listed is strictly between those parties.

TABLE OF CONTENTS

FOREWORD

RESEARCH SAYS YOU'RE LIKELY TO SKIP THIS SECTION. BUT DON'T.

I promise not to merely tell you all about this book, which you can deduce from the "Table of Contents." Nor will I rhapsodize about Steve Laube (great as he is). In short, I want to avoid all the predictable Foreword folderol that might make you abandon it.

You bought this guide, so you could . . .

- avoid rejection slips,
- do your homework, and study the markets,
- find an agent,
- find a publishing house,
- remain a lifelong learner,
- express your faith-based worldview in your writing.

So let's stipulate that you understand what this book is all about and what it's for, and I'll launch you into it with a bit of training.

I have been emphasizing to my online students the importance of a good elevator pitch. If that's a new term to you, it's simply a label for what you would say to literary agents or editors if you found yourself with them on an elevator.

What would you say if you introduced yourself as a writer and they asked what you were working on? You have only until they reach their floor. Your goal is to get them to ask you to send your manuscript.

Two of the most common mistakes I see are: (1) assuming you have time to include character names and plot points for a novel or a list of chapter titles for a nonfiction book and (2) teasing the prospect by posing questions, the way you would try to lure readers with back-cover or advertising copy.

In truth, you shouldn't assume you'll have even sixty seconds. Your elevator pitch must be streamlined to a sentence or two. For my first novel, mine was simply, "I'm writing about a judge who tries a man for a murder the judge committed." That was either going to intrigue a buyer or it wasn't.

I didn't use character names, didn't even tell the judge's gender (which happened to be female) or what happens. The entire premise is obvious: How long could a person stand such an assault on her conscience?

As for avoiding a sales-copy approach, remember that ultimately you're pitching the professional to become your publishing partner. Don't leave that person in the dark. Give answers, not questions.

A bad example: "My nonfiction book is about a man challenged to build a ship in a bottle and make it look professional, though he is not creative or handy. Could he do it? Or will he give up in frustration?"

Rather: "My nonfiction book shows that any adult with two healthy hands can produce a professional-looking ship in a bottle, even if he or she isn't creative or handy."

That pitch tells the potential partner the premise, and it also can serve as a reminder to the writer to stay on point through the entire writing process.

A bad fiction example: "A mysterious threat causes a young prince to abandon the love of his life and confront a danger so great it could mean life or death for him."

That sounds more like a *TV Guide* blurb. The agent or editor doesn't know when this novel is set, what the threat is, what or whom is the love of his life, what the even greater danger is, or whether he succeeds or dies.

Rather: "A medieval prince discovers his fiancée is part of a plot to kill his father, so he can become king and she queen. He leads the fight against her and an army as big as the king's own and, in the process, discovers a new love."

So, cut your elevator pitch to the bone. Be sure it tells more than it asks. And also use it as a mission statement to keep you on point as you finish your book.

In the event you don't find yourself on an elevator with an agent or an editor, find one in this guide and pitch electronically. That proposal can be as long as it needs to be.

If *The Christian Writers Market Guide* plays a part in your selling a piece of your work in 2018, be sure to let Steve Laube and his team know.

Godspeed.

—Jerry B. Jenkins
www.JerryJenkins.com

INTRODUCTION

IT'S AN EXCITING TIME TO BE A WRITER! Numerous opportunities abound for great content from great authors. Traditional methods for publication have expanded due to the diversity of online opportunities. In addition, independent-publication options have made it easy to see your byline on a book, a blog post, or an online magazine.

While it may seem like the industry is shrinking, in reality it is simply changing. Thus you have to research more to find the best place for your work to shine. The problem with general online search engines is the immense number of results you receive. Then the results depend on that site's search-engine optimization. What we have done here is curate the information, so you find what is targeted specifically for the Christian market.

One of the biggest mistakes a writer can make is to ignore the guidelines of an agent, a publisher, or an editor. Some publishers even dropped their listings in this guide due to writers failing to follow the instructions posted on their websites or in here. Editors are looking for writers who understand their periodicals or publishing houses and their unique approaches to the marketplace. This book will help you be such a writer. With a little time and effort, you can meet an editor's expectations, distinguish yourself as a professional, and sell what you write.

A few periodical publishers work only by assigning topics to a select group of writers. If you work hard, you can establish yourself and your reputation among editors and become one of those go-to writers.

When approaching agents, read the material on their websites and look at the authors they represent. Most of the large publishers will work only with agents, so having a good representative is crucial. You'll find a list of agents in this guide to help you with your search.

If you can, I recommend you attend a writers conference. It is good to meet new people and become familiar with the best teachers in the industry. Many faculty members are agents or editors looking for your work even if they work for houses that don't take unsolicited manuscripts. The chapter with conferences will help you locate one.

If this is the first time you've used this guide, read the "How to Use This Book" section. If you run into an unfamiliar term, look it up in the glossary in back and learn the terminology.

May God bless your writing journey. We are on a mission to change the world, word by word. To that end, strive for excellence and make your work compelling and insightful. Great writing is still in demand. But it must be targeted, crafted, edited, critiqued, polished, and proofread until it shines.

My thanks go to Lin Johnson whose incredible work makes this all possible. She keeps tabs all year on market changes, so every listing is accurate to the best of our information. As the administrator of the online edition and the print edition, she is the genius behind the details. In addition, I would also like to acknowledge my wife, Lisa. Her love, support, and encouragement have been incalculable. We make a great team!

Steve Laube
President
The Christian Writers Institute
The Steve Laube Agency
24 W. Camelback Rd. A-635
Phoenix, AZ 85013
www.christianwritersinstitute.com
www.stevelaube.com

To update a listing or to be added to the next edition or online:
admin@christianwritersmarketguide.com

For direct sales questions, email the publisher:
admin@christianwritersinstitute.com

For books and courses on the writing craft, visit The Christian Writers Institute: *www.christianwritersinstitute.com.*

HOW TO USE THIS BOOK

***THE CHRISTIAN WRITERS MARKET GUIDE 2018* IS DESIGNED** to make it easier for you to sell your writing. It will serve you well if you use it as a springboard to become thoroughly familiar with the markets best suited to your writing style and areas of interest and expertise.

Start by getting acquainted with the setup of this guide.

Part 1 lists Christian book publishers with contact information and what they are looking for. Notice that many houses accept manuscripts only from agents or through meeting with their editors at a writers conference. If you need an agent, check the agent listings in Chapter 16.

Since independent book publishing is a viable option today, Part 2 provides resources to help you. Chapter 2 lists independent book publishers, many of which provide all the services you need as packages or à la carte services. If you decide to publish on your own, Chapters 3 and 4 list design, production, and distribution services. You'll also want to hire a professional editor, so see Chapter 19 for help in this area.

Part 3 lists periodical—magazine, newspaper, and newsletter—publishers. Chapter 5 will help you find markets by topics (e.g., marriage, evangelism) and types (e.g., how-to, poetry, personal experience). Although these lists are not comprehensive, they provide a shortcut for finding appropriate markets for your ideas.

Cross-referencing may be helpful. For example, if you have an idea for a how-to article on parenting, look at the lists in both the "how-to" and "parenting" categories. Also, don't overlook writing on the same topic for different periodicals, such as money management for a general adult magazine, a teen magazine, a women's newsletter, and a magazine for pastors. Each would require a different slant, but you would get more mileage from one idea.

If you run into words in the listings that you are not familiar with, check the glossary at the back of the book.

In Part 4, "Specialty Markets," you'll find nonbook, nonperiodical markets like daily devotionals and drama. Here you can explore types of writing you may not have thought about but that can provide a steady writing income.

As a writer, you'll need support to keep going. Part 5 provides information for various kinds of support.

One of the best ways to get published today is to meet editors at writers conferences. Check out Chapter 17 for a conference or seminar near you—or perhaps in a location you'd like to visit. Before deciding which conference to attend, check the websites for who is on faculty, what houses are represented, and what classes are offered that can help you grow your craft and writing business. You may also want to factor in the size of the conference. Don't be afraid to stretch outside your comfort zone.

For ongoing support and feedback on your manuscripts, join a writers group. Chapter 18 lists groups by state. If you can't find one near you, consider starting one or join an online group.

Since editors and agents are looking for polished manuscripts, you may want to hire a professional editor. See Chapter 19 for people who offer a variety of editorial services, including coaching.

Whether you publish your book with a royalty house or go the independent route, you'll need to do most, if not all, of the promotion. If you want to hire a specialist with contacts, check out Chapter 20, "Publicity and Marketing Services." And if you need accounting or legal help, check out Chapter 21.

Entering a writing contest can boost your sales, supplement your writing income, lead to publication, and sometimes give you valuable feedback on your writing. Check out Chapter 22 for a list of contests by genre. Many of them are not Christian oriented, but you can enter manuscripts with a Christian worldview.

Once you get acquainted with this guide, start using it. After you identify potential markets for your ideas and/or manuscripts, read their writers guidelines. If these are available on the website, the URL is included. Otherwise, email or send (with a SASE) for a copy. Also study at least one sample copy of a periodical (information to obtain one is given in most listings) or the book publisher's website to see if your idea truly fits there. Never send a manuscript without doing this market study.

Above all, keep in mind that this guide is only a starting point for your research and that change is the one constant in the publishing industry. It is impossible for any market guide to be 100 percent accurate since editors move around, publications and publishing houses close, and new ones open. But this guide is an essential tool for getting published in the Christian market and making an impact on God's Kingdom with your words.

PART 1

BOOK PUBLISHERS

1

BOOK PUBLISHERS

Before submitting your query letter or book proposal, it's critical that you read and follow a publisher's guidelines exactly. In most cases the guidelines are available on the website and a direct link is given in the listing. If you do not have a literary agent—and even if you do—check out a publisher thoroughly before signing a contract.

1517 MEDIA

See listings for Fortress Press and Sparkhouse Family.

AADEON PUBLISHING COMPANY

PO Box 223, Hartford, CT 06141

www.aadeonmedia.com

Submissions: Mail only. Query first. Nonfiction 140,000-200,000 words. Responds in six weeks. Only considers manuscripts that have been edited by a professional book copy editor.

Types and topics: cultural and moral makeup of society in the US and its impact on Christianity

Guidelines: *www.aadeonmedia.com/submissions.html*

ABINGDON PRESS

2222 Rosa L. Parks Blvd., Nashville, TN 37228-1306 | 615-749-6000

submissions@umpublishing.org | www.abingdonpress.com

Constance Stella, Bible, leadership, and theology

Dawn Woods, Christian living

Paul Franklyn, academic books

Denomination: United Methodist

Submissions: Email proposal with sample chapters. Publishes one hundred twenty titles per year; receives two thousand submissions annually. Fewer than 5% of books from first-time authors. Accepts manuscripts through agents only for Christian living. Bible: CEB.

Royalty: begins at 7.5% on net

Types and topics: seasonal for Advent, Christmas, Mother's Day, and Father's Day; spiritual and personal growth; devotional

Guidelines: *www.abingdonpress.com/submissions.html*

Tip: Looking for "any young and new voices that have active speaking and conference engagements, as well as blog and social-media followers."

ACTA PUBLICATIONS

4848 N. Clark St., Chicago, IL 60640 | 800-397-2282
acta@actapublications.com | *www.actapublications.com*
Greg Pierce, publisher

Denomination: Catholic

Submissions: Mail only with proposal and sample chapter. Accepts unsolicited manuscripts. No electronic submissions.

Royalty: no advances

Types and topics: prayer, devotions, spirituality, personal growth, social justice

Guidelines: *actapublications.com/about-us*

AMBASSADOR INTERNATIONAL

411 University Ridge, Ste. B14, Greenville, SC 29601 | 864-751-4844, 864-751-4847
publisher@emeraldhouse.com | *www.ambassador-international.com*
Sam Lowry, publisher

Submissions: Dedicated to spreading the gospel of Christ and empowering Christians through the written word. Submit proposal with three chapters through the website, email, or mail. Publishes fifty titles per year; receives seven hundred fifty submissions annually. First-time authors: 50%. Accepts manuscripts through agents or authors. Length: 144 pages minimum. Considers simultaneous submissions. Responds in one month. Bible: KJV, NIV, ESV, NKJV, NASB.

Royalty: 15-20% of net, 25% for e-books, no advance

Types and topics: theology, devotionals, biography, inspirational, children's, business, finance, topical, Bible studies; fiction for teens, new adults, and adults

Guidelines: *ambassador-international.com/get-published/submission-guidelines*

Tip: "We're most open to a book that has a clearly defined market and the author's total commitment to the project. We do well with first-time authors. We have full international coverage. Many of our titles sell globally."

AMERICAN CATHOLIC PRESS

16565 State St., South Holland, IL 60473-2025 | 708-331-5485
acp@acpress.org | *www.acpress.org, www.leafletmissal.com*
Father Michael Gilligan, editorial director

Denomination: Catholic
Submissions: Publishes four titles per year; receives ten submissions annually. Query first via mail. Average first printing 3,000. Publication within one year. No simultaneous submissions. Responds in two months. Bible: NAS.
Royalty: pays $25-100 for outright purchases only
Types and topics: only publishes material on the liturgy
Guidelines: *www.americancatholicpress.org/faq.html#faq5*

AMG PUBLISHERS

6815 Shallowford Rd., Chattanooga, TN 37421 | 800-266-4977, 423-894-6060
sales@www.amgpublishers.com | *www.amgpublishers.com*
Amanda Jenkins, author liaison

Parent company: AMG International
Submissions: "God's Word to you is our highest calling." We are unique in that proceeds from our sales are funneled into world missions through our parent organization. Publishes one to five titles per year; receives five hundred submissions annually. Query letter first. Accepts manuscripts through agents or authors. Length: 40,000-60,000 words (128-224 pages) for Bible studies, 60,000-100,000 words (208-400 pages) for trade nonfiction. Prefers accepted manuscript by email. Responds in one to four months. Bible version: prefers NASB 95, NKJV, ESV, or NIV.
Royalty: 10-20% of net, 30-40% for e-books
Guidelines: *www.amgpublishers.com/main/pdf/Prospective_ Author_ Guidelines.pdf*
Types and topics: Bible studies (highly recommended that they fit the Following God series format), devotional, applied theology, apologetics, Bible reference, African-American, Hispanic
Also does: Bible software, Bible CD-ROMs

Imprints: Living Ink Books, God and Country Press

Tip: "Most open to an interactive workbook Bible study geared for small groups that effectively taps into a largely female audience. We are currently placing priority on books with strong bibliocentric focus."

ANCIENT FAITH PUBLISHING

PO Box 748, Chesterton, IN 46304
khyde@ancientfaith.com | www.ancientfaith.com/publishing
Katherine Hyde, editorial director, adult
Jane Meyer, children's book editor, jmeyer@ancientfaith.com

Denomination: Eastern Orthodox

Submissions: Publishes twelve to sixteen adult titles per year; receives one hundred submissions annually. First-time authors: 50%. Length: 40,000-100,000 words. Email query letter only. Responds in three months. Bible: NKJV.

Royalty: 10-15%, no advance

Types and topics: Orthodox life, marriage and family, theology, spirituality, church history, memoir, biography/hagiography, Bible commentary, worship and sacraments, patristics, contemporary issues—all from Eastern Orthodox perspective; children's/YA fiction, nonfiction, picture books

Also does: small booklets

Guidelines: *www.ancientfaith.com/publishing#af-resources*

Tip: "Read and follow the guidelines. Look through our website to see the kinds of books we publish. Do not submit material that is not intended specifically for an Eastern Orthodox audience."

ANEKO PRESS

PO Box 652, Abbotsford, WI 54405
jeremiah@lspbooks.com | www.anekopress.com
Jeremiah Zeiset, president

Parent company: Life Sentence Publishing, Inc.

Submissions: Niche is publishing ministry-related books. Publishes thirty titles per year; receives one hundred fifty. First-time authors: 20%. Length: 50,000 words. Submit through the website. Responds in two weeks. Bible: Jubilee Bible, KJV, ESV, ASV.

Royalty: 30% net, no advance

Types and topics: Christian living, evangelism

Guidelines: *anekopress.com/write-for-us*

Tip: "Make sure that your writing is biblically sound, that you're writing because the Lord clearly led you to do so, and that you have a legitimate method of helping market your book."

ASHBERRY LANE PUBLISHING

PO Box 665, Gaston, OR 97119 | 503-860-5069
christina@ashberrylane.com | *ashberrylane.com*
Christina Tarabochia, acquisitions editor
Sherrie Ashcraft, co-owner

Submissions: Email proposal with first three chapters. Publishes six to nine titles per year; receives seventy submissions annually. First-time authors: 50%. Length: adult novel, 85,000-100,000 words. Responds in one month.

Royalty: 50%, paid twice a year

Types and topics: fiction only, stories that point to God while touching emotions

Guidelines: *ashberrylane.com/submissions-guidelines*

Tip: Reading a newer Ashberry Lane title will reveal what kind of writing appeals to this house.

ASPIRE PRESS

PO Box 3473, Peabody, MA 01961-3473 | 800-358-3111
info@hendricksonrose.com | *www.aspirepress.com*
Lynette Pennings, managing editor

Parent company: Hendrickson Publishers

Submissions: Publishes books that are "compassionate in their approach and rich with Scripture," giving "godly insight and counsel for those personally struggling and for believers who have a heart to minister and encourage others." Need credentials in helping others. Submit manuscripts through *ChristianManuscriptSubmissions.com*.

Types and topics: Christian living, counseling

AVE MARIA PRESS

PO Box 428, Notre Dame, IN 46556
submissions@mail.avemariapress.com | *www.avemariapress.com*
Heidi Hess Saxton, acquisitions editor

Denomination: Catholic

Submissions: Publishes twenty to twenty-five books per year; receives hundreds. Email proposal with first chapter. Responds in three to four weeks.

Guidelines: *www.avemariapress.com/manuscript-submissions*

BAAL HAMON PUBLISHERS

244 Fifth Ave., Ste. T279, New York, NY 10001 | 646-233-4017

publishers@baalhamon.com | *www.baalhamon.com*
Temitope Oyetomi, managing and acquisitions editor

Parent company: Joy and Truth Christian Ministry
Submissions: Publishes twenty to thirty books per year; receives three hundred proposals annually. First-time authors: 30%. Length: 60,000 words. Email proposal with sample chapters. Responds in three to six weeks. Bible version: NKJV.
Royalty: 30% on net, advance sometimes
Guidelines: *www.baalhamonpublishers.com/guidelines.html*
Types and topics: fiction (general, historical), biographies, Christian living, devotionals, general nonfiction, theology, African-American
Tip: "For nonfiction, include a cursory highlight of your book's comparative advantage over similar books."

BAKER ACADEMIC

6030 E. Fulton Rd., Ada, MI 49301 | 616-676-9185
submissions@bakeracademic.com | *bakerpublishinggroup.com/bakeracademic*

Parent company: Baker Publishing Group
Submissions: Publishes fifty titles per year. First-time authors: 10%. Accepts manuscripts through agents, submission services, or editor's personal contacts at writers conferences.
Royalty: standard, advance
Types and topics: religious academic books, professional books for students and church leaders
Guidelines: *bakerpublishinggroup.com/bakeracademic/contact/submitting-a-proposal*

BAKER BOOKS

6030 E. Fulton Rd., Ada, MI 49301 | 616-676-9185
bakerpublishinggroup.com/bakerbooks
Rebekah Guzman, senior acquisitions editor
Brian Thomasson, senior acquisitions editor, nonfiction

Parent company: Baker Publishing Group
Submissions: No unsolicited proposals. Agents only.
Types and topics: family, parenting, business, leadership, marriage, Christian living, spiritual growth, personal growth, self-help, memoir/personal narrative, biography, cultural engagement, theology, apologetics, church life, ministry resources
Guidelines: *bakerpublishinggroup.com/contact/submission-policy*

B&H PUBLISHING GROUP

1 Lifeway Plaza, MSN 188, Nashville, TN 37234
ManuscriptSubmission@lifeway.com | *www.bhpublishinggroup.com*
Jennifer Lyell, senior acquisitions, women's, family, parenting
Michelle Prater Burke, acquisitions and development editor, B&H Kids

Denomination: Southern Baptist
Parent company: LifeWay Christian Resources
Submissions: "Because we believe Every Word Matters, we seek to provide innovative, intentional content that is grounded in biblical truth." Query first. Publishes ninety titles per year; receives thousands of submissions annually. First-time authors: 10%. Responds in two to three months. Bible version: HCSB.
Royalty: on net, advance
Types and topics: Christian living, leadership, reference, women, Bible-study helps, church growth, college textbooks, evangelism, theology, marriage, parenting, worship, children's
Imprints: B&H Books, B&H Kids, B&H Academic, Holman Bible Publishers, Holman Reference, Broadman Church Supplies, B&H Español
Guidelines: *www.bhpublishinggroup.com/consumer-faq/#3*
Tip: "Follow guidelines when submitting. Be informed that the market in general is very crowded with the book you might want to write. Do the research before submitting."

BARBOUR PUBLISHING, INC.

PO Box 719, Uhrichsville, OH 44683 | 740-922-6045
submissions@barbourbooks.com | *www.barbourbooks.com*
Annie Tipton, senior acquisitions editor

Submissions: Fiction proposals only through agents, nonfiction by email. Responds only if interested.
Types and topics: fiction, popular Bible reference, devotions, gift books, Christian classics, children's, practical Christian living
Guidelines: *www.barbourbooks.com/pages/writersguide.aspx*

BEACON HILL PRESS

PO Box 419527, Kansas City, MO 64141
crm@nph.com | *www.nph.com*
René McFarland, submissions editor

Denomination: Nazarene
Types and topics: Christian living, spiritual growth, ministry resources
Guidelines: *www.nph.com/nphweb/html/bhol/FAQ.jsp*

BETHANY HOUSE PUBLISHERS

6030 E. Fulton Rd., Ada, MI 49301
bakerpublishinggroup.com/bethanyhouse
Raela Schoenherr, fiction acquisitions
Jeff Braun, nonfiction acquisitions

Parent company: Baker Publishing Group
Submissions: Publishes biblically based books that encourage evangelicals to grow in relationship with God. Publishes approximately eighty titles per year. First-time authors: 10%. Accepts manuscripts through agents only.
Royalty: negotiable on net, negotiable advance
Types and topics: devotionals, Christian living, spiritual life, relationships, prayer, women's interests, spiritual warfare; fiction: Amish, biblical, contemporary, contemporary romance, historical, romantic suspense, speculative, suspense
Guidelines: *bakerpublishinggroup.com/contact/submission-policy*
Tip: "We do not accept unsolicited queries or proposals."

BLING! ROMANCE

2333 Barton Oaks Dr., Raleigh, NC 27614
editor@blingromance.com | www.blingromance.com
Jessica Nelson, acquisitions editor

Parent company: LPC Books (Lighthouse Publishing of the Carolinas)
Submissions: Publishes eight books per year; receives forty proposals. First-time authors: 50%. Length: 80,000 words. Email proposal with sample chapters. Prefers submissions from agents. Responds in three months. Bible: NIV.
Types of books: POD, e-book
Royalty: 40% net, no advance
Types and topics: romance fiction
Guidelines: *www.blingromance.com/submissions*
Tip: "At Bling! the first thing readers will notice is a solid, entertaining story. Think parables. The primary objective is to entertain and engage the contemporary reader. The stories are simultaneously character- and plot-driven, written by seasoned and debut novelists with unique voices. We seek clean, wholesome stories with God's moral truths woven into the story. Please avoid sermons in stories. Bling! sells into the general market."

BLINK

3900 Sparks Dr. S.E., Grand Rapids, MI 49546 | 616-698-3431
blinkyasubmissions@harpercollins.com | *www.blinkyabooks.com*
Robyn Burwell, acquisitions editor

Parent company: HarperCollins Publishing

Submissions: Query letter only via email, from agents only. All submissions must be PG or PG-13 content with no excessive profanity, violence, drug/alcohol use, etc. First-time authors: 20%. Length 60,000-90,000 words. Replies in four to six weeks. Bible: NIV.

Royalty: depends on the project, advance

Types and topics: YA fiction and nonfiction; novels with great contemporary love stories, serious issues with heart, fun summer reads, laugh-out-loud comedy, unique fantasy or magical realism, psychological suspense (but no horror), and stories featuring characters from diverse backgrounds; plus African-American and Hispanic audiences

Guidelines: none

Tip: "Please note that Blink books do not contain overt Christian content. These books are intended to be 'clean' teen reads aimed toward the ABA market. We seek established authors, authors with growing social-media platforms, and/or authors with strong literary connections. We look for novels that have bestseller or literary award potential. We look for nonfiction by well-known individuals with a strong platform to reach readers."

BMH BOOKS

PO Box 544, Winona Lake, IN 46590 | 800-348-2756, 574-372-3098
lcgates@bmhbooks.com | *www.BMHbooks.com*
Liz Cutler Gates, executive director

Denomination: Grace Brethren

Submissons: Shows preference to Grace Brethren authors who have important and worthwhile messages that need to be heard. Trinitarian theology, dispensational eschatology, emphasis on exegesis. Publishes three to five titles per year; receives thirty submissions annually. First-time authors: 50%. Query first; no unsolicited manuscripts. Requires accepted manuscripts by email. Length: 50,000-75,000 words or 128-256 pages. Prefers not to consider simultaneous submissions. Responds in three months. Bible version: prefers KJV, NIV.

Royalty: 8-10% on retail, rarely pays an advance

Types and topics: primarily used as texts in Bible colleges, Bible institutes, and seminaries; revives and refreshes the classics; Brethren history and doctrine

Guidelines: *bmhbooks.com/faqs*

Tip: "Most open to a small-group study book or text for Bible college/ Bible institute and biblically based, timeless discipleship material."

BOLD VISION BOOKS

PO Box 2011, Friendswood, TX 77549-2011 | 832-569-4282
bvbgloria@gmail.com | *www.boldvisionbooks.com*
Gloria Penwell-Holtzlander, acquisition editor
Karen Porter, managing editor

Submissions: Publishes ten to fifteen titles per year; receives one hundred. First-time authors: 75%. Length: 60,000-70,000 words. Email proposal with sample chapters. Prefers from agents. Responds in three to six months. Bible: no preference.

Royalty: 25-50%, no advance

Types and topics: inspirational, Christian living, contemporary fiction, historical fiction, mystery

Imprints: Nuts 'n Bolts (craft books on arts and business), Optasia Books (books from beloved pastors)

Guidelines: *boldvisionbooks.com/Page_6.html*

Tip: "Follow the guidelines. Give us a fresh look at a timeless truth."

BRAZOS PRESS

6030 E. Fulton Rd., Ada, MI 49301 | 616-676-9185
submissions@brazospress.com | *bakerpublishinggroup.com/brazospress*

Parent company: Baker Publishing Group

Submissions: Publishes books that creatively draw on the riches of our catholic Christian heritage to deepen our understanding of God's creation and inspire faithful reflection and engagement. Authors typically hold advanced degrees and have established publishing platforms.

Guidelines: *bakerpublishinggroup.com/brazospress/contact/submitting-a-proposal*

BREATH OF FRESH AIR PRESS

PO Box 12, St. Clair, NSW, Australia 2759
debporter@breathoffreshairpress.com.au | *www.breathoffreshairpress.com.au*
Deborah Porter, acquisitions/submissions editor

Submissions: Publishes three to four books per year; receives ten proposals per year. First-time authors: 90%. Length:

55,000-80,000 words. Submit proposal with sample chapters by email or through the website. No agents. Responds in two months. Bible: all but KJV.

Types of books: POD only

Royalty: 7.5-15%, $100 advance

Types and topics: fiction, YA fiction, Christian living

Guidelines: *www.breathoffreshairpress.com/for-authors*

Tip: "Always looking for fresh, encouraging, slightly edgy (but not over the edge) authors."

BRIDGE LOGOS

17750 N.W. 115th Ave., Bldg. 200, Ste. 220, Alachua, FL 32615 | 386-462-2525

swooldridge@bridgelogos.com | *www.bridgelogos.com*

Peggy Hildebrand, acquisitions editor, phildebrand@bridgelogos.com

Submissions: Publishes classics, books by Spirit-filled authors, and inspirational books that appeal to the general evangelical market. Publishes forty titles per year; receives two hundred submissions annually. First-time authors: 30%. Accepts manuscripts through agents or authors. Email proposal with three to five chapters. Length: 250 pages. Responds in six weeks. Prefers accepted manuscripts by email.

Royalty: 10% on net, rarely pays advance

Types and topics: Bible study, biographies of notable Christians, business, finance, personal money management, Christian living, contemporary issues, devotionals/personal growth, encouragement, eschatology, evangelism, families and marriage, Messianic work, material on our nation's heritage (history and patriotism), men's issues, political issues, prayer, singles, social issues, Spirit-filled topics, timely topics, unusual outreach ministries, women's issues, youth, African American, Hispanic

Imprint: Synergy

Guidelines: *www.bridgelogos.com/Manuscript_Submission.html*

Tip: "Looking for well-written, timely books that are aimed at the needs of people and that glorify God. Have a great message, a well-written manuscript, and a specific plan and willingness to market your book. Looking for previously published authors with an active ministry who are experts on their subjects."

BRIMSTONE FICTION

1440 W. Taylor St., Ste. 449, Chicago, IL 60607 | 847-845-9302

rowena.brimstonefiction@gmail.com | www.brimstonefiction.com
Rowena Kuo, CEO and executive editor
Keith Osmun, acquisitions editor, keith.brimstonefiction@gmail.com
Meaghan Burnett, CFO and marketing director, brimstonefiction@gmail.com

Submissions: Brimstone Fiction is geared for YA through adult readers who enjoy speculative fiction and chiller thrillers with supernatural or paranormal elements. Publishes eight to twelve books per year; receives sixty proposals. First-time authors: 60%. Length: 60,000-100,000 words. Submit proposal with sample chapters or full manuscript by email or through the website. Prefers submissions from agents. Responds in six to eight weeks. Bible: NIV.

Types of books: POD, e-book

Royalty: 30% of profits, no advance

Types and topics: science fiction, YA fantasy and science fiction, suspense, mystery, action and adventure, romance, supernatural, paranormal, paranormal romance, paranormal suspense, contemporary women's, historical/medieval fiction, and time travel

Also does: short and full-length films

Guidelines: *brimstonefiction.com/submission-guidelines*

Tip: "We welcome new and multipublished authors and/or authors with or without agents. If you have a good story, come and meet us at writers conferences or through our website."

BROADSTREET PUBLISHING

8646 Eagle Creek Cir., Ste. 210, Savage, MN 55378 | 855-935-2000
proposals@broadstreetpublishing.com | www.broadstreetpublishing.com
David Sulka, editorial director

Submissions: Prefers working with agents but will work directly with authors. Publishes more than a hundred titles per year.

Types and topics: biographies, Majestic Expressions adult coloring books, Christian living, fiction, devotionals, and Bible promise books.

Imprint: Belle City Gifts (women's journals, devotional journals, and planners)

Guidelines: *broadstreetpublishing.com/contact*

CANDLELIGHT ROMANCE

2333 Barton Oaks Dr., Raleigh, NC 27614
editor@candlelightfiction.com | www.candlelightfiction.com
Jessica Nelson, acquisitions editor

Parent company: LPC Books (Lighthouse Publishing of the Carolinas)

Submissions: Publishes four books per year; receives twenty proposals. First-time authors: 50%. Length: 60,000-80,000 words. Email proposal with sample chapters. Prefers submissions from agents. Responds in three months. Bible: NIV.

Types of books: POD, e-book

Royalty: 40% net, no advance

Types and topics: inspirational contemporary romance fiction

Guidelines: *www.candlelightfiction.com/submissions*

Tip: "At Candlelight we agree that a romance novel should first entertain. In doing so, the story should have a strong action plot, emotional plot, and faith plot. Candlelight envisions romance as a novel incorporating depth of character as relationships develop. Romance can be exhibited in the worst of trials and circumstances or encased in a lovely evening of moonlight and roses. Candlelight stories may focus on a soft glow, an illumination of heart and soul, a flame of emotion, and/or a light to one's spiritual journey. Our realistic love stories are designed to entertain, encourage, inspire, and enlighten. We seek clean, wholesome stories with God's moral truths woven into the story. Please avoid sermons in stories. Candlelight sells into the general market."

CASCADIA PUBLISHING HOUSE

126 Klingerman Rd., Telford, PA 18969
editor@CascadiaPublishingHouse.com | *CascadiaPublishingHouse.com*
Michael A. King, publisher, editor

Submissions: Query only by mail or email.

Types and topics: creative, thought-provoking, Anabaptist-related material

Guidelines: *www.cascadiapublishinghouse.com/submit.htm*

Tip: "All Cascadia books receive rigorous evaluation and some form of peer or consultant review."

CASTLE GATE PRESS

submissions@castlegatepress.com | *www.castlegatepress.com*
Suzanne Hartman, editorial director

Submissions: Accepts submissions from agents or authors.

Length: 70,000-100,000 words. Email a query with one-page, single spaced synopsis and the first fifty pages, double-spaced.

Royalty: 50%

Types and topics: only fiction, likes speculative fiction or at least a touch of speculative, novellas, adults, new adults, young adults

Guidelines: *www.castlegatepress.com/submissions*

Tip: "We highly recommend that you have your work reviewed by other authors before submitting. We are seeking polished manuscripts with intriguing plots, compelling characters, and an understanding of basic grammar, punctuation, and writing style."

CATHOLIC BOOK PUBLISHING CORP.

77 W. End Rd., Totowa, NJ 07572 | 973-890-2400
info@catholicbookpublishing.com | *www.catholicbookpublishing.com*
Anthony Buono, editor

Denomination: Catholic

Submissions: Primarily assigns books but will look at mailed queries. No simultaneous submissions or submissions from agents. Responds in two to three months. Publication in twelve to fifteen months.

Royalty: no royalty or advances, outright purchases

Imprint: Resurrection Press

Types and topics: liturgical books, Bibles, missals, prayer books; for Resurrection Press: readable nonfiction titles for popular Catholic and general Christian markets in the areas of prayer, healing, and spirituality, as well as pastoral and liturgical resources

Guidelines: *www.catholicbookpublishing.com/faq.php#manuscript*

CHALICE PRESS

483 E. Lockwood Ave., Ste. 100, St. Louis, MO 63119 | 800-366-3383
submissions@chalicepress.com | *chalicepress.com*
Brad Lyons, publisher

Submissions: Open to receiving any publishing proposal that "aligns with our mission to publish resources inviting all people into deeper relationship with God, equipping them as disciples of Jesus Christ, and sending them into ministries as the Holy Spirit calls them. Particularly interested in publishing content by and for women, young adults (age 18 to 35), and racial/ethnic cultures for our academic, congregational leadership, and general audiences." Send email query only initially.

Types and topics: academics (homiletics, biblical studies, theology, Christian education); congregational leadership (preaching, evangelism, hospitality, leadership development, discipleship/equipping ministries); general (faith and life, inspiration/devotion, Bible study/application, mission/evangelism)

Guidelines: *www.chalicepress.com/AuthorGuidelines.aspx*
Tip: "Our theological tradition is evangelistic (we share with others our experience of God), inclusive (we are guests at a table where everyone is welcome), and mission-oriented (our gratitude to God compels us to serve others)."

CHARISMA HOUSE

600 Rinehart Rd., Lake Mary, FL 32746 | 407-333-0600
charismahouse@charismamedia.com | *www.charismamedia.com*
Maureen Eha, acquisitions editor

Submissions: To inspire and equip people to live a Spirit-led life and walk in the divine purpose for which they were called. Accepts proposals only through agents. Publishes one hundred fifty titles per year; receives fifteen hundred submissions annually. First-time authors: 65%. Reprints books. Length: 55,000 words. Responds in one to two months.
Royalty: on net or outright purchase, advance
Topics and types: Charisma House: Charismatic/Pentecostal perspective on Christian living, work of the Holy Spirit, prophecy, prayer, Scripture, adventures in evangelism and missions, popular theology. Siloam: living in good health—body, mind, and spirit, including alternative medicine; diet and nutrition; and physical, emotional, and psychological wellness; prefers manuscripts from certified doctors, nutritionists, trainers, and other medical professionals. Frontline: contemporary political and social issues from a Christian perspective. Realms: adult Christian fiction in the supernatural, speculative genre, 80,000-120,000 words; also considers historical or biblical fiction if supernatural element is substantial. Excel: targeted toward success in the workplace and businesses. Casa Creación: books in Spanish; contact: 800-987-8432; *casacreacion@charismamedia.com*; *www.casacreacion.com*. Publicaciones Casa: same as Creation House but for people who like to copublish in Spanish; contact same as Casa Creación.
Guidelines: *charismahouse.com/index.php/submit-book-proposal*

CHICKEN SOUP FOR THE SOUL BOOKS

See listing in the periodicals section, "**Adult Markets**."

CHOSEN

6030 E. Fulton Rd., Ada, MI 49301 | 616-676-9185
bakerpublishinggroup.com/chosen

Kim Bangs, nonfiction acquisitions editor

Parent company: Baker Publishing Group
Submissions: Email proposal with two chapters.
Types and topics: Charismatic, Spirit-filled life, a few thematic narratives
Guidelines: *bakerpublishinggroup.com/chosen/contact/preparing-a-proposal-for-chosen-books*

CHRISTIAN FOCUS PUBLICATIONS

Geanies House, Fearn, Tain, Ross-shire IV20 1TW, Scotland, UK | 01862 871011
submissions@christianfocus.com | *christianfocus.com*
Catherine Mackenzie, children's editor, Catherine.Mackenzie@christianfocus.com

Submissions: Submit proposal with two chapters by email or mail.
Types and topics: Christian Focus: popular works, including biographies, commentaries, basic doctrine, and Christian living. Mentor: written at a level suitable for Bible college and seminary students, pastors, and other serious readers, including commentaries, doctrinal studies, examination of current issues, and church history. Christian Heritage: classic writings from the past. Children's: Bible story books, devotionals, craft books, puzzle books, activity books, game books, material for family devotions, biography series (Trailblazers for ages 9-14, retells the stories of well-known Christians past and present; Torchbearers for ages 8-11 about real martyrs), and several fiction series.
Guidelines: adults: *www.christianfocus.com/pages/guidelines_adult/-/-* | children: *www.christianfocus.com/pages/guidelines_children/-/-*
Tip: "Read our website please. Don't send us stuff we don't publish."

CISTERCIAN PUBLICATIONS

dutton@ohio.edu | *www.cistercianpublications.org*
Marsha L. Dutton, executive editor

Submissions: Prefers a proposal. All submissions must be accompanied by a summary form that's available on the website. Before submitting a manuscript, request the style sheet and instructions.
Types and topics: studies on the Christian monastic tradition and monographs reflecting contemplative monastic spirituality
Guidelines: *www.cistercianpublications.org/Contact/manuscript*

CLADACH PUBLISHING

PO Box 336144, Greeley, CO 80633 | 970-371-9530
office@cladach.com | *www.cladach.com*
Catherine Lawton, publisher, editor, cathyl@cladach.com

Submissions: Publishes four or five titles per year. First-time authors: 58%. Considers book proposals from authors met at writers conferences or when introduced through present authors or mutual acquaintances, including literary agents. Query letter first, preferably by email in the message. Length: 180-224 pages. Responds in three months. Bible: NIV, NRSV.

Royalty: 7-20% on net, $100 advance

Types and topics: creative nonfiction, memoir, poetry, fiction (historical, frontier, contemporary; prefers stories set in Colorado), nature writings, devotional, relationships, some compilations

Guidelines: *cladach.com/authors*

Tip: "We are family owned and small enough to be entrepreneurial, to take risks on new authors and ideas. Peruse the titles and authors on our website, read our books in your interest area."

CLC PUBLICATIONS

PO Box 1449, Fort Washington, PA 19034
submissions@clcpublications.com | *www.clcpublications.com*
Colleen Kelly, acquisitions

Parent company: CLC Ministries International

Submissions: Publishes sixteen titles per year; receives one hundred fifty submissions. First-time authors: 50%. Length: 150-200 pages. Email proposal with sample chapters. Responds in six to eight weeks. Bible: ESV.

Royalty: 12-16% net, advance sometimes

Types and topics: Christian living, church life, church renewal, marriage, family, relationships, missions, evangelism, prayer, discipleship

Guidelines: *www.clcpublications.com/about/prospective-authors-submissions*

Tip: "We are most open to manuscripts that bring a fresh and unique perspective on timeless subjects that are relevant to the daily lives of Christians. We prefer first-time authors to have an established platform (blogs, social media, affiliations with larger churches and ministries, etc.)."

COLLEGE PRESS PUBLISHING

PO Box 1132, 2111 N. Main St., Ste. C, Joplin, MO 64801 | 800-289-3300
collpressjoplin@gmail.com | *www.collegepress.com*

Denomination: Christian Churches/Churches of Christ
Submissions: Requires a query or proposal first. Responds in two to three months.
Types and topics: Bible studies, topical studies (biblically based), apologetic studies, historical biographies of Christians
Guidelines: *www.collegepress.com/pages/for-authors*

CONCORDIA PUBLISHING HOUSE

3558 S. Jefferson Ave., St. Louis, MO 63118-3968 | 314-268-1080
ideas@chph.org | *www.cph.org*
Rev. Paul T. McCain, publisher, executive director of editorial, paul.mccain@cph.org

Denomination: Lutheran Church, Missouri Synod
Submissions: Send proposal and sample chapters. Publication within two years. Responds in six weeks.
Types and topics: nonfiction, fiction, no longer looking for children's books
Guidelines: *www.cph.org/t-about-faq.aspx*

CROSSLINK PUBLISHING

558 E. Castle Pines Pkwy., Ste. B4117, Castle Rock, CO 80108 | 888-697-4851
publisher@crosslinkpublishing.com | *www.crosslinkpublishing.com*
Rick Bates, managing editor

Parent company: CrossLink Ministries
Submissions: As a small publisher, it is author focused, processes are nimble, and it prides itself on having the most transparent and participative publishing process in the industry. Publishes thirty-five titles per year in paperback. Receives five hundred submissions annually. First-time authors: 85%. Requires manuscript submission on the website. Length: 12,000-60,000 words. Responds in a week.
Royalty: 10% of retail, 20% for e-books, no advance.
Types and topics: adult fiction, Bible studies, devotional, inspirational, meditations, spiritual growth areas
Imprint: New Harbor Press
Guidelines: *www.crosslinkpublishing.com/faq*
Tip: "We are particularly interested in providing books that help Christians succeed in their daily walk (inspirational, devotional, small groups, etc.)."

CROSSRIVER MEDIA GROUP

PO Box 187, Brewster, KS 67732 | 785-269-4730
info@crossrivermedia.com | *www.crossrivermedia.com*
Tamara Clymer, fiction editor, tamara@crossrivermedia.com
Debra L. Butterfield, nonfiction editor, deb@crossrivermedia.com

Submissions: Publishes four to eight titles per year; receives sixty to seventy-five submissions annually. First-time authors: 50%. Accepts but doesn't require submissions through agents. Length: 60,000-80,000 words. Email proposal with sample chapters. Responds in three to four months. Bible: any except NIV.
Royalty: 8-12%, negotiable, no advance
Types and topics: inspirational fiction for adults (contemporary, historical, biblical, romance); Bible studies, Christian living, family and marriage, inspirational, church growth, children
Imprints: CrossRiver, CrossRiver Kids
Guidelines: *www.crossrivermedia.com/about/manuscript-submissions*
Tip: "Read our website, and follow the guidelines."

THE CROSSROAD PUBLISHING COMPANY

submissions@crossroadpublishing.com | *www.crossroadpublishing.com*

Submissions: Open to unsolicited proposals; email submissions only. Responds in six to eight weeks. Accepts submissions from agents or authors.
Royalty: yes, no advance
Types and topics: spirituality, Christian living, theology
Guidelines: *www.crossroadpublishing.com/crossroad/static/for-authors*

CROSSWAY

1300 Crescent St., Wheaton, IL 60187 | 630-682-4300
submissions@crossway.org | *www.crossway.org*
Jill Carter, editorial administrator (submit to her)

Parent company: Good News Publishers
Submissions: Publishes eighty titles per year; receives one thousand plus. First-time authors: 1%. Length: 25,000 words and up. Email, mail, or submit through the website a proposal with sample chapters. Responds in six to eight weeks. Bible: ESV.
Royalty: varies, variable advance
Types and topics: biblical studies, Christian living, current issues
Guidelines: *www.crossway.org/submissions*
Tip: "Be sure to look at our guidelines and see if your project fits. A well-written proposal is vital."

CSS PUBLISHING GROUP, INC.

5450 N. Dixie Hwy., Lima, OH 45807-9559 | 419-227-1818
editor@csspub.com | *www.csspub.com*
Missy Cotrell, managing editor

Submissions: Serves the needs of pastors, worship leaders, and parish program planners in the broad Christian mainline of the American church. Prefers query first but will also look at proposals with a sample chapter(s) by email or mail. Publishes fifteen titles per year; receives five hundred to a thousand submissions annually. First-time authors: 50%. Length: 100-125 pages. Responds in three weeks to six months. Bible version: NRSV.

Royalty: none, no advance, outright purchase

Types and topics: lectionary-based resources for worship, preaching, group study, drama, and use with children (but not children's books); sermons, preaching, and worship resources for special seasons and days of the church year and special themes or emphasis; children's object lessons and sermons; resources for working with youth; pastoral aids, such as materials to assist in counseling; easy-to-perform dramas and pageants for all age groups, primarily for Advent/Christmas/Epiphany and Lent/Easter (no full-length plays), parish-tested materials for use in education, youth ministry, stewardship, and church growth; a few general titles

Guidelines: *store.csspub.com/page.php?Custom%20Pages=10*

Imprints: Fairway Press (see separate listing in "Independent Book Publishers"), B.O.D. (Books On Demand)

Tip: "We're looking for authors who will help with the marketing of their books."

DAVID C. COOK

4050 Lee Vance Dr., Colorado Springs, CO 80918 | 719-536-0100
www.davidccook.org
Alice Crider, senior acquisitions and development editor

Submissions: Accepts proposals only from agents. Publishes forty books per year; receives four hundred proposals. First-time authors: 15%. Responds in one month. Bible: NIV.

Royalty: varies, advance varies

Types and topics: Christian living, discipleship, spiritual growth, marriage, parenting, leadership, women's, men's

Guidelines: *www.davidccook.com/about/Manuscript-Submission*

Tip: "Attend a writers conference to meet agents and editors."

DAWN PUBLICATIONS

12402 Bitney Springs Rd., Nevada City, CA 95959 | 530-274-7775
submission@dawnpub.com | *www.dawnpub.com*
Carol Malnor, acquisitions editor

Submissions: Dedicated to inspiring in children a sense of appreciation for all of life on earth through creative nonfiction. Publishes six titles per year; receives twenty-five hundred submissions annually. New authors: 35%. Accepts manuscripts through agents or authors. Submit complete manuscript by mail or email. Responds in six months.

Royalty: on net, advance

Types and topics: picture books, some chapter books for middle grade

Guidelines: *www.dawnpub.com/submission-guidelines*

Tip: "Most open to creative nonfiction. We look for nature awareness and appreciation titles that promote a relationship with the natural world and specific habitats, usually through inspiring treatment and nonfiction."

DESERT BREEZE PUBLISHING

submissions@desertbreezepublishing.com | *www.desertbreezepublishing.com*
Gail Delaney, editor

Submissions: Novellas 25,000-35,000 (prefers 30,000); super books (more than 100,000 words). Prefers 55,000-80,000 words. Will consider series. No simultaneous submissions. Releases six to twelve titles per month.

Types and topics: romance fiction in a variety of subgenres, women's fiction with or without romance, variety of YA and new-adult fiction

Guidelines: *www.desertbreezepublishing.com/submissions*

Tip: "We are actively seeking inspirational and Christian novels with a bit more real-world flair. It's not always easy being a Christian, and we would like to see novels that express that."

DISCOVERY HOUSE PUBLISHERS

PO Box 3566, Grand Rapids, MI 49501 | 800-653-8333, 616-942-9218
submissions@dhp.org | *www.dhp.org*
Andrew Rogers, acquisitions editor

Parent company: Our Daily Bread Ministries

Submissions: Publishes nonfiction books that feed the soul with the Word of God. Publishes fourteen titles per year; receives three hundred submissions annually. First-time authors: 10%. Accepts manuscripts through agents or authors. Send proposal with sample chapters by email or mail; if by email, put "Attn: Ms Review Editor" in the subject line. Responds in four to six weeks.

Royalty: 10-15% on net, no advance

Types and topics: devotional, Bible study and Bible reference materials, spiritual growth, personal growth, contemporary issues from a Christian viewpoint, memoir, children's

Guidelines: *dhp.org/writers-guidelines* (FAQ#6)

Tip: "Trying to acquire authors who can speak to boomers, millennials, or both. We're looking for compelling nonfiction that drives people to Jesus through the truth of the Bible. We're passing on niche products."

DIVINE MOMENTS BOOKS

See listing in periodicals section, "**Adult Markets**."

DOULOS RESOURCES

195 Mack Edwards Dr., Oakland, TN 38060 | 901-201-4612
submissions@doulosresources.org | *www.doulosresources.org*

Submissions: Requires email query first; no attachments. Responds in one to two months. Publishes four to six titles annually. Publication in twelve to eighteen months.

Types and topics: practical theology, leadership resources, curricula, and resources for dissemination among congregations

Imprint: Kalos Press (literary fiction, memoir, biography, devotional, Christian reflection, nonfiction essays)

Guidelines: *www.doulosresources.org/about/about/submissions.html*

Tip: "We publish works that are theologically consistent with the Westminster Confession of Faith; other traditions and theological trajectories will be considered accordingly. We are not interested in submissions with a polemical tone or an aggressive/antagonistic ethos; axes should be ground elsewhere. Follow our submission guidelines closely."

DOVE CHRISTIAN PUBLISHERS

PO Box 611, Bladensburg, MD 20710-0611 | 240-342-3293
submissions@dovechristianpublishers.com | *www.dovechristianpublishers.com*
Raenita Wiggins, acquisitions editor

Submissions: Submit proposal with full manuscript through the website. Publishes ten books per year; receives six hundred proposals. First-time authors: 90%. Responds in three to four weeks. Length: 200-350 pages. Bible: NIV.

Books: POD, e-books
Royalty: 10-25%, no advance
Types and topics: Christian living, ministry help, devotionals, relationships, fiction (romance, fantasy, suspense, historical, contemporary), poetry, children's, African-American, Hispanic
Guidelines: *www.dovechristianpublishers.com/publish-with-us*
Tip: "Examine and adhere to our website writers guidelines carefully."

EARTHEN VESSEL PUBLISHING

9 Sunny Oaks Dr., San Raphael, CA 94903 | 415-302-1199
kentphilpott@comcast.net | *www.earthenvesseljournal.com*
Kent and Katie Philpott, editors

Denomination: Baptist
Submissions: Publishes three titles per year; receives forty proposals. First-time authors: 50%. Email proposal with sample chapters. Responds in one week. Length: 200 pages. Bible: any.
Types of books: paperback, e-book, POD
Royalty: 50%, no advance
Guidelines: none
Types and topics: theology, Islam, evangelism, testimonies, some fiction, African-American, Hispanic
Tip: "Conversation over the phone."

EERDMANS BOOKS FOR YOUNG READERS

2140 Oak Industrial Dr. N.E., Grand Rapids, MI 49505 | 800-253-7521, 616-459-4591
youngreaders@eerdmans.com | *www.eerdmans.com/youngreaders*
Kathleen Merz, managing editor

Parent company: Wm. B. Eerdmans Publishing Co.
Submissions: Strives to publish books that are honest, wise, and hopeful, books that will stand the test of time. Submit by mail to Acquisitions Editor. For children and teens, send a proposal with three chapters for book length or complete manuscript for picture books. Publishes twelve to eighteen titles per year; receives two to three thousand submissions annually. First-time authors: 10%. Accepts manuscripts through agents or authors. Length: picture books, 1,000 words; middle-grade books, 15,000 words; young adult, 35,000 words. Publication within one year for novels, two to three years for picture books. Responds in three to four months if interested.

Royalty: 5-7% on retail, 7-9% on net, advance varies

Types and topics: picture books, middle-grade and young-adult fiction and nonfiction; looking for stories that celebrate diversity, stories of historical significance, and stories that relate to contemporary social issues

Guidelines: *www.eerdmans.com/Pages/Default.aspx?ContentID=2237&Title=EBYR-Guidelines*

Tip: "We are always looking for well-written picture books and novels for young readers. Make sure that your submission is a unique, well-crafted story, and take a look at our current list of titles to get a sense of whether yours would be a good fit for us."

WM. B. EERDMANS PUBLISHING CO.

2140 Oak Industrial Dr. N.E., Grand Rapids, MI 49505 | 800-253-7521, 616-459-4591
info@eerdmans.com | *www.eerdmans.com*
Lil Copan, senior acquisitions editor

Submissions: Publishes about a hundred titles per year. Accepts manuscripts through agents or authors. Email proposal only. Responds in six weeks.

Royalty: yes, some advances

Topics and types: adult nonfiction, textbooks, reference, biblical studies, theology, religious history and biography, ethics, spirituality, Christian living, ministry, social issues, contemporary cultural issues

Imprint: Eerdmans Books for Young Readers (see separate listing)

Guidelines: *www.eerdmans.com/Pages/About/Submission-Guidelines.aspx*

Tip: "Review submission guidelines carefully and check recent catalogs for suitability. Target readerships range from academic to semipopular. We are publishing a growing number of books in Christian life, spirituality, and ministry."

eLECTIO PUBLISHING

4206 S. Mentor Ave., Springfield, MO 65804 | 972-987-0015
submissions@electiopublishing.com | *www.electiopublishing.com*

Submissions: Publishes sixty to one hundred titles per year; receives a thousand annually. First-time authors: 70-80%. Length: 25,000-100,000 words. Email full manuscript. Responds in three months.

Royalty: 20%, no advance

Types and topics: Christian living, fiction (historical, romance, mystery), Bible studies, memoir, YA, African-American, Hispanic

Guidelines: *www.electiopublishing.com/index.php/submissions*

Tip: "Please read carefully the submissions guidelines listed on website."

ELK LAKE PUBLISHING, INC.

35 Dogwood Dr., Plymouth, MA 02360-3166 | 508-746-1734
Deb@ElkLakePublishingInc.com | *ElkLakePublishingInc.com*
Deb Haggerty, publisher & editor-in-chief

Submissions: Publishes forty-plus titles per year; receives a hundred plus. First-time authors: 80%. Length: 80,000-100,000 words. Email proposal with sample chapters. Prefers submissions from agents. Replies in one week. Bible: NKJV, NASB.

Books: POD, e-book

Royalty: 40%, no advance

Types and topics: 95% fiction (mystery, romance, speculative, historical, suspense, children, middle grade, YA), Christian living

Guidelines: *www.elklakepublishinginc.com/proposal-guidelines*

Tip: "Be different, be good, have an error-free proposal."

ELLECHOR PUBLISHING HOUSE, LLC

Beaverton, OR 97006 | 559-744-3553
contactus@ellechorpublishing.com | *www.ellechorpublishinghouse.com*
Veronika Walker, managing editor
Sharon Jenkins, acquisitions editor

Submissions: Publishes fifteen titles per year; receives two hundred fifty submissions annually. First-time authors: 90%. Submit complete manuscript through the form on the website. Responds in three to four weeks. Prefers no simultaneous submissions. Accepts submissions through agents. Length: 65,000 words or 280 pages. Bible: KJV.

Royalty: 10-30% on net, 30-50% for e-books, no advance

Types and topics: preschool, young adult, and adults; fiction; practical Christian living; questions and issues of contemporary Christian youth; women's concerns; singles

Guidelines: *www.ellechorpublishinghouse.com/faqs.cfm#how-to-submit*

EMPOWERED PUBLICATIONS, INC.

529 County Road 31, Millry, AL 36558 | 251-754-9335
editor@empoweredpublicationsinc.com | *www.empoweredpublicationsinc.com*

Denomination: Conservative Pentecostal (Assemblies of God, Church of God, independent Pentecostals)

Submissions: Publishes thirty-six titles per year; receives five hundred annually. First-time authors: 80%. Length: 35,000 for nonfiction, 65,000- 80,000 for fiction. Email or mail proposal with full manuscript. Replies in two weeks. Bible version: KJV.

Royalty: 8-30%

Types and topics: Christian living; theology; biographies; pneumatology; historical, biblical, contemporary fiction for all ages

Guidelines: *www.empoweredpublicationsinc.com/about-us.html*

Tip: "We prefer submissions from those with an established ministry, but will consider works from a lay person recommended by a minister personally known to us. Potential authors must agree with our Statement of Faith. No prosperity preaching."

ENCLAVE PUBLISHING

24 W. Camelback Rd. A-635, Phoenix, AZ 85013 | 602-336-8910
acquisitions@enclavepublishing.com | *www.enclavepublishing.com*
Steve Laube, publisher and acquisitions editor

Parent company: Gilead Publishing

Submissions: Enclave is the premier publisher of Christian fantasy and science fiction. Publishes twelve titles per year; receives more than three hundred submissions annually. Responds in two to three months. First-time authors: 20-30%. Submit proposal and full manuscript through the website form. Length: 70,000-150,000 words.

Royalty: varies

Types and topics: only speculative fiction (sci-fi, fantasy, supernatural) for adults and YA

Guidelines: *www.enclavepublishing.com/guidelines*

Tip: "Keep word count above 70,000 words and below 150,000. Too often we are sent books that are either far too short or extremely long."

EVERGREEN PRESS

5601-D Nevius Rd., Mobile, AL 36619 | 251-861-2525
brian@evergreenpress.com | *www.evergreenpress.com*
Brian Banashak and Kathy Banashak, editors-in-chief

Parent company: Genesis Communications

Submissions: Publishes books that empower people for breakthrough living by being practical, biblical, and engaging. Publishes thirty titles per year; receives two hundred fifty submissions annually. First-time authors: 40%. Accepts manuscripts through agents or authors. Submit proposal, query, or full manuscript with the "Author and Book Submission Form" on the website. Length: 96-160 pages. Responds in four to six weeks.

Royalty: on net, no advance

Types and topics: Christian living, family and parenting, personal growth, business and finances, humor and pets, children's picture books, youth books, devotional and prayer, health and fitness, and recovery; fiction: allegories, historical, fantasy and science fiction, mysteries, romance, and youth

Also does: booklets

Imprints: Gazelle Press, Axiom Press (POD for short runs)

Guidelines: *evergreenpress.com/for-authors*

Tip: "Most open to books with a specific market (targeted, not general) that the author is qualified to write for and that is relevant to today's believers and seekers. Author must also be open to editorial direction."

FAITH ALIVE CHRISTIAN RESOURCES

1700 28th St. S.E., Grand Rapids, MI 49508-1407 | 800-333-8300, 616-224-0728

rvanderhart@crcna.org | www.faithaliveresources.org

Ruth Vanderhart, managing editor

Denomination: Christian Reformed

Submissions: Submit by mail or email. Responds in one month.

Types and topics: educational curricula for children, teens, and adults; Bible studies; church leadership and training materials

FAITHWORDS

1290 Avenue of the Americas, New York, NY 10104

www.faithwords.com

Keren Baltzer, senior editor

Parent company: Hachette Livre

Submissions: Through agents only. Publishes seventy-five books per year; receives three hundred fifty. First-time authors: 50%. Length: 50,000 words. Responds in one month. Bible: ESV, NIV.

Types of books: offset paperback, hardcover, e-book

Royalty: 10% and up, advance

Types and topics: for Christian women ages 25-45: parenting, marriage, Christian living, social issues, spiritual issues, African-American, Hispanic

Guidelines: *www.hachettebookgroup.com/about/faqs/#submissions*

Tip: "Have a clear, well-written proposal and a solid platform."

FANATIC PUBLISHING, LLC

submissions@fanaticpublishing.com | *www.fanaticpublishing.com*

Submissions: Publishes four books per year, receives a hundred plus proposals per year. First-time book authors: 50%. Length: 108+ pages. Email proposal with complete manuscript. Responds in two weeks. Bible: KJV.

Royalty: negotiable, sometimes offers a negotiable advance

Types and topics: nonfiction and fiction, anything and everything from a biblical perspective no matter how controversial

Guidelines: *www.fanaticpublishing.com/new-authors-wanted*

Tip: "Be yourself, and let God take care of the rest."

FATHER'S PRESS

590 N.W. 1921 St. Rd., Kingsville, MO 64061-9312 | 816-566-0654
mike@fatherspress.com | *www.fatherspress.com*
Mike Smitley, editor

Submissions: Accepts manuscripts only through authors; no agents. Send proposal. Responds in four weeks. Bible versions: KJV, ESV.

Types and topics: fiction (contemporary or historical), historical nonfiction, reference, children's books, biblical studies, theology, ethics, literature, religious history, regional history, cookbooks, self-help, Christian counseling

Guidelines: *fatherspress.com/?page_id=2380*

Tip: "Father's Press is a rapidly-growing, full-service publishing company dedicated to publishing well-written works by dynamic, energetic new authors who are frustrated with the endless barriers that have historically locked talented authors out of the writing profession."

FIREFLY SOUTHERN FICTION

2333 Barton Oaks Dr., Raleigh, NC 27614
fireflysouthernfiction@aol.com | *www.fireflysouthernfiction.com*
Eva Marie Everson, acquisitions editor

Parent company: LPC Books (Lighthouse Publishing of the Carolinas)

Submissions: Publishes six books per year; receives forty proposals. First-time authors: 50%. Length: 65,000-90,000 words. Email proposal with sample chapters. Prefers submissions from agents. Responds in three months. Bible: NIV.

Types of books: POD, e-book

Royalty: 40% net, no advance

Types and topics: southern fiction with family culture, history, and values; also African-American audience

Guidelines: *www.fireflysouthernfiction.com/submissions*

Tip: "Southern fiction is about story, driven by characters who are distinctly southern and/or characters who move to southern settings (which are also characters). Southern fiction is strong in faith and religion and in family, family history, and family values. Characters include people as well as small towns, big cities, houses with wrap-around porches, plantations, farmhouses, and shanties. Landscape is as important to story as plot and character. Sells to the general market."

FIRST STEPS PUBLISHING

PO Box 571, Gleneden Beach, OR 97388
submissions@FirstStepsPublishing.com | *www.FirstStepsPublishing.com*
RJ McRoberts, submissions, account manager

Submissions: Publishes two to six titles per year; receives thirty-five proposals. First-time authors: 80%. Length: children's, 700 words minimum; fiction and nonfiction, 25,000-150,000 words. Email query or proposal with sample chapters through the website. Responds in four to six weeks. Bible: ASV, NKJV.

Types: POD, e-book, offset of 100-500 to start

Royalty: 15-35%, higher for special cases, no advance

Types and topics: fiction (cozy mystery, mystery/suspense, future / fantasy, contemporary, historical romance, historical), historical/ creative, memoir, biography, true stories

Imprints: White Parrot Press (children), West Wind Press (middle grade, young adult, new adult)

Guidelines: *www.firststepspublishing.com/get-published*

Tip: "Please follow our online submission guidelines. Put forth your best effort, offering a well-edited and polished piece that demands to be read."

FOCUS ON THE FAMILY

8605 Explorer Dr., Colorado Springs, CO 80995 | 719-531-5181
www.focusonthefamily.com
Steve Johnson, associate publisher

Submissions: Accepts manuscripts only via established literary agents or manuscript services. Only specific types of books are being considered.

Types and topics: family advice topics, including resources about specific elements of marriage and parenting, encouragement for women, and topics for seniors

Guidelines: *family.custhelp.com/app/answers/detail/a_id/4501/related/1*

FORGET ME NOT ROMANCES

PO Box 8047, Surprise, AZ 85374 | 623-910-4279
cynthiahickey@outlook.com | *www.forgetmenotromances.com*
Cynthia Hickey, editor

Parent company: Winged Publications

Submissions: Publishes twenty-five titles per year; receives fifty annually. First-time authors: 50%. Length: 45,000-80,000 words. Email proposal with sample chapters. Replies in two weeks. Publishes POD. Bible version: NIV.

Royalty: 60%, sometimes gives advance

Types and topics: only fiction: historical romance, contemporary romance, romantic suspense, cozy mystery; clean, wholesome stories

Guidelines: *forgetmenotromances.com/for-authors/submissions*

Tip: "Have a good grasp of the craft; but, most importantly, tell a good story."

FORTRESS PRESS

PO Box 1209, Minneapolis, MN 55440-1209
www.fortresspress.com

Denomination: Evangelical Lutheran Church in America

Parent company: 1517 Media

Submissions: Submit via the online form.

Types and topics: scholarly works in biblical studies, theology, and Christian history

Guidelines: *fortresspress.com/submissions*

FORWARD MOVEMENT

412 Sycamore St., Cincinnati, OH 45202-4110 | 800-543-1813
editorial@forwardmovement.org | *www.forwardmovement.org*

Denomination: Episcopal Church

Submissions: Focuses on discipleship. Submit through email. Responds in four to six weeks. Also does: PDF downloads, smartphone applications

Types and topics: prayer, spiritual practices, stewardship, church traditions, emerging trends, Bible study

Guidelines: *www.forwardmovement.org/Pages/About/Writers_Guidelines.aspx*

FOUR CRAFTSMEN PUBLISHING

PO Box U, Lakeside, AZ 85929-0585 | 928-367-2076
info@fourcraftsmen.com | *www.fourcraftsmen.com*
CeCelia Jackson, editor in chief | *Martin Jackson, publisher*

Submissions: Publishes three books per year; receives five proposals. First-time authors: 100%. Length: 40,000-80,000 words. Submit proposal with sample chapters by email, mail, or website. Responds in three weeks. Bible: all modern versions.

Books: POD, e-book

Royalty: 10-20% print, 50-70% ebook, no advance

Types and topics: testimony, Scripture studies, Christian living, finances, marriage

Guidelines: *fourcraftsmen.com/additional-info*

Tip: "Describe experience illuminating Scripture truth and encouraging hope, faith and active walking by/with the Holy Spirit."

FRANCISCAN MEDIA

28 W. Liberty St., Cincinnati, OH 45202 | 800-488-0488, 513-241-5615
info@franciscanmedia.org | *www.FranciscanMedia.org*
Mark Lombard, director, acquisitions, MLombard@FranciscanMedia.org

Denomination: Catholic

Submissions: Seeks manuscripts that inform and inspire adult Catholics, other Christians, and all who are seeking to better understand and live their faith. Goal is to help people "Live in love. Grow in faith." Not accepting unsolicited manuscripts. Publishes twenty to thirty books per year. Submit proposal by email or mail. Responds in one to three months. Length: 25,000-50,000 words or 100-250 pages. Bible: NRSV. No simultaneous submissions.

Royalty: 10-14% on net, advance $1,000-3,000

Topics and types: Christian living, spiritual growth, fiction

Guidelines: *www.franciscanmedia.org/writers-guide*

FRIENDS UNITED PRESS

101 Quaker Hill Dr., Richmond, IN 47374 | 765-962-7573
friendspress@fum.org | *friendsunitedmeeting.org*

Denomination: Quaker

Submissions: Submit proposal with two or three chapters by mail or email; responds in three to six months. Publishes two to five books per year.

Royalty: 7.5%, no advance

Types and topics: Quaker/Friends history, theology, biography, spirituality, peace, and justice

Guidelines: *shop.fum.org/category_s/38.htm*

GILEAD PUBLISHING

3040 Charlevoix Dr. S.E., Ste. 150, Grand Rapids, MI 49546
www.gileadpublishing.com
Kristen Gearhart, managing editor

Submissions: Submissions from agents only or meeting an editor at a writers conference. Length: 80-100,000 words.

Types and topics: fiction only: contemporary women's, romance, biblical, historical, speculative, mystery/suspense, thrillers

Guidelines: *gileadpublishing.com/submission-guidelines*

Tip: "We are always looking for quality writing, midlist and traditionally published authors in core CBA genres, literary fiction, and new voices with fresh ideas and concepts."

GRACE ACRES PRESS

PO Box 22, Larkspur, CO 80118 | 303-681-9995
Anne@GraceAcresPress.com | *www.GraceAcresPress.com*
Anne R. Fenske, publisher

Submissions: Publishes four to six books per year; receives twenty-five. First-time authors: 85%. Length: 60,000-150,000 words. Email query letter only. Responds in one to three months. Bible: NKJV, NIV.

Royalty: 10-15%, no advance

Types and topics: Bible study, memoir, biography, inspirational, Christian living

Guidelines: *graceacrespress.com/Documents/Prospectus.pdf*

Tip: "Provide a statement of faith with inquiry."

GRACE PUBLISHING

PO Box 1233, Broken Arrow, OK 74013-1233 | 918-346-7960
editorial@grace-publishing.com | *www.grace-publishing.com*
Terri Kalfas, publisher

Submissions: Publishes six to ten titles per year; receives three hundred submissions. First-time authors: 25%. Length: varies, fiction 40,000-125,000 words. For unsolicited work, email query only. However, for a completed manuscript accepts a two-page, double-spaced synopsis, three consecutive sample chapters (double-spaced), and a proposal as email attachments. Responds in three to four months. Bible: any.

Royalty: varies, some flat fees, no advance

Types and topics: Christian living, anthologies, Bible studies, open to fiction

Also does: stewardship program for churches

Guidelines: *grace-publishing.com/manuscript-submission*

Tip: "Attend conferences; know what we publish."

GROUP PUBLISHING, INC.

1515 Cascade Ave., Loveland, CO 80538 | 800-635-0404
PuorgBus@group.com | *www.group.com*

Submissions: Publishes twenty titles per year; receives two hundred submissions annually. First-time authors: 1%. Length: 128-200 pages. Email or mail proposal with sample chapters. No agents. No simultaneous submissions. Responds in six months. Bible: NLT.

Royalty: 8-10% net, advance sometimes

Topics and types: church resources, Christian living

Guidelines: *grouppublishingps.zendesk.com/hc/en-us/articles/211878258-Submissions*

Tip: "Most open to resources that will create experiences that help people grow in relationship with Jesus and each other, which are innovative and involve active/interactive learning."

GUARDIAN ANGEL PUBLISHING, INC.

12430 Tesson Ferry Rd. #186, St. Louis, MO 63128 | 314-276-8482
editorial_staff@guardianangelpublishing.com
www.guardianangelpublishing.com

Submissions: Publishes sixty to seventy-five titles per year; receives six hundred submissions annually. First-time authors: 10-15%. Length: picture book, 500 words; storybook, up to 5,000 words; chapter book, up to 40,000 words. Email manuscript. No simultaneous submissions. Responds in two to four weeks. Bible: no preference. Submit only during August.

Types of books: print, e-books, iBooks enhanced with sound

Royalty: minimum 30%, no advance

Types and topics: all kinds of books for kids ages 0-12, nonfiction and fiction, Spanish and bilingual, African-American audience

Imprints: Wings of Faith, Chapbooks for Tweens, Littlest Angels, Academic Wings, Health & Hygiene, Animals & Pets, Angelic Harmony, Angel to Angel

Guidelines: *www.guardianangelpublishing.com/submissions.htm*

Tip: "Send best submission, not sloppy writing."

GUIDEPOSTS BOOKS

110 William St., Ste. 901, New York, NY 10038 | 212-251-8100
bookeditors@guideposts.org | *www.guideposts.org*
Jon Woodhams, fiction editor
Tarice L. S. Gray, nonfiction editor

Submissions: Extremely limited acquisitions. Accepts manuscripts through agents only. Publishes twenty to thirty titles per year.

Types and topics: inspirational memoir; Christian living; contemporary women's fiction focusing on faith, family, and friendships

GUIDING LIGHT WOMEN'S FICTION

2333 Barton Oaks Dr., Raleigh, NC 27614
editor@guidinglightfiction.com | *www.guidinglightfiction.com*
Jennifer Slattery, acquistions editor

Parent company: LPC Books (Lighthouse Publishing of the Carolinas)

Submissions: Publishes four books per year; receives thirty proposals. First-time authors: 50%. Length: 55,000-60,000 words. Email proposal with sample chapters. Prefers submissions from agents. Responds in three months. Bible: NIV.

Types of books: POD, e-book

Royalty: 40% net, no advance

Types and topics: women's issue-oriented (health, finances, infidelity, relationships, career, etc.) fiction

Guidelines: *www.guidinglightfiction.com/submissions*

Tip: "Guiding Light themes and subjects are deep and serious. Women are the central characters. We seek clean, wholesome stories with God's moral truths woven into the story. Please avoid sermons in stories. Guiding Light sells into the general market."

HANNIBAL BOOKS

313 S. 11th Street, Ste. A, Garland, TX 75040 | 800-747-0738
louismoore@hannibalbooks.com | *www.hannibalbooks.com*
Louis Moore, publisher

Submissions: Not currently accepting new submissions, but check the website for changes in this situation.

Types and topics: missions, marriage and family, critical issues, Bible-study curriculum

HARBOURLIGHT BOOKS

PO Box 1738, Aztec, NM 87410
inquiry@harbourlightbooks.com | *www.pelicanbookgroup.com*
Nicola Martinez, editor-in-chief

Parent company: Pelican Book Group

Submissions: Novels 25,000-80,000 words. Interested in series ideas. Accepts unagented submissions. Responds to queries in one month, full manuscript in three months. Email submissions through the website form.

Royalty: 40% on download, 7% on print, nominal advance

Types and topics: fiction: action-adventure, mystery (cozy or other), suspense, crime drama, police procedural, family saga, westerns, women's fiction

Guidelines: *pelicanbookgroup.com/ec/index.php?main_page=page&id=57*

HARPERCOLLINS CHRISTIAN PUBLISHING

See Thomas Nelson, Tommy Nelson, Zonderkidz, and Zondervan.

HARPERLEGEND

353 Sacramento St. #500, San Francisco, CA 94111-3653 | 415-477-4400
www.harperlegend.com

Parent company: HarperOne

Submissions: Must submit using the online form. Works directly with authors. Preferred length: 50,000-60,000 words. If no response after three months, assume your manuscript has been rejected; you will not receive notice of this.

Type of books: e-books only

Royalty: 25-50%

Types and topics: visionary fiction only. "If you have a novel (or a trilogy or a series) that communicates wisdom, insight, transformation and/or personal growth, bring them on. We want fresh voices, great characters, compelling storylines, and original ideas and approaches. These novels may have many different stripes and flavors including Christian, ... as long it is transformational."

Guidelines: *www.harperone.com/harperlegend/whatarewelookingfor*

HARPERONE

353 Sacramento St. #500, San Francisco, CA 94111-3653 |
415-477-4400
harperone.hc.com
Gideon Weil, editorial director

Parent company: HarperCollins Publishing
Submissions: Requires manuscripts through agents only. Publishes seventy-five titles per year; receives ten thousand submissions annually. First-time authors: 5%. Length: 160-256 pages. Responds in three months.
Royalty: 7.5-15% on retail, advance $20,000-100,000
Types and topics: religion, spirituality

HARRISON HOUSE PUBLISHERS

Box 35035, Tulsa, OK 74153 | 800-888-4126, 918-523-5400
www.harrisonhouse.com
Julie Werner, acquisitions, juliew@harrisonhouse.com

Denomination: Charismatic
Submissions: Not currently accepting any proposals or manuscripts, but check the website for changes in this situation.
Types and topics: children, fiction, Christian living, devotionals, family, finances, health and healing, Holy Spirit, men's and women's issues, ministry resources, prayer, restoration and recover, youth
Guidelines: *www.harrisonhouse.com/assets/clientpages/publishing.aspx*

HARVEST HOUSE PUBLISHERS

PO Box 26311, Eugene, OR 97402-0465 | 800-547-8979
harvesthousepublishers.com
Kathleen Kerr, acquisitions editor
Kyle Hatfield, acquisitions editor, children and family
Todd Hafer, senior acquisitions editor, fiction, nonfiction

Submissions: Requires submissions through agents.
Types and topics: self-help (relationships, family, Christian living), Bible resources (Bible studies, topical studies), and full-color gift and children's books
Guidelines: *www.harvesthousepublishers.com/about/manuscript-submissions*

HENDRICKSEN PUBLISHERS

137 Summit St., PO Box 3473, Peabody, MA 01961

rbrown@hendrickson.com | *www.hendrickson.com*
Rick Brown, publisher

Submissions: Works only through agents or direct contact at various conferences editors attend throughout the year (most notably, the AAR/SBL annual meeting).

Types and topics: academic, Bible studies, marriage and parenting resources, new media and the arts, biblical studies and reference works for both pastors and thoughtful laypersons, devotionals, classic fiction, Christian classics, and prolife resources

Imprints: Aspire Books, Rose Publishing, RoseKidz

Guidelines: *www.hendrickson.com/content/getting-published*

HERITAGE BEACON FICTION

2333 Barton Oaks Dr., Raleigh, NC 27614
LPCHistorical@gmail.com | *www.heritagebeaconfiction.com*
Ann Tatlock, acquisitions editor

Parent company: LPC Books (Lighthouse Publishing of the Carolinas)

Submissions: Publishes eight books per year; receives fifty proposals. First-time authors: 50%. Length: 60,000-80,000 words. Email proposal with sample chapters. Prefers submissions from agents. Responds in three months. Bible: NIV.

Types of books: POD, e-book

Royalty: 40% net, no advance

Types and topics: historical fiction set in the United State or abroad

Guidelines: *www.heritagebeaconfiction.com/submissions*

Tip: "Heritage Beacon Fiction publishes powerful stories that will serve as that vehicle of time travel for those who long to visit the past. For that reason, we choose manuscripts that reveal thorough research into and thorough comprehension of the chosen historical era. The historical setting of each story serves as the backdrop to a compelling plot played out through the choices and actions of memorable characters. Though our stories reveal a Christian worldview, they are not intended to be sermons. Christian themes and messages ought to arise naturally through the unfolding of the storyline and the development of characters. Sells to the general market."

HOPE PUBLISHING HOUSE

PO Box 60008, Pasadena, CA 91106 | 626-792-6123
hopepublishinghouse@gmail.com | *www.hope-pub.com*
Faith A. Sand, publisher

Parent company: Southern California Ecumenical Council

Submissions: Produces thinking books that challenge the faith community to be serious about their pilgrimage of faith. Publishes six titles per year. Query only first. Receives forty submissions annually. First-time authors: 30%. No manuscripts through agents. Length: 200 pages. No simultaneous submissions. Accepts manuscripts by email. Responds in three months. Bible: NRSV.

Royalty: 10% on net, no advance

Types and topics: Christian living, church life, biography, young readers

Tip: "Most open to a well-written manuscript, with correct grammar, that is provocative, original, challenging, and informative."

HOWARD BOOKS

1230 Avenue of the Americas, New York, NY 10020
simonandschusterpublishing.com/howard-books
Beth Adams, executive editor, fiction and nonfiction acquisitions

Parent company: Simon & Schuster

Submissions: Does not accept, review, or return unsolicited manuscripts, except through agents.

Types and topics: inspirational memoir, Christian living, self-help, fiction with authors who have established track records or platforms, growing list of African-American authors

Guidelines: *www.simonandschuster.com/about/publishing#manuscripts*

ILLUMINATEYA

2333 Barton Oaks Dr., Raleigh, NC 27614
illuminateYAfiction@gmail.com | *www.illuminateya.com*
Tessa Hall, acquisitions editor

Parent company: LPC Books (Lighthouse Publishing of the Carolinas)

Submissions: Publishes four books per year; receives twenty proposals. First-time authors: 50%. Length: 50,000-100,000 words. Email proposal with sample chapters. Prefers submissions from agents. Responds in three months. Bible: NIV.

Types of books: POD, e-book

Royalty: 40% net, no advance

Types and topics: YA contemporary-issues, historical, romance fiction

Guidelines: *www.illuminateya.com/submissions*

Tip: "The protagonists in new-adult novels must be between 18-25

years of age. Our YA novels are clean reads; no vulgar language or sex scenes. IlluminateYA seeks to change our culture by publishing books with strong moral values. We will consider inspirational themes but prefer stories that can reach the young, general-market reader."

IMAGE BOOKS

1745 Broadway, New York, NY 10019 | 212-782-9000
imagebooks@randomhouse.com |*crownpublishing.com/imprint/image-catholic-books*
Gary Jansen, director

Parent company: Crown Publishing Group, which is part of Penguin Random House
Denomination: Catholic
Submissions: Takes submissions only from agents.

INTERVARSITY PRESS

PO Box 1400, Downers Grove, IL 60515-1426 | 630-734-4000
email@ivpress.com | *www.ivpress.com*
Al Hsu, senior editor and acquisitions, IVP Books
Jon Boyd, editorial director and acquisitions, academic

Parent company: InterVarsity Christian Fellowship
Submissions: Publishes a hundred titles per year; receives more than one thousand submissions annually. First-time authors: 15%. Accepts manuscripts through agents or if you have had direct contact with an editor. Length: 50,000 words or 200 pages. Bible: NIV, NRSV. Email submissions after acceptance.
Royalty: negotiable on retail or outright purchase, negotiable advance
Types and topics: IVP books are characterized by a thoughtful, biblical approach to the Christian life that transforms the hearts, souls, and minds of readers in the university, church, and the world, on topics ranging from spiritual disciplines to apologetics, to current issues, to theology. Especially looking for ethnic writers (African-American, Hispanic, Asian-American).
Imprints: IVP Academic, IVP Books, IVP Connect (Bible studies and small-group resources), Formatio (spiritual formation), IVP Cresendo (women's books), IVP Praxis (ministry)
Guidelines: *www.ivpress.com/submissions*
Tip: "Most open to books written by pastors (though not collections of sermons) or other church staff, by professors, by leaders in Christian organizations. Authors need to bring resources for publicizing and selling their own books, such as a website, an

organization they are part of that will promote their books, speaking engagements, well-known people they know personally who will endorse and promote their book, writing articles for national publication, etc."

JOURNEY FICTION

3342 Cape Cod Dr., Las Vegas, NV 89122 | 702-570-3433
contact@journeyfiction.com | *www.journeyfiction.com*
Jennifer L. Farey, acquisitions

Submissions: Publishes ten to twenty books per year. First-time authors: 50%. Length: 50,000-90,000 words. Email proposal with sample chapters or full manuscript. Prefers series. Responds in two weeks. Bible: NKJV.

Types of books: POD, e-book

Royalty: 50-60% of net sales, no advance.

Types and topics: fiction only: romance, suspense, mystery, historical, women's fiction, speculative

Guidelines: *www.journeyfiction.com/for-authors*

Tip: "We want to introduce readers to stories that are so compelling they don't want them to end. Because of that, we're especially interested in series of three or more books."

JOURNEYFORTH BOOKS

1430 Wade Hampton Blvd., Greenville, SC 29609 | 864-546-4600
journeyforth@bjupress.com | *www.journeyforth.com*
Nancy Lohr, acquisitions editor

Parent company: BJU Press

Submissions: Publishes ten titles per year; receives 350 submissions. First-time authors: 10%. Length: varies, see guidelines. Email proposal with sample chapters; no multiple submissions. Responds in three months. Bible: KJV, NKJV, ESV, NASB.

Royalty: 10% with escalation at sales benchmarks, variable advance

Types and topics: youth contemporary and historical fiction; youth biographies; teen and adult Christian living, marriage and family, topical expositions/studies (e.g., sanctification, meditation), Bible book or passage studies

Guidelines: *www.bjupress.com/books/freelance.php*

Tip: "Your book needs to complement our catalog of titles and support our mission. The writing must be engaging for the target reader. We are not accepting picture books, speculative fiction, fiction for the adult market, memoirs, or curriculum. Familiarize yourself with our books on our website."

JUDSON PRESS

PO Box 851, Valley Forge, PA 19482-0851 | 800-458-3766
JPAcquisitions@abc-usa.org | *www.judsonpress.com*
Rebecca Irwin-Diehl, editor | *Lisa Blair, editorial associate*

Denomination/parent company: American Baptist Churches USA

Submissions: Publishes ten to twelve titles per year; receives two hundred fifty to three hundred submissions. First-time authors: 50%. Email or mail query or proposal with sample chapters. Responds in three to nine months. Length: 128-244 pages. Bible: NRSV.

Types of books: paperback, hardback, e-book

Royalty: 10% net with escalators, advance sometimes

Types and topics: church resources; pastor resources; Baptist identity and history, especially for theologically moderate Baptists; academic; African-American, Hispanic, intercultural

Guidelines: *www.judsonpress.com/Content/Site189/BasicBlocks/10258Manuscript_00000120345.pdf*

Tip: "Be clear about your audience; be concrete about your marketing plans as a publishing partner; make sure your project is uniquely compelling; and, in general, aim for a book that is practical."

KENDALL NEFF PUBLISHING

PO Box 22, Talladega, AL 35160 | 256-368-1559
publr@KendallNeff.com | *www.KendallNeff.com*
Dr. Tana N. Thompson, publisher

Submissions: Publishes fewer than ten titles per year.

Types and topics: projects that are spiritual, secular, or educational in nature, ranging from print books to digital downloads of audio, video, or text media, including children's picture books, devotionals, self-help works, and children's activity pages

KREGEL PUBLICATIONS

2450 Oak Industrial Dr. N.E., Grand Rapids, MI 49505 | 616-451-4775
kregelbooks@kregel.com | *www.kregel.com*
Steve Barclift, managing editor

Submissions: Evangelical/conservative company. Does not accept unsolicited proposals or manuscripts for review. Submit only through agents or manuscript-review services.

Types and topics: biblical studies, biography, Bible reference, children's, Christian living, church/ministry, fiction (YA, historical, romance, romantic suspense), marriage and family, theology, women's issues, self-help, parenting, Bible studies (prefers topical), discipleship, devotionals

Guidelines: *www.kregel.com/contact-us/submissions-policy*

LAMPLIGHTER MYSTERIES AND SUSPENSE

2333 Barton Oaks Dr., Raleigh, NC 27614
lamplighterlpc@gmail.com | *lamplightermysteries.com*
Darla Crass, managing editor

Parent company: LPC Books (Lighthouse Publishing of the Carolinas)

Submissions: Publishes eight books per year; receives twenty-five proposals. First-time authors: 40%. Length: varies, write tight. Email proposal with sample chapters. Prefers submissions from agents. Responds in one month. Bible: NIV, NKJV.

Types of books: POD, e-book

Royalty: 40% net, no advance

Types and topics: mystery, suspense

Guidelines: *lamplightermysteries.com/submissions*

Tip: "Present a great story in a fresh voice for the general market. Mysteries with unique angles and themes without sermons are highly sought after."

LANGMARC PUBLISHING

PO Box 90488, Austin, TX 78709-0488 | 512-394-0989
langmarc@booksails.com | *www.langmarc.com*
Lois Qualben, publisher

Denomination: Lutheran

Submissions: Focuses on spiritual growth of readers. Not accepting manuscripts at this time; check the website for a change in this situation. Publishes three to five titles per year; receives more than two hundred submissions annually. First-time authors: 60%. Accepts manuscripts directly from authors. Submit proposal with three chapters. Length: 150-300 pages. Responds in three months. Bible: NIV.

Royalty: 10-14% on net, no advance

Types and topics: Christian living, devotionals for teens and adults, Bible studies, humor

Tip: "Most open to inspirational books."

LEAFWOOD PUBLISHERS

ACU, PO Box 29138, Abilene, TX 79699
manuscriptsubmissions@groupmail.acu.edu | *www.leafwoodpublishers.com*
Gary Myers, editor

Parent company: Abilene Christian University
Submissions: Works directly with authors. Email proposal.
Types and topics: Christian living, women's issues, spiritual disciplines, and leadership. We do not accept manuscript submissions for poetry, children's books, or fiction.
Guidelines: *store.acupressbooks.com/pages/author-resources*

LEXHAM PRESS

1313 Commercial St., Bellingham, WA 98225
editor@lexampress.com | *www.lexhampress.com*
Dr. Brannon Ellis, publisher

Parent company: FaithLife Corporation, makers of Logos Bible Software
Submissions: Publishes print, e-books, and innovative resources for Logos Bible Software. Will work directly with authors. Submit proposal and sample chapters through the website.
Types and topics: evangelical scholarly and pastoral works in the areas of biblical studies, including Bible reference and original language resources; biblical, historical, and systematic theology; and ministry resources
Guidelines: *www.lexhampress.com/manuscript-submission*

LIGHTHOUSE PUBLISHING

754 Roxholly Walk, Buford, CA 30518 | 770-709-2268
info@lighthousechristianpublishing.com
www.lighthousechristianpublishing.com
Sylvia Charvet, acquisitions editor

Parent company: Lighthouse eMedia and Publishing
Submissions: Publishes thirty books annually; receives two hundred. First-time authors: 80%. Length: 300-320 pages for fiction. Email proposal with full manuscript. Responds in four to six weeks. Bible: NAS.
Types of books: POD, e-book
Royalty: 50%, no advance
Types and topics: all fiction and nonfiction, also African-American and Hispanic audiences

Also does: audiobooks
Imprint: Lone Oak Publishing (general market)
Guidelines: *lighthousechristianpublishing.com/about_1.html*
Tip: Looking for unique stories.

LIGHTHOUSE PUBLISHING OF THE CAROLINAS

lpcbooks.com
Eddie Jones, founder, CEO

Parent company: Christian Devotions Ministries
Imprints: See Bling! Romance, Candlelight Inspirational Romance, Firefly Southern Fiction, Guiding Light Women's Fiction, Heritage Beacon Fiction, IlluminateYA, Lamplighter Mysteries & Suspense, Smitten Historical Romance, Sonrise Devotionals, Straight Street Books.
Guidelines: lpcb*ooks.com/submissions*
Tip: "Our authors include Christy Award winners, debut novelists, and nonfiction writers. Our fiction points to moral truths and portrays characters with strong beliefs about what's right and wrong. LPC is a traditional, royalty-paying book publisher. We do not offer author advances, nor do we seek full bookstore distribution through Ingram. If you can accept that your book may never find its way onto the shelves of a bookstore, but may sell thousands through Amazon, LPC might be a good fit for you."

LIGHTHOUSE TRAILS PUBLISHING, LLC

PO Box 908, Eureka, MT 59917 | 406-889-3610
david@lighthousetrails.com | *www.lighthousetrails.com*
David Dombrowski, acquisitions editor

Submissions: Publishes books that bring clarity and light to areas of spiritual darkness or deception. Publishes two to four titles per year; receives fifty to seventy-five submissions annually. First-time authors: 30%. Accepts manuscripts directly from authors. Length: 160-300 pages. Email proposal with two sample chapters as attachment, or mail it on a CD. Responds in two months. Bible: KJV.
Royalty: 12-17% of net, 20% of retail
Types and topics: stories of Christians who have risen above incredible and unusual challenges and even their own failures to illustrate God's amazing grace and strength to overcome, books about or by missionaries, fiction for all ages
Guidelines: *www.lighthousetrails.com/content/11-submit-manuscript*

Tip: "Any book we consider will not only challenge the more scholarly reader, but also be able to reach those who may have less experience and comprehension. Our books will include human interest and personal experience scenarios as a means of getting the point across. Read a couple of our books to better understand the style of writing we are looking for. We also have a doctrinal statement on our website that helps to define us."

LION HUDSON

Wilkinson House, Jordan Hill Rd., Oxford OX2 8DR, UK
SubmissionstoLionBooksMonarchLionFiction@LionHudson.com
www.lionhudson.com
Becki Bradshaw, Lion Books
Simon Cox, Monarch Books
Jessica Tinker, Lion fiction

Parent company: AFD Group

Submissions: Publishes internationally; distributed in the US by Kregel Publications. Email or mail a proposal and sample chapters or manuscript; mail only for children's books. If no response in three months, consider it a rejection.

Types and topics: Lion Books, Lion Children's Books, Lion Fiction: accessible books that reflect a Christian worldview to a general audience. Candle Books, Monarch Books: support Christian families, individuals and communities in their devotional and spiritual lives

Guidelines: *www.lionhudson.com/page/contact*

LITTLE LAMB BOOKS

PO Box 211724, Bedford, TX 76021
subs@littlelambbooks.com | *www.littlelambbooks.com*
Rachel Pellegrino, managing editor

Parent company: Lamb Publishing, LLC

Submissions: Publishes two to six books per year; receives one hundred plus proposals. First-time authors: 75%. Length: picture books, 200-500 words; chapter books, 1,000-5,000 words; middle grade, 30,000-60,000 words; YA, 50,000-80,000 words. Email proposal with sample chapters or full manuscript. Responds in six to eight weeks.

Royalty: varies, on retail; no advance

Types and topics: faith-based children's, tween, and teen fiction, action and adventure, contemporary, folktales, historical, humor, inspirational, mystery, sweet romance, science fiction, character traits, patriotic, seasonal/holidays, family values

Guidelines: *littlelambbooks.com/subs*

Other products: digital printables, t-shirts

Tip: "We're an author-friendly press looking for strong, creative, biblically-sound fiction that encourages, entertains, and inspires elementary, middle grade, and young-adult readers. Visit our site, and follow the submission guidelines found online. Remember your audience. Edit your work. Build and grow your reach/platform."

LITURGICAL PRESS

2950 St. John's Rd., PO Box 7500, Collegeville, MN 56321-7500
submissions@litpress.org | *www.litpress.org*

Denomination: Catholic

Submissions: Email or mail proposal, using the downloadable "Project Summary Form" and "Author Biography Form" from the website.

Types and topics: biography, vocation, commentaries, chidren's, church, discipleship, liturgy, marriage and family, prayer, preaching, Bible reference books, theology, spriituality

Guidelines: *www.litpress.org/Authors/submit_manuscript*

LOVE INSPIRED

195 Broadway, 24th floor, New York, NY 10007 | 212-207-7900
harlequin.submittable.com/submit | *www.loveinspired.com*
Tina James, executive editor
Melissa Endlich, senior editor

Parent company: Harlequin, a division of HarperCollins Publishers

Submissions: Publishes one hundred ninety-two titles per year; receives five hundred to one thousand. First-time authors: 15%. Submit proposal with sample chapters or full manuscript through the website. Responds in three months. Length: 55,000 words. Bible: KJV.

Royalty: on retail, competitive advance

Types of books: mass-market paperback

Types and topics: Love Inspired: contemporary romance; Love Inspired Suspense: contemporary romantic suspense

Guidelines: *harlequin.submittable.com/submit*

Tip: "Aspiring Love Inspired writers should familiarize themselves both with our guidelines and our books. By reading our romances, an aspiring writer will get a very good sense of what we're looking to acquire."

LOVE2READLOVE2WRITE PUBLISHING, LLC (L2L2 PUBLISHING)

PO Box 103, Camby, IN 46113 | 317-550-9755
editor@love2readlove2writepublishing.com |
www.love2readlove2writepublishing.com
Michele Israel Harper, acquisitions editor

Submissions: Publishes four to six titles per year POD; receives thirty to fifty proposals. 90% from first-time authors. Length: 60,000-120,000. Email proposal with full manuscript. Replies in six to eight weeks. Bible: NKJV.

Royalty: 50% of net, $50 advance

Types and topics: Christian or clean speculative fiction only: YA fantasy, paranormal, supernatural, dystopian, science fiction; unique writing guides

Guidelines: *www.love2readlove2writepublishing.com/submissions*

Tip: "Be professional, be succinct, and know your audience."

LOYOLA PRESS

3441 N. Ashland Ave., Chicago, IL 60657 | 773-281-1818, 800-621-1008
editorial@loyolapress.com | *www.loyolapress.com*
Joseph Durepos, acquisitions editor, durepos@loyolapress.com

Denomination: Catholic

Submissions: Publishes twenty titles per year; receives five hundred submissions annually. Accepts manuscripts directly from authors. Email proposal with sample chapters. Length: 25,000-75,000 words or 150-300 pages. Considers first-time authors without agents. Responds in three months. Bible: NRSV (Catholic edition).

Royalty: standard, reasonable advance

Types and topics: books that help people experience God in their lives more directly, that introduce the dynamics of the Spiritual Exercises and the Ignatian process of discernment and decision-making, and that open up Scripture as a way of encountering Jesus and books that introduce and explain Catholic tradition and the richness of our faith

Guidelines: *www.loyolapress.com/general/submissions*

Tip: "Looking for books and authors that help make Catholic faith relevant and offer practical tools for the well-lived spiritual life."

MANTLE ROCK PUBLISHING, LLC

2879 Palma Rd., Benton, KY 42025 | 270-493-1560
Erin@mantlerockpublishingllc.com | *mantlerockpublishingllc.com*
Erin Howard, acquisitions
Kathy Cretsinger, owner, kathy@mantlerockpublishingllc.com
Pam Harris, editor, Pam@mantlerockpublishingllc.com

Submissions: Publishes ten to fifteen books per year; receives thirty. First-time authors: 99%. Length: 70,000-80,000 words. Email or submit through the website a proposal with sample chapters. Prefers submissions from agents. Responds in two to four weeks. Bible: NKJV.

Royalty: 12% retail on print, 50% of publisher's royalty on e-book, no advance

Types and topics: Christian fiction only—contemporary romance, historical romance, romantic suspense, fantasy/speculative

Guidelines: *mantlerockpublishingllc.com/submissions*

Tip: "Follow our guidelines, write a clean manuscript with few grammar or punctuation errors, use the font we state in the guidelines, and only send the genres we publish."

MASTER BOOKS

PO Box 726, Green Forest, AR 72638 | 800-999-3777
submissions@newleafpress.net | *www.masterbooks.com*
Craig Froman, acquisitions editor

Parent company: New Leaf Publishing Group

Submissions: Publishes thirty to thirty-five titles per year. First-time authors: 10%. Accepts manuscripts directly from authors. Requires email submission with "Author's Proposal Document" on the website. Responds within three months or isn't interested.

Royalty: varies on net, no advance

Types and topics: young-earth creation material for all ages, including apologetics, homeschool resources, science and the Bible, reference titles, and children's literature

Guidelines: *www.nlpg.com/submissions*

MATERIAL MEDIA, LLC

5150 Broadway #466, San Antonio, TX 71209 | 210-508-5553
Elizabeth@MaterialMedia.com | *www.MaterialMedia.com*
Elizabeth Cauthorn, owner

Submissions: Publishes five books per year. 50% from first-time authors. Not accepting manuscripts at this time, but check the website for changes in this situation. Responds in two months. Average first print run. 2,000. Royalty: 10%, no advance.

Also does: audiobooks.

Types and topics: prayer, contemporary fiction, historical fiction, meditation, memoir

Imprint: New Beginnings

Guidelines: by email

Tip: "We have a significant online presence."

MOODY PUBLISHERS

820 N. LaSalle Blvd., Chicago, IL 60610 | 800-678-8812
www.moodypublishers.com
Ingrid Beck, acquisitions editor
Judy Denagan, women's acquisitions editor

Parent company: Moody Bible Institute

Submissions: Moody Publishers exists to resource the church's work of discipling all people. Publishes fifty to sixty titles per year; receives thousands of submissions annually. First-time authors: 20%. Does not accept unsolicited manuscripts in any category; must be submitted by a literary agent, an author who has published with Moody, a Moody Bible Institute employee, or a contact at a writers conference. Responds in one to two months. Bible: NASB, ESV, NKJV.

Royalty: on net, advances begin at $500

Types and topics: spiritual growth, family/relationships, church leaders, women, Bible studies, next-generation resources, finance

Guidelines: *www.moodypublishers.com/about/contact*

Tip: "Most open to books that (1) have a great idea at the core, (2) are executed well, and (3) can demonstrate an audience clamoring for the content."

MOUNTAIN BROOK INK

26 Moore Rd., White Salmon, WA 98672
mountainbrookink@gmail.com | *www.mountainbrookink.com*
Miralee Ferrell, publisher

Submissions: Publishes fifteen titles per year; receives sixty proposals. First-time authors: 70%. Length: 70,000-95,000 words; speculative fiction can be longer. Email query through the website. Replies in forty-five to sixty days. Bible: KJV, NKJV.

Books: POD, e-book

Royalty: 35-45%, advance varies

Types and topics: fiction—contemporary, historical, mystery, cozy mystery, suspense, biblical, romance, women's, fantasy, sci-fi, possibly paranormal with a Christian worldview, YA; no dystopian; open to clean general-market fiction with a Christian worldview but no specific Christian message

Guidelines: *mountainbrookink.com/submission-guidelines*

Tip: "Make certain your book is ready to submit. Run it by an editor first before submitting. A proposal with errors or craft issues won't get the same attention as a book that's well-written. Read the submissions page on our website thoroughly before submitting."

MULTNOMAH BOOKS

10807 New Allegiance Dr. #500, Colorado Springs, CO 80921 | 719-590-4999

info@waterbrookmultnomah.com | *www.waterbrookmultnomah.com*

Laura Barker, editorial director

Parent company: Crown Publishing Group, a division of Penguin Random House

Submissions: Publishes sixty titles per year. Currently not accepting unsolicited manuscripts, proposals, or queries. Queries will be accepted through literary agents and at writers conferences at which a Multnomah representative is present.

Royalty: on net, advance

Types and topics: Christian living, discipleship and spiritual growth, Bible study, apologetics, popular theology, devotional, evangelism, pastoral helps, leadership, children's, fiction

Guidelines: *waterbrookmultnomah.com/submissions*

MY HEALTHY CHURCH

1445 N. Boonville Ave., Springfield, MO 65802 | 800-641-4310, 417-831-8000

newproducts@myhealthychurch.com | *www.myhealthychurch.com*

Julie Horner, senior director of publishing and marketing

Denomination: Assemblies of God

Submissions: Does not accept unsolicited manuscripts unless represented by an agent. Responds in two to three months.

Types and topics: church resources for kids, youth, and adults; small group studies

Guidelines: *myhealthychurch.com/store/startcat.cfm?cat=tWRITGUID*

Tip: "The content of all our books and resources must be compatible with the beliefs and purposes of the Assemblies of God."

NAVPRESS

3820 N. 30th St., Colorado Springs, CO 80904 | 719-598-1212
inquiries@navpress.com | *www.navpress.com*
Caitlyn Carlson, acquisitions editor
David Zimmerman, acquisitions editor

Parent company: The Navigators

Submissions: Publishes twenty titles per year; receives a thousand proposals annually. First-time authors: 40%. Length: 40,000 words. Submit through the website. Prefers submissions from agents. Responds in two months.

Royalty: 16-22%, advance

Types and topics: Christian living, spiritual growth, devotionals, marriage, prayer, discipleship, parenting/grandparenting, leadership, counseling/psychology, evangelism, missions, apologetics, theology, church/ministry, women, men, relationships, dating, home/family, Bible studies

Guidelines: *www.navpress.com/faq*

Tip: "Proposals with strong discipleship elements are preferred. Authors should have a ministry platform that supports their discipleship elements. NavPress does not accept unsolicited manuscripts."

NEW GROWTH PRESS

PO Box 4485, Greensboro, NC 27404 | 336-378-7775
jwalt@newgrowthpress.com | *www.newgrowthpress.com*
John Walt, director of acquisitions

Submissions: Publishes gospel-centered and Bible-based materials that empower individuals, families, and churches to grow in their love for God, their love for others, and their ability to bring healing and hope to the world. Will work directly with authors and agents.

Types and topics: small-group resources, family, parenting, counseling issues, sexual-identity issues, missions, renewal, fiction, illustrated children's books

Also does: minibooks, short, 24-page booklets that address one specific felt need

NEW HOPE PUBLISHERS

100 Missionary Ridge, Birmingham, AL 35252 | 866-266-8399
proposals@newhopepublishers.com | *www.newhopepublishers.com*
Ramona Richards, associate publisher

Parent company: Iron Stream Media

Submissions: Publishes twelve to fifteen titles per year; receives one hundred plus. First-time authors: 20%. Length 40,000-50,000 words. Email or submit through the website a proposal with sample chapters. New authors must submit full manuscript with proposal. Prefers submissions from agents. Responds in four months. Bible: any.

Royalty: 12-14%, sometimes advance, varies depending on publishing history

Types and topics: spiritual growth, personal growth, leadership, Bible studies, fiction (women's, suspense, romantic suspense, speculative)

Guidelines: *www.newhopepublishers.com/proposals*

Tip: "Proposals must be polished and free of errors. Marketing plans in proposal must show author's knowledge of market, platform, and genre. Please include previous sales figures (if any) and author's biography as related to book topic."

NEW LEAF PRESS

PO Box 726, Green Forest, AR 72638-0726 | 870-438-5288
submissions@newleafpress.net | *www.nlpg.com/imprint/new-leaf-press*
Craig Froman, acquisitions editor

Parent company: New Leaf Publishing Group

Submissions: Publishes thirty to thirty-five titles per year; receives a thousand submissions annually. First-time authors: 10%. Accepts manuscripts directly from authors. Requires email submission with "Author's Proposal Document" on the website. Responds within three months or isn't interested.

Royalty: on net, no advance

Types and topics: Christian living, stewardship, reference titles, church ministry, family issues, some materials in Spanish

Guidelines: *www.nlpg.com/submissions*

Tip: "Always follow our online guidelines before submitting."

NORTH WIND PUBLISHING

PO Box 3655, Brewer, ME 04412 | 207-922-8435
info@northwindpublishing.com | *www.northwindpublishing.com*
Janet Robbins, publisher

Submissions: Email or mail proposal with sample chapters. Responds in three months. Publishes six to ten titles per year; receives twenty. First-time authors: 50%. Length: no preference. Bible: no preference.

Type of book: POD

Royalty: 10-30%, no advance
Types and topics: devotionals, Christian living
Guidelines: none
Tip: "You must have an established audience."

NORTHWESTERN PUBLISHING HOUSE

1250 N. 113th St., Milwaukee, WI 53226 | 800-662-6022, 414-615-5710
millert@nph.wels.net | *www.nph.net*
Terry Miller, administrative assistant

Denomination: Wisconsin Evangelical Lutheran Synod
Submissions: Mail proposal and manuscript, Attn: Manuscript Submissions.
Types and topics: devotions, family and personal guidance, church history, Scripture studies like the popular People's Bible commentary series and the People's Bible Teachings series on doctrine
Guidelines: *online.nph.net/manuscript-submission*

OLIVIA KIMBRELL PRESS

PO Box 470, Fort Knox, KY 40121-0470 | 859-577-1071
admin@oliviakimbrellpress.com | *www.oliviakimbrellpress.com*
G. B. Williams, submissions
Heather McCurdy, editor
Gregg Bridgeman, editor-in-chief

Submissions: Specializes in true-to-life, meaningful Christian fiction and nonfiction titles intended to uplift the heart and engage the mind. Primary focus on "Roman Road" small-group guides or reader's guides to accompany nonfiction and fiction. Fiction: finished manuscript only. Nonfiction: primarily completed and an outline. Email submission.
Types and topics: adult devotionals, family, Christian living, healthy living, cookbooks, fasting/feasts; fiction: speculative/science fiction, fantasy
Imprints: CAVË (historical fiction from the periods immediately before, during, or after the time of Christ), Sign of the Whale (biblical and/or Christian fiction primarily with speculative fiction, science fiction, fantasy, or other futuristic and/or supernatural themes), House of Bread (biblical and/or traditional foods; clean foods; fasting; feasts; and healthy, nutritious information presented in an educational and entertaining manner)

Guidelines: *www.oliviakimbrellpress.com/submission.html*
Tip: "Must meet our stated editorial standards. Follow our submission guidelines. Fiction series preferred over standalone titles. Complete manuscripts only."

OUR SUNDAY VISITOR, INC.

200 Noll Plaza, Huntington, IN 46750-4303 | 260-356-8400, 800-348-2440
www.osv.com
Greg Willits, editorial director

Submissions: To assist Catholics to be more aware and secure in their faith and capable of relating their faith to others. Submit proposal through the website. Publishes thirty to forty titles per year; receives more than five hundred submissions annually. First-time authors: 10%. Prefers not to work through agents. Responds in six to eight weeks.
Royalty: 10-12% of net, average advance $1,500
Also does: pamphlets and booklets
Types and topics: prayer—books and devotionals that help readers draw nearer to God; Scripture—books about how to read, understand, pray, and apply Scripture; family and marriage—books that reflect on the nature of marriage and practical books on family life; saints and heritage—informative and inspiring stories about Mary, the saints, and Catholic identity; faith and culture—books about the intersection of faith and contemporary culture; service—practical application of the call to serve the needy and love our neighbor; evangelization, apologetics, and catechetics—books that help readers explain, defend, and share their faith with others; worship—books about understanding and experiencing the graces of the sacraments, especially the eucharist; parish—books that help pastors, leaders, and parishioners conduct parish life more effectively
Guidelines: *osv.submittable.com/submit*
Tip: "All books published must relate to the Catholic Church; unique books aimed at our audience. Give as much background information as possible on author qualification, why the topic was chosen, and unique aspects of the project. Follow our guidelines. We are expanding our religious education product line and programs."

PACIFIC PRESS

PO Box 5353, Nampa, ID 83653-5353 | 208-465-2500
booksubmissions@pacificpress.com | *www.pacificpress.com*
Scott Cady, acquisitions editor

Denomination: Seventh-day Adventist

Submissions: Books of interest and importance to Seventh-day Adventists and other Christians of all ages. Publishes thirty-five to forty titles per year; receives five hundred submissions annually. First-time authors: 5%. Email or mail query. Accepts manuscripts directly from authors. Length: 40,000-90,000 words, 128-320 pages. Responds in one to three weeks. Requires requested proposal with three chapters by email or mail, manuscript by email.

Royalty: 12-16% of net, advance $1,500

Also does: booklets

Types and topics: adults: inspiration/Christian life, prayer, doctrine and Bible study, church history, Ellen White, topics and issues, biographies and true stories, story collections, cookbooks, health and nutrition, marriage and parenting, books for sharing and gospel outreach; children: picture books illustrating a distinctive Adventist belief for ages 1-3; true or based-on-truth, contemporary or historical stories with Christian themes (usually in a series) for ages 6-8 and 9-12; sets of Bible stories for ages 8-108

Guidelines: *www.pacificpress.com/index.php?pgName=newsBookSub#PPPAPubs*

Tip: "Most open to spirituality, inspirational, and Christian living. Our website has the most up-to-date information, including samples of recent publications. Do not send full manuscript unless we request it after reviewing your proposal."

P&R PUBLISHING

1102 Marble Hill Rd., Phillipsburg, NJ 08865 | 908-454-0505
editorial@prpbooks.com | *www.prpbooks.com*
Amanda Martin, editorial director
Melissa Craig, children's editor

Denomination: Reformed

Submissions: Devoted to stating, defending, and furthering the gospel in the modern world. Download the submission form from the website, and email it with an outline and two or three chapters. Publishes forty-five titles per year; receives four hundred submissions annually. First-time authors: fewer than 10%. Length: 140-240 pages. Responds in one to four months.

Royalty: 10-15% of net, advance

Types and topics: apologetics, Bible study aids, biography, Christian issues and ethics, Christian living, church history, church resources, commentary, counseling, fiction for children and teens, theology, women's resources, youth resources

Guidelines: *www.prpbooks.com/manuscript-submissions*

Tip: "Direct biblical/Reformed content. Clear, engaging, and insightful applications of Reformed theology to life. Offer us fully developed proposals and polished sample chapters. Check our website to see the categories we publish."

PARACLETE PRESS

PO Box 1568, Orleans, MA 02653 | 508-255-4685
submissions@paracletepress | www.paracletepress.com
Jon Sweeney, publisher and editor-in-chief

Denomination: Catholic and Protestant

Submissions: Email proposal and two or three sample chapters as single attached Word file. Responds in one month.

Types and topics: prayer, faith formation, spirituality, grief, Advent/Christmas or Lent/Easter picture books; poetry by invitation only

Guidelines: *www.paracletepress.com/Pages/About/Submission-Guidelines.aspx*

PARSONS PUBLISHING HOUSE

PO Box 410063, Melbourne, FL 32941 | 850-867-3061
diane@parsonspublishinghouse.com | www.parsonspublishinghouse.com
Diane Parsons, chief editor

Submissions: Email proposal. Responds in six to eight weeks. Publishes five to ten titles per year; receives thirty submissions annually. First-time authors: 90%. Length: 35,000-60,000 words. No agents. Bible: any.

Royalty: 10%, no advance

Types and topics: prayer, Christian living, spiritual warfare, spiritual growth, marriage

Guidelines: on the website

Tip: Looking for "books that share the GOOD news of the Gospel and the victory in following Jesus, which rely on the Bible as the inspired Word of God. Looking for sincere, genuine authors with a message or an experience and inspire others to live a godly life."

PAULINE BOOKS & MEDIA

50 Saint Paul's Ave., Boston, MA 02130-3491 | 617-522-8911
editorial@paulinemedia.com | *www.pauline.org*
Sean Mayer, FSP, acquisitions editor, adults
Marilyn Monge, FSP, and Jaymie Stuart Wolfe, editors, children and teens

Denomination: Catholic/Daughters of St. Paul
Submissions: Publishes twenty titles per year; receives more than three hundred submissions annually. First-time authors: 10%. Accepts manuscripts directly from authors. Length: 10,000-60,000 words. Email proposal as an attachment, or mail it. Responds in two months. Bible: NRSV.
Royalty: 5-10% on net, advance
Types and topics: adults: spirituality, prayer, lives of saints, faith formation, theology, family life; children: prayer books, lives of saints, Bible stories, activity books, easy reader and middle-grade fiction, board books, picture books; YA: fiction and nonfiction
Guidelines: *www.pauline.org/Publishing/Submit-a-Manuscript*
Tip: Looking for well-documented historical fiction and graphic novels for middle grade and YA.

PAULIST PRESS

997 Macarthur Blvd., Mahwah, NJ 07430-9990
submissions@paulistpress.com | *www.paulistpress.com*
Trace Murphy, editorial director

Denomination: Catholic
Submissions: Email proposal and sample chapters, pages for children's chapter books, or full manuscript for other children's books. Responds in two months.
Types and topics: academic, children's, popular, and professional or clergy books
Guidelines: *www.paulistpress.com/Pages/Center/auth_res_0.aspx*

PELICAN BOOK GROUP

See Harbourlight Books, Pure Amore, Watershed Books, and White Rose Publishing.

PRAYERSHOP PUBLISHING

3525 S. 3rd Pl., Terre Haute, IN 47802 | 812-238-5504
jong@harvestprayer.com | *www.prayershoppublishing.com*
Jonathan Graf, publisher

Parent company: Harvest Prayer Ministries, Church Prayer Leaders Network

Submissions: Our ministry is to disciple people in prayer and grow praying churches. We only do resources that will move an individual or church deeper in prayer. Publishes four to six titles per year; receives ten to fifteen submissions annually. First-time authors: 15%. Accepts manuscripts directly from authors. Length: 30,000-50,000 words, 128-144 pages. Email or mail proposal with sample chapters. Reports in six to eight weeks. Bible: prefers NIV.

Royalty: 10-15% of net, no advance

Types and topics: practical books on prayer that show how to pray or provide guides to help people learn to pray, Bible studies/small-group resource

Also does: short booklets on one practical prayer topic, media packs that might include teaching seminar CD/DVD plus booklet

Tip: "Currently looking for book manuscripts, booklets, and materials that can be formatted via CD and print into training kits. We are mostly interested in products that will in some way enhance the prayer life of a local church."

PRISM BOOK GROUP

contact@prismbookgroup.com | www.prismbookgroup.com
Jacqueline Hopper, acquisitions editor, jhopper@prismbookgroup.com
Susan Baganz, acquisitions editor, sbaganz@prismbookgroup.com
Paula Mowery, acquisitions editor, pmowery@prismbookgroup.com

Submissions: Publishes clean and wholesome fiction. Publishes twenty-four to sixty titles annually. Query by email only. Proofread your finished manuscript thoroughly before querying the general address. When a manuscript is requested, it is important to include your real name and email on the title page; manuscripts without this information may be deleted.

Royalty: paid quarterly

Types and topics: fiction: romance, Christian romance, Christian fiction, young adult

Imprints: Diamond (clean and wholesome romance), Inspired (Christian romance), Illuminate (Christian fiction), Shine (uplifting young-adult fiction)

Guidelines: *prismbookgroup.com/store/index.php?main_page=page&id=55*

Tip: "Our books offer clean and compelling reads for the discerning reader. We will not publish graphic language or content and look for well-written, emotionally charged stories, intense plots, and captivating characters. We are especially interested in western/cowboy romances, regency romance, romantic suspense, and contemporary romance in both Diamond and Inspired imprints. We would also love to see more historical, biblical fiction."

PURE AMORE

PO Box 1738, Aztec, NM 87410
customer@pelicanbookgroup.com | *pelicanbookgroup.com*
Nicola Martinez, editor-in-chief

Parent company: Pelican Book Group
Submissions: Length: 40,000-45,000 words. Accepts unagented submissions. Responds to queries in one month, full manuscripts in four months. Email submissions only through the website.
Royalty: yes, advance
Types and topics: only contemporary Christian romance, sweet in tone and in conflict, emotionally driven tales of youthful Christians between the ages of 21 and 33 who are striving to live their faith in a world where Christ-centered choices may not fully be understood
Guidelines: *pelicanbookgroup.com/ec/index.php?main_page=page&id=69*
Tip: "Pure Amore romances emphasize the beauty in chastity, so physical interactions, such as kissing or hugging, should focus on the characters' emotions, rather than heightened sexual desire; and scenes of physical intimacy should be integral to the plot and/or emotional development of the character or relationship."

RANDALL HOUSE PUBLICATIONS

114 Bush Rd., Nashville, TN 37217 | 615-361-1221
michelle.orr@randallhouse.com | *www.randallhouse.com*
Michelle Orr, senior acquisitions editor

Denomination: Free Will Baptist
Submissions: Publishes books to make Christ known, from a conservative perspective. Email or mail proposal with sample chapters. Responds in ten to twelve weeks. Publishes ten to twelve titles per year; receives several hundred submissions annually. First-time authors: 25%. Accepts manuscripts directly from authors. Length: 96-152 pages. Bible: NKJV, ESV.
Types of books: offset paperback, POD, e-book, first run 5,000
Royalty: 14-16% on net, advance sometimes

Types and topics: Christian living, parenting, family ministry, small-group studies, church leadership, theology, academic
Imprints: Randall House (ministry leaders, parents), Randall House Academic (college and seminary students and professors, ministry leaders)
Guidelines: by email
Tip: "Author platform is a key component for book selection."

REGNERY FAITH

300 New Jersey Ave., N.W., Ste. 500, Washington, DC 20001
submissions@regnery.com | *www.regnery.com*
Gary Tereshita, editor-in-chief

Parent company: Regnery Publishing, Salem Media Group
Submissions: Regnery Faith imprint is dedicated to developing new faith-based projects for Christian readers. Only accepts manuscripts and proposals from agents.

RESOURCE PUBLICATIONS

See Wipf and Stock Publishing.

RESURRECTION PRESS

77 West End Rd., Totowa, NJ 07572 | 973-890-2400
info@catholicbookpublishing.com | *www.catholicbookpublishing.com*
Anthony Buono, editor

Denomination: Catholic
Parent company: Catholic Book Publishing Corp.
Submissions: Mail proposal and two chapters. Responds in four to six weeks.
Royalty: negotiable
Types and topics: prayer, healing, spirituality, pastoral and liturgical resources
Guidelines: *www.catholicbookpublishing.com/faq.php#manuscript*

REVELL BOOKS

6030 E. Fulton Rd., Ada, MI 49301 | 616-676-9185
www.bakerpublishinggroup.com/revell
Lonnie Hull Dupont, nonfiction acquisitions editor
Kelsey Bowen, fiction acquisitions editor

Parent company: Baker Publishing Group
Submissions: Publishes inspirational fiction and nonfiction for the broadest Christian market. Accepts proposals only

through agents, meeting an editor at a writers conference, or *ChristianManuscriptSubmissions.com.*

Types and topics: apologetics/world religions, Bible study, biography/ memoir, Christian living, Christianity and culture, church life, marriage and family, Spirit-filled, fiction, children and youth fiction and nonfiction

Guidelines: *bakerpublishinggroup.com/contact/submission-policy*

ROSE PUBLISHING

PO Box 3473, Peabody, MA 01961-3473 | 800-358-3111
info@hendricksonrose.com | *www.hendricksonrose.com*
Lynette Pennings, managing editor

Parent company: Hendrickson Publishers

Submissions: Publishes resources that help believers love God by deepening their understanding of who God is. Submit through *ChristianManuscriptSubmissions.com.*

Types and topics: reference products packed with charts, timelines, and simple summaries to make the Bible and its teachings easy to understand

Also does: pamphlets, wall charts

ROSEKIDZ

PO Box 3473, Peabody, MA 01961-3473 | 800-358-3111
info@hendricksonrose.com | *www.hendricksonrose.com*
Brenda Noel, managing editor

Parent company: Hendrickson Publishers

Submissions: Email samples of work first.

Types and topics: reproducible Bible lesson material for children, including age-appropriate Sunday-school activities, instant Bible lessons, girls and boys devotionals, fiction; nursery, toddler, preschool, kindergarten, elementary, and preteen

SAINT CATHERINE OF SIENA PRESS

4812 N. Park Ave., Indianapolis, IN 46205 | 888-232-149
tzander@indy.rr.com | *www.saintcatherineofsienapress.com*

Denomination: Catholic

Types and topics: small-group study guides that put the reader in contact with the sources of Catholic doctrine: The Holy Bible, the Fathers of the Church, papal and conciliar documents, and the Catechism of the Catholic Church

SCEPTER PUBLISHERS

PO Box 360694, Strongsville, OH 44136 | 800-322-8773, 212-354-0670
info@scepterpublishers.org | *www.scepterpublishers.org*
Nathan Davis, editor

Denomination: Catholic

Submissions: Publishes Catholic books that help men and women find God in ordinary life and to realize sanctity in their work, family life, and everyday activities. Send a one- or two-page proposal with cover letter by mail or email.

SERENADE BOOKS

340 S. Lemon Ave. #1639, Walnut, CA 91789
info@serenadebooks.com | *www.serenadebooks.com*
Erin Taylor Young, editor, erin@serenadebooks.com
Regina Jennings, editor, regina@serenadebooks.com

Submissions: Uses innovative marketing and adaptive strategies to help published authors connect with readers who want more romance from voices they love. Publishes six to eight titles per year. First-time authors: 10%. Hometown Romance, 20,000-65,000 words; Timeless, 45,000-110,000 words. Published authors email a proposal with three sample chapters; debut authors email a proposal with the complete manuscript. Responds in two months. Slots for debut authors are extremely limited.

Types of books: e-books only

Royalty: paid monthly, no advance

Types and topics: Frontier romance, historical romance, and romance. Timeless: features previously published books brought back to the market for a new generation of readers. Primary consideration is the power of a memorable story. The romance thread needs to be strong, but that doesn't mean the book has to fit squarely into the romance genre. A bent toward romantic suspense or historical, etc., would not exclude a great story from consideration. Hometown Romance: Story needs to be original, memorable, and of exceptional craftsmanship, with a strong sense of setting and community. While stories can be contemporary or historical, the romance must be the primary focus.

Guidelines: *www.serenadebooks.com/about-us*

Tip: "We only accept submissions at certain times of the year. Please check our website before submitting."

SERVANT BOOKS

See Franciscan Media.

SMITTEN HISTORICAL ROMANCE

2333 Barton Oaks Dr., Raleigh, NC 27614
smitten@lpcbooks.com | *smittenromance.com*
Pegg Thomas, managing editor

Parent company: LPC Books (Lighthouse Publishing of the Carolinas)

Submissions: Publishes eight books per year; receives fifty proposals. First-time authors: 25%. Length: 75,000-95,000 words. Email proposal with sample chapters. Prefers submissions from agents and writers met at writers conferences. Responds in three months. Bible: NIV.

Types of books: POD, e-book

Royalty: 40% net, no advance

Types and topics: historical romance

Guidelines: *smittenromance.com/submissions*

Tip: "Smitten seeks well-written novels with fascinating characters who are engaging with the history of their time period. Historical facts and authenticity are important but do not trump the story. We're not looking for documentaries. This is historical romance. We seek clean, wholesome stories that grab our readers by the heart and present characters with strong moral values."

SMYTH & HELWYS BOOKS

6316 Peake Rd., Macon, GA 31210-3960 | 478-757-0564
proposal@helwys.com | *www.helwys.com*

Submissions: Submit both a hard and digital copy of the complete proposal and two to four sample chapters. Responds in several months.

Types and topics: Christian living, ministry/leadership, biblical studies

Guidelines: *www.helwys.com/submit-a-manuscript*

SONFIRE MEDIA PUBLISHING, LLC

120 West Grayson Street, Ste. 350, Galax, VA 24333 | 276-233-0276
www.sonfiremedia.com
Vie Herlocker, editor, vie.herlocker@sonfiremedia.com
Mary Beth Dahl, editor, mbdahl@taberahpress.com

Submissions: Publishes two to five titles per year, POD. Receives fifty per year. First-time authors: 95%. Length: 40,000-80,000 for nonfiction, 70,000-100,000 for fiction. Email query letter only. Replies in one to two months. Bible: prefers NIV but open to others.

Royalty: 10-20%

Types and topics: devotionals; Christian living; writing instruction; YA and adult fantasy, science fiction, speculative; open to other types of fiction except romance

Imprints: Sonfire Media (nonfiction), Taberah Press (Christian fiction)

Guidelines: *www.sonfiremedia.com/submit.html*

Tip: "We are open to new writers if they are serious about their craft, understand the need for author marketing, and have a 'message that matters.'"

SONRISE DEVOTIONALS

2333 Barton Oaks Dr., Raleigh, NC 27614
csproleslpcacquisitions@gmail.com | *www.sonrisedevotionals.com*
Cindy Sproles, managing editor

Parent company: LPC Books (Lighthouse Publishing of the Carolinas)

Submissions: Publishes six books per year; receives forty proposals. First-time authors: 50%. Length: 50,000-100,000 words. Email proposal with sample chapters. Prefers submissions from agents. Responds in three months. Bible: NIV.

Types of books: POD, e-book

Royalty: 40% net, no advance

Types and topics: daily devotionals, also African-American and Hispanic audiences

Guidelines: *www.sonrisedevotionals.com/submissions*

Tip: "Our goal is to shed light on positive and inspiring books that encourage, educate, and inform from beginning to end. We do not shy away from reflecting today's culture, yet we do so in a way that promotes values, love, and inspiration. Our devotionals touch personal needs, answer life questions, and portray our world with a thread of hope. "Our authors are familiar with the current market and understand how they will reach their target audience. They should have a platform via social media and must regularly engage with their tribe. While we assist in marketing efforts, authors must create and follow through with their own marketing plans.

We prefer 365-day devotionals but will consider 30-, 60-, 90-day devotionals."

SPARKHOUSE FAMILY

510 Marquette Ave., Minneapolis, MN 55403
sparkhousefamily.submittable.com | *www.sparkhouse.org*
Andrew DeYoung, acquisitions

Parent company: 1517 Media
Denomination: Evangelical Lutheran Church in America
Submissions: Publishes twenty-four books per year; receives two hundred fifty. First-time authors: 50%. Length: 500 words for picture book. Submit proposal with sample chapters or full manuscript through the website. Responds in three months. Bible: NIV, CEB.
Royalty: varies, advance
Types and topics: board books for ages birth-3, picture books for ages 3-8, activity books for ages 3-8, early reader and first chapter books for ages 5-9, nonfiction books for ages 5-9 and 8-12, fiction for ages 8-12, activity books for families, devotionals for ages 0-12 and families
Guidelines: *sparkhousefamily.submittable.com/submit/65108/sparkhouse-family-submissions*
Tip: "Look at what we've published before. Read a few of our books before submitting."

STRAIGHT STREET BOOKS

2333 Barton Oaks Dr., Raleigh, NC 27614
csproleslpcacquisitions@gmail.com | *www.straightstreetbooks.com*
Cindy Sproles, managing editor

Parent company: LPC Books (Lighthouse Publishing of the Carolinas)
Submissions: Publishes six books per year; receives forty proposals. First-time authors: 50%. Length: 50,000-100,000 words. Email proposal with sample chapters. Prefers submissions from agents. Responds in three months. Bible: NIV.
Types of books: POD, e-book
Royalty: 40% net, no advance
Types and topics: Christian living, business, family issues, mental and physical disabilities, sports, biographies, prayer, marriage, women's issues, discipleship
Guidelines: *www.straightstreetbooks.com/submissions*

Tip: "Straight Street Books covers current topics and issues from a Christian worldview. Our books touch personal needs, answer life questions, and portray our world with a thread of hope. Authors are familiar with the current market and understand how they will reach their target audience. We do not accept Bible studies."

SUNPENNY PUBLISHING

Urbanització Tossal Gross, 90-1, La Font d'en Carròs, 46717, Valencia Communidad, Spain (based in England too)
writers@sunpenny.com | *www.sunpenny.com*
Jo Holloway, editor

Submissions: Email brief synopsis and short author bio included in the body of the email with a one- to two-page synopsis attached. Publishes fifteen to twenty titles per year. First-time authors: 50%. Accepts manuscripts directly from authors. Responds in one to two weeks to queries, one to two months to proposals, two to three months to manuscripts.
Royalty: sliding scale, beginning at 15%
Types and topics: wit and humor, entertainment, travel, adventure, historical novels, romance, women's fiction, courage, challenges, overcoming, gift books, coffee-table books, children and young teens, self-help, memoir, biography
Imprints: Rose & Crown Books (Christian romance), ChristLight Books (Christian fiction and nonfiction in all genres)
Guidelines: *www.sunpenny.com/#!submissions*

THOMAS NELSON PUBLISHERS

PO Box 141000, Nashville, TN 37214-1000 | 615-889-9000
www.thomasnelson.com
Becky Monds, acquisitions editor, fiction
Debbie Wickwire, acquisitions, W Publishing
Jessica Wong, acquisitions, Thomas Nelson
Joel Kneedler, publisher, Emanate Books

Parent company: HarperCollins Christian Publishing
Submissions: Only accepts proposals through agents or direct contact with editors. Does not accept or review any unsolicited queries, proposals, or manuscripts. Publishes fewer than one hundred titles per year.
Types and topics: Christian living, church and ministry resources, Bible reference, commentaries, Bible book studies, business and leadership, biography, women's devotionals, fiction for adults and YA, gift books

Imprints: Nelson Books (spiritual growth and practical living), W Publishing Group (memoir, help and hope for doing life better, and leading pastoral voices, with select practical living), Grupo Nelson (Spanish), Tommy Nelson (children and teens; see separate entry), Emanate Books (Charismatic)

Guidelines: *www.harpercollinschristian.com/write-for-us*

TOMMY NELSON

PO Box 141000, Nashville, TN 37214-1000 | 615-889-9000
www.tommynelson.com
Mackinzie Howard, children's acquisitions editor

Parent company: Thomas Nelson Publishers

Submissions: Only accepts proposals through agents or direct contact with editors. Does not accept or review any unsolicited queries, proposals, or manuscripts.

Types and topics: board books, picture books, Bible story books, devotionals for middle grade and teens

Guidelines: *www.harpercollinschristian.com/write-for-us*

THE TRINITY FOUNDATION

PO Box 68, Unicoi, TN 37692 | 423-743-0199
tjtrinityfound@aol.com | *www.trinityfoundation.org*
Thomas W. Juodaitis, president

Submissions: Publishes books to promote the logical system of truth found in the Bible. Publishes two to three titles per year; receives five proposals. First-time authors: 10%. Length: 50-400 pages. Email or mail a proposal with sample chapters. Responds in one week. Bible version: KJV, NKJV.

Types of books: hardcover, paperback, e-books

Royalty: none, no advance, flat fee $1,000-2,000

Types and topics: theology, philosophy

Guidelines: none

Tip: "Look at the content of our website and be in agreement with that content."

TYNDALE HOUSE PUBLISHERS

351 Executive Dr., Carol Stream, IL 60188 | 630-668-8300
www.tyndale.com
Sarah Atkinson, senior acquisitions, nonfiction
Jon Farrar, acquisitions director, devotionals
Jan Stob, fiction director

Submissions: Publishes one to two hundred titles per year. First-time authors: 5%. Only reviews manuscripts submitted by professional literary agents, Tyndale authors, authors known to them from other publishers, or other people in the publishing industry. Responds in three to six months. Bible: NLT. Fiction length: 75,000-100,000 words.

Types of books: offset paperback, hardback, e-book

Types and topics: home and family, Christian beliefs, finance, leadership, career, parenting, marriage, memoir, biography, devotionals, counseling; fiction with evangelical message: biblical, contemporary, futuristic, historical, romance, suspense/thriller

Imprint: Tyndale Kids (see separate entry), Tyndale Español (Spanish)

Guidelines: *www.tyndale.com/faq*

TYNDALE KIDS

351 Executive Dr., Carol Stream, IL 60188 | 630-668-8300
www.tyndale.com/kids
Jesse Doogan, acquisitions editor

Submissions: Publishes twenty to twenty-five books per year. Proposals only from agents, Tyndale authors, authors known to them from other publishers, or other people in the publishing industry.

Types and topics: picture books, first-chapter books, middle grade, YA, Bible stories, fiction, nonfiction

Guidelines: *www.tyndale.com/faq*

WARNER PRESS

1201 E. 5th St., Anderson, IN 46012 | 800-741-7721
editors@warnerpress.org | *www.warnerpress.org*
Karen Rhodes, editorial director

Denomination: Church of God

Submissions: Email manuscript. Receives more than a hundred submissions annually. Accepts manuscripts directly from authors. Responds in six to eight weeks. Publication within one year. Bible: KJV, NIV.

Royalty: based on the author and type of book, advance

Types and topics: evangelism, discipleship, missions, pastoral leadership, Christian living, devotionals, Bible-study guides on specific subjects or a Bible book, teaching resource books; short books that are inspirational, devotional, and encouraging and help others deal with life's challenging situations; also see entry in

"Miscellaneous."

Guidelines: *www.warnerpress.org/submission-guidelines*

WATERBROOK PRESS

10807 New Allegiance Dr. #500, Colorado Springs, CO 80921

719-590-4999

info@waterbrookmultnomah.com | *www.waterbrookmultnomah.com*

Shannon Marchese, senior editor, fiction

Andrew Stoddard, acquisitions editor

Parent company: Crown Publishing Group, a division of Penguin Random House

Submissions: Publishes sixty titles per year. Currently not accepting unsolicited manuscripts, proposals, or queries. Queries will be accepted through literary agents and at writers conferences at which a WaterBrook representative is present.

Types of books: hardcover, trade paperbacks, e-books

Royalty: on net, advance

Types and topics: practical life, inspiration and encouragement, devotional, relationships and parenting, biography, memoir, topical Bible study, justice, spiritual warfare, fiction, children's books

Imprint: Shaw (Fisherman Bible study guides)

Guidelines: *waterbrookmultnomah.com/submissions*

WATERFALL PRESS

waterfall-inquiries@brilliancepublishing.com | *www.brilliancepublishing.com/waterfall.html*

Sheryl Zajchowski, acquisitions

Parent company: Brilliance Publishing, *Amazon.com*

Submissions: Publishes twenty to thirty titles per year.

Types and topics: Christian living

WATERSHED BOOKS

PO Box 1738, Aztec, NM 87410

customer@pelicanbookgroup.com | *www.pelicanbookgroup.com*

Nicola Martinez, editor-in-chief

Parent company: Pelican Book Group

Submissions: Email submissions only through the website. Length: 25,000-60,000 words. Accepts unagented submissions. Responds to queries in one month, full manuscript in three months. Email submissions only.

Royalty: 40% on download, 7% on print, nominal advance

Types and topics: young-adult fiction that features young-adult characters; action-adventure, mystery (amateur sleuth or other), romance, science fiction, fantasy, supernatural, suspense, crime drama, police procedural, teen angst, coming-of-age, westerns; interested in series ideas

Guidelines: *pelicanbookgroup.com/ec/index.php?main_page=page&id=60*

WESTMINSTER/JOHN KNOX PRESS

100 Witherspoon St., Louisville, KY 40202-1396
submissions@wjkbooks.com | *www.wjkbooks.com*
Jessica Miller Kelley, acquisitions editor

Denomination: Presbyterian

Parent company: Presbyterian Publishing Corporation

Submissions: Publishes approximately sixty books and other resources each year. Prefers emailed proposals but will take them by mail. Responds in two to three months.

Types and topics: children, theology, biblical studies, preaching, worship, ethics, religion and culture, and other related fields for four main markets: scholars and students in colleges, universities, seminaries, and divinity schools; preachers, educators, and counselors working in churches; members of mainline Protestant congregations; and general readers

Imprint: Geneva Press (books specifically related to the Presbyterian Church USA)

Guidelines: *www.wjkbooks.com/Pages/Item/1345/Author-Relations.aspx*

WHITAKER HOUSE

1030 Hunt Valley Cir., New Kensington, PA 15068 | 724-334-7000
publisher@whitakerhouse.com | *www.whitakerhouse.com*
Tom Cox, managing editor
Christine Whitaker, fiction acquisitions editor

Denomination: Charismatic

Submissions: Only reviews proposals from agents or by request from a house representative. Email a proposal or mail to Author Liaison. Responds in six months. Publishes seventy titles per year; receives fifty to one hundred submissions annually. First-time authors: 15-20%. Length: 40,000-70,000 words, 96-336 pages.

Royalty: 6-20% on net, 25% on e-books, variable advance

Types and topics: biography/autobiography, Charismatic interest, Christian living, devotions, fiction, gender-specific issues for men or women, inspiration, marriage, family, relationships, prayer, spiritual growth, spiritual warfare, theology, African-American, Hispanic

Imprints: Banner Publishing, Resolute Books

Guidelines: *www.whitakerhouse.com/downloads/WhitakerManuscriptSubmissionGuidelines.pdf*

Tip: "Looking for quality nonfiction and fiction by authors with a national marketing platform. Most open to high-quality, well-thought-out, compelling pieces of work. Review the guidelines and submit details as thoroughly as possible for publication consideration."

WHITE ROSE PUBLISHING

PO Box 1738, Aztec, NM 87410
customer@pelicanbookgroup.com | *www.pelicanbookgroup.com*
Nicola Martinez, editor-in-chief

Parent company: Pelican Book Group

Submissions: Email submissions only through the website. Length: short stories, 10,000-20,000 words (e-book); novelettes, 20,000-35,000 words (e-book); novellas, 35,000-60,000 words (e-book); novels, 60,000-80,000 words (e-book and print). Accepts unagented submissions. Responds to queries in one month, full manuscript in three months. Email submissions only.

Royalty: 40% on download, 7% on print, nominal advance

Types and topics: only romance, interested in series ideas

Guidelines: *pelicanbookgroup.com/ec/index.php?main_page=page&id=58*

WHITEFIRE PUBLISHING

13607 Bedford Rd. N.E., Cumberland, MD 21502 | 866-245-2211
www.whitefire-publishing.com
Roseanna White, senior editor, r.white@whitefire-publishing.com
Wendy Chorot, senior nonfiction editor, w.chorot@whitefire-publishing.com

Submissions: Publishes nine to twelve POD titles per year; receives one hundred annually. First-time authors: 50%. Length: 60,000-125,000. Email query letter only. Replies in two to four weeks. Bible: KJV for historicals, no preference for contemporaries.

Royalty: 50% on e-books, 10% on print, advance sometimes

Types: memoir, Christian living, inspirational; fiction: historical,

historical romance, romantic suspense, contemporary romance, contemporary, suspense, open to speculative and young adult

Guidelines: *whitefire-publishing.com/wordpress/sample-page/submissions*

Tip: "Embrace the motto of 'Where Spirit Meets the Page.' Looking for stories or nonfiction with a unique angle; don't shy away from difficult subjects."

WILLIAM CAREY LIBRARY

626-720-8210
submissions@WCLBooks.com | *www.missionbooks.org*
Aidan Lewis, editor

Submissions: Publishes scholarly and professional or educational books, all related to missions. "We especially seek to assist the work of the mission executive, field missionary, church leader, and the student of world mission." Responds in three to six months. Send a maximum two-page query letter initially. No unsolicited manuscripts.

Types and topics: ethnography, biography, educational, nonfiction, missions, missiology

Guidelines: *missionbooks.org/submissions*

Tip: "Read our publishing focus carefully. We only publish literature promoting world missions, specifically among unreached and unengaged peoples."

WIPF AND STOCK PUBLISHERS

199 W. 8th Ave., Ste. 3, Eugene, OR 97401-2960 | 541-344-1528
proposal@wipfandstock.com | *www.wipfandstock.com*
Rodney Clapp, editor, rodney@wipfandstock.com
Dr. Chris Spinks, editor, chris@wipfandstock.com

Submissions: Email proposal with proposal form from the website. Responds in eight weeks. It is your responsibility to submit a manuscript that has been fully copyedited by a professional copy editor. Publishes more than four hundred books per year, short-run and e-books.

Types and topics: primarily academic

Imprint: Resource Publications (for leaders and pastors in ministries, faith-based resources for personal growth and use by educators)

Guidelines: *wipfandstock.com/submitting-a-proposal?hl=1*

WORTHY KIDS / IDEALS

6100 Tower Cir., Ste. 210, Franklin, TN 37067 | 615-932-7600
IdealsInfo@worthypublishing.com |
worthypublishing.com/product-category/worthy-kids-ideals
Peggy Schaefer, publisher

Parent company: Worthy Publishing Group
Submissions: Publishes thirty titles per year; receives six hundred annually. First-time authors: fewer than 1%. Length: 200 words for board books, 800 words for picture books. Email proposal with full manuscript. Responds only to manuscripts of interest. Bible: NLT.
Royalty: 5-7%, advance sometimes
Types and topics: fiction and nonfiction children's books for birth through age 8: inspiration/faith, patriotism, and holidays, particularly Easter and Christmas; relationships and values; general fiction; Ideals Christmas and Ideals Easter: poetry and prose for annual issues for all ages, should be optimistic and can be nostalgic, inspirational, or humorous
Guidelines: *worthypublishing.com/wp-content/uploads/2017/03/SUBMISSION-GUIDELINES-PDF.pdf*
Tip: "Editors review complete manuscripts only; do not send query letters or proposals. Previous publications, relevant qualifications or background, and a brief synopsis of your manuscript may be included in a cover letter."

WORTHY PUBLISHING GROUP

134 Franklin Rd., Ste 200, Brentwood, TN 37027 | 615-932-7600
www.worthypublishing.com
Jeana Ledbetter, acquisitions, Worthy Publishing
Marilyn Jansen, acquisitions, Worthy Inspired

Submissions: Publishes thirty-six titles per year. Requires submission by agents; unsolicited manuscripts returned unopened.
Royalty: for Worthy Books, flat fee for some of Worthy Inspired, advance
Types and topics: broad spectrum of genres, including current events, pop culture, biography, fiction, spiritual growth, and Bibles; Worthy Inspired: felt-need personal growth, inspirational, devotional, for professional women
Imprints: Worthy Books, Worthy Inspired, Worthy Kids/Ideals (see separate listing), Ellie Claire (gifts, see separate listing), Museum of the Bible Books (engagement with the Bible)

WRITE INTEGRITY PRESS

PO Box 702852, Dallas, TX 75370
MarjiLaine@WriteIntegrity.com | *www.WriteIntegrity.com*
Marji Laine Clubine, executive editor

Submissions: Publishes twenty-four titles per year; receives two hundred fifty. First-time authors: 20%. Length: 55,000-80,000 words. Email proposal with first three chapters. No simultaneous submissions. Responds in two months. Bible: any version.

Books: POD, e-book

Royalty: 40-50%; no advance

Types and topics: clean, wholesome fiction (contemporary, suspense, historical romance; crime drama, cozy mystery, action and adventure; 1900s historical; contemporary, romance, dystopian YA; contemporary, action and adventure, mystery and detective, 1900s historical middle grade); evangelical/redemptive children's picture books; Christian living; devotions; Bible studies

Imprints: Pix-N-Pens Publishing (Christian living and children's evangelistic picture books)

Guidelines: *www.writeintegrity.com/submissions*

Tip: "Follow submission guidelines. Make sure your manuscript is clean. Utilize critique groups, partners, or freelance editors before submitting your project."

YOUTH SPECIALTIES

5320 W. 23rd St., Ste. 130, Minneapolis, MN 55416 | 888-346-4179
publishing@youthspecialties.com | *youthspecialties.com*
Jacob Eckeberger, director of resource development

Submissions: Not currently looking for books, but check the website to see if this situation changes. Email proposal and sample chapters as attached file. Responds in three months.

Types and topics: youth ministry, parenting, meeting plans and programming ideas for middle school and high school, game books

Guidelines: *youthspecialties.com/about/write-for-us*

YWAM PUBLISHING

PO Box 55787, Seattle, WA 98155 | 800-922-2143
books@ywampublishing.com | *www.ywampublishing.com*

Parent company: Youth With A Mission

Submissions: Email or mail proposal, following the template on the website. Will not respond to submissions that deviate from proposal guidelines.

Types and topics: evangelism, mission adventures, missions for kids,

Bible studies, devotionals, leadership, relationships; no longer accepts fiction or children's literature

Guidelines: *www.ywampublishing.com/t-submission.aspx*

ZONDERKIDZ

3900 Sparks Dr. S.E., Grand Rapids, MI 49512 | 616-698-6900

ZonderkidzSubmissions@harpercollins.com | *www.zonderkidz.com*

Robyn Burwell, acquisitions editor, Robyn.Burwell@harpercollins.com

Parent company: HarperCollins Christian Publishing

Submissions: Requires submissions only through agents.

Types and topics: children's fiction and nonfiction, teen fiction and nonfiction, children's Bibles

Guidelines: *www.harpercollinschristian.com/write-for-us*

Tip: "We are seeking fresh fiction and nonfiction for children ages 0-18. Under our Zonderkidz and Zondervan imprints, we look for engaging picture books and board books, timeless storybook Bibles, faith-centric fiction from established authors, and nonfiction from key voices in the Christian sphere."

ZONDERVAN

3900 Sparks Dr. S.E., Grand Rapids, MI 49512 | 616-698-6900

www.zondervan.com

Carolyn McCready, trade acquisitions editor

Molly Hodgin, gift books

Parent company: HarperCollins Christian Publishing

Submissions: Requires submissions only through agents. Publishes one hundred twenty trade titles per year. Bible version: NIV.

Types and topics: spiritual growth, marriage, family, social issues, leadership, finance, biography, commentaries, church and ministry, fiction (contemporary, mystery, historical, romance, science fiction, fantasy, suspense)

Imprints: Zonderkidz (see separate entry), Editorial Vida (Spanish), Zondervan Academic

Guidelines: *www.harpercollinschristian.com/write-for-us*

PART 2

INDEPENDENT BOOK PUBLISHING

2

INDEPENDENT BOOK PUBLISHERS

PUBLISHING A BOOK YOURSELF NO LONGER CARRIES THE STIGMA self-publishing has had in the past—if you do it right. Even some well-published writers are now hybrid authors, with independently published books alongside their royalty books. Others have built their readerships with traditional publishers, then moved to independent publishing where it is possible to make more money per sale.

Independent book publishers require the author to pay for part of the publishing costs or to buy a certain number of books. They call themselves by a variety of names, such as book packager, cooperative publisher, self-publisher, custom publisher, subsidy publisher, or simply someone who helps authors get their books printed. Services vary from including different levels of editing and proofreading to printing your manuscript as is.

Whenever you pay for any part of the production of your book, you are entering into a nontraditional relationship. Some independent publishers also offer a form of royalty publishing, so be sure you understand the contract they give you before signing it.

Some independent publishers will publish any book, as long as the author is willing to pay for it. Others are as selective about what they publish as a royalty publisher is. Some independent publishers will do as much promotion as a royalty publisher—for a fee. Others do none at all.

If you are unsuccessful in placing your book with a royalty publisher but feel strongly about seeing it published, an independent publisher can make printing your book easier and often less expensive than doing it yourself. POD, as opposed to a print run of 1,000 or more, could save you upfront money, although the price per copy is higher. Having your manuscript produced only as an e-book is also a less-expensive option.

Entries in this chapter are for information only, not an endorsement of publishers. For every complaint about a publisher, there can be several other authors who sing the praises of it. Before you sign with any company, get more than one bid to determine whether the terms you are offered are competitive. A legitimate independent publisher will provide a list of former clients as references. Also buy a couple of the publisher's previous books to check the quality of the work—covers, bindings, typesetting, etc. See if the books currently are available through any of the major online retailers.

Get answers before committing yourself. You may also want someone in the book-publishing industry to review your contract before you sign it. Some experts listed in the "**Editorial Services**" chapter review contracts.

If you decide not to use an independent publisher but do the work yourself, at least hire an editor, proofreader, cover designer, and interior typesetter-designer. The "**Editorial Services**" and "**Design and Production Services**" chapters will help you locate professionals with skills in these areas, as well as printing companies. Plus the "**Distribution Services**" and "**Publicity and Marketing Services**" chapters can help you solve one of the biggest problems of independent publishing: getting your books to readers.

AARON BOOK PUBLISHING

1104 Bristol Caverns Hwy., Bristol, TN 37620 | 423-212-1208
info@aaronbookpublishing.com | *www.AaronBookPublishing.com*
Lidany Rouse, acquistions editor

Types: hardcover, paperback, gift book, POD
Services: book covers, formatting, substantive editing, copyediting, proofreading, marketing, packages of services, à la carte options
Tip: Prefers manuscript by email. Submission guidelines are on the website.

ACW PRESS

PO Box 110390, Nashville, TN 37222 | 800-21-WRITE
acwriters@aol.com | *www.acwpress.com*
Reg A. Forder, publisher

Types: hardcover, offset and POD paperback, gift book
Services: design, substantive editing, copyediting, proofreading, packages of services
Production time: two to four months
Tip: "We offer a high-quality publishing alternative to help Christian authors get their material into print. High standards, high quality. If authors have a built-in audience, they have the best chance to make self-publishing a success."

ALTEN INK

1888 Montara Way, San Jacinto, CA 92583 | 951-327-3698
AltenInk3@gmail.com | www.AltenInk.com
Deborah L. Alten

Types: paperback, e-book, picture book
Services: substantive editing, proofreading, design, promotional materials, online bookstore, publishing packages of services, à la carte options
Production time: six months
Tip: "Email us. You will get a quicker response."

AMPELOS PRESS

951 Anders Rd., Lansdale, PA 19446 | 484-991-8581
mbagnull@aol.com | writehisanswer.com/ampelospress
Marlene Bagnull, publisher

Types: e-book, POD
Services: manuscript evaluation, design, substantive editing, copyediting, proofreading
Production time: six months
Books per year: one or two
Tip: "Especially interested in helping authors independently publish books about missions, issues, and the needs of children. Not actively soliciting manuscripts, but accepts them from writers she meets at conferences."

BK ROYSTON PUBLISHING, LLC

PO Box 4321, Jeffersonville, IN 47131 | 502-802-5385
publishnow@bkroystonpublishing.com | www.bkroystonpublishing.com
Julia A. Royston, CEO

Types: hardcover, offset and POD paperback, e-book
Services: copyediting, proofreading, distribution
Also does: ghostwriting, coaching, royalty contracts
Production time: one to four months

BOOKBABY

7905 N. Crescent Blvd., Pennsauken, NJ 08110 | 877-961-6878
info@bookbaby.com | www.bookbaby.com

Types: paperback, hardcover, e-book, POD, gift book, picture book, cookbook, comic book, yearbook, many other formats
Services: manuscript evaluation, design, substantive editing,

copyediting, proofreading, promotional materials, marketing, distribution, author website, online bookstore

Production time: as quick as five days

Tip: Has e-book and printed book distribution network for self-published authors around the globe.

BOOKS BY THE BUNDLE

9217 W. River Rd., Brooklyn Park, MN 55444 | 612-968-9301
Jamie@booksbythebundle.org | *www.booksbythebundle.org*
Jamie Morrison, executive publisher; Kelly, office manager

Types: paperback, hardcover, e-book, POD, picture book

Services: manuscript evaluation, design, substantive editing, copyediting, proofreading, distribution, à la carte options

Production time: six weeks to nine months

Tip: "We make publishing your book easy."

BROWN CHRISTIAN PRESS

16250 Knoll Trail Dr., Ste. 205, Dallas, TX 75248 | 972-381-0009
email through website | *www.brownbooks.com/christian.php*

Types: hardcover, paperback, gift book, e-book

Services: substantive editing, copyediting, proofreading, ghostwriting, design, marketing, distribution, author website

Publication time: six months

Tip: "We are a relationship publisher and work with our authors from beginning to end in the journey of publishing."

CARPENTER'S SON PUBLISHING

307 Verde Meadow Dr., Franklin, TN 37067 | 615-472-1128
larry@christianbookservices.com | *www.carpenterssonpublishing.com*
Larry Carpenter, president-CEO, editor

Types: offset and POD paperback, hardcover, e-book, audiobook, gift book, picture book

Services: manuscript evaluation, design, substantive editing, copyediting, proofreading, indexing, promotional materials, marketing, distribution, author website, à la carte options

Production time: four to six months

Books per year: one hundred

Tip: "Get books that are the same quality as those coming from traditional publishers but with more control over your book and more profit through our custom-publishing program."

CHRISTIAN FAITH PUBLISHING

832 Park Ave., Meadville, PA 16335 | 800-955-3794
contact@christianfaithpublishing.com | *www.Christianfaithpublishing.com*
Chris Rutherford, president; Jason Murray, executive vice president

Types: offset and POD paperback, hardcover, e-book
Services: manuscript evaluation, design, copyediting, indexing, promotional materials, marketing, distribution, author website, packages of services, à la carte options
Also offers: royalty contracts
Production time: eight to ten months
Books per year: twelve hundred
Tip: "Be mindful of the fact that it is quite challenging to publish a book and have commercial success."

CHRISTIAN WRITER'S EBOOK

PO Box 446, Ft. Duchesne, UT 84026 | 435-772-3429
editor@writersebook.com | *www.writersebook.com*
Linda Kay Stewart Whitsitt, editor-in-chief

Type: e-book
Services: design, author website, marketing, online bookstore
Production time: six months
Tip: "Make sure your work is polished and ready for print. The books we publish are sold in our online store at Amazon and eBay."

CLM PUBLISHING

Building G, Ste. 5, Countryside Shopping Village, Box 1217 GT, Grand Cayman, Cayman Islands KY11108 | 345-926 2507
production@clmpublishing.com | *www.clmpublishing.com*
Karen E. Chin, managing editor

Types: paperback, hardcover, e-book, POD, gift book, picture book
Services: manuscript evaluation, design, substantive editing, copyediting, proofreading, promotional materials, marketing, distribution, author website, online bookstore, publishing packages of services, à la carte options
Production time: three months
Also does: royalty contracts
Tip: "Even after many rejection letters, never stop writing. There is always a publisher for you."

COVENANT BOOKS

11661 Hwy. 707, Murrells Inlet, SC 29576 | 843-507-8373
info@covenantbooks.com | *www.covenantbooks.com*
Denice Hunter, president

Types: offset and POD paperback, hardcover, e-book
Services: design, copyediting, indexing, marketing, distribution, online bookstore
Also does: royalty contracts
Production time: six months
Books per year: five hundred
Tip: "Publishing a book should be done for the author's satisfaction, pride, and desire to share a story or spread the word about something—not for the purpose of making a profit. The publishing process should be an enjoyable, fun, and satisfying one for the author but is often not likely to result in a financial gain for the author. Any author who engages in the process with this in mind will find it to be a most satisfying experience."

CREATION HOUSE

600 Rinehart Rd., Lake Mary, FL 32746-4872 | 407-333-0600
creationhouse@charismamedia.com | *www.creationhouse.com*

Types: hardcover, paperback, gift book
Services: "We use the term 'co-publishing' to describe a hybrid between conventional royalty publishing and self- or subsidy publishing, utilizing the best of both worlds. We produce a high-quality book for our own inventory, market it, distribute it, and pay the author a royalty on every copy sold. In return, the author agrees to buy, at a deep discount, a portion of the first print run."
Production time: two to four months
Tip: Our purpose is "to inspire and equip people to live a Spirit-led life and to walk in the divine purpose for which they were created."

CREATIVE ENTERPRISES STUDIO

PO Box 224, Fort Worth, TX 76095 | 817-312-7393
AcreativeShop@aol.com | *CreativeEnterprisesStudio.com*
Mary Hollingsworth, publisher and managing director

Types: hardcover, paperback, gift book, e-book, audiobook, POD
Services: coaching, ghostwriting, editing, proofreading, typesetting, marketing, warehousing, shipping, website creation, video trailers
Production time: six months

Tip: "With 30 years of experience, CES is the best alternative to traditional publishing and self-publishing, offering first-class, custom publishing services from manuscript through printed books to help Christian authors powerfully glorify God in print."

CREDO HOUSE PUBLISHERS

2200 Boyd Ct. N.E., Grand Rapids, MI 49525-6714 | 616-363-2686
publish@credocommunications.net | *www.credohousepublishers.com*
Timothy J. Beals, publisher

Types: hardcover, paperback, gift book, e-book, POD
Services: Exists to "bring words to life" by working with Christian ministry leaders and organizations to develop life-changing books, Bible-related products, and other Christian resources. Can assist you in all phases of the publishing process—from concept sheets and prototypes to simple proofreading or complex content editing.

CROSSHAIR PRESS

PO Box 154, Haven, KS 67543 | 316-214-9818
acquisitions@crosshairpress.com | *www.crosshairpress.com*
Amy Davis, acquisitions manager

Types: paperback, e-book, audiobook, POD
Services: manuscript evaluation, design, substantive editing, copyediting, proofreading, distribution
Production time: one year
Tip: "View our submission guidelines online for our reading period dates. Email submissions only."

DCTS PUBLISHING

PO Box 40216, Santa Barbara, CA 93140 | 805-570-3168
dennis@dctspub.com | *www.dctspub.com*
Dennis Stephen Hamilton, editor

Types: print and e-book
Services: editing, design
Production time: six to eight months
Tip: "For authors who want quality low-cost publishing, we will partner with you in producing a fantastic marketable book that will sell anywhere in the world. Please contact me for more details."

DEEP RIVER BOOKS

PO Box 310, Sisters, OR 97759 | 541-549-1139
info@deepriverbooks.com | *www.deepriverbooks.com*

Bill and Nancie Carmichael, publishers;
Andy Carmichael, associate publisher

Types: hardcover, offset paperback, e-book, audiobook, gift book
Services: manuscript evaluation, design, substantive editing, copyediting, proofreading, promotional materials, marketing, distribution, packages of services
Production time: nine to twelve months
Books per year: thirty-five to forty
Tip: "All manuscripts submitted go to our editorial review team. Send manuscript synopsis; a paragraph or two about you, your platform, and credentials; and two or three sample chapters."

DEEPER REVELATION BOOKS

PO Box 4260, Cleveland, TN 37320-4260 | 423-478-2843
email through website | *www.deeperrevelationbooks.org*
Mike Shreve

Types: POD, e-book
Services: editing, proofreading, design, marketing, distribution promotional materials, author website

DESTINY IMAGE PUBLISHERS

PO Box 310, Shippensburg, PA 17257 | 800-722-6774, 717-532-3040
manuscripts@norimediagroup.com | *www.destinyimage.com*
Mykela Krieg, executive acquisitions director

Types: hardcover, paperback, e-book
Services: evaluation, editing (whatever level is necessary), proofreading, design, marketing
Production time: one year
Tip: Requires prepurchase of 1,000 to 3,000 copies. Major topics include dreams/dream interpretation, supernatural God encounters, healing/deliverance, and prophecy. No poetry, art, or children's stories; limited fiction. Prefers 40,000-60,000 words. "Most open to books on the deeper life or of charismatic interest."

EABOOKS PUBLISHING

1567 Thornhill Cir., Oviedo, FL 32765 | 407-712-3431
info@eabookspublishing.com | *www.eabookspublishing.com*
Cheri Cowell, owner-publisher

Types: POD, e-book, audiobook, gift book
Services: manuscript evaluation, design, substantive editing, copyediting, proofreading, promotional materials, marketing,

distribution, author website, online bookstore, packages of services, à la carte options

Production time: forty-five to ninety days

Books per year: forty-five

Tip: "Send and email through website with contact info. Or see us at a Christian writers conference; see the list on our website. We want to help you get your message into the world."

ELECTRIC MOON PUBLISHING, LLC

PO Box 466, Stromsburg, NE 68666 | 402-366-2033

info@emoonpublishing.com | *www.emoonpublishing.com*

Laree Lindburg, owner

Types: offset and POD paperback, hardcover, e-book, audiobook, gift book, picture book

Services: manuscript evaluation, design, substantive editing, copyediting, proofreading, promotional materials, marketing, distribution, author website, packages of services, à la carte options

Production time: six to eight months

Books per year: twelve plus

Tip: "Ask the publisher for submission guidelines, and follow them. Take your time with your book, and do all steps with excellence. You will never regret a well-executed project."

ELM HILL

836 S. Western Dr., Bloomington, IN 47403 | 800-254-2735

email through website | *elmhill books.com*

Types: POD, hardcover, e-book

Services: manuscript evaluation, substantive editing, copyediting, design, marketing, promotional materials, author website, video trailer, distribution assistance, packages of services, à la carte options

Tip: Parent company is Harper-Collins Christian Publishing in collaboration with Accurance, a production services company.

ESSENCE PUBLISHING

20 Hanna Ct., Belleville, ON K8P 5J2, Canada | 800-238-6376, 613-962-2360

info@essence-publishing.com | *www.essence-publishing.com*

Sherrill Brunton, manager of publishing department

Types: offset and POD paperback, gift book, e-book, picture book

Services: manuscript evaluation, design, substantive editing,

copyediting, proofreading, indexing, promotional materials, marketing, distribution, online bookstore, packages of services, à la carte options, book trailers, sell sheets

Production time: three months

Books per year: one hundred fifty

Tip: "Request our free author's information package, and submit a copy of your manuscript for your free evaluation. There is no cost, and you are under no obligation."

FAIRWAY PRESS

5450 N. Dixie Hwy., Lima, OH 45807-9559 | 800-241-4056, 419-227-1818

david@csspub.com | *www.fairwaypress.com*

Missy Cotrell, acquisitions editor

Types: hardcover, paperback, POD, e-book

Services: mechanical edit (spelling, grammar, punctuation, etc.), formatting, proofreading, cover design, printing (average print run five hundred copies, minimum fifty), ISBN, bar coding, copyright filing. No email submissions.

Production time: six to nine months

Books per year: ten to fifteen

Tip: This is the subsidy division of CSS Publishing Company. No longer does color illustrations or four-color books.

FAITH BOOKS & MORE PUBLISHING

PO Box 1024, Athens, OH 45701 | 678-232-6156

publishing@faithbooksandmore.com | *www.faithbooksandmore.com*

Nicole Antoinette Smith, author advocate

Types: hardcover, offset and POD paperback, picture book

Services: manuscript evaluation, design, substantive editing, copyediting, proofreading, promotional materials, marketing, distribution, author website, packages of services, à la carte options

Also does: author coaching, ghostwriting

Production time: three months

Books per year: ten

Tip: "Understand the anatomy of a book, and develop a marketing plan for your book."

FIESTA PUBLISHING

1219 E. Colter St. #16, Phoenix, AZ 85014 | 602-795-5868

julie@fiestapublishing.com | www.fiestapublishing.com
Julie Castro, owner

Types: offset and POD paperback, e-book, hardcover
Services: manuscript evaluation, design, substantive editing, copyediting, proofreading, promotional materials, marketing, distribution, online bookstore, à la carte options
Production time: depends on author's timeline
Tip: "The book you write should be the best it can be. Each book is unique and should be treated as such."

FILLED BOOKS / EMPOWERED PUBLICATIONS, INC.

529 County Road 31, Millry, AL 36558 | 888-278-2547
editor@empoweredpublications.com | www.filledbooks.com
Bridgett Henson, acquisitions editor

Types: offset and POD paperback, hardcover, e-book
Services: manuscript evaluation, design, substantive editing, copyediting, proofreading, promotional services, marketing, distribution, author website, online bookstore, packages of services, à la carte options
Also does: royalty contracts
Production time: five weeks
Books per year: six
Tip: "We are a conservative, Pentecostal publisher for ministers who agree with our trinitarian statement of faith. All authors must submit their testimonies of salvation and baptism of the Holy Ghost."

FIRST STEPS PUBLISHING

PO Box 571, Gleneden Beach, OR 97388 | 541-961-7641
publish@firststepspublishing.com | www.FirstStepsPublishing.com
Suzanne Fyhrie Parrott, publisher

Types: POD, hardcover, e-book
Services: manuscript evaluation, design, substantive editing, copyediting, proofreading, promotional materials, marketing, online bookstore
Also does: royalty contracts
Production time: twelve to eighteen months
Books per year: four to five
Tip: "Our goal is to publish books of high quality, including those that may have trouble finding homes in traditional markets. We love working with authors who are passionate about their work and have

a desire to publish to the world. Are you writing a book you would like to see published? We have years of publishing experience as well as being authors ourselves. We know the quality and service you want from a publisher; and as your publisher, we seek to work with undiscovered and talented authors with the desire and potential to grow to success, whose work is exciting and fresh."

FRUITBEARER PUBLISHING, LLC

PO Box 777, Georgetown, DE 19947 | 302-856-6649
info@fruitbearer.com | www.fruitbearer.com
Candy Abbott, owner

Types: offset and POD paperback, hardcover, e-book, gift book, picture book
Services: manuscript evaluation, design, substantive editing, copyediting, proofreading, indexing, promotional materials, marketing, distribution, online bookstore, author websites, à la carte options
Also does: royalty contracts
Production time: three to six months
Books per year: six
Tip: "To inquire, complete the Submission Guidelines form on the website. Expect a reply within two weeks."

HALO PUBLISHING INTERNATIONAL

1100 N.W. Loop 410, Ste. 700-176, San Antonio, TX 78213 | 877-705-9647
contact@halopublishing.com | www.halopublishing.com
Lisa M. Umina, publisher

Types: hardcover, offset and POD paperback, e-book, picture book
Services: manuscript evaluation, copyediting, proofreading, design, promotional materials, distribution, marketing, author website, online bookstore, packages of services
Production time: one month
Books per year: three hundred fifty
Tip: "We highly recommend hiring an editor for your manuscript before publishing." Also publishes in Spanish.

HEALTHY LIFE PRESS

702 S Wolff St., Denver, CO 80219 | 877-331-2766
info@healthylifepress.com | www.HealthyLifePress.com
Dr. David Biebel, publisher

Types: hardcover, POD, e-book, gift book, picture book
Services: manuscript evaluation, design, substantive editing, copyediting, proofreading, promotional materials, marketing, online bookstore
Also does: royalty contracts
Production time: three to six months
Books per year: eight to twelve
Tip: "Healthy Life Press is a cooperative (author-subsidized) and collaborative company, sharing costs and net proceeds equitably. We welcome well-written, edited, and ready-for-design manuscripts on topics the author is passionate about and about which he or she is able to provide a new, different, unique, or original perspective. Submit book proposal plus three sample chapters; inquiries and manuscripts by email only. Do not inquire by phone, except for clarification."

HOLY FIRE PUBLISHING

5016 Spedale Ct., Ste. 199, Spring Hill, TN 37174 | 843-285-3130
publisher@holyfirepublishing.com | *www.holyfirepublishing.com*
Vanessa Hensel, COO

Types: hardcover, paperback, e-book
Services: design, copyright service, bookstore advertising, distribution, online bookstore, packages of services
Tip: "Our contract can be canceled at any time for any reason with a 60-day written notice. It's that simple."

HONEYCOMB HOUSE PUBLISHING LLC

New Cumberland, PA
dave@fessendens.net | *davefessenden.com*
David E. Fessenden, publisher

Types: POD, e-book
Services: manuscript evaluation, design, substantive editing, copyediting, proofreading, promotional materials, marketing, distribution, author website, packages of services, à la carte options
Production time: three to six months
Tip: "Prepare a book proposal, even if you plan to self-publish, and use it as a guideline for your book project."

MCDOUGAL PUBLISHING

PO Box 3595, Hagerstown, MD 21742 | 301-797-6637
publishing@mcdougal.org | *www.mcdougalpublishing.com*

Types: POD, offset printing
Services: manuscript critiquing, editing, cover design, typesetting

MORGAN JAMES PUBLISHING

5 Penn Plaza, 23rd Floor, New York City, NY 10001 | 516-900-5711
terry@morganjamespublishing.com | *www.morganjamespublishing.com*
W. Terry Whalin, acquisitions editor, Morgan James Faith

Types: hardcover, offset and POD paperback, e-book, audiobook, picture book
Services: design, distribution, marketing, promotional materials, online bookstore
Also does: royalty contracts
Production time: three to six months
Books per year: one hundred fifty
Tip: "General-market publisher that does 45 to 50 Christian books per year. Our books have been on *The New York Times* bestseller list more than twenty-five times (broad distribution). Requires authors to purchase 2,500 copies at print costs plus $2 over lifetime of agreement. Pays 20-30% royalties on sales; pays small advance. Email proposal with sample chapters or full manuscript. Only 30% of authors have agents."

NORDSKOG PUBLISHING

4562 Westinghouse St., Ste. E, Ventura, CA 93003 | 805-642-2070
email through website | *nordskogpublishing.com*
Desta Garrett, managing editor

Types: paperback, hardcover
Services: editing, design, marketing
Tip: "Looking for the best in sound theological and applied Christian faith books, both nonfiction and fiction."

OAKS BOUGH PUBLISHING, LLC

9119 Highway 6 S., Ste. 230, PMB 380, Missouri City, TX 77459 | 832-671-8906
marykaarto@marykaarto.com | *marykaarto.com*
Mary Kaarto, publisher

Types: paperback, e-book
Services: proofreading
Production time: one book at a time, one author at a time
Tip: Submit three sample chapters, book proposal, table of contents, and SASE.

PARSON PLACE PRESS, LLC

PO Box 8277, Mobile, AL 36689-0277 | 251-643-6985
info@parsonplacepress.com | *www.parsonplacepress.com*
Michael L. White, managing editor

Types: POD, hardcover, e-book
Services: substantive editing, proofreading
Production time: three months
Tip: "Read the author guidelines on the publisher's website before querying the editor."

POSITIVE PUBLISHING

116 Maurice Ave. N.W., Fort Walton Beach, FL 32548 | 712-259-1381
joanieandjennib@positivenotenetwork.com | *www.positivenotenetwork.com/positive-publishing.html*
Joanie Beaver, publisher

Types of books: offset paperback, POD, hardcover, e-book, audiobook, gift book, picture book
Services: manuscript evaluation, design, substantive editing, copyediting, proofreading, promotional materials, marketing, distribution, author websites, online bookstore, packages of services, à la carte options
Production time: six to twelve months
Books per year: ten plus
Tip: "Query first either in body of email or as attachment, and really sell your story."

REDEMPTION PRESS

1730 Railroad St., Enumclaw, WA 98022 | 360-226-3488
info@redemption-press.com | *www.redemption-press.com*
Athena Dean Holtz, publisher; Brenda Anderson, accounts manager

Types: offset and POD paperback, hardcover, e-book, audiobook, gift book, picture book, DVD packaging, workbook
Services: manuscript evaluation, design, substantive editing, copyediting, proofreading, indexing, promotional materials, marketing, distribution, author website, online bookstore, à la carte options
Production time: three to four months, expedited forty-five days
Books per year: more than one hundred
Tip: "If you're going to indie publish, the last thing you want to do is look self-published. Don't skimp on having your work evaluated

and refined to be the best it can possibly be. Our service is a custom strategy to insure you have all the services you need and no more or less. As you look for a publisher, be sure to do your due diligence and insure the contract aligns with what you're told over the phone. In Mark Levine's *Fine Print of Self Publishing*, 6th Edition, Redemption Press was rated #1 over Westbow and Xulon. Connect with us for more information."

SALVATION PUBLISHER AND MARKETING GROUP

PO Box 40860, Santa Barbara, CA 93140 | 805-252-9832
opalmaedailey@aol.com
Dr. Opal Mae Dailey, editor

Types: hardcover, offset paperback, e-book
Services: manuscript evaluation, design, substantive editing, copyediting, proofreading
Production time: six to nine months
Books per year: five to seven
Tip: "Turning taped messages into book form for pastors is a specialty of ours. We do not accept any manuscript we would be ashamed to put our name on."

SERMON TO BOOK • SPEAK IT TO BOOK

424 W. Bakerview Rd., Ste. 105 #215, Bellingham, WA 98226 | 360-223-1877
info@sermontobook.com | *www.sermontobook.com*
Caleb Breakey, lead book director

Types: paperback, e-book, audiobook, POD
Services: design, substantive editing, copyediting, proofreading, promotional materials, marketing, distribution, author website, online bookstore, packages of services, à la carte options
Production time: six to ten months
Tip: "To schedule a call with Caleb Breakey, go to *calendly.com/sermontobook/30min*."

SPLASHDOWN BOOKS

4/11 Hall Rd, Glenfield, Auckland, New Zealand 0629 | +6-422-472-2301
grace@splashdownbooks.com | *www.splashdownbooks.com*
Grace Bridges, managing editor

Types: paperback, e-book, POD
Services: manuscript evaluation, design, substantive editing,

copyediting, proofreading, distribution, à la carte options, hybrid publishing

Production time: depends on how much editing is needed and how long the author needs to implement changes and learn about publishing, etc.

Tip: "Speculative genres only: science fiction, fantasy, paranormal, or a combination. No preaching or excessively overt content."

STONEHOUSE INK

Boise, ID | 208-608-8325
stonehousepress@hotmail.com | *stonehouseink.net*
Aaron Patterson, editor-publisher

Types: paperback, e-book

Tip: Specializes in fiction, including thrillers, mystery, and YA. Interested in published authors looking to publish backlist titles or to rebrand and relaunch titles.

STRONG TOWER PUBLISHING

PO Box 973, Milesburg, PA 16863 | 814-206-6778
strongtowerpubs@aol.com | *www.strongtowerpublishing.com*
Heidi L. Nigro, publisher

Types: paperback, e-book, POD

Services: manuscript evaluation, copyediting, proofreading, substantive editing, design, online bookstore

Production time: three to four months

Books per year: one or two

Tip: Specializes in books on end-times topics from the prewrath rapture perspective.

TEACH SERVICES, INC.

11 Quartermaster Cir., Fort Oglethorpe, GA 30742-3886
706-504-9192
publishing@teachservices.com | *www.teachservices.com*
Timothy Hullquist, author advisor

Types: offset and POD paperback, hardcover, e-book, gift book, picture book, landscape hardback and mechanical binding

Services: manuscript evaluation, design, substantive editing, copyediting, proofreading, indexing, promotional materials, marketing, distribution, author websites, online bookstore, packages of services, à la carte options

Also does: royalty contracts

Production time: one to four months
Tip: "We specialize in marketing our titles to Seventh-day Adventists."

TESTIMONY PUBLICATIONS

5625 Pearl Dr., Ste. F-123, Evansville, IN 47712 | 812-602-3031
mkough@testimonypublications.com | *www.testimonypublications.com*
Marj Kough, CEO

Types: paperback, hardcover, e-book, POD
Services: manuscript evaluation, design, substantive editing, copyediting, proofreading, promotional materials, marketing, distribution, author websites, online bookstore, packages of services, à la carte options
Also does: royalty contracts
Production time: three to six months
Tip: "We publish fiction or nonfiction books or materials with a Christian focus."

TMP BOOKS

1420 Martha Berry Blvd. Unit 1241, Rome, GA 30165
info@tmpbooks.com | *www.TMPbooks.com*
Tracy Ruckman, publisher

Types: POD, e-book, audiobook, picture book, large print
Services: manuscript evaluation, design, substantive editing, copyediting, proofreading, promotional materials, marketing, distribution, packages of services, à la carte options, coaching, consultations
Production time: two to six months
Books per year: twelve plus
Tip: "Study the craft of writing and the book industry as you write your book. Determine your audience before you start writing."

T2PNEUMA PUBLISHERS LLC

PO Box 230564, Centreville, VA 20120 | 703-973-8898
T2Pneuma@gmail.com | *www.T2Pneuma.com*
Stephen W. Hiemstra, publisher

Types: paperback, e-book
Services: manuscript evaluation
Production time: one year
Tip: "We focus on nonfiction, Christian books in English and Spanish. Check website for details before submitting manuscript ideas."

TRAIL MEDIA

PO Box 387, La Mirada, CA 90637
admin@ChisholmTrailMedia.com | www.chisholmtrailmedia.com
Christine "CJ" Simpson, director of publishing

Types: POD, e-book, gift book, picture book
Services: manuscript evaluation, substantive editing, copyediting, proofreading, promotional materials, marketing, packages of services, à la carte options
Production time: negotiable
Tip: "Our goal is to help new authors publish their work by coordinating the services needed with experts in the field and publish in a co-op fashion under the Trail Media imprint, so 100% of the revenue generated goes to ministry of the authors. In many cases, we find scholarships and grants to help missionaries and those in the persecuted church. Trail Media is a ministry of modified tentmaking models."

TRUTH BOOK PUBLISHERS

900 S. Main St., Jacksonville, IL 62650 | 217-243-8880
truthbookpublishers@yahoo.com | www.truthbookpublisher.com

Types: POD, e-book
Services: editing, design, marketing
Production time: one month
Tip: "We are missionary minded and desire to help the body of Christ mature."

TULPEN PUBLISHING

11043 Depew St., Westminster, CO 80020 | 303-438-7276
tulpenpublishing@gmail.com | TulpenPublishing.com
Sandi Rog, acquisitions editor

Types: paperback, e-book, POD
Services: manuscript evaluation, design, substantive editing, copyediting, proofreading, distribution, online bookstore, marketing
Production time: twelve to twenty months
Tip: Only accepts submissions via email. See the website for submission guidelines.

WESTBOW PRESS

1663 Liberty Dr., Bloomington, IN 47403 | 866-928-1240
email through website | www.westbowpress.com

Types: hardcover, paperback, e-book, audiobook
Services: manuscript evaluation, substantive editing, copyediting, design, illustrations, indexing, Spanish translation, marketing, video trailer, distribution
Tip: Independent publishing division of Thomas Nelson and Zondervan.

WORD ALIVE PRESS

131 Cordite Rd., Winnipeg, MB R3W 1S1, Canada | 866-967-3782
publishing@wordalivepress.ca | *www.wordalivepress.ca*

Types: hardcover, offset and POD paperback, e-book, gift book
Services: packages of services, editing, design, marketing, distribution, online bookstore
Production time: four to five months

XULON PRESS

2301 Lucien Way, Ste. 415, Maitland, FL 32751 | 407-339-4217, 866-381-2665
email through website | *www.xulonpress.com*
Donald Newman, director of sales

Types: hardcover, paperback, e-book, POD
Services: manuscript review, editorial critique, developmental editing, copyediting, design, packages of services, à la carte options, color illustrations, back-cover copy, ghostwriting, translation, marketing, promotional materials, publicity, video trailer, 100% net royalty, online bookstore
Production time: three to six months

YO PRODUCTIONS, LLC

PO Box 32329, Columbus, OH 43232 | 614-452-4920
info_4u@yoproductions.net | *www.yoproductions.net*
Yolonda Tonette Sanders, founder and CEO

Types: POD, e-book
Services: manuscript evaluation, design, substantive editing, copyediting, proofreading, packages of services, à la carte options
Also does: royalty contracts
Production time: three to six months, six months to a year royalty
Books per year: six plus, two royalty
Tip: "Books considered for traditional publishing must be exceptionally well-written prior to submission. In addition, manuscripts cannot contain any foul or vulgar language."

ZOË LIFE PUBLISHING

PO Box 871066, Canton, MI 48187 | 888-400-4922
info@zoelifepub.com | *www.zoelifepub.com*
Sabrina Adams, publisher

Types: hardcover, paperback, e-book
Services: packages of services, editing, design, rights and registrations, warehousing, promotion, distribution and fulfillment, online bookstore
Also does: royalty contracts
Production time: one year
Also does: royalty publishing

3

DESIGN AND PRODUCTION SERVICES

ARTBYPAGE.COM | PAGE POWELL
3712 N. Rosser St., Apt. 102, Alexandria, VA 22311 | 703-671-4131
paige@artbypaige.com | *artbypaige.com*

Contact: email, phone
Services: book-cover design, book-interior design, website design
Charges: flat fee, hourly rate
Credentials/experience: See *artbypaige.com/paige-powell-book-covers.html* and *artbypaige.com/paige-powell-web-design.html.*

AUTHOR SUPPORT SERVICES | RUSSELL SHERRARD
Carmichael, CA | 916-967-7251
russellsherrard@reagan.com | *www.sherrardsebookresellers.com/WordPress/author-support-services-professional-services-affordable-prices-by-russell-sherrard-june-21-2016*

Contact: email
Services: Kindle e-book formatting, e-book linked table of contents, PDF creation, book-cover design, copyediting, proofreading
Charges: flat fee
Credentials/experience: Writing and editing since 2009; currently providing freelance services for multiple clients.

BETHANY PRESS INTERNATIONAL
6820 W. 115th St., Bloomington, MN 55438 | 888-717-7400
info@bethanypress.com | *www.bethanypress.com*

Contact: email, phone, website form
Services: short-run digital printing and long-run (minimum 500 copies) printing, only with files created by a professional book designer; e-book conversion, only with corresponding print order
Charges: flat fee

Credentials/experience: Printer for the majority of Christian publishing houses since 1997. "We partner with publishers and ministries to create, produce, and distribute millions of life-changing Christian books each year. We invest our proceeds in training and sending missionaries through Bethany International."

BLUE LEAF BOOK SCANNING

618 Crowsnest Dr., Ballwin, MO 63021 | 314-606-9322
blue.leaf.it@gmail.com | *www.blueleaf-book-scanning.com*

Contact: email, phone, website form
Services: book and document scanning to multiple formats, e-book and audio conversions
Charges: flat fee
Credentials/experience: The first book-scanning service for consumers. Accurate optical character recognition (more than 99.6% accurate on ideal conditions) with excellent format retention. Can scan nearly 200 languages.

BRAYV | ROBERT CRUM

8617 66th St., Kenosha, WI 53142 | 719-351-4968
bob@brayv.co | *brayv.co*

Contact: email, phone
Services: book-cover design, book-interior design, illustrations
Charges: flat fee
Credentials/experience: A full-time illustrator and designer with more than twenty years of experience with authors in the young-adult fiction market, as well as graphic novels and comics.

BREADBOX CREATIVE | ERYN LYNUM

1437 N. Denver Ave. #167, Loveland, CO 80538 | 970-308-3654
eryn@breadboxcreative.com | *www.breadboxcreative.com/creators*

Contact: website form
Services: website design, social-media assistance
Charges: flat fee
Credentials/experience: "At Breadbox Creative, we have more than twenty years of experience in web design. The owner, Eryn Lynum, is an author herself and marries her passion for writing with her passion for web design to come alongside writers and speakers and help them further spread the messages God has laid on their hearts. Breadbox Creative works with businesses, writers, and speakers by creating professional WordPress websites, as well as assisting with

SEO and social-media platforms. We also offer assistance with preparing book proposals and writing consulting."

CASTELANE, INC. | KIM MCDOUGALL

Whitehall, PA | 647-281-1554
kimm@castelane.com | *www.castelane.com*

Contact: email
Services: book-cover design, e-book conversion, book video trailers
Charges: flat fee
Credentials/experience: "I have made more than five hundred book video trailers and three hundred book covers since 2009. Samples and references are available on the website."

CELEBRATION WEB DESIGN BY SKWD | BRUCE SHANK

PO Box 471068, Celebration, FL 34747 | 610-989-0400
info@celebrationwebdesign.com | *CelebrationWebDesign.com*

Contact: email, phone, website form
Services: website design
Charges: flat fee, hourly rate
Credentials/experience: In business since 2002.

CHRISTIANPRINT.COM

6820 W. 115th St., Bloomington, MN 55438 | 888-201-1322
info@bethanypress.com | *www.christianprint.com*

Contact: email, phone, website form
Services: prints ancillary products, such as business cards, brochures, booklets, banners, postcards, posters, and signs
Charges: flat fee
Credentials/experience: A division of Bethany Press, founded in 1997.

CROWN LAID DOWN DESIGNS | HOLLY SMITH

College Station, TX | 719-482-5523
chrishollysmith@msn.com | *www.crownlaiddowndesigns.com*

Contact: email
Services: website design
Charges: hourly rate
Credentials/experience: Seven years of experience as a designer/ developer for WordPress and Blogger sites for publications and entrepreneurs.

DESIGN CORPS | JOHN WOLLINKA
Colorado Springs, CO | 719-260-0500
john@designcorps.us | *designcorps.us*

Contact: email
Services: book-cover design, book-interior design, typesetting, e-book conversion, illustrations, website design, printing, marketing
Charges: flat fee
Credentials/experience: Design Corps has been serving Christian publishers, denominations, ministries, and organizations for more than twenty years.

THE DESIGN IN YOUR MIND • FINDLEY FAMILY VIDEO PUBLICATIONS | MARY C. FINDLEY
Tulsa, OK | 918-805-0669
mjmcfindley@gmail.com | *elkjerkyforthesoul.wordpress.com*

Contact: email
Services: book-cover design, book-interior design, e-book conversion, illustrations
Charges: flat fee
Credentials/experience: Designer and formatter for six years for many indie authors and many genres, including illustrated children's books, graphics in layouts, illustrated e-books, print for fiction, and curriculum.

DIGGYPOD | KEVIN OSWORTH
301 Industrial Dr., Tecumseh, MI 49286 | 877-944-7844
kosworth@diggypod.com | *www.diggypod.com*

Contact: email
Services: book-cover design, printing
Charges: based on the number of books/pages being printed; website has an active quote calculator that provides 100% accurate pricing
Credentials/experience: DiggyPOD has been printing books since 2001. All facets of the book printing take place in its facility.

EDENBROOKE PRODUCTIONS | MARTY KEITH
Franklin, TN | 615-415-1942
johnmartinkeith@gmail.com | *www.edenbrookemusic.com/booktrailers*

Contact: email
Services: book trailers with custom music
Charges: flat fee
Credentials/experience: Has produced music for everyone from CBS TV to Discovery Channel.

FAITH & FANTASY ALLIANCE | SCOTT AND BECKY MINOR
Pottstown, PA | 610-906-6266
scottminor@comcast.net | *www.faithandfantasyalliance.com*

Contact: email
Services: illustration, audiobook narration, video book trailer
Charges: hourly rate
Credentials/experience: Scott is a professional actor, audiobook producer/narrator, full-cast audiobook producer, and video producer/editor. Becky is a professional illustrator, animator, and author. Both have BFA degrees from The University of the Arts, Philadelphia, Pennsylvania.

FISTBUMP MEDIA, LLC | DAN KING
Sarasota, FL | 941-780-4179
dan@fistbumpmedia.com | *fistbumpmedia.com*

Contact: email
Services: book-cover design, book-interior design, typesetting, e-book conversion, website design
Charges: flat fee, hourly rate
Credentials/experience: See the website for references and portfolio. Specializes in design and formatting for print-on-demand.

FIVE J'S DESIGN | JEFF AND JOY MILLER
Aubrey, TX
info@fivejsdesign.com | *fivejsdesign.com* | *secondbreakfastmedia.com*

Contact: email
Services: book-cover design, book-interior design, typesetting, e-book conversion, website design
Charges: hourly rates or flat fees based on project needs
Credentials/experience: "We have been designing books and websites since 2008, including the website, typesetting, and cover design for *The Christian Writers Market Guide* and The Christian Writers Institute website."

THE FOREWORD COLLECTIVE, LLC |
MOLLY KEMPF HODGIN, NICOLE CORSE LEVINE
1726 Charity Dr., Brentwood, TN 37027
info@theforewordcollective.com | *www.theforewordcollective.com*

Contact: email, website form
Services: book-cover design, book trailers
Charges: custom rate

Credentials/experience: "We employ a wide variety of creative professionals on a per-project basis, including editors, copyeditors, designers, writers, photographers, marketers, and public-relations pros. We have more than thirty years of publishing experience between us, and we want to put that experience to work for you. Molly was most recently the associate publisher for the specialty division of HarperCollins Christian Publishing, directing the design of some of the most-coveted covers in the Christian market. Nicole was most recently the editorial director at InSight Publishing , directing the design of books for kids and teens."

HL CREATIVE | LAURA PATTERSON

PO Box 570606, Houston, TX 77257 | 281-915-4358
laura@hl-creative.com | *www.hlcreative.com*

Contact: email
Services: book-cover design, book-interior design, typesetting, illustrations, website design
Charges: flat fee, hourly rate
Credentials/experience: Thirteen years of advertising and graphic-design experience.

JOANNA MARIE ART | JOANNA MARIE

PO Box 30664, Mesa, AZ 85275 | 520-686-1088
joanna@joanamarieart.com | *www.joannamarieart.com*

Contact: email
Services: book-cover design, illustrations, website design
Charges: flat fee
Credentials/experience: More than ten years in fine art/illustration work, five years web design.

KEN RANEY

Wichita, KS | 316-737-9724
kenraney@mac.com | *kenraneydesign.blogspot.com*

Contact: email, phone
Services: book-cover design, book-interior design, e-book conversion, illustrations
Charges: flat fee, hourly rate
Credentials/experience: More than forty years of experience in graphic design and illustration.

MADISON BOOK COVER DESIGNS | RUTH DERBY

220 W. Elm St., Hanford, CA 93230 | 559-772-2489
rmadison_1@hotmail.com | *www.ruthiemadison.com*

Contact: email
Services: book-cover design
Charges: flat fee
Credentials/experience: More than three years of experience and has had mentors in this field.

MCLENNAN CREATIVE | ALISON MCLENNAN

1933 Geraldson Dr., Lancaster, PA 17601 | 717-572-2585
alison@mclennancreative.com | *www.mclennancreative.com*

Contact: email, phone, website contact form
Services: book-cover design, e-book conversion, website design
Charges: flat fee, hourly rate, customized packages
Credentials/experience: More than twenty years of experience in the publishing industry.

MELINDA MARTIN

Palestine, TX | 903-948-4893
support@melindamartin.me | *melindamartin.me*

Contact: email
Services: book-cover design, book-interior design, typesetting, e-book conversion
Charges: flat fee
Credentials/experience: Four years of working with clients' manuscripts to achieve a design that is best for their platforms.

PROFESSIONAL PUBLISHING SERVICES | CHRISTY CALLAHAN

PO Box 461, Waycross, GA 31502 | 912-809-9062
professionalpublishingservices@gmail.com | *www.ChristyCallahan.com*

Contact: email
Services: book-interior design, typesetting, e-book conversion
Charges: flat fee, custom
Credentials/experience: "We offer typesetting with quick turnaround times and reasonable rates to traditional and independent book publishers, as well as indie authors. Christy graduated Phi Beta Kappa from Carnegie Mellon University, where she first learned how to use Adobe software and worked as an assistant in the Language Learning Resource Center and the psychology

department. While she earned her MA in Intercultural Studies from Fuller Seminary, she edited sound files for distance-learning classes for the Media Center and designed ads as Women's Concerns Committee chairperson. Christy is proficient in using Adobe InDesign software, leveraging her expertise as an editor and proofreader and extensive knowledge of *Chicago* style to create professional-looking interior book layouts."

ROSEANNA WHITE DESIGNS | ROSEANNA WHITE

Cumberland, MD | 410-571-1678
roseannamwhite@gmail.com | *www.RoseannaWhiteDesigns.com*

Contact: email
Services: book-cover design, book-interior design
Charges: flat fee
Credentials/experience: Designed covers for several small publishers and a slew of independent authors since 2011. Covers have been finalists in several book-cover award contests.

SCREE, LLC | LANDON OTIS

Sandpoint, ID | 208-290-4624
landon@scree.it | *scree.it*

Contact: email
Services: website design, website development
Charges: hourly rate
Credentials/experience: Professional, full-time web developer at a local design and marketing firm. Websites include *veritasincorporated.com* and *mineralchurch.org*.

STARCHER DESIGNS | KARA STARCHER

PO Box 93, Chloe, WV 25235 | 330-705-3399
info@starcherdesigns.com | *www.starcherdesigns.com*

Contact: website form
Services: book-cover design, book-interior design, typesetting
Charges: custom fee
Credentials/experience: BA in publishing, more than fifteen years typesetting and designing book covers.

TLC GRAPHICS | TAMARA DEVER

Austin, TX | 512-669-5744
tamara@tlcgraphics.com | *www.TLCGraphics.com*

Contact: email

Services: book-cover design, book-interior design, typesetting, e-book conversion, printing, publishing consulting, editorial
Charges: custom pricing according to project needs
Credentials/experience: "Award-winning design firm and author guidance with more than twenty-five years of publishing experience. Small, caring team working with you, taking your raw manuscript through editorial, design, and printing to provide a beautiful and salable book you'll be proud to represent. Services are à la carte with design contract. Also publishers of My Publishing Journal, a guided, illustrated journal for authors."

TRILION STUDIOS | BRIAN WHITE

Lawrence, KS | 785-841-5500
brian@TriLionStudios.com | *www.TriLionStudios.com*

Contact: email, phone
Services: book-cover design, illustrations, web design
Charges: flat fee, hourly rate
Credentials/experience: Twenty years in the design/web design/ branding industry. Has worked with nonprofits and churches for more than fifteen years.

VIVID GRAPHICS | LARRY VAN HOOSE

523 E. Stuart Dr., Ste. 2, Galax, VA 24333 | 276-233-0276
larry@vivid-graphics.com | *www.vivid-graphics.com*

Contact: email
Services: book-cover design, book-interior design, e-book conversion, typesetting
Charges: hourly rate
Credentials/experience: Graphic, magazine, and book designer with more than twenty years of succcessful and award-winning experience.

WRITERS' TABLET, LLC | TERRI WHITEMORE

4371 Roswell Rd. #315, Marietta, GA 30062 | 770-648-4101
WritersTablet@gmail.com | *www.WritersTablet.org*

Contact: email
Services: book-cover design, book-interior design, typesetting, e-book conversion, illustrations, website design
Charges: flat fee
Credentials/experience: Graphic design, BS in computer science, testimonials from local and national businesses and authors. Copywriter for G5. Five years of experience.

YO PRODUCTIONS, LLC | YOLONDA TONETTE SANDERS

PO Box 32329, Columbus, OH 43232 | 614-452-4920
info_4u@yoproductions.net | *www.yoproductions.net*

Contact: email, phone, website form
Services: book-interior design, typesetting, e-book conversion
Charges: flat fee, custom fee
Credentials/experience: More than thirteen years of professional experience, editor and writer for a national publication, traditionally published author.

> **Note:** See **"Editorial Services"** and **"Publicity and Marketing Services"** for help with these needs.

4

DISTRIBUTION SERVICES

BOOKMASTERS

30 Amberwood Pkwy., Ashland, OH 44805 | 419-281-5100
info@bookmasters.com | *www.bookmasters.com*

Offers a wide range of fulfillment and distribution services. Contact an account executive through the website.

CBA MAILING LISTS OF CHRISTIAN BOOKSTORES

1365 Garden of the Gods Rd., Ste. 105, Colorado Springs, CO 80907 | 800-252-1950
info@cbaonline.org | *www.cbaonline.org*

Three different lists are available for rental: nonmember stores, 2,500 addresses, $349; member stores, 675 addresses, $499; combination of all stores, 3,500 addresses, $549. Prices and numbers are subject to change. Call for full details.

CHRISTIAN BOOK DISTRIBUTORS

PO Box 7000, Peabody, MA 01961-7000 | 800-247-4784, 978-977-5000
email through website | *www.christianbook.com*

Sometimes distributes independently published books.

PATHWAY BOOK SERVICE

PO Box 89, Gilsum, NH 03448 | 800-345-6665
pbs@pathwaybook.com | *www.pathwaybook.com*

Provides warehousing, order fulfillment, and trade distribution. It is a longtime distributor to Ingram and Baker & Taylor, the vendors of choice for most bookstores. Pathway uploads new-title spreadsheets to Ingram and Baker & Taylor, as well as to *Amazon.com*, Barnes & Noble, Books-A-Million, and Indigo/Chapters (Canada) databases on a weekly basis. Distribution outside of North America is available through Gazelle Book Services in the United Kingdom. Also provides the option of having Pathway add titles to their Amazon Advantage account, which is at a lower discount and often a lower shipping cost per book than individual accounts.

PART 3

PERIODICAL PUBLISHERS

5

TOPICS AND **TYPES**

This chapter is not an exhaustive list of types of manuscripts and topics editors are looking for, but it is a starting place for some of the more popular ones. For instance, almost all periodicals take manuscripts in categories like Christian living, so they are not listed here. Plus writers guidelines tend to outline general areas, not every specific type and topic an editor will buy.

CONTEMPORARY ISSUES

Brio
Catholic Sentinel
Christian Herald
Christianity Today
Citizen Magazine
City Light News
The Covenant Companion
Eureka Street
Faith Today
Holiness Today
Light + Life Magazine
Ministry
New Frontier Chronicle
Now What?
Our Sunday Visitor Newsweekly
Perspectives
Presbyterians Today
St. Anthony Messenger
War Cry

DEVOTIONALS

FCA Magazine
Focus on the Family
The Gem
Gems of Truth
Girlz 4 Christ Magazine
Halo Magazine
Keys to Living
Mature Living
ParentLife
Presbyterians Today
Reach Out, Columbia

ESSAY

America
Believers Bay
The Canadian Lutheran
Catholic Digest
The Christian Century
Christian Communicator
Christian Librarian
Commonweal
The Cresset
CrossCurrents
Faith Today
Image
Liguorian

Our Sunday Visitor Newsweekly
The Penwood Review
Poets & Writers Magazine
Relief Journal
Sharing
U.S. Catholic
The Writer
The Writer's Chronicle
Writer's Digest

EVANGELISM

Christian Research Journal
CommonCall
Decision
Evangelical Missions Quarterly
The Gem
Indian Life
Just Between Us
Lutheran Witness
Mature Living
Message of the Open Bible
Net Results
New Identity Magazine
On Mission
Outreach
War Cry

FAMILY

Boundless
Celebrate Life Magazine
Citizen Magazine
Columbia
CommonCall
Evangelical Missions Quarterly
Faith & Friends
Focus on the Family
HomeLife
Joyful Living Magazine
Ministry
The Mother's Heart
ParentLife
Power for Living
St. Anthony Messenger
SHINE brightly
Southwest Kansas Faith and Family
Sparkle
Thrive Connection
YouthMinistry.com

FICTION

See **Short Stories**.

FILLER

Angels on Earth
Bible Advocate
Children's Ministry
Christian Living in the Mature Years
Creation Illustrated
Eternal Ink
FellowScript
Focus on the Family Clubhouse
Focus on the Family Clubhouse Jr.
Freelance Writer's Report
The Gem
Girlz 4 Christ Magazine
Guideposts
Indian Life
The Lutheran Digest
The Mother's Heart
The Newsletter Newsletter
SHINE brightly
Sparkle
War Cry
Words for the Way
Your Voice
YouthMinistry.com

FINANCES/MONEY

Boundless

Children's Ministry
Christian Living in the Mature Years
Christian Standard
Columbia
Joyful Living Magazine
Just Between Us
Living Better
MTL Magazine
Net Results
WritersWeekly.com

HOW-TO

Canada Lutheran
Catechist
Catholic Digest
Celebrate Life Magazine
Children's Ministry
Christian Communicator
Christian Living in the Mature Years
Christian Standard
Citizen Magazine
CommonCall
Creation Illustrated
Enrichment
Evangelical Missions Quarterly
Faith Today
Focus on the Family
Focus on the Family Clubhouse
Girlz 4 Christ Magazine
Highway News and Good News
Homeschooling Today
InSite
Joyful Living Magazine
Just Between Us
Leading Hearts
Live
Living Better
Lutheran Witness
Mature Living
Ministry
Ministry Today
The MOPS Magazine
The Mother's Heart
MTL Magazine
Mutuality
Net Results
New Identity Magazine
The Newsletter Newsletter
Outreach
ParentLife
Parish Liturgy
Poets & Writers Magazine
Psychology for Living
SAConnects
Teachers of Vision
Vibrant Life
The Writer
The Writer's Chronicle
Writer's Digest
Writing Corner
YouthMinistry.com

INTERVIEW/PROFILE

The Arlington Catholic Herald
Brio
byFaith
Canada Lutheran
Catholic Sentinel
Celebrate Life Magazine
Charisma
Christ Our Hope
The Christian Century
Christian Communicator
The Christian Herald
The Christian Journal
The Christian Ranchman

Christianity Today
Citizen Magazine
City Light News
Columbia
CommonCall
The Covenant Companion
Creation
The Cresset
DTS Magazine
Evangelical Missions Quarterly
Faith & Friends
Faith Today
FCA Magazine
Friends Journal
Gems of Truth
Girlz 4 Christ Magazine
Good News, Etc.
History's Women
Homeschooling Today
Image
InSite
International Journal of Frontier Missiology
Joyful Living Magazine
Kansas City Metro Voice
Leading Hearts
Leaves
Leben
Light + Life Magazine
Liguorian
Lutheran Witness
Ministry Today
The Mother's Heart
MTL Magazine
Our Sunday Visitor Newsweekly
Outreach
Parish Liturgy
Poets & Writers Magazine
Point
Power for Living
Prairie Messenger
Reach Out, Columbia
St. Anthony Messenger
St. Mary's Messenger
Testimony Magazine
Today's Christian Living
U.S. Catholic
Vibrant Life
War Cry
The Writer's Chronicle
Writer's Digest

LEADERSHIP/MINISTRY

Children's Ministry
Christian Standard
CommonCall
Enrichment
Facts & Trends
Holiness Today
Just Between Us
Message of the Open Bible
Ministry
Ministry Today
Mutuality
Net Results
Outreach
YouthMinistry.com

MARRIAGE

Boundless
Catholic Digest
Converge Magazine
Faith & Friends
Focus on the Family
Joyful Living Magazine
Mature Living
St. Anthony Messenger
Thrive Connection

NEWSPAPER

The Anglican Journal
The Arlington Catholic Herald
Catholic New York
Catholic Sentinel
Christian Courier
The Christian Herald
Christian News Northwest
City Light News
The Good News (Florida)
The Good News (New York)
Good News, Etc.
The Good News Journal
Indian Life
Kansas City Metro Voice
The Messianic Times
New Frontier Chronicle
Our Sunday Visitor Newsweekly
Prairie Messenger
Southwest Kansas Faith and Family

PARENTING

Catholic Digest
Columbia
Focus on the Family
The Gem
Just Between Us
Parenting Teens
ParentLife
Reach Out, Columbia
War Cry

PERSONAL EXPERIENCE

Angels on Earth
The Anglican Journal
Authentik Magazine
Bible Advocate
The Breakthrough Intercessor
Canada Lutheran
Catholic Digest
Catholic New York
Catholic Sentinel
Celebrate Life Magazine
Chicken Soup for the Soul Book Series
Christ Our Hope
Christian Living in the Mature Years
Christian Standard
Christianity Today
Converge Magazine
Creation Illustrated
Decision
Divine Moments Book Series
DTS Magazine
EFCA Today
Faith & Friends
Friends Journal
The Gem
Guideposts
Halo Magazine
Highway News and Good News
Holiness Today
Joyful Living Magazine
Just Between Us
Leading Hearts
Leaves
Live
The Lutheran Digest
Lutheran Witness
Mature Living
Message of the Open Bible
The MOPS Magazine
The Mother's Heart
MTL Magazine
Mutuality
Mysterious Ways

A New Heart
New Identity Magazine
Now What?
Point
Power for Living
Psychology for Living
Purpose
SAConnects
Sharing
Sister Soldiers in Christ
Standard
Teachers of Vision
Testimony Magazine
Thrive Connection
Today's Christian Living
Vibrant Life
Words for the Way

POETRY

America
Believers Bay
Bible Advocate
The Breakthrough Intercessor
Chicken Soup for the Soul Book Series
The Christian Century
Christian Communicator
Christian Courier
Commonweal
Creation Illustrated
The Cresset
CrossCurrents
Eternal Ink
Eureka Street
Focus on the Family Clubhouse Jr.
Friends Journal
The Gem
Gems of Truth
Girlz 4 Christ Magazine
Halo Magazine
Image
Leaves
Live
The Lutheran Digest
The Lutheran Journal
The Messenger
Mutuality
A New Heart
The Penwood Review
Perspectives
Poets & Writers Magazine
Positive Note Magazine
Power for Living
Prairie Messenger
Purpose
Relief Journal
St. Anthony Messenger
St. Mary's Messenger
Sharing
SHINE brightly
Sojourners
Sparkle
Teachers of Vision
Time Of Singing
U.S. Catholic
Words for the Way
Young Salvationist
Your Voice

PROFILES

See **Interviews**.

REVIEWS

The Anglican Journal
byFaith
The Canadian Lutheran
Canadian Mennonite
Charisma
The Christian Century

Christian Communicator
Christian Courier
The Christian Herald
The Christian Journal
Christian Librarian
Christian Retailing
Christianity Today
The Covenant Companion
Creation Research Journal
Evangelical Missions Quarterly
Faith Today
FellowScript
The Good News (New York)
Good News, Etc.
Indian Life
Kansas City Metro Voice
Leading Hearts
The Living Church
The Messianic Times
Ministry
MTL Magazine
Mutuality
New Frontier Chronicle
On Mission
Perspectives
Sojourners
Time Of Singing
U.S. Catholic

SCIENCE

Answers
Creation
Nature Friend Magazine

SEASONAL

The Anglican Journal
Answers
Believers Bay
Brio
Canadian Lutheran
Catechist
Catholic Digest
Catholic New York
Celebrate Life Magazine
Charisma
Children's Ministry
The Christian Century
Christian Communicator
Christian Courier
Christian Living in the Mature Years
Christian Standard
Columbia
Decision
Divine Moments Book Series
DTS Magazine
EFCA Today
Eternal Ink
Faith Today
Focus on the Family Clubhouse
Focus on the Family Clubhouse Jr.
Freelance Writer's Report
The Gem
Gems of Truth
Girlz 4 Christ Magazine
Guide
Halo Magazine
Indian Life
Insight
InSite
Keys to Living
Liguorian
Live
Living Better
The Lutheran Digest
Message of the Open Bible
The Messenger
The Mother's Heart

Nature Friend Magazine
The Newsletter Newsletter
Our Little Friend
Outreach
Poets & Writers Magazine
Prairie Messenger
Presbyterians Today
Primary Treasure
Reach Out, Columbia
St. Anthony Messenger
St. Mary's Messenger
Simple Grace
Standard
Testimony Magazine
Time Of Singing
U.S. Catholic
War Cry
Words for the Way
Writer's Digest
WritersWeekly.com

SHORT STORY/ FICTION

The Anglican Journal
Believers Bay
Brio
Cadet Quest
CrossCurrents
Eureka Street
Focus on the Family Clubhouse
Focus on the Family Clubhouse Jr.
The Gem
Gems of Truth
Girlz 4 Christ Magazine
Halo Magazine
Havok
Image
The Kids' Ark
Liguorian
Live
Living Better
Mature Living
Nature Friend Magazine
Positive Note Magazine
Relief Journal
St. Anthony Messenger
St. Mary's Messenger
SHINE brightly
Spark
Sparkle
Splickity
Standard
U.S. Catholic
War Cry
Your Voice

TAKE-HOME PAPER

The Gem
Gems of Truth
Guide
Insight
Live
Our Little Friend
Power for Living
Primary Treasure
Purpose
Seek
Standard

THEOLOGY

byFaith
The Canadian Lutheran
Christianity Today
Faith & Friends
Lutheran Witness
Mature Living
The Messenger
Presbyterians Today

6

ADULT MARKETS

AMERICA

106 W. 56th St., New York, NY 10019-3803 | 212-581-4640
articles@americamagazine.org | *www.americamagazine.org*
Kevin Clarke, senior editor
Joseph Hoover, S.J., poetry editor, jhoover@americamagazine.org

Denomination: Catholic
Parent company: America Media, Jesuit Conference of the United States and Canada
Type: weekly print magazine plus online content; 36 pages, circulation 46,000
Audience: primarily Catholic, two-thirds are laypeople, college educated
Purpose: to provide a smart Catholic take on faith and culture
Submissions: Only accepts complete manuscripts submitted through the website. Unsolicited freelance: 100%. Responds in two weeks.
Types: Articles, 2,500 words maximum. "Faith in Focus," personal essays, 800 to 1500 words. "Short Take" opinion essays, 500-600 words. Poetry, 30 lines maximum.
Topics: Catholic take on a political, social, cultural, economic, or ecclesial news event or historical/cultural trend; essays on joys and challenges of living out one's faith in the midst of real life
Rights: first, electronic
Payment: competitive rates, on acceptance
Guidelines: *americamedia.submittable.com/submit*
Sample: download from the website
Tip: "We are known across the Catholic world for our unique brand of excellent, relevant, and accessible coverage. From theology and spirituality to politics, international relations, arts and letters, and the economy and social justice, our coverage spans the globe."

ANGELS ON EARTH

110 William St., Ste. 901, New York, NY 10038 | 212-251-8100
submissions@angelsonearth.com |
www.guideposts.org/brand/angels-on-earth-magazine
Colleen Hughes, editor-in-chief

Parent company: Guideposts
Type: bimonthly print and digital magazine, circulation 550,000
Purpose: to tell true stories of heavenly angels and earthly ones who find themselves on a mission of comfort, kindness, or reassurance
Submissions: Submit complete manuscript through the website, by email, or by mail with SASE. Responds in two months or isn't interested. Unsolicited freelance: 90%. Articles to 1,500 words, 40-60 per year; short anecdotes similar to full-length articles, 50-250 words. All stories must be true.
Types of manuscripts: personal experience, recipes, fillers
Topics: true stories about God's angels and humans who have played angelic roles on earth; "Angel Sightings," pictures of angels
Rights: all
Payment: $25-500, on publication, 20% kill fee on assignments
Guidelines: *www.guideposts.org/writers-guidelines*
Sample: 7x10 SASE with four stamps
Tip: "We are not limited to stories about heavenly angels. We also accept stories about human beings doing heavenly duties."

THE ANGLICAN JOURNAL

80 Hayden St., Toronto, ON M4Y 3G2, Canada | 416-924-9199
jthomas@national.anglican.ca | *www.anglicanjournal.com*
Janet Thomas, assistant to editor

Denomination: Anglican
Parent company: Anglican Church of Canada
Type: monthly (except July and August) print and digital newspaper, circulation 123,000, takes ads
Audience: denomination
Purpose: to share compelling news and features about the Anglican Church of Canada and the Anglican Communion and religion in general
Submissions: No unsolicited manuscripts; email query as attachment. Length: 500-600 words. Freelance: 5%. Seasonal at least two months in advance. Responds in two weeks. Bible: NRSV.
Types of manuscripts: personal experience, short stories, news, reviews

Topics: Christian life, spiritual issues
Rights: first
Payment: $75-100, on acceptance
Guidelines: *www.anglicanjournal.com/about-us/writers-guidelines*
Sample: on website
Tip: Looking for "local church/parish news stories, book reviews, spiritual reflection."

ANSWERS

PO Box 510, Hebron, KY 41048 | 800-350-3232
editor@answersmagazine.com | *answersingenesis.org/answers/magazine*
Mike Matthews, editor in chief

Parent company: Answers in Genesis
Type: bimonthly print and digital magazine, circulation 50,000, takes ads
Audience: Christian laypeople interested in a biblical worldview from a young-earth creation perspective
Purpose: to illustrate the importance of Genesis in building a creation-based worldview and to equip readers with practical answers, so they can confidently communicate the gospel and biblical authority with accuracy and gracioiusness
Submissions: Email query letter. Once accepted, email article as an attachment. Responds in two weeks. Length: 300-2,500 words. Seasonal six months in advance. Buys ninety articles/year. Bible: ESV.
Types of manuscripts: teaching, wide range of scientific and theological analysis
Topics: creation-evolution, biblical authority
Rights: all
Payment: varies, on publication, kill fee sometimes
Sample: email Connie Par-Due at *conniep@answersingenesis.org*
Tip: "Science writing from a knowledge of young-earth creationism. We normally carry articles by specialists in a scientific field. We do not carry devotionals or general apologetics for creation over evolution. Rather, we cover specific topics from a biblical creation perspective."

THE ARLINGTON CATHOLIC HERALD

200 N. Glebe Rd, Ste. 600, Arlington, VA 22203 | 703-841-2590
editorial@catholicherald.com | *www.catholicherald.com*
Ann M. Augherton, editor

Denomination: Catholic
Parent company: Arlington, VA Diocese
Type: weekly print and digital newspaper, circulation 70,000, takes ads
Audience: denomination
Purpose: to support the Church's mission to evangelize by providing news from a Catholic perspective
Submissions: Email a query with a story idea.
Types of manuscripts: news, feature articles, profiles
Guidelines: *www.catholicherald.com/contact_us.html*
Sample: on the website

AUTHENTIK MAGAZINE (FORMERLY SHATTERED MAGAZINE)

600 Boulevard South S.W., Ste. 104, Huntsville, AL 35802
256-783-8350
rachael@shatteredmagazine.net | *shatteredmagazine.net*
Rachael Jackson, editor-in-chief

Type: quarterly print and digital magazine, takes ads
Audience: general
Purpose: to celebrate our unique, God-given stories
Submission: Looking for testimonies of encountering Jesus to use in the features, life, community, and mission sections. "Where did He meet you? Where does He continue to meet you? How has He used what others intended for evil in your life for good? How has He taken what you have screwed up and redeemed for His glory? How has He used community to be a part of your story? Or, how has your community been a part of a larger story? Has God moved you to share Him with others? What has that looked like?" Query through the website.
Types of manuscripts: personal experience
Guidelines: *authentikmag.com/want-to-write-for-shattered*

BELIEVERS BAY

1202 S. Pennsylvania St., Marion, IN 46953 | 765-997-173
editor@BelieversBay.com | *www.BelieversBay.com*
Tim Russ, editor

Type: weekly online magazine
Purpose: to share the love of God with common sense
Submissions: Articles 500-1,000 words, columns 300-500 words. Open to new columns; query type and topic. Freelance: 100%; accepts as many manuscripts as are submitted. Seasonal at least two weeks ahead.

Types of manuscripts: articles, short stories, essays, poetry
Topics: almost anything
Rights: onetime electronic, permanently archives pieces
Payment: none
Guidelines: *www.believersbay.com/submissions*
Tip: "Easy to break in with quality writing; share something that shares the love of God with common sense, or share something that would be of value to the average person."

BIBLE ADVOCATE

PO Box 33677, Denver, CO 80233
bibleadvocate@cog7.org | *baonline.org*
Sherri Langton, associate editor

Denomination: Church of God (Seventh Day)
Type: bimonthly print and digital magazine, circulation 11,000
Audience: denomination, general
Purpose: to advocate the Bible, represent the Church, and glorify the God of grace and truth
Submissions: Email complete manuscript. Unsolicited freelance: 30%. Buys twenty manuscripts per year. Length: 1,100-1,500 words. Responds in four to ten weeks. No Christmas or Easter manuscripts. Accepts simultaneous submissions. Bible: NKJV.
Types: teaching, poetry, personal experience, fillers
Topics: theme related, Christian life
Rights: first, reprint (tell when/where appeared), electronic
Payment: articles, $25-65; poems, $20; on publication
Guidelines and theme list: *baonline.org/write-for-us*
Sample: 9x12 envelope with three stamps
Tip: "Fresh writing with keen insight. All areas are open to freelancers. Be sure to support your points with Scripture. No Christmas or Easter pieces, please."

THE BREAKTHROUGH INTERCESSOR

PO Box 121, Lincoln, VA 20160-0121 | 540-338-4131
breakthrough@intercessors.org | *www.intercessors.org*
Noelle Garnier, editor

Parent company: Breakthrough
Type: quarterly print magazine, circulation 4,000
Audience: adults interested in growing their prayer lives
Purpose: to encourage people to pray and to equip them to do so more effectively

Submissions: Email complete manuscript. Length: articles, 600-1,000 words; poetry, 12 lines maximum.
Types of manuscripts: personal experience, teaching, poetry
Topic: prayer
Rights: first, onetime, nonexclusive electronic
Payment: none
Guidelines: *www.intercessors.org/media/downloads/Guidelines%20&%20PermissionForm.pdf*
Sample copy: download from the website

byFAITH

1700 N. Brown Rd., Ste. 105, Lawrenceville, GA 30043 | 678-825-1005
editor@byfaithonline.com | byfaithonline.com
Dick Doster, editor, ddoster@byfaithonline.com

Denomination: Presbyterian Church in America
Type: online magazine
Audience: denomination
Purpose: to provide news of the PCA, to equip readers to become a more active part of God's redemptive plan for the world, and to help them respond biblically and intelligently to the questions our culture is asking
Submissions: Email complete manuscripts. Articles 500-3,000 words.
Types: profiles, teaching, reviews, news
Topics: true stories of people living out their faith, practical theology, biblical perspective on arts and culture, reviews of current books and movies, Christian living, PCA news
Guidelines: *byfaithonline.com/about*
Tip: "Theologically, the writers are Reformed and believe the faith is practical and applicable to every part of life. Most of our writers (though not all) come from the PCA."

CANADA LUTHERAN

600-177 Lombard Ave., Winnipeg, MB R3B 0W5, Canada | 888-786-6707
www.elcic.ca
British Columbia Synod, Jude Whaley, editor, deacjudy09@yahoo.ca
Synod of Alberta and the Territories, Colleen McGinnis, editor, mail@caelinartworks.com
Saskatchewan Synod, sksynod@elcic.ca
Manitoba/Northwestern Ontario Synod, Rick Scherger, editor, rscherger@elcic.ca

Eastern Synod, Beverley Cunnigham, editor, beverley@cunninghamcommunications.ca

Denomination: Evangelical Lutheran Church in Canada
Type: monthly print magazine (8x), circulation 14,000
Audience: denomination
Purpose: to engage the Evangelical Lutheran Church in Canada in a dynamic dialogue in which information, inspiration, and ideas are shared in a thoughtful and stimulating way
Submissions: Especially looking for articles for "Practising Our Faith," stories and ideas about how you or the people around you handle life's challenges and opportunities through faith. Length: 650 words. Also takes documentary articles and profiles of people of interest to readers (normally ELCIC members), seasonal, advice in how-to lists, and articles highlighting ministry in the synods. Email submissions.
Types of manuscripts: personal experience, profile, documentary, how-to
Topics: seasonal, Christian living, ELCIC ministries
Rights: onetime
Guidelines: *www.elcic.ca/clweb/contributing.html*
Tip: "As much as is possible, the content of the magazine is chosen from the work of Canadian writers. The content strives to reflect the Evangelical Lutheran Church in Canada in the context of our Canadian society."

THE CANADIAN LUTHERAN

3074 Portage Ave., Winnipeg, MB R3K 0Y2, Canada | 800-588-4226, 204-895-3433
communications@lutheranchurch.ca | *www.lutheranchurch.ca/canluth.php*
Matthew Block, editor-in-chief

Denomination: Lutheran Church—Canada
Type: bimonthly print magazine, circulation 20,000
Audience: denomination
Purpose: to inspire, motivate and inform
Submissions: Email complete manuscript with "Canadian Lutheran article" in the subject line. Looking for Christian reflections on current events, teaching articles about our theology, discussions of contemporary culture in the light of faith, and more.
Types of manuscripts: news, teaching, essay
Topics: theology, contemporary culture, congregational and district news (submit to appropriate district editor and include photo)

Rights: first (but reserves the right to reprint)
Payment: none for unsolicited manuscripts
Guidelines: *www.canadianlutheran.ca/submissions*
Sample: download from the website
Tip: "All feature articles with doctrinal content must go through doctrinal review to ensure fidelity to the Scriptures. As a result, authors may occasionally be asked to rewrite some sections of their article before publication."

CANADIAN MENNONITE

490 Dutton Dr., Unit C5, Waterloo, ON N2L 6H7, Canada | 519-884-3810
submit@canadianmennonite.org | *www.canadianmennonite.org*
Ross W. Muir, managing editor

Denomination: Mennonite Church Canada
Type: biweekly print magazine
Audience: denomination
Purpose: to educate, inspire, inform, and foster dialogue on issues facing Mennonites in Canada as it shares the good news of Jesus Christ from an Anabaptist perspective
Submissions: Email query first. Email manuscripts as attachments or mail them.
Types: theological reflections, sermons, opinion pieces, letters, reviews (books, music, movies), personal stories, news
Topics: theme-related
Payment: none for unsolicited articles, 10¢/word for solicited articles
Guidelines and theme list: *www.canadianmennonite.org/submissions*
Sample: download from the website

CATECHIST

2 W. Hill Dr., Worcester, MA 01609
pat.gohn@bayard-inc.com | *www.catechist.com*
Pat Gohn, editor

Parent company: Bayard, Inc.
Type: monthly (7x during school year) print and digital magazine, digital newsletter; print circulation 42,000; takes ads
Audience: catechists, directors of religious education, catechetical leaders
Purpose: to support the work of catechists through formation, lessons, activities, and resources
Submissions: Must be Catholic-focused. Freelance: 10%. Buys 200

manuscripts/year. Seasonal: six months in advance. Query first. Email as an attachment. Responds in one week. Length: 500-1,500 words. Bible: NABRE.

Types of manuscripts: lessons and activities for K-12 students or adults

Topics: Catholic faith, sacraments, liturgical year

Rights: first

Payment: $75-350, on acceptance

Guidelines: *www.catechist.com/about-catechist*

Sample: on the website

Tip: "Query editor with your ideas first. We work most with writers who are catechists themselves or specialists in this field."

CATHOLIC DIGEST

1 Montauk Ave., New London, CT 06320
queries@catholicdigest.com | *www.catholicdigest.com*
Paul McKibben, managing editor

Denomination: Catholic

Type: print magazine, 9x a year; takes ads

Audience: denomination

Purpose: to encourage and support Catholics in a variety of life stages and circumstances

Submissions: Query for feature articles. Accepts simultaneous submissions. Articles 1,500 words. Seasonal four to five months ahead. Departments: "Last Word" personal essay, 550-700 words; "Open Door" first-person stories about conversion to or recovering the Catholic faith, 350-600 words; send to *opendoor@catholicdigest.com*. Email complete manuscript for departments.

Types of manuscripts: how-to, essay, personal experience

Topics: marriage, practical spirituality, parish/work, parenting, grandparenting, homemaking, relationships, beauty

Rights: first

Payment: $100-500, on publication

Guidelines: *www.catholicdigest.com/writers-guidelines*

CATHOLIC NEW YORK

1011 First Ave., Ste. 1721, New York, NY 10022 | 212-688-2399
jwoods@cny.org | *www.cny.org*
John Woods, editor-in-chief

Denomination: Catholic

Parent company: Ecclesiastical Communications Corp.

Type: biweekly print newspaper, circulation 127,000, takes ads
Audience: denomination
Purpose: to publish news and information of interest to Catholics in the Archdiocese of New York
Submissions: Email query or complete manuscript as attachment. Unsolicited freelance: 2%. Accepts five to ten manuscripts/year. Length: 600 words. Responds in one month. Seasonal two weeks in advance. Bible: NAB.
Types of manuscripts: news reports, personal experience, teaching
Topics: state news, Christian living, moral issues
Rights: onetime
Payment: $125, on publication
Guidelines: none
Sample: written request
Tip: "We use freelancers from New York to cover evening and weekend events."

CATHOLIC SENTINEL

5536 N.E. Hassalo, Portland, OR 97213 | 503-281-1191
sentinel@CatholicSentinel.org | *www.CatholicSentinel.org*
Ed Langlois, managing editor

Denomination: Catholic
Parent company: Archdiocese of Portland
Type: bimonthly print newspaper
Audience: Catholics who live in Oregon
Purpose: to feature Oregon people and Oregon issues that relate to Catholics
Submissions: Articles 600-1,500 words. Query first. Feature stories about Catholics living out their faith. Columns about local, national, or international issues of interest with a local connection.
Types of manuscripts: profiles, personal experience
Topics: Christian living, issues
Payment: variable rates for articles, none for columns
Guidelines: *www.catholicsentinel.org/main.asp?SectionID=15&SubSectionID=60&ArticleID=11770*

CELEBRATE LIFE MAGAZINE

PO Box 1350, Stafford, VA 22555 | 540-659-4171
clmag@all.org | *www.clmagazine.org*
William Mahoney, editor

Denomination: Catholic

Parent company: American Life League
Type: quarterly print and digital magazine, circulation 7,500, takes ads
Audience: pro-life
Purpose: to inspire, encourage, and educate pro-life activists
Submissions: Covers all respect-for-life matters according to the Catholic Church's teaching. Email complete manuscript as an attachment. Freelance: 25%. Accepts six manuscripts/year. Articles 800-1,800 words. Seasonal six months ahead. Responds in one to two months. Bible: *Jerusalem Bible.*
Types of manuscripts: personal experience, interviews, how-to, teaching
Topics: matters concerning the sanctity of life and human personhood in harmony with the teachings of the Catholic Church; see specific list in guidelines
Rights: first
Payment: 10-25¢/word, on publication, sometimes kill fee
Guidelines: *www.clmagazine.org/submission-guidelines*
Sample: email for copy
Tip: "Most in need of timely investigative reports and personal experiences."

CHARISMA

600 Rinehart Rd., Lake Mary, FL 32746 | 407-333-0600
charisma@charismamedia.com | *www.charismamag.com*
Christine D. Johnson, managing editor

Denomination: Pentecostal/Charismatic
Type: monthly print and digital magazine, circulation 90,000
Audience: passionate, Spirit-filled Christians
Purpose: to empower believers for life in the Spirit
Submissions: Query only through the online form. If accepted, prefers email submission. Responds in two to three months. Seasonal five months ahead. Assigned: 80%. Needs articles that reflect on the work of a particular ministry, Christian author or artist, 700 words maximum; product reviews of newly released books, music, and movies/DVDs (assigned); in-depth feature stories to 2,600 words. Bible: MEV. Prefers third-person.
Types: profiles, interviews, reviews, feature stories
Topics: prayer, healing, spiritual warfare, end times, the prophetic and Israel, Christmas, Easter
Rights: all
Payment: on publication

Guidelines: *www.charismamag.com/about/write-for-us*
Sample: on the website
Tip: "Please take time to read—even study—at least one or two of our recent issues before submitting a query. Sometimes people submit their writing without ever having read or understood our magazine or its readers, and sometimes people will have read our magazine years ago and think it's the same as it has always been; but magazines undergo many changes through the years."

CHICKEN SOUP FOR THE SOUL BOOK SERIES

PO Box 700, Cos Cob, CT 06807
www.chickensoup.com
Amy Newmark, editor-in-chief

Parent company: Chicken Soup for the Soul Publishing, LLC
Type: trade paperback books, about a dozen yearly
Purpose: to share happiness, inspiration, and hope
Submissions: Submit complete manuscript only through the website. Unsolicited freelance: 98%. Length: 1,200 words maximum. "A Chicken Soup for the Soul story is an inspirational, true story about ordinary people having extraordinary experiences. . . . These stories are personal and often filled with emotion and drama." Poems tell a story; no rhyming. Accepts submissions from children and teens for some books. No reprints.
Types: personal experiences, poetry
Topics: *www.chickensoup.com/story-submissions/possible-book-topics*
Payment: $200, one month after publication, plus ten copies of the book
Tip: "The most powerful stories are about people extending themselves or performing an act of love, service, or courage for another person."

CHILDREN'S MINISTRY

1515 Cascade Ave., Loveland, CO 80538 | 970-669-3836
puorgbus@group.com | *childrensministry.com/about-our-magazine*
Jennifer Hooks, managing editor, jhooks@group.com

Parent company: Group
Type: bimonthly print and digital magazine
Audience: children's ministry workers
Purpose: to help leaders encourage children to grow spiritually
Submissions: Feature articles, 1,000-2,200 words; teacher and parent tips, games, crafts, activities, 200 words. Regular columns on age-

level development, outreach, family ministry, leading volunteers, special needs, and discipline. Email or mail full manuscript. Responds in eight to ten weeks. Seasonal ten months ahead.

Types of manuscripts: how-to, tips, crafts, activities

Topics: working with volunteers; discipline; understanding children; communicating with children about faith, morals, money, friends, grades, and choices

Rights: all

Payment: features $75-400, tips and fillers $40

Guidelines: *grouppublishingps.zendesk.com/hc/en-us/articles/211878258-Submissions*

CHRIST OUR HOPE

16555 Weber Rd., Crest Hill, IL 60403 | 815-221-6100
magazine@dioceseofjoliet.org |
www.dioceseofjoliet.org/magazine/sectioncontent.php?secid=1
Carlos Briceño, editor

Denomination: Catholic

Parent company: Diocese of Joliet, Illinois

Purpose: to tell inspiring stories of faith and share information with the goal of educating and evangelizing others

Type: monthly print magazine

Submissions: Query by email.

Types: news, personal experiences, profiles

Topics: Catholic life, local news

Payment: none

Sample: on the website

THE CHRISTIAN CENTURY

104 S. Michigan Ave., Ste. 1100, Chicago, IL 60603-5901
312-263-7510
submissions@christiancentury.org | *www.christiancentury.org*
Debra Bendis, senior editor
Elizabeth Palmer, books editor
Jill Peláez Baumgaertner, poetry editor, poetry@christiancentury.org

Type: biweekly print magazine, takes ads

Audience: ecumenical, mainline ministers, educators, and church leaders

Purpose: to explore what it means to believe and live out the Christian faith in our time

Submissions: Email query first. Responds in four to six weeks. Unsolicited freelance: 90%. Seasonal four months in advance.

Articles 1,500-3,000 words, buys 150 per year; poetry (free verse, traditional) to 20 lines. Bible version: NRSV.

Types of manuscripts: essays, humor, interviews, opinion, book reviews (assigned), poetry

Topics: poverty, human rights, economic justice, international relations, national priorities, popular culture, critiques of individual religious communities

Rights: all, reprint (tell where and when published)

Payment: articles $100-300, poems $50, reviews to $75, on publication

Guidelines and theme list: *www.christiancentury.org/submission-guidelines*

Sample: $3.50

Tip: "Keep in mind our audience of sophisticated readers, eager for analysis and critical perspective that goes beyond the obvious. We are open to all topics if written with appropriate style for our readers."

CHRISTIAN COURIER

2 Aiken St., St. Catherines, ON L2N 1V8, Canada | 800-969-4838, 905-937-3314

editor@christiancourier.ca | *www.christiancourier.ca*

Angela Reitsma Bick, editor-in-chief, editor@christiancourier.ca

Monica Kronemeyer deRegt, features editor, ccmonicaderegt@gmail.com

Brian Bork, review editor, bbork41@gmail.com

Denomination: Christian Reformed

Type: biweekly print newspaper, circulation 2,500, takes ads

Purpose: to connect Christians with a network of culturally savvy partners in faith for the purpose of inspiring all to participate in God's renewing work with His creation

Submissions: Email queries and manuscripts to the appropriate editor. Articles 700-1,200 words, book and movie reviews 750 words. Responds in one to two weeks, only if accepted. Seasonal three months ahead. Accepts simultaneous submissions. Uses some sidebars. Prefers NIV.

Types of manuscripts: editorials, reviews, columns, features, news, poetry

Rights: onetime, reprint (tell when/where appeared)

Payment: $45-$70, 30 days after publication; no pay for reprints

Guidelines: *christiancourier.ca/writeForUs.php*

Tip: "Suggest an aspect of the theme which you believe you could cover well, have insight into, could treat humorously, etc. Show that you think clearly, write clearly, and have something to say that we should want to read. Have a strong biblical worldview and avoid moralism and sentimentality."

THE CHRISTIAN HERALD

PO Box 68526, Brampton, ON L6R 0J8, Canada | 905-874-1731
info@christianherald.ca | *christianherald.ca*

Type: monthly print newspaper
Purpose: to present an informed Christian perspective on current local, regional, and international issues, news and events
Audience: greater Toronto area
Submissions: Email query first.
Types of manuscripts: news, profiles, reviews
Topics: newsmaker profiles, including Christians in ministry, politics, sports, media, and business; book, music, concert, theatre, and movie reviews; travel destination profiles
Guidelines: *christianherald.ca/editorial.html*

THE CHRISTIAN JOURNAL

1032 W. Main, Medford, OR 97501 | 541-773-4004
info@thechristianjournal.org | *www.TheChristianJournal.org*
Chad McComas, senior editor

Type: monthly print and digital magazine
Audience: both Christians and non-Christians
Purpose: to share encouragement with the body of Christ in the Rogue Valley, Oregon
Submissions: Each article needs to inspire the reader to reconnect with God and his or her faith. Length: 300–500 words, average around 400 words. Email manuscript.
Types of manuscripts: feature articles, testimonies, profiles, reviews
Topics: hope, encouragement, theme-related articles, profiles of local ministries and Christian personalities, children's stories
Rights: onetime
Payment: none
Guidelines: *thechristianjournal.org/writers-information/guidelines-for-writers*

CHRISTIAN LIBRARIAN

PO Box 4, Cedarville, OH 45314 | 937-766-2255
trobinson@whitworth.edu | *www.acl.org*

Tami Robinson, managing editor

Parent organization: Association of Christian Librarians
Type: biannual print journal
Audience: primarily Christian librarians in institutions of higher learning
Purpose: to publish articles, provide a membership forum, and encourage writing
Submissions: Mail or email manuscripts. Shorter articles, 1,000-3,000 words, are generally preferable for practical and nonresearch papers; scholarly articles to 5,000 words, some longer. Include a 100-word abstract.
Types of manuscripts: teaching, reviews, bibliographies
Topics: Christian interpretation of librarianship, theory and practice of library science, bibliographic essays, reviews, and human-interest articles relating to books and libraries
Rights: first, with signed grant of license
Payment: none
Guidelines: *www.acl.org/index.cfm/publications/the-christian-librarian/tcl-author-guidelines-5-3-17*

CHRISTIAN LIVING IN THE MATURE YEARS

2222 Rosa L Parks Blvd., Nashville, TN 37228
matureyears@umpublishing.org | *www.adultbiblestudies.com/MatureYears*
Rachel Mullen, features and acquisitions editor

Denomination: United Methodist
Parent company: United Methodist Publishing House
Type: quarterly print magazine
Audience: ages 50 and older
Purpose: to help older adults with opportunities and challenges related to aging
Submissions: Submit through *www.matureyears.submittable.com*. Responds in two to four months. Seasonal one year in advance. Length: 250-2,000 words. Buys fifty manuscripts per year. Unsolicited freelance: 100%. Bible: CEB.
Types of manuscripts: how-to, short memoir, personal experience, recipe, religious reflection/meditation, filler, puzzle
Topics: grandparenting, Christian life, general interest, health, money, retirement, aging, Bible lessons
Rights: first
Payment: 7¢/word, on acceptance
Guidelines: by email

Sample: email for a PDF
Tip: "Our 'Fragments of Life' section always needs new writers. It is a short memoir section; four pieces needed each quarter. We do not accept articles about 'the good old days' or pieces that focus on negativity and death over health, wellness, and life."

CHRISTIAN MOTORSPORTS ILLUSTRATED

PO Box 790, Quinlan, TX 75474 | 607-742-3407
www.christianmotorsports.com
Roland Osborne, publisher

Type: print magazine
Audience: people interested in all types of motorsports racing, bike rallies, aftermarket manufacturers, car clubs, auto museums, sanctioning bodies, tracks, and event sites
Purpose: to meet the spiritual needs of the motorsports community
Submissions: Articles 650-1,200 words. Query through the website.
Topics: uplifting and positive stories relating to all forms of motorsports
Payment: none
Guidelines: *www.christianmotorsports.com/index.php/from-the-editor*

CHRISTIAN NEWS NORTHWEST

PO Box 974, Newberg, OR 97132 | 503-537-9220
cnnw@cnnw.com | *www.cnnw.com*
John Fortmeyer, editor

Type: monthly print newspaper, circulation 29,000
Audience: people living in western and central Oregon and southwest Washington
Purpose: to inform about ministry news in the target area
Submissions: Email news and commentaries pertinent to ministry concerns in the Northwest. Length: 700 words.
Payment: none
Tip: "Top priority is given to writers living in Oregon and Washington."

THE CHRISTIAN ONLINE MAGAZINE

PO Box 262, Wolford, VA 24658
submissions@christianmagazine.org | *www.ChristianMagazine.org*
Darlene Osborne, publisher, darlene@christianmagazine.org

Type: monthly e-zine
Audience: general

Purpose: to bring readers the best Christian information on the net
Submissions: Email manuscript. Length: 700 words maximum. Articles should be practical, having a distinct Christian perspective throughout.
Topics: anything that builds faith
Rights: electronic
Payment: none
Guidelines: *www.christianonlinemagazine.com/submit_an_article_writer_guidelines*
Tip: "Most open to solid Christian articles founded on the Word of God."

THE CHRISTIAN RANCHMAN

PO Box 7557, Fort Worth, TX 76111 | 817-236-0023
ranchman@cowboysforchrist.net | *www.CowboysforChrist.net*
Dr. David Harvey, editor

Parent company: Cowboys for Christ
Type: bimonthly print tabloid, circulation 23,000
Purpose: to share the gospel with cowboys and cowgirls and those who are drawn by the cowboy image and way of life
Submissions: Email query or complete manuscript. Length: 350-1,000 words.
Types of manuscripts: testimonies, profiles
Topics: related to the cowboy way of life
Payment: none
Sample: on the website

CHRISTIAN RESEARCH JOURNAL

PO Box 8500, Charlotte, NC 28271-8500 | 704-887-8200
emiller@equip.org | *www.equip.org*
Elliot Miller, editor-in-chief
Melanie Cogdill, managing editor

Parent company: Christian Research Institute
Type: bimonthly print journal
Audience: thoughtful laypeople, academics, scholars
Purpose: to equip Christians with the information they need to discern doctrinal errors; to evangelize people of other faiths; to present a strong defense of Christian beliefs and ethics; and to provide comprehensive, definitive responses to contemporary apologetic concerns
Submissions: Email query or a manuscript that follows formatting

guidelines. Responds in four months. Articles should reflect a command of the subject at hand, including its history, the key personalities involved, the beliefs and/or practices surrounding the controversy, and the criticisms that have been made concerning the subject. Feature articles 2,200 or 3,500 words as assigned; include 250-300-word synopsis with main facts and arguments. Summary critique review 1,700 words, effective evangelism 1,700 words, viewpoint 1,700 words, movie and book reviews 800 words. All articles must be within 25 words of these word counts.

Types of manuscripts: feature articles, news stories, viewpoint, book reviews, and summary critiques

Topics: apologetics, evangelism, cults and new religions, the occult, New Age movement, aberrant Christian movements and teachings

Rights: first, reprint

Payment: $125-500, kill fee 50%

Guidelines: *www.equip.org/PDF/WriterGuidelines.2017.pdf*

Tip: "Almost nothing can better prepare you to write for the Christian Research Journal than familiarity with the Journal itself. If you are not a regular reader of the Journal, you should read all the articles in recent issues that correspond to the type of article you wish to write."

CHRISTIAN RETAILING

600 Rinehart Rd., Lake Mary, FL 32746 | 407-333-0600
retailing@charismamedia.com | *www.christianretailing.com*
Christine D. Johnson, editor, chris.johnson@charismamedia.com

Parent company: Charisma Media

Type: bimonthly print and digital trade journal

Audience: retailers, church bookstores, publishers, music labels, distributors, and others working and volunteering in the Christian products industry

Purpose: to champion the world of Christian resources and to provide critical information and insight to advance business and ministry

Submissions: Query only. Prefers third-person point of view. Bible: MEV.

Types of manuscripts: features, news stories, columns, reviews

Topics: all aspects of running a bookstore, trends in publishing, new-product reviews

Payment: varies by assignment

Guidelines: *christianretailing.com/index.php/general/28335-writers-guidelines*

CHRISTIAN STANDARD

16965 Pine Ln., Ste. 202, Parker, CO 80134 | 800-543-1353
CS@christianstandardmedia.com | *www.christianstandard.com*
Michael C. Mack, editor
Jim Nieman, managing editor

Denomination: Christian Churches, Churches of Christ
Parent company: Christian Standard Media
Type: monthly print and digital magazine, circulation 13,000
Audience: Christian leaders
Purpose: to resource Christian leaders
Submissions: Email queries (preferred) and manuscripts as attachments. Length: 500-2,000 words. Freelance: 5-10%. Buys fifteen manuscripts per year. Seasonal six to eight months in advance. Responds in one to three months. Bible: NIV.
Types of manuscripts: theme-related, how-to, meditations, sidebars
Topics: church and ministry leadership, church finances, intergenerational ministry, urban and rural ministry, international ministry and missions, Communion meditations
Rights: first, reprint (tell when/where published)
Payment: $50-250, on acceptance, kill fee sometimes
Guidelines: *www.christianstandard.com/contact-us/submit-articles*
Theme list: *www.christianstandard.com/wp-content/uploads/2016/06/CS-Cover-Themes-for-2018.pdf*
Sample: by email
Tip: "We are looking for well-written articles especially by and about independent Christian churches (Restoration Movement churches). Success stories are great, of course, but we want real stories about real people who rely on God's grace and power to overcome adversity and grow in Christlikeness. How is the church/ministry/leader living out and carrying out the mission?"

CHRISTIANITY TODAY

465 Gundersen Dr., Carol Stream, IL 60188-2498 | 630-260-6200
cteditor@christianitytoday.com | *www.christianitytoday.com*
Mark Galli, editor-in-chief

Type: monthly (10x) print and digital magazine, takes ads
Audience: intentional Christians who seek to thoughtfully integrate their faith with responsible action in the church and world
Purpose: to provide evangelical thought leaders a sense of community, coherence, and direction through thoughtful, biblical commentary on issues and through careful, caring reporting of the news
Submissions: Query first through the website. Requires published

credits. Responds in three weeks or not interested. Articles must be well supported, provide a fresh perspective, and connect the eternal message of the gospel with current trends, culture, events, and news. First-person articles should apply your personal experience to a broader concept of faith and biblical truth.

Types of manuscripts: profiles, interviews, feature stories, book reviews, opinion pieces, personal experience

Topics: Christians living out their faith in unique ways that impact the world for the better and communicate truth in a way that is deep, nuanced, and challenging

Rights: first, electronic

Payment: not specified

Guidelines: *www.christianitytoday.com/ct/help/about-us/writers-guidelines.html*

Tip: "We publish articles by and for evangelical Christians. Our readers are typically in some form of leadership or ministry—whether volunteer or professional—in their churches and communities."

THE CHURCH HERALD & HOLINESS BANNER

7407 Metcalf, Overland Park, KS 66212
editor@heraldandbanner.com | *www.heraldandbanner.com*
Dr. Gordon L. Snider, editor

Denomination: Church of God (Holiness)

Parent company: Herald and Banner Press

Type: monthly print and digital magazine

Audience: denomination

Submissions: Email through the website for current needs. Includes various teaching articles each month that will inspire you in your Christian walk, help you understand more about a biblical topic, etc. Also featured are various articles promoting Christian ideals, such as the importance to live with gratitude, etc.

Types of manuscripts: teaching

Topics: biblical teaching, Christian living from a holiness perspective

CITIZEN MAGAZINE

8605 Explorer Dr., Colorado Springs, CO 80920 | 719-531-3400
citizeneditor@focusonthefamily.com |
www.focusonthefamily.com/socialissues/citizen-magazine
Karla Dial, editor in chief

Parent company: Focus on the Family

Type: monthly (10x) print magazine

Audience: to equip today's Christian with often-unreported facts and the resources to dig deeper; inspire subscribers "to love and good works"; and provide ways to engage with friends, colleagues, and neighbors who may have an opposing worldview

Submissions: Balancing truth and grace, each article is carefully researched and reported on from a biblical worldview.

Types of manuscripts: teaching, profiles, news

Topics: contemporary issues, popular culture, government policy

Sample: link at *www.focusonthefamily.com/socialissues/promos/subscribe-to-citizen-magazine*

Tip: "Our working agenda has been 'hope, how-to, and hot national topics.' We aim to provide hope by telling the stories of people and organizations that have successfully made a difference in their sphere of influence—and how they did it—so others can follow their example. When it comes to hot national topics, we provide an in-depth perspective from a Christian point of view that readers can't get from the mainstream media."

CITY LIGHT NEWS

459 Astoria Cres. S.E., Calgary, AB T2J 0Y6, Canada | 403-640-2011
editor@Calgarychristian.com | *www.calgarychristian.com*
Peter McManus, editor

Type: monthly print newspaper

Audience: youth to seniors who live in Southern and Central Alberta

Purpose: to report on newsworthy activities, ministries, and issues from a Christian perspective; provide thought-provoking commentary; advance the Kingdom of God by uniting and strengthening the Body of Christ through encouraging and informative stories, events, and testimonies

Submissions: Freelance: 50%. Deadline: no later than the 15th of the month prior to publication date.

Types of manuscripts: news reports, commentary, columns, profiles, testimonies

Topics: anything of interest to Christians in Alberta

Guidelines: *www.calgarychristian.com/adventures/guidelines.htm*

Sample: *www.calgarychristian.com/archives.htm*

COLUMBIA

1 Columbus Plaza, New Haven, CT 06510-3326 | 203-752-4398
columbia@kofc.org | *www.kofc.org/Columbia*
Alton J. Pelowski, editor-in-chief

Denomination: Catholic
Parent company: Knights of Columbus
Type: monthly print and digital magazine
Audience: general Catholic family
Submissions: Query first by email or mail. Length: 700-1,500 words. Seasonal six months in advance.
Types of manuscripts: feature articles, profiles
Topics: current events, social trends, family life, parenting, social problems, health and nutrition, finances, Catholic practice and teaching, church programs, institutions, personalities
Rights: first, electronic
Payment: varies, on acceptance
Guidelines: *www.kofc.org/un/en/columbia/guidelines.html*
Sample: *www.kofc.org/un/en/columbia/archive/columbia.html#*

COMMONCALL

PO Box 259019, Plano, TX 75025 | 214-630-4571 x1012
kencamp@baptiststandard.com | *www.baptiststandard.com*
Ken Camp, managing editor

Denomination: Baptist
Type: quarterly print magazine
Purpose: to aid and support the denomination
Submissions: Looking for stories about everyday Christians who are putting their faith into action.
Types of manuscripts: profiles, how-to
Topics: missions, evangelism, family life, leadership, effective church ministry, Texas Baptist history

COMMONWEAL

475 Riverside Dr., Rm. 405, New York, NY 10115 | 212-662-4200
editors@commonwealmagazine.org | *www.commonwealmagazine.org*
Paul Baumann, editor

Denomination: Catholic
Type: biweekly (20x) print and digital magazine
Audience: educated, committed Catholics, as well as readers from other faith traditions
Purpose: to provide a forum for civil, reasoned debate on the interaction of faith with contemporary politics and culture
Submissions: Email queries and manuscripts as attachments or through the website. Mail poetry; buys thirty per year. Articles fall into these categories: (1) "Upfronts," 1,000-1,500 words,

brief, newsy, and reportorial, giving facts, information, and some interpretation behind the headlines of the day. (2) Longer articles, 2,000-3,000 words, reflective and detailed, bringing new information or a different point of view to a subject, raising questions, and/or proposing solutions to the dilemmas facing the world, nation, church, or individual. (3) "Last Word" column, a 750-word reflection, usually of a personal nature, on some aspect of the human condition: spiritual, individual, political, or social.

Types of manuscripts: essays, features, news with interpretation, poetry

Topics: public affairs, religion, literature, the arts

Rights: all

Payment: on publication

Guidelines: *www.commonwealmagazine.org/contact-us*

Sample: $5

Tip: "Articles should be written for a general but well-educated audience. While religious articles are always topical, we are less interested in devotional and churchy pieces than in articles which examine the links between 'worldly' concerns and religious beliefs."

CONVERGE MAGAZINE

301-291 2nd Ave., Vancouver, BC V5T 1B8, Canada | 604-558-1982
info@convergemagazine.com | *www.convergemagazine.com*
Leanne Janzen, editor

Type: quarterly print and digital magazine

Audience: millennials

Purpose: to influence a growing number of people through daily content that is intelligent, authentic, and that stimulates hope in God

Submissions: Email queries and manuscripts. Articles 500-1,000 words. If no response in six weeks, assume no interest.

Types of manuscripts: personal experience

Topics: life, relationships, experiences, work, culture, faith

Guidelines: *convergemagazine.com/write*

Sample: see link at *convergemagazine.com/magazine*

Tip: "We write for those in transition: between school and work, singleness and marriage, freedom and responsibility, doubt and faith. We write as friends on the journey together, rather than one coaching another down the path. We share what we've learned through experience, rather than what we've heard or been taught. Our stories, like our lives, don't need to be tidy, with all the right answers."

THE COVENANT COMPANION

8303 W. Higgins Rd., Chicago, IL 60631 | 773-907-3328
editor@covchurch.org | *covenantcompanion.com*
Cathy Norman Peterson, director of editorial services

Denomination: Evangelical Covenant Church
Type: monthly (10x) print magazine
Audience: denomination
Purpose: to inform, stimulate thought, and encourage dialogue on issues that impact the church and its members
Submissions: Email or mail. Length: 1,200-1,800 words.
Types of manuscripts: news, profiles, book reviews
Topics: Christian life, the church (local, denominational, and universal), spirituality, contemporary issues, social justice, outreach ministry
Rights: onetime
Payment: $35-100, two months after publication
Guidelines: *covenantcompanion.com/submit-story*
Tip: "We are interested in what is happening in local churches, conferences, and other Covenant institutions and associations, as well as reports from missionaries and other staff serving around the world. Human interest stories are also welcome."

CREATION

PO Box 4545, Eight Mile Plains, QLD 4113, Australia
editors@creation.info | *creation.com/creation-magazine*

Parent company: Creation Ministries International
Type: quarterly print and digital magazine
Audience: families, homeschoolers
Purpose: to refute evolution and give answers to defend your faith and uphold the true history of the world found in Genesis
Submissions: Email manuscript as an attachment in .rtf format. Length: maximum 1,800 words, prefers 250 to 1,600 words.
Types of manuscripts: interviews with creationists, teaching
Topics: creation science, evolution's errors, nature, Genesis, Noah's Ark, the Flood
Rights: all
Payment: none
Guidelines: *creation.com/creation-magazine-writing-guidelines*
Sample: on the website

Tip: "Except in technical articles, we like to see simple words, short sentences, and short paragraphs."

CREATION ILLUSTRATED

PO Box 7955, Auburn, CA 95604 | 530-269-1424
ci@creationillustrated.com | *www.creationillustrated.com*
Tom Ish, editor

Type: quarterly print magazine
Audience: families
Purpose: to share the wonders of God's creation
Submissions: Email queries (preferred) and manuscripts. Length: 1,500-2,000 words; children's stories 500-1,000 words. Bible: KJV, NKJV.
Types of manuscripts: teaching, personal experience, children's stories, poetry, profile, fillers (crafts, games, puzzles, hikes, activities), how-to
Topics: nature, outdoor adventures, creatures, a creation day from Genesis
Rights: first, electronic, reprint
Payment: articles $100, children's stories $50-75, poetry $15; 30 days after publication; kill fee 25%
Tip: "Write for the reader. Inspire the reader to be in awe of the Creator. Help generate a worshipful spirit. Glorify God the Creator. Make your story uplifting and positive, rather than confrontive or argumentative."

THE CRESSET

Lindwood House, Valparaiso University, 1320 S. Campus Dr., Valparaiso, IN 46383
cresset@valpo.edu | *thecresset.org*
Heather Grennan Gary, editor
Marci Rae Johnson, poetry editor

Parent company: Valparaiso University
Type: print journal, 5-6x per year
Audience: general readers interested in religious matters, mostly college teachers
Purpose: to comment on literature, the arts, and public affairs and explore ideas and trends in contemporary culture from a perspective grounded in the Lutheran tradition of scholarship, freedom, and faith while informed by the wisdom of the broader Christian community
Submissions: Email query first. Prefers submissions through the website but also takes them by email or mail.

Types of manuscripts: essays, poetry, interviews
Guidelines: *thecresset.org/submissions.html*
Sample: on the website
Tip: "The Cresset is not a theological journal, but a journal addressing matters of import to those with some degree of theological interest and commitment. Authors are encouraged to reflect upon the religious implications of their subject."

CROSSCURRENTS

475 Riverside Dr., Ste. 1945, New York, NY 10115 | 212-864-5439
cph@crosscurrents.org | *www.aril.org*
Charles Henderson, executive editor

Parent company: The Association for Religion and Intellectual Life
Type: quarterly print magazine
Audience: thoughtful activists for social justice and church reform
Submissions: Accepts emailed and mailed submissions with SASE. Responds in four to eight weeks. No unsolicited book reviews, reprints. Articles 3,000-5,000 words.
Types of manuscripts: essays, poetry, fiction
Payment: none
Guidelines: *www.aril.org/submissions.htm*
Sample: on the website

CRW MAGAZINE

1710 Evergreen St., Duarte, CA 91010 | 800-309-4466
managing.editor@ptm.org | *www.ptm.org/magazine.htm*
Greg Albrecht, senior editor

Parent company: Plain Truth Ministries
Type: quarterly print and digital magazine
Audience: general
Purpose: to combat legalism and give hope, inspiration, and encouragement to those burned out by religion
Submissions: Queries only. Types of manuscripts: teaching
Guidelines: by email
Sample: on the website

DECISION

1 Billy Graham Pkwy., Charlotte, NC 28201 | 704-401-2246
decision@bgea.org | *billygraham.org/decision-magazine*

Parent company: Billy Graham Evangelistic Association
Type: monthly (11x) print and digital magazine
Audience: general

Purpose: to set forth the Good News of salvation in Jesus Christ with such clarity that readers will be drawn to make a commitment to Christ; to encourage, teach, and strengthen Christians to walk daily with Christ and reach out to others for Christ; and to inform readers about the ministry of the Billy Graham Evangelistic Association

Submissions: Query first. Freelance: 5%. Articles 400-1,500 words. "Finding Jesus" (people who became Christians through Billy Graham ministries), 500-900 words. Prefers queries. Seasonal six months in advance.

Types of manuscripts: testimonies, personal experience

Topics: salvation, evangelism

Payment: $200-500, on publication

DIVINE MOMENTS BOOK SERIES

102 Corbett Ln., Black Mountain, NC 28711 | 828-231-1963
yvonnelehman3@gmail.com | *www.yvonnelehman.com/moments*
Yvonne Lehman, compiler and editor

Parent company: Grace Publishing

Purpose: to show how faith works in everyday life experiences

Audience: general and Christian

Type: two books per year

Submissions: Accepts fifty articles per book. Email complete manuscript as attachment. Length: 500-2,000. Seasonal: six months in advance. Responds in one day. Bible: no preference.

Types of manuscripts: personal experience

Topics: theme-related, Christmas, romance, brokenness, questioning

Rights: onetime

Payment: none, royalties donated to Samaritan's Purse

Guidelines and theme list: *www.yvonnelehman.com/moments-2*

Tip: Needs stories for Christmas and personal overcoming.

DTS MAGAZINE

3909 Swiss Ave., Dallas, TX 75204
dtsmagazine@dts.edu | *www.dts.edu/magazine*
Raquel Wroten, editor

Parent company: Dallas Theological Seminary (DTS)

Type: quarterly print and digital magazine

Audience: evangelical laypeople, students, alumni, donors, and friends

Purpose: to offer articles rich in biblical and theological exposition, tell stories of how God is working through students and alumni, and update friends on God's work at DTS

Submissions: Email query first; email or mail submission. Responds in six to eight weeks. Seasonal six months in advance. Articles: alumni profiles; exposition, usually authored by DTS faculty or similarly qualified individuals; Christian living, personal experience that encourages average Christians in how to live out their faith in the world and includes some exposition that ends with application of truth. Length: 2,000 words with 200-word sidebar.

Types: profiles, teaching, personal experience

Rights: first, reprint

Payment: up to $500 for first, $150 for reprints, $50 for sidebars

Guidelines: *www.dts.edu/magazine/policy*

Sample: see the link on the website

Tip: "DTS Magazine is a ministry of Dallas Theological Seminary. We prefer articles written by our alumni, faculty, students, staff, board members, donors and their families."

EFCA TODAY

PO Box 315, Charlottesville, VA 22902 | 434-961-2500
editor@efca.org | *www.efcatoday.org*
Diane J. McDougall, editor

Denomination: Evangelical Free Church in America

Type: quarterly digital magazine

Audience: EFCA pastors, elders, Sunday-school teachers, ministry volunteers

Purpose: to unify church leaders around the overall mission of the EFCA by bringing its stories and vision to life and to sharpen those leaders by generating conversations over topics pertinent to faith and life

Submissions: Email query with published clips. Freelance: 30%. Seasonal six months in advance. Length: 500-2,000 words.

Types of manuscripts: teaching, personal experience

Topics: theme-related

Rights: first, reprint

Payment: 23¢/word, on acceptance after editing; less for reprints

Guidelines: *go.efca.org/resources/document/writing-guidelines*

Sample: on the website

ENRICHMENT: A JOURNAL FOR PENTECOSTAL MINISTRY

1445 N. Boonville Ave., Springfield, MO 65802 | 417-862-2781, x4095

enrichmentjournal@ag.org | www.enrichmentjournal.ag.org
Rick Knoth, managing editor

Denomination: Assemblies of God
Type: quarterly print journal, circulation 33,000
Audience: Assembly of God ministers and other Pentecostal/ Charismatic leaders
Purpose: to enrich and encourage Pentecostal ministers to equip and empower Spirit-filled believers for effective ministry
Submissions: Email or mail complete manuscript with SASE.
Unsolicited freelance: 15%. Responds in eight to twelve weeks. Articles 1,200-2,100 words, program and ministry how-tos 200-500 words. Prefers NIV.
Types of manuscripts: how-to, sermon outlines and illustrations
Topics: preaching, pastoral practice, ministry
Rights: first
Payment: up to 10¢/word, on publication
Guidelines: *www.enrichmentjournal.ag.org/extra/EJ_Writer_Guidelines.pdf*
Sample: download from the website for a fee

ETERNAL INK

4706 Fantasy Ln., Alton, IL 62002 | 618-466-7860
sonsong@charter.net | eternallyours8@groups.facebook.com
Mary-Ellen Grisham, editor

Type: biweekly digital newsletter, circulation 400
Audience: general
Purpose: to edify and inspire
Submissions: Email manuscript in the body of the message. Unsolicited freelance: 10-15%. Accepts twenty-four to thirty manuscripts per year. Length: 500-700 words. Seasonal: one month in advance. Responds in a day. Bible: NIV. Some themes that follow the Christian year.
Types of manuscripts: devotions, meditations, feature articles, poetry, fillers, humor
Topics: all
Rights: author's choice
Payment: none
Guidelines: by email
Sample: by email
Tip: Looking for features, short Christian humor, and brief devotions.

EUREKA STREET

PO Box 553, Richmond, VIC 3121, Australia
editor@eurekastreet.com.au | *www.eurekastreet.com.au*
Tim Kroenert, editor
Poetry editor, poetry@eurekastreet.com.au

Denomination: Catholic
Parent company: Australian Jesuits
Type: bimonthly digital journal
Audience: denomination
Purpose: to analyze, comment on, and reflect on current issues in the worlds of politics, religion, and culture
Submissions: Submit articles using the online form. Email poetry. Articles should provide humane, ethical analysis or commentary on politics, religion, popular culture, or current events in Australia or the world. Length: 800 words. Short fiction and creative nonfiction up to 1,000 words. Simultaneous submissions for poetry only.
Types of manuscripts: feature articles, poetry
Topics: politics, religion, popular culture, current events
Rights: first
Payment: $200 AUD; poetry, portion of $50 allotted per week
Guidelines: *eurekastreet.com.au/article.aspx?aeid=33927#.WB5nsvQoFUU*
Sample: on the website

EVANGELICAL MISSIONS QUARTERLY

PO Box 794, Wheaton, IL 60187 | 630-752-7158
emq@wheaton.edu | *www.emqonline.com*
A. Scott Moreau, editor
Marcus Dean, book review editor, emq.book.reviews@wheaton.edu

Parent company: Billy Graham Center for Evangelism
Type: quarterly print journal
Audience: missionaries; mission executives, scholars, professors, students, pastors, and supporters; missionary candidates; lay leaders
Purpose: to increase the effectiveness of the evangelical missionary enterprise
Submissions: Email query first. Articles 3,000 words; book reviews 400 words.
Types of manuscripts: reports, profiles, how-to, book reviews
Topics: world missions, evangelism, trends, missionary family life

Rights: first
Payment: $100, on publication.
Guidelines: *emqonline.com/submit-an-article*

FACTS & TRENDS

1 Lifeway Plaza, Nashville, TN 37234 | 615-251-2000
factsandtrends@lifeway.com | *www.factsandtrends.net*
Carol Pipes, editor

Denomination: Southern Baptist
Parent company: LifeWay Christian Resources
Type: quarterly print magazine, circulation 65,000
Audience: pastors, church staff, denominational leaders
Purpose: to provide information, insight, and resources for effective ministry
Submissions: Query only. Email for current needs.
Sample: click Archives page on the website

FAITH & FRIENDS

The Salvation Army, 2 Overlea Blvd., Toronto, ON M4H 1P4, Canada | 416-422-6226
faithandfriends@can.salvationarmy.org | *salvationist.ca/editorial-publications/faith-and-friends*
Ken Ramstead, editor

Denomination: Salvation Army
Type: monthly print magazine
Audience: general
Purpose: to show Jesus Christ at work in the lives of real people and to provide spiritual resources for those who are new to the Christian faith
Submissions: Email query or manuscript as attached file. Looking for stories about people whose lives have been changed through an encounter with Jesus: conversion, miracles, healing, faith in the midst of crisis, forgiveness, reconciliation, answered prayers, and more. Profiles of people who have found hope and healing through their ministries, including prisoners, hospital patients, nursing-home residents, single parents in distress, addicts, the unemployed, or homeless. Length: 750-1,200 words. Ten departments with 750-word narratives. Bible: TNIV.
Types of manuscripts: testimonies, personal experience, profiles
Topics: changed lives, marriage, family relationships, missionaries, theology
Payment: none

Guidelines: *salvationist.ca/files/salvationarmy/Magazines/FAITH-FRIENDS.pdf*
Sample: on the website

FAITH TODAY

PO Box 5885, West Beaver Creek PO, Richmond Hill, ON
L4B 0B8, Canada
editor@faithtoday.ca | www.faithtoday.ca
Bill Fledderus, senior editor
Karen Stiller, senior editor

Parent company: The Evangelical Fellowship of Canada
Type: bimonthly print and digital magazine, print circulation 20,000, takes ads
Audience: Canadian evangelicals
Purpose: to connect, equip, and inform by offering analysis of trends in society and church groups, news, profiles, book reviews, ministry tips, opinion columns, and more
Submissions: Email query with clips first. Responds in one week. Seasonal four months in advance. Length: 300-1,800. Freelance: 10%. Buys one hundred manuscripts per year.
Types of manuscripts: analysis of trends in church and society, news, profiles, reviews of books and music, tips for lay ministry, how-to, journalistic features, essays
Topics: societal issues and trends, church issues and trends
Rights: first, onetime, electronic, reprint (tell when/where published)
Payment: 15-25¢ per word CAD, on acceptance, kill fee sometimes
Guidelines: *www.faithtoday.ca/writers*
Sample: *www.faithtoday.ca/digital*
Tip: "What is the Canadian angle? How does your approach include diverse Canadian voices from different churches, regions, generations, etc.?"

FOCUS ON THE FAMILY

8605 Explorer Dr., Colorado Springs, CO 80920
focusmagazinesubmissions@family.com |
www.focusonthefamily.com/magazine
Sheila Seifert, editorial director

Parent company: Focus on the Family
Type: bimonthly print magazine
Audience: parents, primarily of ages 4-12
Purpose: to encourage, teach, and celebrate God's design for the family

Submissions: Email or mail to submissions editor. Responds in eight weeks or not interested. Departments: "Family Stages," 50-200 words, practical applications for parents of preschoolers, school-aged children, tweens, and teens; send complete manuscript. "Family Faith," 150 words, devotionals that explore how a biblical principle applies to marriage, 1,200-word articles that show how to help kids understand important biblical truths; send complete manuscript. Features, 1,200-1,500 words; send complete manuscript. "Family Living," 450 words on marriage and parenting; query.

Types of manuscripts: how-to, devotional, teaching

Topics: marriage, parenting

Rights: first

Payment: 25¢/word, $50 for "Family Stages," on acceptance

Guidelines: *www.focusonthefamily.com/magazine/call-for-submissions*

Tip: "Looking for stories about how parents have dealt with challenges and come up with active, practical ways (beyond explaining or talking) of solving those problems."

FRIENDS JOURNAL

1216 Arch St., Ste. 2A, Philadelphia, PA 19107 | 215-563-8629
martink@friendsjournal.org | *www.friendsjournal.org*
Martin Kelly, senior editor

Denomination: Religious Society of Friends

Type: monthly (11x) print and downloadable journal

Audience: denomination

Purpose: to communicate Quaker experience in order to connect and deepen spiritual lives

Submissions: Submit poetry through the website, maximum three. Feature articles 1,200-2,500 words, related to themes. Departments, around 1,500 words or fewer: "Celebration," "Earthcare," "Faith and Practice," "First-day School," "Friends in Business," "History," "Humor," "Life in the Meeting," "Lives of Friends," "Pastoral Care," "Q&A," "Reflection," "Religious Education," "Remembrance," "Service," "Witness."

Types of manuscripts: poetry, testimonies, teaching, profiles, personal experience

Topics: most issues are themed

Rights: first

Payment: none

Guidelines: *www.friendsjournal.org/submissions*

Theme list: on the website

THE GEM

PO Box 926, Findlay, OH 45839-0926 | 419-424-1961
communications@cggc.org | *www.cggc.org*
Rachel Foreman, editor

Denomination: Churches of God, General Conference
Type: weekly take-home paper, circulation 8,500
Audience: denomination
Purpose: to encourage the Church with inspirational stories
Submissions: Articles 200-1,000 words. Seasonal three months in advance. For fiction, it is important that characters are true to life and solutions to problems are genuine. Email complete manuscript as Word attachment or in body of message. Responds in two months. Simultaneous OK. Accepts manuscripts from children and teens too. Freelance: 100%. Buys one hundred fifty per year. Bible: NIV.
Types of manuscripts: personal experience with a spiritual application, devotionals, games, short stories, poetry, fillers
Topics: Christian life, parenting, evangelism, inspirational
Rights: onetime, reprint, all, electronic
Payment: $10-15 on publication
Guidelines: *www.cggc.org/ministries/denominational-communications/the-gem*
Sample: by email
Tip: "We prefer true-to-life stories with a spiritual emphasis."

GEMS OF TRUTH

7407 Metcalf Ave., Overland Park, KS 66204 | 913-432-0331
www.heraldandbanner.com/shop/sunday-school-literature/the-way-truth-and-life-series/adults/gems-truth

Denomination: Church of God (Holiness)
Type: weekly take-home paper
Audience: denomination
Submissions: Send complete manuscript or query. Email through the website. Fiction 1,000-2,000 words. Seasonal six to eight months in advance. Bible: KJV.
Types of manuscripts: biographies, profiles, short stories, devotionals, poetry, teaching

GOOD NEWS

PO Box 132076, The Woodlands, TX 77393-2076 | 832-813-8327
info@goodnewsmag.org | *www.goodnewsmag.org*
Steve Beard, editor-in-chief

Denomination: United Methodist
Type: bimonthly print magazine
Audience: Methodists seeking spiritual renewal
Purpose: to encourage United Methodist renewal
Submissions: Articles 1,500-1,850 words. Email for current needs.
Rights: onetime
Payment: $100-150, on publication

THE GOOD NEWS (FLORIDA)

PO Box 670368, Coral Springs, FL 33067 | 954-564-5378
www.goodnewsfl.org
Shelly Pond, editor

Type: monthly print and digital newspaper
Audience: Dade, Broward and Palm Beach, Florida areas
Submissions: Query through the website. Articles 500-800 words.
Payment: 10¢/word

THE GOOD NEWS (NEW YORK)

PO Box 18204, Rochester, NY 14618 | 585-271-4464
info@TheGoodNewsNewYork.com | *www.thegoodnewswny.com*
Alexandre V. Boutakov, editor

Type: bimonthly print newspaper
Audience: New York state
Submissions: Email query.
Types: articles, reviews
Sample: on the website

GOOD NEWS, ETC .

PO Box 2660, Vista, CA 92085 | 760-724-3075
goodnewseditor@cox.net |*www.goodnewsetc.com*
Rick Monroe, editor

Type: monthly print and digital newspaper
Audience: San Diego area
Purpose: to provide local Christian news and features to believers and seekers in San Diego County
Submissions: Articles 500-900 words. Query first.
Types of manuscripts: interviews, news, reviews
Payment: $40-150
Sample: on the website

THE GOOD NEWS JOURNAL

PO Box 170069, Austin, TX 78717-0069 | 512-461-2964
goodnewsjournal10@gmail.com | *www.thegoodnewsjournal.net*
Evelyn W. Davison, publisher

Type: bimonthly print and digital newspaper
Audience: Capital MetroPlex and Central Texas areas
Purpose: to provide leadership to individuals and corporations with a positive, patriotic, godly perspective
Submissions: Articles 350 words. Email query first.
Payment: none
Sample: on the website

GRACECONNECT

PO Box 544, Winona Lake, IN 46590 | 574-268-1122
lcgates@bmhbooks.com | *www.graceconnect.us*
Liz Cutler Gates, managing editor

Denomination: Grace Brethren
Type: quarterly print and digital magazine
Audience: pastors, elders, and other leaders
Purpose: to build bridges of communication between the people and churches of the denomination
Submissions: Email through the website. Feature stories should have a Grace Brethren connection. Length: 1,000-1,500 words, sometimes 600-800 words or up to 2,000 words.
Topics: theme-related
Guidelines: *graceconnect.us/grace-stories/submit-a-story-idea*
Sample: on the website

GUIDEPOSTS

110 William St., Ste. 901, New York, NY 10038 | 212-251-8100
submissions@guideposts.com |
www.guideposts.org/our-magazines/guideposts-magazine
Edward Grinnan, editor

Type: bimonthly print and digital magazine
Audience: general
Purpose: to help readers find peace of mind, solve tough personal problems, and build satisfying relationships
Submissions: Publishes true, first-person stories about people who have attained a goal, surmounted an obstacle, or learned a helpful lesson through their faith. A typical story is a first-person narrative

with a spiritual point the reader can apply to his or her own life. Buys forty to sixty per year. Length: 1,500 words. Submit queries and manuscripts through the online form. If no answer in two months, not interested. Freelance: 40%. Short anecdotes similar to full-length articles, 50-250 words, for departments: "Someone Cares," stories of kindness and caring, *sc@guideposts.com*; "Mysterious Ways," "Family Room," "What Prayer Can Do." Also takes inspiring quotes for "The Up Side," *upside@guideposts.com*.

Types of manuscripts: personal experiences

Rights: all

Payment: $100-500, on acceptance, kill fee: 20% but not to first-time freelancers

Guidelines: *www.guideposts.org/writers-guidelines*

Tip: "Be able to tell a good story with drama, suspense, description, and dialog. The point of the story should be some practical spiritual help that the subject learns through his or her experience. Use unique spiritual insights, strong and unusual dramatic details."

HALO MAGAZINE

PO Box 1402, Sterling, VA 20167 | 540-877-3568
halomag@aol.com | *www.halomag.com*
Marian Newman Braxton, senior editor

Type: quarterly print magazine, takes ads

Audience: Christians and unbelievers

Purpose: to minister to the unsaved and encourage the Christian

Submissions: Articles 500-1,000 words, devotionals 200-500 words, poems no more than six stanzas with four lines per stanza, fiction 2,500 words maximum. Freelance: 100%. Email manuscript; prefers attached file. Accepts submissions from teens too. Responds in two weeks. Seasonal two months ahead. Accepts simultaneous submissions. Bible version: NIV, NASV, KJV.

Types of manuscripts: testimonies, personal experience, poetry, Bible study, quizzes, short stories, recipes, devotionals, sidebars

Topics: prayer, salvation, encouragement, spiritual growth, practical Christian living, vacation spots, church activities, counseling

Rights: one-time, reprint (tell when/where it appeared)

Payment: none

Sample: large envelope with $3 postage

Tip: "We welcome submissions in any category. We urge writers to submit their best, not their first draft."

HAVOK

2306 Southview Dr., Bettendorf, IA 52722
submissions@splickety.com | *www.splickety.com*
Avily Jerome, lead editor
Kristen Stieffel, associate editor

Parent company: Splickety Publishing Group
Type: quarterly print and digital magazine, circulation 2,000+, takes ads
Audience: speculative flash-fiction readers
Purpose: to publish the best speculative flash fiction in the world
Submissions: Length: 1,000 words maximum. All stories must fit quarterly theme and be submitted at least three months in advance. Email complete manuscript as attachment only. Unsolicited freelance: almost 100%. Buys forty to fifty manuscripts per year. Responds in a week.
Types of manuscripts: short stories; also query at *blog@Splickety.com* for possible nonfiction posts
Topics: speculative flash fiction
Rights: first, all for six months after publication
Payment: 2¢/word, on publication
Guidelines: *splickety.com/submission-guidelines*
Theme list: *splickety.com/submission-guidelines/upcoming-themes*
Sample: subscribe for free on website
Tip: "Follow our submission guidelines, write for our themes, and write brilliant flash fiction. We publish stories solely on merit."

HEARTBEAT

PO Box 9, Hatfield, AR 71945 | 870-389-6196
heartbeat@cmausa.org | *www.cmausa.org/cma_national/heartbeat.asp*
Misty Bradley, editor

Parent company: Christian Motorcyclists Association
Type: monthly print and digital magazine
Purpose: to inspire leaders and members to be the most organized, advanced, equipped, financially stable organization, full of integrity in the motorcycling industry and the Kingdom of God
Submissions: Email manuscript.
Topics: related to motocycling

HIGHWAY NEWS AND GOOD NEWS

PO Box 117, Marietta, PA 17547-0117 | 717-426-9977
editor@transportforchrist.org | *www.transportforchrist.org/highway*
Inge Koenig, managing editor

Parent company: Transport for Christ, International
Type: monthly print and digital magazine
Audience: truck drivers and their families
Purpose: to lead truck drivers, as well as the trucking community, to Jesus Christ and help them grow in their faith
Submissions: Especially looking for human interest stories concerning truck drivers. Length: 600-800 words. Rarely publishes poetry or fiction (600-800 words), but on occasion considers both if they focus on the trucking life. Prefers email submissions.
Types of manuscripts: personal experience, reports, how-to
Topics: spiritual growth, salvation, testimonies
Rights: first, reprint
Payment: none
Guidelines: *www.transportforchrist.org/highway/WritersGuidelines.pdf*
Sample: download from the website
Tip: "Articles submitted for publication do not have to be religious in nature; however, they should not conflict with or oppose guidelines and principles presented in the Bible."

HISTORY'S WOMEN

22 Williams St., Batavia, NY 14020 | 585-297-3009
submissions@historyswomen.com | *www.historyswomen.com*
Patti Chadwick, editor

Type: monthly print newsletter, circulation 21,000
Audience: women
Purpose: to make history come alive for women from a Christian worldview
Submissions: Looking for articles highlighting the extraordinary achievements of women throughout history that have made life better for their families and the societies in which they lived. Articles 400-1,200 words. Requires email submissions with no attachments; put "Article Submission" in the subject line.
Types of manuscripts: profiles, interviews
Topics: women of faith, social reformers, the Arts, early America, women rulers, life lessons for women, amazing moms, women in sports
Payment: none but offers alternative compensation
Guidelines: *historyswomen.com/writers-guidelines*
Tip: "Interviews or features about women who are making a difference in their world today are also welcomed and probably the most sought after."

HOLINESS TODAY

17001 Prairie Star Pkwy., Lenexa, KS 66220 | 913-577-0500
holinesstoday@nazarene.org | *www.holinesstoday.org*
Charles W. Christian, managing editor
Jordan Eigsti, assistant editor

Denomination: Nazarene
Type: bimonthly print and digital magazine, circulation 11,000, takes ads
Audience: Nazarene laity
Purpose: to connect Nazarenes with our heritage, vision, and mission through stories of God at work in the world
Submissions: Email manuscript as attachment. Also accepts submissions from children and teens. Freelance: 30%. Buys six to eight manuscripts/year. Length: 700-1,100 words. Responds in one day. Bible: NIV.
Types of manuscripts: personal experience, sidebars, columns
Topics: Christian ministry, theological teaching, denomination insights on real-world issues
Rights: first, reprint (tell when/where published)
Payment: $135, on publication, pays kill fee
Guidelines and theme list: by email
Sample: self-addressed 9x12 envelope with $1.00 postage
Tip: "We are always interested in hearing from Nazarene pastors, lay leaders, and experts in their fields. We are a Nazarene publication that wants our articles to be relevant and applicable to real-life scenarios and the world we live in."

HOMELIFE

1 Lifeway Plaza, Nashville, TN 37234-0172 | 615-251-2196
homelife@lifeway.com | *tinyurl.com/y8oznjzp*
David Bennett, managing editor

Parent company: LifeWay Christian Resources
Denomination: Southern Baptist
Type: monthly print magazine
Audience: families
Purpose: to equip and challenge families to experience dynamic, healthy, Christ-centered homes
Submissions: Manuscripts by assignment. Email résumé, bio, and clips. Offers practical, real world solutions toward maintaining the spiritual health of family members amid school, sports, work, play, and more.

Payment: unspecified
Guidelines: by email
Sample: on the website

HOMESCHOOLING TODAY

PO Box 1092, Somerset, KY 42502 | 606-485-4105
editor@homeschoolingtoday.com | homeschoolingtoday.com
Ashley Wiggers, executive editor

Type: quarterly print and digital magazine, circulation 5-6,000, takes ads
Audience: homeschooling parents
Purpose: to encourage the hearts of homeschoolers and give them tools to instill a love of learning in their children
Submissions: Does not accept queries; email full manuscript as an attachment with "Article Submission" in the subject line. Responds in six months or not interested. Feature articles include information about a topic, unit study, encouragement, challenge, or an interview, 900-1,200 words. Departments: "Faces of Homeschooling," true stories about real homeschooling families, 600-900 words; "The Home Team," physical education, 600-900 words; "Homeschooling around the World," 600-900 words; "Language Learning," foreign languages, 600-900 words; "Thinking," logic, critical thinking, 600-900 words; "Unit Study," 800-1500 words; "Family Math," 600-900 words.
Types of manuscripts: how-to, unit studies, profiles, interviews
Topics: education, homeschooling
Rights: first, nonexclusive electronic
Payment: 10¢/published word
Guidelines: *homeschoolingtoday.com/wp-content/uploads/pdf/HST-Writers-Guidelines.pdf*

IMAGE

3307 Third Ave. W., Seattle, WA 98119 | 206-281-2988
mkenagy@imagejournal.org | imagejournal.org
Mary Kenagy Mitchell, managing editor

Type: quarterly print literary journal
Purpose: to demonstrate the continued vitality and diversity of contemporary art and literature that engage with the religious traditions of Western culture
Submissions: Email queries. Submit manuscripts through the website or by mail. Responds in three months. Accepts simultaneous submissions. Poetry: no more than five poems or ten pages total.

Fiction, essays, and other nonfiction: 3,000-6,000 words.

Types of manuscripts: poetry, fiction, essays, interviews, artist profiles

Topics: related to art and literature

Rights: first

Payment: unspecified

Guidelines: *imagejournal.org/journal/submit*

Tip: "All the work we publish reflects what we see as a sustained engagement with one of the western faiths—Judaism, Christianity, or Islam. That engagement can include unease, grappling, or ambivalence as well as orthodoxy; the approach can be indirect or allusive, but for a piece to be a fit for *Image*, some connection to faith must be there."

INDIAN LIFE

188 Henderson Hwy., Winnipeg, MB R2L 1L6, Canada | 800-665-9275, 204-661-9333

ilm.editor@indianlife.org | *www.newspaper.indianlife.org*

Jeanette Littleton, editor

Parent company: Indian Life Ministries

Type: bimonthly print and digital newspaper, circulation 12,000, takes ads

Audience: Native Americans, First Nations, and interested parties; also distributed in prisons and on reservations

Purpose: to present positive news of the First Nations/Native American world, encourage, and evangelize

Submissions: Email as attachment the complete manuscript or query letter with clips. Accepts simultaneous submissions. Unsolicited freelance and number of manuscripts accepted: open. Seasonal six months in advance. Response time varies. Bible: First Nations, NIV.

Types of manuscripts: news, features, reviews, columns, fillers, testimonies

Topics: evangelism, issues related to Native Americans/First Nations

Rights: onetime

Payment: varies from donation to small stipend, on publication

Guidelines: by email

Sample: on website

Tip: "Testimonies from Native Americans/First Nations are the ones we need most. The difference between our newspaper and other Native-focused newspapers is that we also want the reader to know about Christ and grow in the grace and knowledge of Christ."

INSITE

PO Box 62189, Colorado Springs, CO 80962-2189 | 888-922-2287
editor@ccca.org | *www.ccca.org/ccca/Publications.asp*
Kris Hardy, editor

Parent company: Christian Camp and Conference Association
Type: bimonthly print and digital magazine, circulation 8,500
Audience: professionals serving in the Christian camp and conference community
Purpose: to help our members maximize their ministries by learning and staying inspired while serving God's people
Submissions: Email query first. Responds within one month. Seasonal six months ahead. Profiles and features, 1,200-1,500 words; how-to articles, 1,000-1,200 words; sidebars, 250-500 words. Unsolicited freelance: 15%; assigned: 85%. Bible: NIV.
Types of manuscripts: profiles, interviews, how-to
Topics: all aspects of camping ministry, business, relationships
Rights: first, electronic
Payment: 20¢/published word, on publication
Guidelines and theme list: download from *www.ccca.org/ccca/Publications.asp*
Sample: $4.99
Tip: "Profiles/interviews are the best bet for newcomers and freelancers. It is crucial to study a sample copy first and then query."

INTERNATIONAL JOURNAL OF FRONTIER MISSIOLOGY

1605 E. Elizabeth St., Pasadena, CA 91104 | 734-765-0368
editors@ijfm.org | *www.ijfm.org*
Rory Clark, editor

Parent company: International Society for Frontier Missiology
Type: quarterly print journal
Audience: mission professors, executives, and researchers; missionaries; young-adult mission mobilizers
Purpose: to cultivate an international fraternity of thought in the development of frontier missiology
Submissions: Query first. Articles 2,000-6,000 words.
Types: profiles, teaching
Topics: missiological perspective and principles, calls to commitment and involvement in frontier missions
Payment: none
Guidelines: *www.ijfm.org/IJFM%20guidelines.pdf*
Sample: download from website

JOYFUL LIVING MAGAZINE

PO Box 311, Palo Cedro, CA 97073 | 530-247-7500
Cathy@joyfullivingmagazine.com | *joyfullivingmagazine.com*
Cathy Jansen, editor-in-chief

Type: quarterly print and digital magazine, takes ads
Audience: general
Purpose: to share encouragement and hope; to help readers grow spiritually and emotionally, and to help them in their everyday lives with practical issues
Submissions: Email articles as attachments. Length: 200-700 words.
Types of manuscripts: profiles, personal experience, recipes, how-to
Topics: making dreams come true, family, marriage, work, singleness, recovery, finances, health, dealing with loss, depression, aging, physical fitness, overcoming obstacles, healthy eating, and more
Payment: none
Guidelines: *www.joyfullivingmagazine.com/writers-info*
Sample: download from website

JUST BETWEEN US

777 S. Barker Rd., Brookfield, WI 53045 | 262-786-6478
jbu@justbetweenus.org | *www.justbetweenus.org*
Shelly Esser, executive editor

Parent organization: Elmbrook Church
Type: quarterly print magazine, circulation 8,000
Audience: women
Purpose: to encourage and equip women for a life of faith and service
Submissions: Prefers emailed manuscripts as attachments but also takes them by mail. Responds in six to eight weeks. Articles, 500 1,500 words; testimonies, 450 words. Bible version: NIV.
Types of manuscripts: how-to, testimony, personal experience
Topics: balance, intimacy with Christ, handling criticism, friendship, conflict, faith, church life, prayer, evangelism, change, Spirit-filled living, finances, forgiveness, God's will, spiritual warfare, staying committed to Christ no matter what, parenting, pain, fighting weariness, church wounds, ministry helps
Payment: none
Guidelines: *justbetweenus.org/writers-guidelines*
Sample: *justbetweenus.org/sample-issue*
Tip: "Articles should be personal in tone, full of real-life anecdotes as well as quotes/advice from noted Christian professionals, and be biblically based. Articles need to be practical and have a distinct Christian and serving perspective throughout."

KANSAS CITY METRO VOICE

PO Box 1114, Lee's Summit, MO 64063 | 816-524-4522
dwight@metrovoicenews.com | *www.metrovoicenews.com*
Dwight Widamon, editor

Type: monthly print and digital newspaper, takes ads
Audience: Kansas City metropolitan area and Topeka/Northeast Kansas
Purpose: to inform and encourage the evangelical community in the area
Submissions: Email for current needs. Takes articles and reviews.
Types of manuscripts: profiles, reviews, opinion pieces, news reports
Sample: download from the website

KEYS TO LIVING

105 Steffens Rd., Danville, PA 17821 | 570-437-2891
owcam@verizon.net | *www.new-keystoliving.com*
Connie Mertz, editor
Collesce Beck, associate editor

Type: quarterly print newsletter
Purpose: to glorify God through nature and present inspirational writing for Christians
Submissions: Email complete manuscript in body of message. Accepts simultaneous submissions. Unsolicited freelance: about 30%. Buys twelve manuscripts per year. Length: 500 words maximum. Also considers high-quality photos to accompany devotionals. Responds in one month. Bible: NIV, KJV.
Type of manuscripts: devotionals
Topics: theme-related
Rights: first, reprint (tell where/when published)
Payment: none
Guidelines: *www.new-keystoliving.com/Writers--Guidelines.html*
Theme list: *www.new-keystoliving.com/Themes.html*
Sample: by email
Tip: "Always open to a seasonal nature story. Seldom is poetry published—only if it pertains to the theme and nature. Devotionals that are theme-related stand the best chance of being published."

LEADING HEARTS

PO Box 6421, Longmont, CO 80501 | 303-835-8473
amber@leadinghearts.com | *leadinghearts.com*
Amber Weigland-Buckley, editor

Parent company: Right to the Heart Ministries
Type: bimonthly digital magazine, circulation 60,000, takes ads
Audience: women who lead hearts at home, church, work, and community; ages 35-50
Submissions: Articles on assignment only. To audition for an assignment, email an article of 1,200 words maximum and a short résumé. Gives preferred consideration to members of AWSA. Articles 800 words maximum. Columns 250-500 words. Bible version: NIV.
Types of manuscripts: personal experience, how-to, profiles, reviews
Topics: based on theme list
Rights: first, reprint
Payment: none
Guidelines: *leadinghearts.com/wp-content/uploads/2014/06/WritersGuidelines.pdf*
Sample: download from the website

LEAVES

PO Box 87, Dearborn, MI 48121-0087 | 313-561-2330
editor.leaves@mariannhill.us | *www.mariannhill.us/leaves.html*
Father Thomas Heier, CMM, editor-in-chief

Denomination: Catholic
Type: bimonthly print magazine
Audience: Catholics, primarily in the Detroit, Michigan, area
Purpose: to promote devotion to God and His saints
Submissions: Articles about personal, spiritual experiences; petitions and thanksgivings; lives of saints and other holy people; timely spiritual topics; and prayers and edifying poems. Length: 500 words. Unsolicited freelance: 25%.
Types of manuscripts: personal experience, profiles, prayers, poetry
Rights: onetime
Payment: none
Sample: write, email, or call for a copy

LEBEN

2150 River Plaza Dr., Ste. 150, Sacramento, CA 95833 | 916-473-8866
editor@leben.us | *www.leben.us*
Wayne C. Johnson, editor

Parent company: City Seminary of Sacramento, California
Type: quarterly print journal
Audience: general

Purpose: to tell the stories of the people and events that make up the Reformation tradition

Submissions: We are a popular history publication that aims at a general readership. Query first. Length: 500-2500 words.

Types of manuscripts: profiles

Topics: Protestant Reformers and those who have followed in their footsteps

Payment: not specified

Guidelines: *leben.us/write-for-leben*

Tip: "Focus on lesser-known events and people. We have no shortage of submissions about Luther, Calvin, Zwingli, etc."

LIGHT + LIFE MAGAZINE

770 N. High School Rd., Indianapolis, IN 46214 | 317-244-3660
jeff.finley@fmcusa.org | *fmcusa.org/lightandlifemag*
Jeff Finley, managing editor
Mark Crawford, assistant editor

Denomination: Free Methodist

Type: monthly print magazine, circulation 38,000

Audience: general

Purpose: to offer encouragement, provide resources, deal with contemporary issues, share denominational news, and offer faith to unbelievers

Submissions: Articles: main article that provides a more detailed examination of the issue's theme, approximately 2,100 words, primarily in third person; action article that shares the story of someone living out the theme and sometimes serves as an instructional piece detailing how to take action, 1,000 words; discipleship, for use by a weekly small group or for individual study, 800 words, reflecting the theme plus two or three group discussion questions. Query first. Responds in two months. Unsolicited freelance: 50%. Bible: NIV.

Types of manuscripts: teaching, profile, Bible study

Topics: theme-related

Rights: first, onetime, occasional reprint (tell when/where appeared)

Payment: $100 for feature articles, $50 for others, on publication

Guidelines: *fmcusa.org/lightandlifemag/writers*

Themes: email *mark.crawford@fmcusa.org*

Tip: "We search for authors who write competently, provide clear information, and employ contemporary style and illustrations."

LIGUORIAN

1 Liguori Dr., Liguori, MO 63057 | 636-223-1538
liguorianeditor@liguori.org | *www.liguorian.org*
Elizabeth Herzing, editor

Denomination: Catholic
Type: monthly print and digital magazine
Audience: denomination
Purpose: to reinforce spiritual beliefs with inspiration and insight
Submissions: Articles must not exceed 2,200 words. Personal essays should be limited to 1,000. Fiction submissions should be approximately 2,000 words. Seasonal articles and stories must be received eight months in advance. Email query. Email manuscripts as attachments or mail them on a CD. Responds in two to three months.
Types of manuscripts: essay, feature, short stories, interviews
Topics: explanations of Church teachings, theological insights, Christian living
Rights: first
Payment: 12-15¢/published word, on acceptance
Guidelines: *www.liguorian.org/submissions-and-rights-and-permissions*
Sample: 9x12 SASE with three stamps

LIVE

1445 N. Boonville Ave., Springfield, MO 65802-1894 | 417-862-2781
wquick@ag.org | *www.gospelpublishing.com*
Wade Quick, editor

Denomination: Assemblies of God
Type: weekly take-home paper, circulation 30,000
Audience: denomination
Purpose: to encourage Christians in living for God through stories that apply biblical principles to everyday problems
Submissions: Prefers emailed submissions as attachments but will accept mailed manuscripts. Stories should be encouraging, challenging, and/or humorous. Even problem-centered stories should be upbeat. Stories should not be preachy, critical, or moralizing. They should not present pat, trite, or simplistic answers to problems. No Bible fiction or sci-fi. Length: cover stories, 800-1,200 words; inside stories, 200-600 words; poetry, 12-25 lines. Seasonal eighteen months in advance.
Types of manuscripts: personal experiences, short stories, how-to, poetry, first-person anecdotes, short humor

Topics: all kinds of stories that show how God works in people's lives
Rights: first, reprint
Payment: 10¢/word for first, 7¢/word for reprint, $35-60 for poetry
Guidelines: *gospelpublishing.com/store/startcat.cfm?cat=tWRITGUID*#Live
Tip: "Make sure the stories have a strong Christian element, are written well, have strong takeaways, but do not preach."

LIVING BETTER

1265 W. 14th St., San Pedro, CA 90731 | 504-617-2107
carol@livingbetter50.com | *LivingBetter50.com*
Carol Doyel, editor
Carri Prior-Faith, carri@livingbetter50.com

Parent company: Living Better LLC
Type: monthly digital magazine, 100,000 hits/month
Audience: women ages 50 and older
Purpose: to inspire women to live better physically, emotionally, financially, and spiritually
Submissions: Email manuscript or query. Freelance: 50%. Accepts twelve to twenty-four manuscripts per year. Length: 600-700 words. Seasonal one month in advance. Responds in one to two weeks. Bible: NKJV.
Types of manuscripts: how-to, tips, short stories
Topics: beauty to business
Payment: none
Guidelines: *livingbetter50.com/guest-blogging-guidelines*
Sample: on website
Tip: Looking for "fashion and beauty, lifestyle, and faith-based content."

THE LIVING CHURCH

PO Box 510705, Milwaukee, WI 53203-0121 | 414-292-1240
jschuessler@livingchurch.org | *www.livingchurch.org*
John Schuessler, managing editor

Denomination: Episcopal
Type: biweekly print magazine
Audience: denomination
Purpose: to seek and serve the Catholic and evangelical faith of the one Church, to the end of visible Christian unity throughout the world
Submissions: Email for current needs.
Types: articles, reviews

THE LOOKOUT

16965 Pine Ln., Ste. 202, Parker, CO 80134 | 800-543-1353
lookout@christianstandardmedia.com | *www.lookoutmag.com*
Shawn McMullen, editor

Parent company: Christian Standard Media
Type: monthly print magazine, circulation 40,000
Audience: ordinary Christians who want to grow in their faith
Purpose: to provide Christian adults with true-to-the-Bible teaching to help them mature as believers and live in the world as faithful witnesses of Christ
Submissions: Assignment only. Bible: NIV.
Topics: theme-related
Rights: first
Payment: up to 11¢/word
Guidelines and theme list: *www.lookoutmag.com/about-us/write-for-us*
Sample: *www.lookoutmag.com/sample*

THE LUTHERAN DIGEST

PO Box 100, Princeton, MN 55371
editor@lutherandigest.com | *www.lutherandigest.com*
Nick Skapyak, editor

Denomination: Lutheran
Type: quarterly print magazine
Audience: denomination
Purpose: to entertain and encourage believers and to subtly persuade nonbelievers to embrace the Lutheran-Christian faith
Submissions: Prefers manuscripts by mail with SASE but will look at emailed submissions as attachments and respond only if accepted. Unsolicited freelance: 30%. Will consider simultaneous submissions but prefers not to. Length: 3,000-7,000 characters. Popular stories show how God has intervened in a person's life to help solve a problem. Seasonal six months in advance. Poetry one or two stanzas. Interested in poems that can be sung to the melodies of familiar hymns. Submit maximum three poems in a month.
Types of manuscripts: personal experience, seasonal, poetry, recipes, jokes
Topics: Christian living, God's presence in nature
Rights: onetime, reprint (tell when/where last appeared)
Payment: $35, on publication, none for poetry and fillers
Guidelines: *lutherandigest.com/write-for-us*

Tip: "Stories frequently reflect a Lutheran-Christian perspective but are not intended to be 'lecturing' sermonettes."

LUTHERAN FORUM

PO Box 327, Delhi, NY 13753-0327 | 607-746-7511
editor@lutheranforum.org | alpb.org/forum-package
Sarah Hinlicky Wilson, editor

Denomination: Lutheran
Parent company: American Lutheran Publicity Bureau
Type: quarterly print journal
Submissions: Articles 2,000-3,000 words. Email query or complete manuscript. Responds in three months.
Rights: first
Payment: none
Guidelines: *alpb.org/writers-guidelines*
Sample: *alpb.org/free-issue*
Tip: "Prospective writers are encouraged to reflect on what moves them most, intellectually and spiritually, and then, armed with adequate research and forethought, put their ideas to paper."

THE LUTHERAN JOURNAL

PO Box 28158, Oakdale, MN 55128 | 651-702-0176
christianad2@msn.com | thelutheranjournal.com

Denomination: Lutheran
Type: annual print magazine
Audience: families
Purpose: to provide wholesome and inspirational reading for the enjoyment and enrichment of Lutherans
Submissions: Email for current needs.
Types of manuscripts: articles, poetry, prayers
Payment: none
Sample: *online.fliphtml5.com/adnv/nksx/#p=1*

LUTHERAN WITNESS

1333 S. Kirkwood Rd., St. Louis, MO 63122-7226 | 800-248-1930
lutheran.witness@lcms.org | blogs.lcms.org/category/lutheran-witness
Rachel Bomberger, managing editor, rachel.bomberger@lcms.org

Denomination: Luthern Church Missouri Synod (LCMS)
Type: monthly (11x) print and digital magazine, circulation 185,000
Audience: denomination
Purpose: to provide Missouri Synod laypeople with stories and information that complement congregational life, foster personal

growth in faith, and help interpret the contemporary world from a Lutheran Christian perspective

Submissions: Prefers complete manuscript instead of a query. Submit by email or mail. Length: 500, 1,000, or 1,500 words. Bible: ESV.

Types of manuscripts: profiles, how-to, teaching, humor, personal experience, Bible studies

Topics: current events; theology; LCMS missions, ministries, members, history; evangelism, outreach, spiritual growth

Rights: first, electronic

Guidelines: *blogs.lcms.org/the-lutheran-witness/writers-guidelines-for-the-lutheran-witness*

Sample: on the website

Tip: "Because of the magazine's long lead time and because main features are planned at least six months in advance of the publication date, your story should have a long-term perspective that keeps it relevant several months from the time you submit it."

MATURE LIVING

1 Lifeway Plaza, MSN 136, Nashville, TN 37234-0175 | 615-251-2000
matureliving@lifeway.com | *tinyurl.com/y8byez6d*
Debbie Dickerson, managing editor

Parent company: LifeWay Christian Resources

Denomination: Southern Baptist

Type: monthly print magazine

Audience: ages 55 and older

Purpose: to equip mature adults as they live a legacy of leadership, stewardship, and discipleship

Submissions: Email for current needs. Buys articles and slice-of-life accounts addressing various issues like marriage, adult children, and caregiving.

Types of manuscripts: personal experience, how-to, teaching, devotional, short stories, recipes

Topics: marriage, caregiving, evangelism, theology, relationship with adult children, grandchildren

Sample: on the website

MESSAGE OF THE OPEN BIBLE

2020 Bell Ave., Des Moines, IA 50315 | 515-288-6761
andrea@openbible.org | *www.openbiblemessage.org*
Andrea Johnson, managing editor

Denomination: Open Bible Churches

Type: bimonthly print and digital magazine, circulation 3,300, takes ads
Audience: denomination
Purpose: to inform, educate, and inspire
Submissions: Email as attachment. Freelance: 1%. Accepts thirty manuscripts/year. Length: 600 words. Seasonal four months in advance. Responds in three weeks. Bible: NIV.
Types of manuscripts: personal experience, sidebar
Topics: Christian life, discipleship, outreach, evangelism, leadership development
Rights: onetime
Payment: none
Guidelines: by email
Sample: SASE
Tip: Looking for "well-written articles that target people not accustomed to church."

THE MESSENGER

440 Main St., Steinbach, MB R5G 1Z5, Canada | 204-326-6401
messenger@emconference.ca | *www.emconference.ca/the-messenger*
Terry Smith, editor

Denomination: Evangelical Mennonite Conference (EMC)
Type: monthly print and digital magazine, circulation 3,000
Audience: denomination with a range of educational and cultural backgrounds
Purpose: to inform concerning events and activities in the denomination, instruct in godliness and victorious living, and inspire to earnestly contend for the faith
Submissions: Email as attachment or mail query or complete manuscript with cover letter. Simultaneous submissions OK. Unsolicited freelance: low. Buys thirty manuscripts per year. Also accepts manuscripts from children and teens. Length: 1,200 words maximum. Seasonal one month in advance. Responds in one week. Bible: NIV.
Types of manuscripts: articles, poetry
Topics: theology, discipleship, community
Rights: first
Payment: $135 CAD for 1,200 words, on publication, kill fee always
Guidelines: *www.emconference.ca/the-messenger/submission-guidelines*
Theme list: not available but follow the church year
Sample: *www.emconference.ca/the-messenger/past-issues*
Tip: Looking for Evangelical Anabaptist perspectives.

THE MESSIANIC TIMES

PO Box 10943, Pensacola, FL 32524 | 866-612-7770
editor.messianictimes@gmail.com | *www.messianictimes.com*
David Tokajer, Dylan Mathew, managing editors

Parent company: Times of the Messiah Ministries
Denomination: Messianic
Type: bimonthly print and digital newspaper
Audience: Messianic community
Purpose: to provide accurate, authoritative, and current information to unite the international Messianic Jewish community, teach Christians the Jewish roots of their faith, and proclaim that Yeshua is the Jewish Messiah
Submissions: Query preferred. Email for current needs.
Types of manuscripts: analysis; opinion pieces; book, music, and film reviews; news

METHODIST HISTORY

36 Madison Ave., Madison, NJ 07940 | 973-408-3189
atday@gcah.org | *www.gcah.org*
Alfred T. Day, III, general secretary

Denomination: United Methodist
Type: annual print journal
Audience: denomination
Submissions: Only email manuscripts as attachments. Articles on the history of other denominations and subjects will be considered when there are strong ties to events and persons significant to the history of the United Methodist tradition. Manuscripts pertaining to strictly local, as opposed to national or international interest, are not accepted. Length: maximum 5,000 words.
Topics: United Methodist history
Payment: none
Guidelines: *www.gcah.org/resources/guidelines-for-publication*

MINISTRY

12501 Old Columbia Pike, Silver Spring, MD 20904 | 301-680-6518
ministrymagazine@gc.adventist.org | *www.ministrymagazine.org*
Pavel Goia, editor

Denomination: Seventh-day Adventist
Type: monthly print and digital magazine, circulation 18,000
Audience: pastors, professors, administrators, chaplains, pastoral students, lay leaders of all denominations

Purpose: to deepen spiritual life, develop intellectual strength, and increase pastoral and evangelistic effectiveness of all ministers in the context of the three angels' messages of Revelation 14:6-12

Submissions: For all submissions, include completed biographical information form. Send all submissions as email attachments. Articles to 2,500 words, book and resources reviews to 500 words.

Types of manuscripts: biblical studies, how-to, teaching, reviews

Topics: personal needs of the minister (spiritual, physical, emotional), pastor-spouse team and ministry relationships, pastoral family needs, pastoral skills, biblical studies for sermon preparation, theological studies, worship, current issues

Rights: all

Payment: not specified, on acceptance

Guidelines: *www.ministrymagazine.org/article-submissions*

Sample: click Archives page on the website

Tip: "Writers should ask themselves: What do I expect the reader to do with my manuscript?"

MINISTRY TODAY

600 Rinehart Rd., Lake Mary, FL 32746 | 407-333-0600
ministrytoday@charismamedia.com | *www.ministrytodaymag.com*
Christine D. Johnson, managing editor

Denomination: Pentecostal/Charismatic

Parent company: Charisma Media

Type: quarterly print and digital magazine, circulation 30,000

Audience: pastors, ministry leaders, business leaders

Purpose: to inspire and assist ministry leaders

Submissions: Email query through the online submission form. If no response in two weeks, assume not interested. Email (preferred) or mail manuscript after query if requested. Bible version: MEV. Most open to departments: "Ministry Life," "Leadership," "Outreach," and "Facilities." Length: to 700 words. Also buys more in-depth features; length to 2,500 words.

Types of manuscripts: how-to, interviews, teaching

Topics: anything related to church ministry and leadership

Rights: all

Payment: unspecified, on publication

Guidelines: *ministrytodaymag.com/write-for-us*

Sample: download at *www.ministrytodaymag.com/index.php/ministry-today-digital*

Tip: "Most open to departments. Please take time to read—even study—at least one or two of our recent issues before submitting a query."

THE MOPS MAGAZINE

2370 S. Trenton Way, Denver, CO 80231-3822 | 303-733-5353, 888-910-6677
magazines@mops.org | *www.MOPS.org/blog*
Candice Santaferraro, editorial project manager

Parent Company: MOPS International (Mothers of Preschoolers)
Type: quarterly print magazine
Audience: mothers of preschoolers and school-age kids
Purpose: to inspire moms and nurture the woman who still exists inside the mother
Submissions: Email complete manuscript as an attachment or in the body of the message.
Types of manuscripts: how-to, personal experience
Topics: Calls for submissions quarterly based on the needs of the magazine. Go to *blog.mops.org/we-love*, and look for "Call for Submissions."
Rights: first
Guidelines: *www.mops.org/writers-guidelines*
Tip: "We always love a good laugh or tearjerker!"

THE MOTHER'S HEART

PO Box 275, Tobaccoville, NC 27050
editor@TMHMag.com | *www.the-mothers-heart.com*
Kym Wright, editor and publisher

Parent company: alWright! Publishing
Type: bimonthly digital magazine, circulation under 20,000, takes ads
Audience: mothers/wives, fathers/husbands, homeschool families
Purpose: to serve and encourage mothers in the many facets of staying at home and raising a family, with the underlying theme of Family First
Submissions: Email query or manuscript as attachment (preferred) or in the body of the message. Seasonal six months ahead. Unsolicited freelance: 30%. Buys thirty to forty-five manuscripts per year. Length: shorts, 750 words; 1,500-2,000 words. Responds in two months.
Types of manuscripts: personal experience, profile, how-to, sidebar, filler
Topics: motherhood, homeschooling, home environment,

organization, living in God's strength, encouragement, homemaking, child-raising, getting it all done, father's viewpoint and roles, and other topics related to Titus 2 and Proverbs 31 living

Rights: first, electronic, reprint (tell when/where published), on publication

Payment: $10-75 or 1/8 page advertising space, on publication

Guidelines: *the-mothers-heart.com/Writers%20Guidelines%202016-2019.pdf*

Sample: *the-mothers-heart.com/subscribe.htm*

Tip: "Study the magazine. Begin with a topic of interest to our readers. Write an outline. Have a good hook. Please keep the tone positive, real-life, with hope and a good ending. Personal experiences or other anecdotes which relate to the article topic make great lead-ins."

MTL (MORE TO LIFE) MAGAZINE

200 W. Bay Dr., Largo, FL 33770 | 727-596-7625
info@mtlmagazine.com | *mtlmagazine.com*
Andrea Stock, editor

Parent company: Munce Marketing Group

Type: online magazine with five print issues a year, takes ads

Audience: women

Purpose: to address the felt needs of women and connect those to products at local Christian bookstores

Submissions: Query ideas.

Types of manuscripts: personal experiences, testimonies, how-to, interviews, reviews

Topics: finances, home, relationships, spiritual growth, health

Sample: on the website

MUTUALITY

122 W. Franklin Ave., Ste. 218, Minneapolis, MN 55404 | 612-872-6898
cbe@cbeinternational.org |
www.cbeinternational.org/content/mutuality-magazine
Tim Krueger, editor

Parent company: Christians for Biblical Equality

Type: quarterly print magazine

Audience: evangelicals in professional and volunteer ministry, seminary faculty and students, male and female leaders, and laypeople interested in egalitarian theory (Bible and theology) and practice (application in churches and homes)

Purpose: to provide inspiration, encouragement, and information on topics related to a biblical view of mutuality between men and women in the home, church, and world

Submissions: Query first through the online contact form. Also submit requested manuscript through that form. Responds in one month or more. Length: first-person narratives and feature articles, 800-1,800 words; book, movie, or music reviews, 500-800 words. Bible: NIV.

Types of manuscripts: personal experience, how-to, biblical reflection, poetry, reviews

Topics: theme-related

Rights: first with electronic

Payment: one-year CBE membership ($49–$59 value) or up to three CBE recordings (up to $30 value)

Guidelines: *www.cbeinternational.org/content/mutuality-writers-guidelines*

Theme list: *www.cbeinternational.org/content/upcoming-mutuality-themes*

Sample: download PDF from guidelines page

MYSTERIOUS WAYS

110 William St., Ste. 901, New York, NY 10038 | 212-251-8100
www.guideposts.org/our-magazines/mysterious-ways-magazine
Diane Aydin, editor

Parent company: Guideposts

Type: bimonthly print and digital magazine

Audience: general

Purpose: to encourage through true stories of extraordinary moments and everyday miracles that reveal a spiritual force at work in our lives

Submissions: Submit complete manuscript through the online form. Looking for true stories of unexpected and wondrous experiences that reveal a hidden hand at work in our lives. The best stories are those that present a credible, well-detailed account that can even leave skeptics in awe and wonder. Length: 750-1,500 words. Also buys news stories and short material, 50-350 words, for recurring features like "Wonderful World," "His Humorous Ways," and "Dreams & Premonitions."

Types of manuscripts: personal experiences

Payment: varies, after scheduled for publication

Guidelines: *www.guideposts.org/write-for-mysterious-ways*

Tip: "A typical Mysterious Ways story is written in dramatic style, with an unforeseen twist that inspires the reader to look for miracles in his or her own life. It may be told from a 1st-person or 3rd-person perspective, and can be your own experience or someone else's story. We are also on the lookout for recent experiences."

NET RESULTS

308 West Blvd. N., Columbia, MO 65203 | 888-470-2456
bill@netresults.org | *netresults.org*
Bill Tenny-Brittian, managing editor

Parent company: The Effective Church Group
Type: bimonthly print and digital magazine
Audience: pastors, church volunteers, and Christian organizations
Purpose: to share great ideas for vital ministry among leaders
Submissions: Email query first; email manuscripts as attached file. Responds in eight weeks. Practical and relevant articles on innovative ways to do mission and ministry, 1,750 words. Bible: TNIV. Takes reprints from noncompetitive periodicals with letter of release from original publication.
Types of manuscripts: how-to, teaching
Topics: evangelism, service, planning, trust-building, leadership and organizational development, worship, preaching, hospitality, Christian education, faith formation, mentoring, training, partnerships, property and technology development, fund-raising, financial planning, stewardship, communications, marketing
Rights: all print and electronic
Payment: on publication
Guidelines: *netresults.org/writers*
Theme list: *netresults.org/writers/upcoming-themes*
Sample: on the website
Tip: "We look for practical, hands-on ministry ideas that an individual can put into practice. The best ideas are those the author has actually used successfully."

NEW FRONTIER CHRONICLE

180 E. Ocean Blvd., 4th Fl., Long Beach, CA 90802 | 562-491-8723
new.frontier@usw.salvationarmy.org | *www.newfrontierchronicle.org*
Christin Davis Thieme, editor-in-chief

Parent company: The Salvation Army Western Territory
Type: monthly print newspaper
Audience: denomination in the territory
Purpose: to empower Salvationists to communicate and engage with the Army's mission

Submissions: Query first. Shares information from across The Salvation Army world, reports that analyze effective programs to identify the unique features and trends for what works, tips to help local congregations better engage in the issues of today, and influential voices on relevant (and sometimes controversial) matters.

Types: articles, reviews

Guidelines: *www.newfrontierchronicle.org/submit*

A NEW HEART

PO Box 4004, San Clemente, CA 92674-4004 | 949-496-7655
HCFUSA@gmail.com | *www.HCFUSA.com*
Aubrey Beauchamp, editor

Parent company: Hospital Christian Fellowship

Type: quarterly print magazine

Audience: healthcare givers

Submissions: Query or submit complete manuscripts. Length: 600-1,800 words. Unsolicited freelance, 20%; assigned, 10%. Limited poetry.

Types of manuscripts: personal experiences, poetry

Rights: onetime

Payment: none

Tip: "Most open to real-life situations which may benefit and encourage healthcare givers and patients. True stories with medical and evangelical emphasis."

NEW IDENTITY MAGAZINE

PO Box 1002, Mount Shasta, CA 96067 | 310-947-8707
submissions@newidentitymagazine.com | *www.newidentitymagazine.com*
Cailin Briody Henson, editor-in-chief

Type: quarterly print and digital magazine

Audience: new believers

Purpose: to provide diverse, Bible-centered content to help lead new believers and seekers to a fuller understanding of the Christian faith

Submissions: Query first; prefers by email. Email requested manuscript. Responds in two to four weeks. Length: 500-3,500 words. Departments: "Grow," teaching new believers and seekers about different Christian perspectives on topics, understanding Christian concepts, jargon, disciplines, practical application of Scripture, etc.; "Connect," encouraging new believers and seekers with testimonies, articles about relationships, fellowship, church, community, discussions and expressions of faith; "Live," engaging new believers and seekers to live out their faith in the real world, with stories of people actively pursuing God and their passions, organizations and resources to apply one's gifts, talents and desires to serve God and others, sharing the love of Christ in everyday arenas.

Types of manuscripts: personal experience, teaching, testimonies, how-to, opinion

Topics: spiritual growth, applying Scripture, relationships, salvation, church, service, evangelism

Rights: first, electronic, sometimes reprint (tell when/where appeared)

Payment: none

Guidelines: *www.newidentitymagazine.com/WritersGuidelines.pdf*

Sample: on the website

Tip: "Articles need creative, well-thought-out ideas that offer new insight. We value well researched, factually and biblically supported content."

THE NEWSLETTER NEWSLETTER

PO Box 36269, Canton, OH 44735 | 800-992-2144
service@newsletternewsletter.com | *www.newsletternewsletter.com*
Stephanie Martin, senior editor

Parent company: Communication Resources, Inc.

Purpose: to help church secretaries and newsletter editors prepare high-quality publications

Type: monthly print and online newsletter

Submissions: Email query first. Responds in four weeks. Articles 800-1,000 words, buys twelve per year. Seasonal four months ahead.

Types of manuscripts: how-to, puzzles, games, activities, snacks, crafts, fillers, quizzes

Rights: all

Payment: $50-150, on acceptance

Sample: risk-free trial, online samples

Tip: "Most open to how-to articles on various aspects of producing newsletters and e-newsletters—writing, layout and design, distribution, etc."

NOW WHAT?

PO Box 33677, Denver, CO 80233

nowwhat@cog7.org | nowwhat.cog7.org
Sherri Langton, associate editor

Denomination: Church of God (Seventh Day)
Type: monthly digital magazine
Audience: unchurched
Purpose: to offer hope and help for life's struggles
Submissions: Each issue is built around a personal experience, with articles related to the topic. Personal experiences show a person's struggle that either led him to faith in Christ or deepened his walk with God. Unsolicited freelance: 100%. Buys ten to fifteen per year. Email manuscripts and queries. Responds in four to ten weeks. Length: 1,100-1,500 words. Bible: prefers NKJV. Avoid unnecessary jargon or technical terms. No Christmas or Easter pieces.
Types of manuscripts: personal experience, sidebar
Topics: salvation, issues
Rights: first, electronic, reprint (tell when/where appeared)
Payment: $25-65, on publication
Guidelines: *nowwhat.cog7.org/send_us_your_story*
Tip: "All topics are open for freelancers. Be able to tell a good story, using fiction techniques. Don't just recount what happened. Make the story come alive to readers with depth of detail and feeling."

OMS OUTREACH

941 Fry Rd., Greenwood, IN 46142 | 317-881-3333
editor@onemissionsociety.org | onemissionsociety.org/give/outreach
Susan Griswold Loobie, editor, sloobie@onemissionsociety.org

Parent company: One Mission Society
Type: triannual print and digital magazine
Purpose: to equip Christians to make disciples of Jesus Christ through informative, inspiring, and involvement-driven articles, which leads to deeper mission participation by serving, giving, and praying
Submissions: Articles 500-600 words to inform the public of ministry opportunities and report on ministry of various mission teams. Email for current needs. Bible version: ESV.
Sample: click link on the website

ON MISSION

4200 N. Point Pkwy., Alpharetta, GA 30022-4176 | 770-410-6000
fmorgan@namb.net | www.namb.net/on-mission-magazine
K. Faith Morgan, editor

Denomination: Southern Baptist
Parent company: North American Mission Board
Type: quarterly magazine
Audience: Christians who are impacting their world for Christ
Purpose: to highlight the work of missionaries and help readers be on mission where they work and live
Submissions: Open to freelance articles and reviews. Email for current needs.
Topics: missions, evangelism
Sample: download from website

OUR SUNDAY VISITOR NEWSWEEKLY

200 Noll Plaza, Huntington, IN 46750 | 800-348-2440, 260-356-8400
oursunvis@osv.com | *www.osv.com/OSVNewsweekly.aspx*
Gretchen R. Crowe, editor-in-chief

Denomination: Catholic
Type: weekly print and digital newspaper
Audience: denomination
Purpose: to provide timely coverage of important national and international religious events reported from a Catholic perspective
Submissions: Query and send manuscript only through the online form. Responds in four to six weeks. Articles: news analysis, 950-1,100 words, including sidebars, but occasionally as short as 500 words or as long as 2,000 words; "In Focus," a package of articles totaling 3,000-4,000 words by one or more authors, query first; features linked to current events and trends of the day, 1,350 words; essays on relevant issues of the day, 500-750 words; profiles, 500-750 words; Q&A interviews, 1,200 words. Bible: RSV.
Types of manuscripts: news, essays, interviews
Topics: Catholic perspective on issues and news
Payment: unspecified, within four to six weeks of acceptance
Guidelines: *www.osv.com/OSVNewsweekly/More/WritersGuidelines.aspx*
Tip: "Our mission is to examine the news, culture, and trends of the day from a faithful and sound Catholic perspective—to see the world through the eyes of faith. Especially interested in writers able to do news analysis (with a minimum of three sources) or news features."

OUTREACH

Story Ideas, 5550 Tech Center, Colorado Springs, CO 80919
tellus@outreachmagazine.com | *www.outreachmagazine.com*
James P. Long, editor

Type: bimonthly magazine

Audience: senior pastors and church leadership, as well as laypeople who are passionate about outreach

Purpose: to be the gathering place of ideas, insights, and stories for churches focused on reaching out to their community—locally and globally—with the love of Christ

Submissions: Email or mail query or complete manuscript with cover letter and published clips. Seasonal six months ahead. Responds in eight weeks. Articles, 1,200-2,500 words; features, 1,500-2,500 words; "Pulse" stories of what churches and individuals are doing, 200-300 words; ideas for outreach events, 300 words; and "Soulfires" profiles of people who are passionate about reaching others for Christ, 600 words.

Types of manuscripts: profiles, how-to

Topics: what's new in ministry, evangelism training, focus on retention, small groups, keeping visitors engaged

Rights: first, reprint (tell when/where published)

Payment: $700-1,000 for feature articles

Guidelines: *www.outreachmagazine.com/magazine/3160-writers-guidelines.html*

Tip: "While most articles are assigned, we do accept queries and manuscripts on speculation. Please don't query us until you've studied at least one issue of *Outreach*."

PARENTING TEENS

1 Lifeway Plaza, Nashville, TN 37234-0172 | 615-251-2196
mike.wakefield@lifeway.com | *tinyurl.com/ycv9p5z3*
Mike Wakefield, editorial team leader

Parent company: LifeWay Christian Resources

Denomination: Southern Baptist

Type: monthly print magazine

Audience: parents of teens

Purpose: to give parents encouragement and challenge them in their relationship with Christ, so they, in turn, can guide their teens

Submissions: Manuscripts by assignment. Email résumé, bio, and clips. Offers timely information, encouragement, expert insight, and practical advice to parents of teens. Bible: HCSB.

Payment: unspecified

Guidelines: by email

Sample: on the website

PARENTLIFE

1 Lifeway Plaza, Nashville, TN 37234-0172 | 615-251-2196
parentlife@lifeway.com | *tinyurl.com/y7yx8des*
Nancy Cornwell, content editor

Parent company: LifeWay Christian Resources
Denomination: Southern Baptist
Type: monthly print magazine
Audience: parents of children birth to preteen
Purpose: to encourage and equip parents with biblical solutions that will transform families
Submissions: Serves as a springboard for parents who may feel exasperated or overwhelmed with information by offering a biblical approach to raising healthy, productive children. Offers practical ideas and information for individual parents and couples. Query first by email. Email requested manuscript as an attachment. Include one to three sidebars. Responds in six to twelve months. Length: 500-1,500 words. Bible: HCSB.
Types of manuscripts: how-to, teaching, family devotional, sidebars
Topics: parenting, health, development, education, discipline, spiritual growth
Payment: unspecified
Guidelines: by email
Sample: on the website

PARISH LITURGY

16565 S. State St., South Holland, IL 60473 | 708-331-5485
acp@acpress.org | *www.americancatholicpress.org/parLit.html*
Rev. Michael Gilligan, executive director

Denomination: Catholic
Parent company: American Catholic Press
Type: quarterly magazine, circulation 950
Audience: parish priests and musicians
Purpose: to support parish leaders in planning the liturgy, resources for Sunday Mass
Submissions: Query by email or mail. Responds in eight weeks.
Unsolicited freelance: 10%. Articles 400 words. Bible: NAB. Email for current needs.
Types of manuscripts: teaching, how-to, profiles
Topics: liturgy, sermons, petitions, music suggestions
Rights: all
Payment: not specified, on publication

Tip: "We use articles on the liturgy only—period. Send us well-informed articles on the liturgy."

PENTECOSTAL MESSENGER

PO Box 211866, Bedford, TX 76095 | 817-554-5900
communications@pcg.org | *www.pcg.org/pentecostal-messenger*
Lloyd L. Natan, editor in chief

Denomination: Pentecostal Church of God (PCG)
Type: quarterly print magazine
Audience: denomination
Purpose: to impart the message of Jesus Christ, strengthen believers, resource the church, and promote the essential values of the PCG
Submissions: Email for current needs.
Sample: *www.pcg.org/pm-digital-dowload*

THE PENWOOD REVIEW

PO Box 862, Los Alamitos, CA 90720-0862
submissions@penwoodreview.com | *www.penwoodreview.com*
Lori M. Cameron, editor

Type: biannual journal
Audience: general
Purpose: to embrace high quality poetry of all kinds and to provide a forum for poets who want to write intriguing, energetic, and disciplined poetry as an expression of their faith in God
Submissions: Email only; no attachments. Unsolicited freelance: 100%. Submit up to five poems or two essays at a time. Poems may be up to two pages in length, essays five pages.
Types of manuscripts: poetry, essays
Payment: $4 off a subscription
Guidelines: *www.penwoodreview.com/submissions*
Tip: "We want serious, disciplined, high quality poetry. We do not want light verse, doggerel, or greeting card-style poetry. Avoid religious platitudes, preaching, and simplistic answers."

PERSPECTIVES: A JOURNAL OF REFORMED THOUGHT

PO Box 441130 #94102, Detroit, MI 48244-1130
submissions@perspectivesjournal.org, editors@perspectivesjournal.org | *www.perspectivesjournal.org*
Sara Sybesma Tolsma, Jason Lief, editors
Deborah Van Duinen, Jon Witt, review editors
Rose Postma, poetry editor

Denomination: Reformed
Type: bimonthly print journal
Audience: academics; pastors; and thoughtful, literate laypeople
Purpose: to express the Reformed faith theologically and to engage issues that Reformed Christians meet in personal, ecclesiastical, and societal life
Submissions: Articles: scholarly and general-interest articles, including spiritual autobiography, 3,000 words maximum; editorial commentary, 1,500 words maximum; fiction, 3,000 words maximum; and book and film reviews, 1,200 words maximum. Departments: "Inside Out," brief biblical reflection/ commentary, 600 words maximum; "As We See It," reflections on faith/culture, 500-750 words. Email manuscripts with cover letter as attachments. Prefers PDF for poetry.
Types: feature articles, opinion, autobiography, stories, reviews, poetry
Guidelines: *perspectivesjournal.org/writers-guidelines*
Tip: "Because we are committed to mentoring and guiding future leaders in the church and academy, we encourage thoughtful contributions from students and emerging writers. It is part of our theological tradition to value good writing and thought, and as such we seek to encourage both rigor and freshness."

THE PLAIN TRUTH

1710 Evergreen St., Duarte, CA 91010 | 800-309-4466
managing.editor@ptm.org | *www.ptm.org/pt-magazine*
Laura Urista, managing editor

Parent company: Plain Truth Ministries
Type: quarterly digital magazine
Audience: general
Purpose: to discover authentic Christianity without all the religious "stuff"
Submissions: Queries only.
Types of manuscripts: teaching
Guidelines: by email
Sample: on the website

POINT

11002 Lake Hart Dr., Orlando, FL 32832 | 407-563-6083
mickeyseward@converge.org | *www.converge.org/point-magazine*
Mickey Seward, editor

Denomination: Baptist General Conference
Type: quarterly print and digital magazine

Audience: denomination

Purpose: to increase movement awareness, ownership, and involvement by publishing captivating God-stories of Converge people and regional ministries

Submissions: Open to freelance submissions. Email query with clips. Articles 300-1,400 words.

Types: personal experiences, profiles, reports

Rights: first, reprint, electronic

Payment: $60-280, on publication

Sample: on the website

POSITIVE NOTE MAGAZINE

116 Maurice Ave. N.W., Fort Walton Beach, FL 32548 | 712-259-1382
joanieandjennib@positivenotenetwork.com
www.positivenotenetwork.com/the-magazine
Joanie Beaver, editor

Parent company: Positive Note Network

Type: bimonthly digital magazine, circulation 1,500, takes ads

Audience: women ages 25-50

Purpose: to deliver your daily, weekly, monthly, and lifetime dose of positive

Submissions: Email complete manuscript as attachment. Simultaneous OK. Also accepts submissions from children and teens. Freelance: 100%. Buys more than thirty manuscripts per year. Length: 300-400. Responds in two days. Bible: NIV, NLT.

Types of manuscripts: articles, short stories, poetry, columns

Topics: theme-related

Rights: all

Payment: none

Guidelines and theme list: *www.positivenotenetwork.com/the-magazine*

Sample: on the website

Tip: "Be yourself. Write in your own style. Keep Jesus at the center of your piece. Interpret the theme; it doesn't always have to be literal. Again, just be yourself."

POWER FOR LIVING

4050 Lee Vance Dr., Colorado Springs, CO 80918 | 800-708-5550, 719-536-0100
Powerforliving@davidccook.com | *shop.davidccook.org*
Karen Bouchard, managing editor

Parent company: David C. Cook

Type: weekly take-home paper
Audience: general
Purpose: to connect God's truth to real life
Submissions: Looking for inspiring stories and articles about famous and ordinary people whose experiences and insights show the power of Christ at work in their lives. Length: 750-1,000 and 1,400-1,600 words. Poetry related to matters of faith and biblically based, twenty lines. Accepts reprints but prefers original work. Accepts simultaneous submissions provided the dates of publication are different. Bible: NIV, KJV.
Types of manuscripts: personal experiences, interviews, poetry
Topics: diverse range of subjects, from world missions to simple, relatable experiences with family and life
Rights: first, onetime, reprint
Payment: $125-$375 for articles, $50 for poems, on acceptance

PRAIRIE MESSENGER

PO Box 190, Muenster, SK S0K 2Y0, Canada | 306-682-1772
pm.canadian@stpeterspress.ca | *www.prairiemessenger.ca*
Maureen Weber, Canadian news editor

Denomination: Catholic
Parent company: Benedictine Monks of St. Peter's Abbey
Type: weekly print newspaper
Audience: primarily prairie Catholics but ecumenical and interfaith with a liberal slant
Purpose: to make the people of God aware of their local, national, and international presence and responsibilities and to keep them informed of the concerns of all the church—its laity, teachers, scholars, and pastors
Submissions: Looking for well-written human-interest stories about a person, program, place, or experience, accompanied by several good photos. Length: 850 words maximum. Buys a few seasonal manuscripts, poetry, comment, and features. Email query and manuscripts. Responds to submissions only if accepted. Unsolicited freelance, 10%; assigned, 90%. Accepts simultaneous submissions. Prefers NRSV.
Types of manuscripts: profiles, poetry, news
Topics: ecumenism, social justice, prairie concerns
Rights: first, reprint (tell when/where appeared)
Payment: $60, $85 with photo, $25 for reprint or poem, on publication

Guidelines: *www.prairiemessenger.ca/writers_guidelines.html*
Sample: on the website
Note: Last issue will be May 2018.

PRESBYTERIANS TODAY

100 Witherspoon St., Louisville, KY 40202-1396 | 800-728-7228
editor@pcusa.org | www.presbyterianmission.org/ministries/today
Sam Washburn, editor

Denomination: Presbyterian Church (USA)
Type: bimonthly print and digital magazine
Audience: denomination
Purpose: to explore practical issues of faith and life, tell stories of Presbyterians who are living their faith, and cover a wide range of church news and activities
Submissions: Query first. Responds in two weeks. Prefers to work with published writers. Length: 1,000-1,800 words. Seasonal three months in advance. Freelance: 25%. Bible: NRSV.
Topics: features about Presbyterians, theology, Bible study, devotional helps, church's role in society
Payment: $75-300, on acceptance
Sample: *pt.epubxp.com/t/9766-presbyterians-today#*

PSYCHOLOGY FOR LIVING

PO Box 661900, Arcadia, CA 91066-1900
chibma@ncfliving.org | ncfliving.org/psychology-for-living-literature/psychology-for-living-magazine.html
Cynthia Hibma, editor

Parent company: Narramore Christian Foundation
Type: annual print journal
Audience: general
Purpose: to apply sound biblical and psychological principles to everyday issues of life
Submissions: Publishes articles that cover a wide range of personal and relational needs. Submit complete manuscript. Length: 1,200-1,700 words or fewer.
Types of manuscripts: how-to, teaching, personal experience
Topics: relationships, psychology, communication, emotions
Rights: first, reprint
Payment: $75-200
Guidelines: *ncfliving.org/psychology-for-living-literature/writers-guidelines.html*

Sample: *ncfliving.org/psychology-for-living-literature/psychology-for-living-magazine.html*

Tip: "Articles need to be written with laypeople in mind; technical terminology needs to be kept to a minimum. Also please avoid 'Christianeze' and suggestions that have a 'preachy' tone. Instead, give insight and understanding with practical applications that are well illustrated."

PURPOSE

718 N. Main St., Newton, KS 67114 | 316-281-4412
PurposeEditor@mennomedia.org | *www.faithandliferesources.org/periodicals/purpose*
Mary Ann Weber, managing editor

Denomination: Mennonite
Type: monthly take-home paper
Audience: denomination
Purpose: to encourage discipleship living
Submissions: Buys short, personal, true stories, 450-700 words, and poems/verse, 12 lines maximum. Both should illustrate practical ways Christians apply their faith in daily life; biblical understandings that support discipleship; and stress loyalty to the church and its peacemaking, missional, and related ministries. Prefers email submissions.
Types of manuscripts: personal experience, poetry
Topics: theme-related
Rights: onetime
Payment: $25-$50, $10-$20 for poetry
Guidelines: *www.faithandliferesources.org/periodicals/purpose/docs/Purpose_Guidelines_Oct2017.pdf*
Theme list: click from *www.faithandliferesources.org/periodicals/purpose*

REACH OUT, COLUMBIA

1051 Key Rd, Unit 57, Columbia, SC 29201
Lori@ReachOutColumbia.com | *www.ReachOutColumbia.com*
Lori Hatcher, editor

Type: monthly (9x) print magazine, circulation 20,000, takes ads
Audience: Christians and seekers
Purpose: to celebrate Jesus Christ by spotlighting local (SC) and national/international ministries and Christian leaders
Submissions: Email as attachment. Unsolicited freelance: 75%. Buys fifty manuscripts per year. Length: 500-1,250 words. Seasonal four to six months in advance. Responds in two weeks. Bible: NIV.

Types of manuscripts: profile, teaching, devotional, testimony
Topics: Christian living, parenting
Rights: onetime
Payment: none
Guidelines: *www.reachoutcolumbia.com/roc-info/article-submissions*
Sample: by mail with $3.00 for postage
Tip: "We are most open to fresh ideas that relate to everyday Christian life."

RELEVANT

55 W. Church St., Ste. 211, Orlando, FL 32801 | 407-660-1411
editorial@relevantmagazine.com | relevantmediagroup.com
Andre Henry, managing editor, andre@relevantmediagroup.com

Type: bimonthly print and digital magazine
Audience: millennials
Purpose: to challenge people to go further in their spiritual journey, live selflessly and intentionally, care about positively impacting the world around them, and find the unexpected places God is speaking in life, music, and culture
Submissions: Email query and complete manuscript as attachment. Responds in one to two weeks or not interested. Length: 750-1,000 words.
Topics: faith, culture, and intentional living
Payment: $100-400
Guidelines: *www.relevantmagazine.com/how-write-relevant*

RELIEF JOURNAL

Reade Center 122, Taylor University, 236 W. Reade Ave., Upland, IN 46989
hannah@reliefjournal.com | www.reliefjournal.com
Hannah Haney, managing editor

Type: biannual print literary journal
Audience: general
Purpose: to promote full human flourishing in faith and art
Submissions: Looking for poetry and stories that reflect reality as honestly as Scripture reflects reality. Submit manuscript through the website only during October 1 to March 31. Costs $2 to submit a manuscript. Length: stories 8,000 words maximum; poetry 1,000 words maximum; creative nonfiction, exploratory essays with an emotional arc that may or may not be narrative, 5,000 words maximum

Types of manuscripts: short stories, creative nonfiction, poetry
Rights: first, electronic
Payment: none
Guidelines: *www.reliefjournal.com/submit*

SACONNECTS

440 W. Nyack Rd., West Nyack, NY 10994-1739 | 845-620-7200
saconnects.org
Robert Mitchell, managing editor

Denomination: Salvation Army
Type: monthly print and digital magazine
Audience: denomination in the eastern territory
Submissions: Manuscripts only from people who live in the eastern territory. Email manuscripts as attachments through the website.
Types of manuscripts: news, how-to, personal experience
Guidelines: *saconnects.org/submission-guidelines-magazine*

ST. ANTHONY MESSENGER

28 W. Liberty St., Cincinnati, OH 45202-6498 | 513-241-5615
MagazineEditors@Franciscanmedia.org | *www.FranciscanMedia.org*
John Feister, editor

Denomination: Catholic
Type: monthly print and digital magazine
Audience: family-oriented, majority are women ages 40-70
Purpose: to offer readers inspiration from the heart of Catholicism—the Gospels and the experience of God's people
Submissions: Query only by email. Responds in eight weeks. Email manuscripts as attachments. Seasonal one year in advance. Length: about 2,000 words or shorter pieces. Fiction 2,000-2,500 words; buys twelve per year. Stories should be about family relationships and about people struggling and coping with problems, triumphing in adversity, persevering in faith, overcoming doubt, or coming to spiritual insights. Poetry 20 lines maximum. Bible: NAB.
Types of manuscripts: profiles, biblical teaching, short stories, poetry
Topics: church, sacraments, education, spiritual growth, family, marriage, social issues
Rights: first, electronic
Payment: 20¢/word, $2/line for poetry with minimum of $20, on acceptance
Guidelines: *www.franciscanmedia.org/writers-guide*

SCP JOURNAL

PO Box 40015, Pasadena, CA 91114 | 510-540-0300
scp@scp-inc.org | *www.scp-inc.org*
Tal Brooks, editor

Parent company: Spiritual Counterfeits Project
Type: quarterly print journal
Audience: general
Purpose: to provide a biblical perspective on new religions and spiritual trends
Submissions: Query only. No unsolicited manuscripts. Articles analyze and discern the inside workings of new spiritual trends.
Guidelines: click "Information" tab

SEEK

4050 Lee Vance Dr., Colorado Springs, CO 80918 | 800-323-7543
seek@standardpub.com | *www.Standardpub.com*
Margaret Williams, editor

Parent company: David C. Cook
Type: weekly take-home paper
Audience: young and middle-age adults
Purpose: to encourage adults in their walk with Jesus Christ
Submissions: Buys articles and stories tied to specific Scriptures. Bible: KJV.
Topics: related to Sunday-school Scripture passages/themes.
Guidelines: by email

SHARING

PO Box 780909, San Antonio, TX 78278-0909 | 877-992-5222
sharing@orderofstluke.org | *orderofstluke.org/en/sharing-magazine.html*

Parent company: International Order of St. Luke the Physician
Type: bimonthly print magazine
Audience: general
Purpose: to inspire, educate, and inform about Christian healing of body, soul, and spirit
Submissions: Share your stories, experiences, thoughts, insights, inspirational poems, and testimonies of God's amazing power to heal. Length: articles 200-1,500 words, poetry 30-50 words. Prefers emailed submissions as attachments but will take them by mail.
Types of manuscripts: personal experience, testimonies, teaching, essays, poetry

Topics: theme-related
Rights: onetime
Payment: none
Guidelines: *orderofstluke.org/images/documents/Submission_Guidelines_0117.pdf*
Theme list: by email

SIMPLE GRACE

270 Sylvan Ave., Englewood Cliffs, NJ 07632 | 201-569-6699
costergard@bauerpublishingcom | *www.simplegrace.com*
Carey Ostergard, editor

Parent company: Bauer Media Group
Type: monthly print magazine, circulation 100,000, takes ads
Audience: women
Purpose: to be a daily dose of hope
Submissions: Email manuscript as attachment. Unsolicited freelance: 5%. Buys one or two unsolicited inspirational stories per year. Length: 1,000 words for features. Seasonal four months in advance. Responds in three weeks. Bible: ESV.
Rights: all
Payment: $1.50 per word, on publication, pays kill fee
Guidelines: by email
Sample: email *help@simple grace.com*
Tip: "We're looking for real-life stories that deliver hope and inspiration."

SISTER SOLDIERS IN CHRIST

800 W. Ave. D #2 N.E, San Angelo, Texas 76903 | 817-228-2415
Info@SisterSoldiersInChrist.com | *SisterSoldiersInChrist.com*
Janis James, managing editor

Type: monthly digital magazine, circulation 1,000, takes ads
Audience: women
Purpose: to inspire, encourage, and equip women warriors for Christ
Submissions: Submit manuscripts through the website. Unsolicited freelance: 25%. Buys twelve articles per year. Length: 700 words maximum. Responds in two to four weeks. Bible version: KJV, NKJV, NIV.
Types of manuscripts: personal experiences
Topics: overcoming "a life challenge from a Christian-based perspective that will encourage and inspire other women"
Rights: electronic

Payment: none
Guidelines: *www.sistersoldiersinchrist.com/write-for-us*
Sample: on the website
Tip: "We need stories of courage and inspiration that will inspire other women to persevere in the faith. We want to hear your 'survival story' on how you overcame a life challenge from a Christian-based perspective. Every story must ultimately end with Jesus as Lord."

SOJOURNERS

408 C St. N.E., Washington, DC 20002 | 202-328-8842
queries@sojo.net, reviews@sojo.net | *www.sojo.net*
Jim Rice, editor

Type: monthly print and digital magazine
Audience: community influencers
Purpose: to explore the intersections of faith, politics, and culture; uncover in depth the hidden injustices in the world around us; and tell the stories of hope that keep us grounded, inspired, and moving forward
Submissions: Query only with no attachments. Responds in six to eight weeks. Feature articles are typically 1800-2000 words. Mail poetry. Length: 25-40 lines. Often tries to use poetry geared toward particular seasons.
Types of manuscripts: feature articles, reviews, poetry
Topics: social justice, popular culture, spirituality
Rights: all
Payment: unspecified, $25 per poem, on publication
Guidelines: *sojo.net/about-us/what-we-cover/write-us*

SOUTHWEST KANSAS FAITH AND FAMILY

PO Box 1454, Dodge City, KS 67801 | 620-225-4677
stan@swkfaithandfamily.org | *www.swkfaithandfamily.org*
Stan Wilson, publisher

Type: monthly print newspaper
Audience: residents of the area
Purpose: to share the Word of God and news and information that honors Christian beliefs, family traditions, and values that are the cornerstone of our nation
Submissions: Email query or complete manuscript.
Topics: any Christian or family issue
Guidelines: *www.swkfaithandfamily.org/submitarticle.html*

SPARK

2306 Southview Dr., Bettendorf, IA 52722
submissions@splickety.com | *www.splickety.com*
Kimberly Duffy, lead editor
Leslie McKee, associate editor

Parent company: Splickety Publishing Group
Type: quarterly print and digital magazine, circulation 2,000+, takes ads
Audience: romance flash-fiction readers
Purpose: to publish the best romance flash fiction in the world
Submissions: All stories must fit quarterly theme and be submitted at least three months in advance. Email complete manuscript as attachment only. Freelance: almost 100%. Buys forty to fifty per year. Length: 1,000 words maximum. Responds in a week.
Types of manuscripts: short stories; also query at *blog@Splickety.com* for possible nonfiction posts
Rights: first, all for six months after publication
Payment: 2¢/word
Guidelines: *splickety.com/submission-guidelines*
Theme list: *splickety.com/submission-guidelines/upcoming-themes*
Tip: "Write incredible romance flash fiction, follow our prescribed submission guidelines, and make sure your story fits the theme for the issue you're submitting to. We publish solely on merit."

SPLICKETY

2306 Southview Dr., Bettendorf, IA 52722
submissions@splickety.com | *www.splickety.com*
Lauren Hildebrand, editor

Parent company: Splickety Publishing Group
Type: quarterly print and digital magazine, circulation 2,000+, takes ads
Audience: general market flash-fiction readers
Purpose: to publish the best flash fiction in the world
Submissions: Email complete manuscript as attachment only. Freelance: almost 100%. Buys forty to fifty per year. Length: 1,000 words maximum. Responds in a week. All stories must fit quarterly theme and be submitted at least three months in advance.
Types of manuscripts: short stories; also query at *blog@Splickety.com* for possible nonfiction posts
Topics: related to theme
Rights: first, all for six months after publication

Payment: 2¢/word
Guidelines: *splickety.com/submission-guidelines*
Theme list: *splickety.com/submission-guidelines/upcoming-themes*
Sample: subscribe on website for free
Tip: "Write a brilliant flash-fiction story, and follow our submission guidelines when sending it in. We publish solely on the story's merit."

SPORTS SPECTRUM

PO Box 2037, Indian Trail, NC 28979 | 866-821-2971
jon@sportsspectrum.com | *sportsspectrum.com*
Jon Ackeman, senior editor

Type: quarterly print and digital magazine
Audience: sports fans, predominantly male, ages 20-55
Purpose: to reach non-Christians with the gospel through the testimonies and experiences of sports figures
Submissions: If you are an experienced sports writer, send information about yourself with clips to get an assignment. Query only for article ideas. Articles generally run 1,500-2,000 words plus one or two sidebars of 150 words. Works five months in advance. Bible: NIV.
Rights: all
Payment: at least 21¢/word plus reasonable expenses
Sample: on the website
Tip: "It is essential that the athletes featured in *Sports Spectrum* demonstrate a strong Christian testimony. The fact that they occasionally talk about God or attend chapel is not enough to go on."

STANDARD

PO Box 843336, Kansas City, MO 64184-3336 | 816-931-1900
standard.foundry@gmail.com | *www.nph.com*
Jeanette Gardner Littleton, editor

Denomination: Wesleyan-Arminian
Parent company: The Foundry (formerly Nazarene Publishing House)
Type: weekly take-home paper, circulation 40,000
Audience: denomination
Purpose: to encourage and inspire our audience and to reinforce curriculum
Submissions: Email query letter or complete manuscript with cover letter as attachment. Accepts simultaneous submissions. Makes assignments. Unsolicited freelance: 20%. Buys one hundred four

manuscripts per year. Length: 400 and 800-900 words. Seasonal one year in advance. Response time varies. Bible: NIV.

Types of manuscripts: personal experience, short stories, open to other styles

Topics: theme-related

Rights: first, reprint, all

Payment: $35 and $50, on acceptance

Writers guidelines and theme list: by email

Sample: email for PDF

Tip: "Writers should know basics of Wesleyan-Arminian theological perspective. Write to the theme list; please indicate which theme you're proposing it for. Nonfiction cannot be preachy; fiction cannot be trite. Put full contact information in the body of the manuscript, not only in the email. It helps to know if you're Nazarene or another Wesleyan/holiness denomination."

TEACHERS OF VISION

PO Box 45610, Westlake, OH 44145 | 888-798-1124
tov@ceai.org | ceai.org/teachers-of-vision-magazine
Doreen Madere, editorial director
Dawn Molnar, managing editor

Parent organization: Christian Educators Association International

Type: quarterly magazine, circulation 6,500, takes ads

Audience: Christian educators, primarily in public school

Purpose: to encourage, equip, and empower Christians serving in public and private schools and to demonstrate God's love to the educational community

Submissions: Email submission as attached file. Minifeatures, 400-800 words; theme-based features, 800-1,000 words; personal interest and methodology, 400-1,000 words.

Types of manuscripts: personal experience, how-to, poetry, inspirational

Topics: theme-based, educational success story, teaching techniques, news

Rights: first, including web copy

Payment: not specified

Guidelines: *ceai.org/wp-content/uploads/2016/01/2016-writers-guidelines.pdf*

Sample: download from website

TESTIMONY MAGAZINE

2450 Milltower Ct., Mississauga, ON L5N 5Z6, Canada | 905-542-7400
testimony@paoc.org | *www.testimonymag.ca*
Stephen Kennedy, editor

Parent company: Pentecostal Assemblies of Canada
Type: bimonthly print magazine
Audience: general
Purpose: to celebrate what God is doing in and through the Fellowship, while offering encouragement to believers by providing a window into the struggles that everyday Christians often encounter
Submissions: Query first by email. Length: 800-1,000 words. Responds in six to eight weeks. Seasonal four months ahead. Bible: NIV.
Types of manuscripts: personal experience, interviews, sidebars
Rights: first
Payment: unspecified
Guidelines: *testimony.paoc.org/submit*
Tip: "Our readership is 98% Canadian. We prefer Canadian writers or at least writers who understand that Canadians are not Americans in long underwear. We also give preference to members of this denomination, since this is related to issues concerning our fellowship."

THRIVE CONNECTION

PO Box 151297, Lakewood, CO 80215 | 303-985-2148
thriveministry.org/magazine
Megan Lenhausen, communications director

Type: digital magazine, circulation 10,000
Audience: women in cross-cultural work overseas
Purpose: to empower and encourage women in cross-cultural work
Submissions: Articles 500-1,000 words. All submissions must be sent through the website. Writers must be women who are or have been in cross-cultural missions.
Types of manuscripts: personal experience, recipes
Topics: cross-cultural experiences, singleness, marriage, family, spiritual formation, relationships; see subtopics on the website
Rights: first, onetime (with permission to archive permanently)
Payment: none
Sample: on the website

TIME OF SINGING: A JOURNAL OF CHRISTIAN POETRY

PO Box 5276, Conneaut Lake, PA 16316
timesing@zoominternet.net | *www.timeofsinging.com*
Lora Homan Zill, editor

Parent organization: Wind & Water Press
Type: quarterly print journal, circulation 250
Audience: general
Purpose: to reflect on our walk with God through the art and craft of poetry, to create a community of creative people who loves both the written and Living Word and shares a Christian worldview
Submissions: Prefers poems without religious jargon, that "show" and don't "tell" and take creative chances with faith and our walk with God. Unsolicited freelance: 95%. Length: 40 lines maximum. Send complete manuscript by mail or email. Responds in three months. Seasonal six months ahead. Accepts simultaneous submissions. Accepts 150 per year.
Types of manuscripts: poetry, assigned reviews of poetry books published by *Time Of Singing* poets
Topics: our walk with God, nature, the "human condition," any topic
Rights: first, reprint (tell when/where published)
Payment: none
Guidelines: *www.timeofsinging.com/guidelines.html*
Sample: $4 each or 2/$7 (checks, money orders payable to Wind & Water Press)
Tip: "Study the craft of poetry. If you don't read poetry, you can't write it. I don't publish sermons that rhyme or greeting-card type poetry. *Time Of Singing* is a literary poetry journal. I love poets who think outside the theological box and challenge my assumptions. We don't write or read poetry to find answers but to wrestle with the questions."

TODAY'S CHRISTIAN LIVING

PO Box 5000, Iola, WI 54945 | 800-223-3161, 715-445-5000
dan@cross-life.us | *www.todayschristianliving.org*
Dan Brownell, editor

Type: bimonthly print and digital magazine
Audience: general
Purpose: to challenge Christians in their faith, so they may be strengthened to fulfill the call of God in their lives
Submissions: Prefers complete manuscripts; discourages queries. Personality and ministry profiles, 1,400-1,600 words plus sidebar of 150-250 words. Personal story/anecdote 670-700 words.

"Grace Notes," how important biblical principles and attributes are illustrated in everyday life, 650-700 words. Hospitality, inspirational story plus recipe, 700-1,500 words. Humorous anecdotes, 50-200 words.

Types of manuscripts: personal experience, profiles, recipes, humor

Rights: all

Payment: $25-150, after publication

Guidelines: *todayschristianliving.org/writers-guidelines*

Sample: on the website

U.S. CATHOLIC

205 W. Monroe St., Chicago, IL 60606 | 312-544-8169
submissions@clairetians.org (articles, essays),
literaryeditor@clairetians.org (poetry, fiction) | *www.uscatholic.org*
Meghan Murphy-Gill, managing editor

Denomination: Catholic

Type: monthly print magazine

Audience: denomination

Submissions: Email manuscripts. Responds in six to eight weeks. Seasonal six months in advance. Features that go beyond basic reporting by offering analysis and interpretation of the issues, 2,500-3,500 words. Essays, 800 to 1,600 words, present thoughtful reflections or opinions on concerns Catholics face in everyday life. "Practicing Catholic," 1,100 words with short sidebar, reflects on the meaning of a particular prayer practice. "Sounding Board" opinion piece, 1,400 words. Profiles, 800 words; reviews, 315 words; fiction, 1,500 words.

Types of manuscripts: essays, profiles, features, short stories, poetry, reviews

Payment: $75-500

Guidelines: *www.uscatholic.org/writers-guide*

VIBRANT LIFE

PO Box 5353, Nampa, ID 83653-5353 | 208-465-2584
heather.quintana@pacificpress.com | *www.vibrantlife.com*
Heather Quintana, editor

Denomination: Seventh-day Adventist

Type: bimonthly print magazine

Audience: general

Purpose: to promote physical health, mental clarity, and spiritual balance from a practical, Christian perspective

Submissions: Send complete manuscript by email as attachment or by mail. Short articles, 450-650 words; feature articles, to 1,000 words plus a sidebar if informational.

Types of manuscripts: teaching, interviews, profiles, personal experiences, how-to, sidebar

Topics: health, exercise, nutrition

Rights: first, reprint

Payment: $100-300, on acceptance

Guidelines: *www.vibrantlife.com/?page_id=1369*

Tip: "Information must be reliable—no faddism. Articles should represent the latest findings on the subject, and if scientific in nature, should be properly documented. (References to other lay journals are generally not acceptable.)"

WAR CRY

615 Slaters Ln., PO Box 269, Alexandria, VA 22314 | 703-684-5500
sapubs.knack.com/home#submissions | *magazine.thewarcry.org*
Lt. Colonel Allen Satterlee, editor-in-chief

Denomination: Salvation Army

Type: monthly print and digital magazine plus special Christmas and Easter issues; circulation 180,000 in general, 1.4 million at Christmas, 750,000 at Easter; takes ads

Audience: denomination plus general

Purpose: to represent the Army's mission of preaching the gospel of Jesus Christ and meeting human needs in His name without discrimination

Submissions: Length: 500-1,500 words. Seasonal six months in advance. Unsolicited freelance: 25%. Buys eighty per year. Email complete manuscript through online form. Responds in one month. Simultaneous OK. Seasonal six months ahead. Bible: NLT.

Types of manuscripts: features, short stories, fillers, sidebars, testimony

Topics: parenting, Christian life, evangelism, profiles, Christ and culture, contemporary issues, apologetics from Wesleyan perspective

Rights: first, reprint (tell when/where published), electronic

Payment: 35¢/word, 15¢/word for reprints, on acceptance

Guidelines and theme list: *www.sanationalpublications.org/submission-guidelines*

Sample: *www.sanationalpublications.org*

Tip: Needs Thanksgiving and other seasonal articles.

WORD&WAY

PO Box 1771, Jefferson City, MO 65102-1771 | 573-635-5939
editor@wordandway.org | *wordandway.org*
Brian Kaylor, editor

Denomination: Baptist
Type: monthly magazine
Audience: denomination, general
Purpose: to accurately inform Baptists and others of relevant news, promote the work of Christ, and encourage inspirational living
Submissions: Email for needs.
Sample: *www.wordandway.org/images/Advertising/March2017issue.pdf*

YOUR VOICE

116 Maurice Ave. N.W., Fort Walton Beach, FL 32548 | 712-259-1381
joanieandjennib@positivenotenetwork.com | *www.positivenotenetwork.com*
Joanie Beaver, owner-editor

Parent company: Positive Note Network
Type: bimonthly print and digital magazine, circulation 1,000, takes ads
Audience: women ages 25-50
Purpose: a literary magazine that allows people to relax and embrace the magic of storytelling
Submissions: Submit as email attachment. Simultaneous OK. Also accepts manuscripts from teens and children. Unsolicited freelance: 90%. Accepts one hundred eighty manuscripts per year. Word count: up to 2,000. Bible: NIV, NLT, *The Message*. Responds in two days.
Types of manuscripts: memoir, short stories, poetry, sidebars, columns, fillers
Topics: any topic that fits the theme
Rights: all
Payment: none
Writers guidelines and theme list: *www.positivenotenetwork.com/yourvoice*
Sample: on the website
Tip: "It's a literary magazine, so we love fiction short stories in any genre. We want to see you have a passion for writing, so make sure that comes across. All writers, first time and otherwise, are welcome."

YOUTHMINISTRY.COM

1515 Cascade Ave., Loveland, CO 80538 | 970-669-3836
puorgbus@group.com | *youthministry.com*

Type: website
Audience: youth workers and leaders
Purpose: to help leaders encourage teens to grow spiritually
Submissions: Email full manuscript. Length: 300-1,000 words.
Types of manuscripts: how-to, lesson plans, fillers, Bible studies
Topics: successful youth ministry strategies, including youth-led ministry ideas; understanding kids and youth culture; recruiting/training/keeping adult leaders; family ministry; staff issues; serving and training parents; professionalism; self-nurture; how-to articles on personal spiritual growth, time management, issues vital to working with young people, leadership skills (listening, discussion-leading), worship ideas, handling specific group problems, fun and experiential programming ideas, and active-learning meeting plans and retreats
Rights: all
Payment: $80, on acceptance
Guidelines: *grouppublishingps.zendesk.com/hc/en-us/articles/211878258-Submissions*
Note: Replaces *Group* magazine.

7

TEEN/YOUNG ADULT MARKETS

BOUNDLESS

8605 Explorer Dr., Colorado Springs, CO 80920 | 719-531-3400
editor@boundless.org | *www.boundless.org*
Lisa Anderson, director

Parent company: Focus on the Family
Type: website and articles; circulation 300,000 visitors per month
Audience: single young adults in 20s and 30s
Purpose: to help Christian young adults grow up, own their faith, date with purpose, and prepare for marriage and family
Submissions: Rarely accepts unsolicited articles but open to considering new writers. To get an assignment, send a sample or two of your writing, a link to your blog, and a proposal of what you're interested in writing about. Length: 1,200 words. Accepts unsolicited blog posts 500-800 words; email manuscript.
Bible: prefers ESV
Types of manuscripts: articles and blog posts
Topics: fit in these three categories: (1) adulthood: being single, career, family, money; (2) faith: spiritual growth, ministry; (3) relationships: dating, marriage, sexuality, community
Rights: all
Guidelines: *www.boundless.org/about/write-for-us*
Tip: "Aim to engage our readers' hearts, as we're primarily in the business of affecting lives, not changing society. Use personal stories as illustrations and to spark our readers' imaginations."

THE BRINK

See entry in "**Daily Devotional Booklets and Websites.**"

BRIO

8605 Explorer Drive, Colorado Springs, CO 80920 | 719-531-3400
submissions@briomagazine.com | *www.briomagazine.com*
Pam Woody, editorial director, editor@briomagazine.com

Parent company: Focus on the Family
Type: monthly magazine (10x), circulation 60,000
Audience: girls ages 13-16
Purpose: to provide inspiring stories, fashion insights, fun profiles, and practical tips, all from a biblical worldview
Submissions: Email as Word attachment. Fiction must be complete mansuscript.
Types of manuscripts: fiction, articles, profiles, crafts
Topics: health and beauty, ordinary girls doing extraordinary things, spiritual health, seasonal, relationships, pertinent cultural issues
Rights: onetime
Payment: minimum 20¢/word
Guidelines: *tinyurl.com/ycv3qna6*
Tip: "We want parents to trust that Brio provides relevant, educational material with scriptural or moral insight. Your job, then, as a writer, is to create work that pleases both parents and teens."

DEVOZINE

See entry in "**Daily Devotional Booklets and Websites**."

FCA MAGAZINE

8701 Leeds Rd., Kansas City, MO 64129 | 800-289-0909
mag@fca.org | *www.fca.org/magazine*
Clay Meyer, editor

Parent company: Fellowship of Christian Athletes
Type: bimonthly magazine
Audience: teen and college athletes and their coaches
Purpose: to serve as a ministry tool of the Fellowship of Christian Athletes by informing, inspiring, and involving coaches, athletes, and all whom they influence, that they may make an impact for Jesus Christ
Submissions: Email manuscripts through the website.
Types of manuscripts: sports stories, interviews, devotionals
Topics: stories applicable to campus, camps, or coaches; devotionals that apply biblical truths to the competitive mindset and sports atmosphere
Guidelines: *www.fca.org/quick-links/submit-a-devotional*

GIRLZ 4 CHRIST MAGAZINE

G4Csubmissions@gmail.com | Girlz4Christ.org
Jessica Lippe, editor-in-chief, Girlz4christ@yahoo.com
Lily Garay, assistant editor

Type: quarterly digital magazine, circulation 2,000, takes ads
Audience: teen girls (also preteen and college)
Purpose: to provide uplifting quality media options to girls around the world
Submissions: Email complete manuscript as attachment. Simultaneous submissions OK. Accepts submissions from teens. Freelance: 100%. Accepts fifty manuscripts per year. Length: 100-1,000 words. Seasonal: two to three months in advance. Responds in two days.
Types of manuscripts: devotional, interviews, games, how-to, short stories, poetry, sidebars, columns, fillers
Topics: fit one of these sections: "Godly Girlz," "Girlz in Action," "Beautiful Girlz," "Fun 4 Girlzfashion"; beauty, health, service projects
Rights: author's choice
Payment: free or discounted advertising and other free or discounted G4C merchandise
Guidelines: *girlz4christ.org/submissions*
Sample: sign up for a free digital subscription on the website
Tip: "Deliver what teens want: fashion/beauty, Christian celebrities, things to do, etc."

INSIGHT

PO Box 5353, Nampa, ID 83653-5353 | 301-393-4038
insight@rhpa.org | www.insightmagazine.org
Omar Miranda, editor, omar.miranda@pacificpress.com

Denomination: Seventh-day Adventist
Parent company: Pacific Press Publishing Association
Type: weekly take-home paper; 18 pages, takes ads
Audience: ages 13-19
Purpose: to help teenagers grow in a friendship with God, solve life's problems, and choose positive Christian values and principles to live by
Submissions: Articles 1,200-1,700 words. Email submissions. Seasonal six months ahead.
Rights: first
Payment: $50-85, on publication
Guidelines: send SASE

TAKE FIVE PLUS

See entry in "**Daily Devotional Booklets and Websites**."

YOUNG SALVATIONIST

615 Sisters Ln., Alexandria, VA 22314 | 703-684-5500
YS@usn.salvationarmy.org | *www.youngsalvationist.org*
Captain Pamela Maynor, editor

Denomination: The Salvation Army
Type: monthly (10x) print and digital magazine; 28 pages
Audience: teens and young adults
Purpose: to help young people develop a mature faith, a personal ministry, and a Christian perspective on everyday life
Submissions: Email complete manuscript through the website. Articles to 500 words. Responds in six weeks or isn't interested. Submit at least two months in advance of theme issue. Bible: NLT.
Types of manuscripts: articles, poems
Topics: related to theme
Rights: first, one-time, reprint
Payment: 35¢/word, 15¢ for reprints
Guidelines and theme list: *www.youngsalvationist.org/contribute-to-ys-2*

8

CHILDREN'S MARKETS

CADET QUEST

1333 Alger St. S.E., Grand Rapids, MI 49507 | 616-241-5616 x4
submissions@CalvinistCadets.org | *www.CalvinistCadets.org*
Steve Bootsma, executive director

Parent company: Dynamic Youth Ministries
Type: print magazine, 7x/year; 24 pages, circulation 6,000
Audience: boys ages 9-14
Purpose: to show how God is working in the lives of boys and in the world around them
Submissions: Unsolicited freelance: 10%. Buys 25 per year. Mail complete manuscript, or email it in body of message. Selections made in May for the following September—May; responds in June. Accepts simultaneous submissions. Accepts manuscripts from kids and teens. Length: 750-1,500 words. Bible: NIV.
Types of manuscripts: articles, short stories
Topics: Christian athletes, outdoor activities, nature, relating Christian values to boys' lives
Rights: first, reprint
Payment: minimum 5¢/word, on acceptance
Guidelines and theme list: *counselors.calvinistcadets.org/submissionshelp/quest-authors-info*
Sample: order online, $4.00 (US), including postage
Tip: "Don't be too preachy or write with clichés. Try to think like an 11-year-old boy. Always looking for nonfiction bios of sports heroes, musicians, and other people the boys would know about."

COMPASSION EXPLORER

12290 Voyager Pkwy., Colorado Springs, CO 80921 | 800-336-7676
compassionkids@compassion.com | *www.compassion.com/kids-magazine.htm*
Leanna Summers, editor-in-chief;
Willow Welter, managing editor

Parent company: Compassion International
Type: triannual print magazine, PDF download, online
Audience: children
Purpose: to broaden American children's perspective as they learn about children from the developing world in a fun, engaging way, creating a desire to help those in need
Submissions: email for current needs

DEVOKIDS

See entry in "**Daily Devotional Booklets and Websites.**"

FOCUS ON THE FAMILY CLUBHOUSE

8605 Explorer Dr., Colorado Springs, CO 80920 | 719-531-3400
editor@clubhousemagazine.com | *www.clubhousemagazine.com*
Jesse Florea, editorial director, youth publications
Kate Jameson, editorial assistant (submit to)

Parent company: Focus on the Family
Type: monthly print magazine with online extras; 32 pages, circulation 73,000, takes ads
Audience: children ages 8-12
Purpose: to helps kids grow closer to Christ through entertaining fiction, personality, and Christian-worldview stories
Submissions: Unsolicited freelance: 20%. Length: 500-2,000 words. Buys fifty manuscripts per year. Mail complete manuscript, or email it as attachment. Responds in three months. Seasonal six to eight months ahead. Accepts submissions from teens. Bible: HCSB.
Types of manuscripts: nonfiction, short stories, crafts, recipes
Topics: animal fact stories, personality stories of ordinary kids doing something extraordinary, Christian living and worldview
Rights: nonexclusive license
Payment: 15-20¢ per word, on acceptance, kill fee sometimes
Guidelines: *www.clubhousemagazine.com/submission-guidelines.aspx*
Theme list: by email
Sample: 9x12 SASE with check for $2.50 made out to Focus on the Family
Tip: "See writers guidelines on website. Know the audience and treat young readers with respect."

FOCUS ON THE FAMILY CLUBHOUSE JR.

8605 Explorer Dr., Colorado Springs, CO 80920 | 719-531-3400
editor@clubhousejr.com | *www.clubhousejr.com*
Jesse Florea, editorial director, youth publications
Kate Jameson, editorial assistant (submit to)

Parent company: Focus on the Family
Type: monthly print magazine with online extras; 32 pages, circulation 45,000, ads
Audience: children ages 3-7
Purpose: to build a child's faith in Jesus through entertaining fiction, animal, personality, and Bible stories
Submissions: Unsolicited freelance, 15%. Buys fifty manuscripts per year. Length: 150-800 words. Mail complete manuscript, or email it as attachment. Responds in three months. Seasonal six to eight months ahead. Bible: NIrV.
Types of manuscripts: nonfiction, animal factoid, recipes, crafts, short stories, poetry, rebus
Topics: ordinary kids doing something extraordinary, Christian life
Rights: nonexclusive license
Payment: 20-25¢ per word, on acceptance, kill fee sometimes
Guidelines: *www.clubhousejr.com/submission-guidelines.aspx*
Theme list: by email
Sample: 9x12 SASE with check for $2.50 made out to Focus on the Family
Tip: "See online writers guidelines. Be creative and funny. Stories should help children develop educationally and spiritually."

GUIDE

PO Box 5353, Nampa, ID 83653-5353
guide.magazine@pacificpress.com | *www.guidemagazine.org*
Randy Fishell, editor

Denomination: Seventh-day Adventist
Parent company: Pacific Press Publishing
Type: weekly take-home paper; 32 pages, circulation 26,000
Audience: ages 10-14
Purpose: to show readers, through stories that illustrate Bible truth, how to walk with God now and forever
Submissions: Prefers complete manuscript. Submit online or by mail with SASE. Responds in four to six weeks. Seasonal eight months in advance. Accepts submissions from teens 14 and older. Bible: NKJV.

Types of manuscripts: true stories 1,000-1,200 words (some shorter pieces 450 words and up), sometimes accepts quizzes and other unique nonstory formats; must include a clear spiritual element

Topics: adventure, personal growth, humor, inspiration (answers to prayer, biblical narratives, mission stories, and examples of young people living out their Christian beliefs), biography, nature

Rights: first, reprint (tell when and where published)

Payment: 7-10¢ per word, $25-40 for games and puzzles, on acceptance

Guidelines: *www.guidemagazine.org/writersguidelines*

Sample: download from guidelines page

Tip: "Use your best short-story techniques (dialogue, scenes, a sense of plot) to tell a true story starring a kid ages 10-14. Bring out a clear spiritual/biblical message. We publish multipart true stories regularly, two to twelve parts, 1,200 words each. All topics indicated need to be addressed within the context of a true story."

KEYS FOR KIDS

See entry in "**Daily Devotional Booklets and Websites.**"

KIDS ANSWERS

PO Box 510, Hebron, KY 41048

jupchurch@answersingenesis.com | *answersingenesis.org/kids/answers/magazine*

John UpChurch, editor

Parent company: Answers in Genesis

Type: quarterly mini print magazine in *Answers* magazine; 8 pages

Audience: children

Purpose: to highlight the wonders of God's creation with kid-friendly information and images

Submissions: Only accepts one-paragraph article proposals with author's qualifications (300 words) via email or through the website. Once accepted, email article as an attachment. Responds in one month.

Types of manuscripts: nonfiction

Topics: themed

Rights: all

Payment: $75-125

Guidelines: *answersingenesis.org/answers/magazine/contact*

Sample: on the website

THE KIDS' ARK

PO Box 3160, Victoria, TX 77903 | 800-455-1770
thekidsarksubmissions@yahoo.com | *thekidsark.com*
Beth Haynes, senior editor

Type: quarterly print magazine; 36 pages
Audience: ages 4-12
Purpose: to enlighten children with the love and power of God through Jesus Christ and to provide children with a solid biblical foundation on which to base their choices in life
Submissions: Email complete manuscript as a Word attachment. Responds in eight to ten weeks. Freelance: 100%. Length: 650 words maximum. Buys sixteen per year. Also accepts submissions from children and teens. Bible: NIV.
Types of manuscripts: nonfiction, short stories, games, puzzles
Topics: theme-related
Rights: first, electronic, reprint
Payment: $100 for first plus electronic, $25 for reprints, on publication
Guidelines and theme list: *thekidsark.com/guidelines.htm*
Sample: *www.thekidsark.com/images/sample.pdf*
Tip: "Write for the 6- to 10-year-old reading level."

NATURE FRIEND MAGAZINE

4253 Woodcock Ln., Dayton, VA 22821 | 540-867-0764
editor@naturefriendmagazine.com | *www.naturefriendmagazine.com*
Kevin Shank, editor

Parent company: Dogwood Ridge Outdoors
Type: monthly print magazine; 28 pages, circulation 10,000
Audience: ages 6-16
Purpose: to increase awareness of God and appreciation for God's works and gifts, to teach accountability toward God's works, and to teach natural truths and facts
Submissions: Freelance: 50-80%. Mail complete manuscript with SASE, or email as attachment. Length: 500-800 words. Buys forty to fifty per year. Seasonal four months in advance. Accepts simultaneous submissions.
Bible: KJV only
Rights: first, reprint
Payment: 5¢/edited word, 3¢/word for reprints, on publication
Types: crafts, projects, experiments, fiction, articles, photo features
Topics: nature-related, science experiments, stories about people

interacting with nature or about an animal, nature-friendly gardening, nature photography lessons, survival/wilderness first-aid, weather, astronomy, flowers, marine life

Guidelines: *www.naturefriendmagazine.com/index.pl?linkid=12;class=gen*

Sample: *www.naturefriendmagazine.com/index.pl?linkid=4;class=gen*

Tip: "While talking animals can be interesting and teach worthwhile lessons, we have chosen to not use them in *Nature Friend.* Excluded are puzzle-type submissions such as 'Who Am I?'"

OUR LITTLE FRIEND

PO Box 5353, Nampa, ID 83653
anita.seymour@pacificpress.com | www.ourlittlefriend.com
Anita Seymour, managing editor

Denomination: Seventh-day Adventist
Parent company: Pacific Press Publishing
Type: weekly take-home paper, circulation 16,000
Audience: ages 2-5
Purpose: to teach about Jesus and the Christian life
Submissions: Length: 1-2 double-spaced pages. Mail complete manuscript, or email it as attached file. Seasonal seven to eight months ahead. Responds in four to six weeks. Buys fifty-two per year. Bible: ICB or NIrV.
Payment: $30-40, on acceptance
Rights: first, reprint (tell when/where published)
Type of manuscripts: true stories
Topics: Christian life, God's love, seasonal, nature, see list in guidelines
Guidelines: *ourlittlefriend.com/?page=authors*
Theme list: by mail with SASE
Sample: for 9 x 12 SAE
Tip: "We need true, age-appropriate stories that teach about the Christian life."

POCKETS

See entry in "**Daily Devotional Booklets and Websites.**"

PRIMARY TREASURE

PO Box 5353, Nampa, ID 83653
anita.seymour@pacificpress.com | www.primarytreasure.com
Anita Seymour, managing editor

Denomination: Seventh-day Adventist

Parent company: Pacific Press Publishing
Type: weekly take-home paper, circulation 14,000
Audience: ages 6-9
Purpose: to teach children about the love of God and the Christian life through true stories
Submissions: Freelance: 80%. Buys 104 per year. Mail complete manuscript, or email it as attached file. Length: 3-5 double-spaced pages. Seasonal eight months ahead. Responds in four to six weeks.
Rights: first, reprint (tell when/where published)
Payment: $40-60, on acceptance
Type of manuscripts: true stories
Topics: Christian life, seasonal, nature, see list in guidelines
Guidelines: *primarytreasure.com/?page=authors*
Theme list: by mail with SASE
Sample: for 9 x 12 SAE
Tip: "We need age-appropriate stories that teach about Jesus and the Christian life."

SHINE BRIGHTLY

1333 Alger St. S.E., Grand Rapids, MI 49507 | 616-241-5616 x2
shinebrightly@gemsgc.org | *gemsgc.org/shinebrightly*
Kelli Gilmore, managing editor, kelli@gemsgc.org

Parent company: GEMS Girls Clubs
Type: monthly (September—May) print magazine; 28 pages, circulation 13,000+
Audience: girls ages 9-12
Purpose: to equip, motivate, and inspire girls in grades 4-8 to become activists for Christ
Submissions: Unsolicited freelance: 15%. Email complete manuscript; no attachments. Buys fifteen manuscripts per year. Responds in six to eight weeks. Length: 200-800 words. Bible: NIV.
Types of manuscripts: articles, short stories, sidebars, poetry, fillers
Topics: animals, sports, music, movies, musicians, personal care, fashion, famous people, interaction with family/friends/siblings, cross-cultural experiences, international issues, service projects, dealing with schoolwork, crafts
Rights: first, reprint (tell when/where published)
Payment: 3-5¢/word up to $35, on publication, kill fee sometimes
Guidelines and theme list: *gemsgc.org/shine-brightly-writers-guideline*
Sample: $1 plus 9 x 12 SASE with three stamps, Attn: Hannah/ Sample Copy Request

Tip: "Stay away from Christianize language or Pollyanna endings. We want real stories that relate to real girls. Most of their time is spent at school, in sports, in afterschool activities, with friends, dealing with peer problems/pressure, with family, in church groups, and learning to reach out beyond their immediate world. Manuscript topics should build girls up in Christian character, but they should not be preachy. Pollyanna endings, where everything turns out perfectly, are not always realistic; and our readers want realistic stories. Our readers have a great sense of humor, so your manuscripts should be fun, as well as educational and inspirational. Stretch our readers by challenging them to new vision, new experiences, and setting new goals."

SPARKLE

1333 Alger St. S.E., Grand Rapids, MI 49507 | 616-241-5616 x2
sparkle@gemsgc.org | *gemsgc.org/sparkle-magazine*
Kelli Gilmore, managing editor, kelli@gemsgc.org

Parent company: GEMS Girls Clubs

Type: monthly (October—March) print magazine; circulation 8,000+

Audience: girls grades 1-3

Purpose: to help girls in grades 1-3 discover who God is and how He works in their lives, striving to give girls the building blocks to create a living and dynamic faith in Jesus

Submissions: Unsolicited freelance: 10%. Length: 100-400 words. Email complete manuscript, no attachments. Buys eight to ten manuscripts per year. Responds in six to eight weeks. Bible: NIV. Accepts submissions from teens.

Types of manuscripts: articles, short stories, sidebars, poetry, fillers, quizzes, puzzles, crafts

Topics: animals, activities, games, sports, music, famous people, interaction with family/friends/siblings, cross-cultural experiences, exciting service projects, and issues relating to school

Rights: first, reprint (tell when/where published)

Payment: 3-5¢/word up to $35, on publication, kill fee sometimes

Guidelines and theme list: *gemsgc.org/writers-guideline-sparkle-magazine*

Sample: $1 plus 9 x 12 SASE with three stamps, Attn: Hannah/ Sample Copy Request

Tip: "Stay away from Christianize language or Pollyanna endings. We want real stories that relate to real girls. Also make sure the wording is age appropriate for a young audience. We are looking for manuscripts that are fresh, that present a realistic look at life, and that cause young readers to see how God's Word—His Truth—applies to their daily lives. Each season, *Sparkle* dedicates its pages to the exploration of an annual theme."

ST. MARY'S MESSENGER

310 Birch St., Green River, WY 82935 | 270-325-3061
submissions@stmarysmessenger.com | *stmarysmessenger.com*
Kris Weipert, senior editor

Denomination: Catholic
Type: quarterly print magazine, 32 pages
Audience: ages 7-12
Purpose: to enlighten, entertain, and educate children about their Catholic faith
Submissions: Email or mail query for nonfiction, complete manuscript for fiction. Responds to queries in one to two weeks, to manuscripts in two to four weeks. Length: 300-900 words. Seasonal four months in advance. Accepts simultaneous submissions.
Types of manuscripts: nonfiction articles, short stories, poems, puzzles, games, activities, crafts, projects, recipes
Topics: biographies of saints, historical figures, or Catholic leaders in today's world; personal stories from kids, their families, or teachers, especially about works of mercy or helping other kids live their faith; articles about individuals who exemplify humility, Christ's love, and other virtues; articles about fun, interesting things that kids are doing; Catholic traditions in different cultures, rites, and countries; interviews or profiles of Catholics who are famous or well-known but also live their faith
Rights: first, reprint
Payment: $25-100 for article or story
Guidelines and theme list: *stmarysmessenger.com/submission-guidelines*
Tip: "We don't want every article to be explicitly religious, of course, nor do you have to be a Catholic to share your work."

9

WRITERS MARKETS

CHRISTIAN COMMUNICATOR

9118 W. Elmwood Dr., Ste. 1G, Niles, IL 60714-5820 | 847-296-3964
submissions@wordprocommunications.com | *www.ACWriters.com*
Lin Johnson, managing editor
Sally Miller, poetry editor, sallymiller@ameritech.net
samples, advertising, and subscriptions, ACWriters@aol.com

Description: To help Christian communicators improve their writing craft and speaking ability, provide practical information about the business, publishing, and freelance side of writing; keep them informed about markets; and encourage them in their ministries. Published by American Christian Writers. Bimonthly magazine, 20 pages, circulation 1,000. Subscription $29.95. Ads.

Submitting: Unsolicited freelance: 50%. Queries or complete manuscript (prefers attachment) by email only. Pays $5-10 on publication for first or reprint (tell when/where appeared) rights. Responds in eight weeks. Seasonal six months ahead. No simultaneous submissions.

Guidelines: *regaforder.wordpress.com/articles/guidelines-ad-rates*

Sample: *regaforder.wordpress.com/articles*, or send a 9 x 12 SASE with three stamps to ACW, PO Box 110390, Nashville, TN 37222

Manuscripts: How-to articles, 750-1,000 words, eighteen per year. Reviews of books on writing, publishing, and speaking, 250-350 words; query title first. Some sidebars. Prefers NIV. Poems to twenty lines on writing, publishing, and speaking only, ten per year; send maximum of two poems. Interviews with well-published, Christian authors with unique angles or with Christian editors, 750-1,000 words, six per year, query first. Anecdotes for "A Funny Thing Happened on the Way to Becoming a Communicator" humor column, 75-300 words, eighteen per year.

Tip: Greatest needs are anecdotes for the "Funny Thing Happened" column and articles on research, creativity, and writing nonfiction.

FELLOWSCRIPT

PO Box 99509, Edmonton, AB T5B 0E1, Canada
fellowscripteditor@gmail.com | *www.inscribe.org/fellowscript*
Nina Morey, editor-in-chief

Description: For, by, and about writers and writing. Quarterly newsletter, 30 pages, circulation 150-200. Subscription with InScribe membership. Ads.

Submitting: Submit complete manuscript by email. Pays 2.5¢ per word (Canadian funds) for onetime rights, 1.5¢ per word for reprint rights, extra .5¢ for publication with author's permission on the website for no more than three months. Pays by PayPal on publication. Themes listed on website.

Guidelines: *inscribe.org/fellowscript/#1464585100450-da2d1a9f-62ed*

Manuscripts: Feature articles, 750 words; columns, 300-600 words; reviews, 150-300 words; fillers/tips, 25-500 words; general articles, 700 words. Responds in four weeks. Submission deadlines are January 1, April 1, July 1, and October 1. Plans six months ahead.

Tip: "We always prefer material specifically slanted toward the needs and interests of Canadian Christian writers. We give preference to members and to Canadian writers."

FREELANCE WRITER'S REPORT

PO Box A, North Stratford, NH 03590 | 603-922-8338
submissions@writers-editors.com | *www.writers-editors.com*
Dana K. Cassell, editor

Description: To help serious, professional freelance writers—whether full-time or part-time—improve their earnings and profits from their editorial businesses. The bulk of the content is market news and marketing information—how to build a writing/editing business, how to maximize income. Monthly newsletter, 8 pages. Subscription $39.

Submitting: Freelance: 25%. Complete manuscript by email as attachment or copied into message. Pays 10¢ per word on publication for onetime rights. Responds within one week. Seasonal two months ahead. Accepts simultaneous submissions and reprints (tell when/where appeared).

Guidelines: *www.writers-editors.com/Writers/Membership/ Writer_Guidelines/writer_guidelines.htm*

Sample: *www.writers-editors.com/Writers/Membership/FWR_Online/fwr_online.htm*

Manuscripts: Articles to 900 words, 50 per year. Prose fillers to 400 words.

Tip: "No articles on the basics of freelancing since readers are established freelancers. Looking for marketing and business-building for freelance writers, editors, and book authors."

POETS & WRITERS MAGAZINE

90 Broad St., Ste. 2100, New York, NY 10004-2272 | 212-226-3586
editor@pw.org | *www.pw.org*
Melissa Faliveno, senior editor

Description: Professional trade journal for poetry, fiction, and nonfiction writers. Bimonthly magazine, circulation 100,000. Subscription $15.95. Ads.

Submitting: Query with clips via email or mail. Pays $150-500 for exclusive worldwide, periodical publication and syndication rights in all languages and nonexclusive reprint rights shared 50/50 thereafter. Pays when scheduled for production. Responds in four to six weeks. Seasonal four months ahead. Some kill fees at 25%.

Guidelines: *www.pw.org/about-us/about_poets_&_writers_magazine*

Sample: sold at large bookstores and online

Manuscripts: "News & Trends," 500-1,200 words; "The Literary Life," essays, 1,500-2,500 words; "The Practical Writer," how-to and advice, 1,500-2,500 words; profiles and interviews, 2,000-3,000 words (35 per year).

Tip: Most open to "News & Trends," "The Literary Life," and "The Practical Writer."

WORDS FOR THE WAY

5042 E. Cherry Hills Blvd., Springfield, MO 65809 | 417-812-5232
Ozarks@yahoo.com | *www.ozarksacw.org*
James Cole-Rous, managing editor
Jeanetta Chrystie, assistant acquisitions editor

Description: To encourage and educate Christians to follow their call to write and learn to write well. Published by Ozarks Chapter of American Christian Writers. Bimonthly (5x) print and digital newsletter, circulation 60. Subscription $10. Ads.

Submitting: Freelance: 95%. Buys forty-five manuscripts per year. Seasonal two months in advance. Responds in one month. Email query or complete manuscript with brief bio and photo. No payment for reprint and electronic rights. Responds in three weeks. Seasonal two months ahead.

Guidelines: *www.OzarksACW.org/guidelines.php*

Sample: email for sample

Manuscripts: Length: 300-1,000 words. All submissions must speak to writing, the writing life, how to write better, etc., including any poetry or fillers. How to write well, market your writing, blog, etc. Personal experience: writing stories that teach something about the writing life. Encouragement to follow God's call to write. Poetry, sidebars, columns, fillers. Stories only from spring contest. Any Bible version.

Tip: "Write clearly about writing. Focus on a single topic per submission. Think 'What would help or encourage Christian writers and want-to-be writers?' and write your piece to help them."

THE WRITE MARKETS REPORT

200 2nd Avenue S. #526, St. Petersburg, FL 33710 | 305-768-0261
Angela@writersweekly.com | *www.writersweekly.com*
Angela Hoy, publisher

Description: Features new and updated paying markets for writers. Published by *WritersWeekly.com*. Monthly (11x) digital magazine. Circulation 1,500.

Submitting: Freelance: 5%. Email query letter in body of the message; don't send manuscript until requested. Responds in two days. Pays $10 per market on acceptance and only via PayPal for all rights. Sometimes pays kill fee.

Manuscripts: Seeking writers to assist with researching and compiling paying markets. (See tip for details.) Length: 150 words.

Guidelines: *writersweekly.com/writersweekly-com-writers-guidelines*

Sample: *booklocker.com/books/677.html*

Tip: "Please review the sample issue and contact us if you're interested in researching and creating market listings for us. We will need to review your résumé and discuss the work with you prior to providing instructions, our questionnaire, and template. If we can work with you, we will pay $10 per market listing and all market listings must be approved by the editor or publisher of each publication featured. All markets must pay respectable fees to writers."

THE WRITER

Editorial, Madavor Media, 25 Braintree Hill Office Park, Ste. 404, Braintree, MA 02184
tweditorial@madavor.com | *www.writermag.com*
Nicki Porter, senior editor

Description: Dedicated to expanding and supporting the work of professional and aspiring writers with a straightforward presentation of industry information, writing instruction, and professional and personal motivation. Monthly magazine, 60-68 pages; circulation 30,000. Subscription $28.95. Ads.

Submitting: Unsolicited freelance: 80%. Query first with short bio. Query for features six months ahead. No reprints. Pay varies by type and department on acceptance for first rights. If no response in two weeks, probably not interested.

Guidelines: *www.writermag.com/the-magazine/submission-guidelines*

Manuscripts: Primarily looking for how-to articles on the craft of writing. Also has a variety of columns and departments: "Breakthrough," first-person articles about a writer's experience in breaking through to publication, 1,000 words; "Freelance Success," tips on the business of freelancing, 1,000 words; "Writing Essentials," basics of the craft of writing, 1,000 words plus a short sidebar of resources; "Market Focus," reports on specific market areas, 1,000 words; "Off the Cuff," essays on a particular aspect of writing or the writing life, 1,000 words; "Poet to Poet," how-to on writing poetry, 500-750 words; "Take Note," topical items of literary interest, 200-500 words; "Writer at Work," specific writing problem and how it was successfully overcome on the way to publication, 750-1,500 words. Uses some sidebars.

Tips: "Personal essays must provide takeaway advice and benefits for writers. Include plenty of how-to, advice, and tips on techniques. Be specific. All topics must relate to writing."

THE WRITER'S CHRONICLE

The Association of Writers & Writing Programs, George Mason University, MSN 1E3, 4400 University Dr., Fairfax, VA 22030-4444 | 703-993-4301

chronicle@awpwriter.org | *www.awpwriter.org/magazine_media/writers_chronicle_overview*

Supriya Bhatnagar, editor

Description: Provides diverse insights into the art of writing that are accessible, pragmatic, and idealistic for serious writers. Articles are used as teaching tools. Magazine published six times during the academic year, 96 pages, circulation 35,000. Subscription $20. Ads.

Submitting: Ninety percent unsolicited freelance. Submit only from February 1 through September 30 via website portal or mail. Pays $18 per 100 words for first and electronic rights on publication. Responds in three months. No simultaneous submissions.

Guidelines: *www.awpwriter.org/magazine_media/submission_guidelines*

Manuscripts: Interviews, 4,000-7,000 words; essays on teaching writing, 2,500-7,000 words; appreciations of contemporary writers, 2,000-5,000 words; essays on the craft of writing, 2,000 to 6,000 words; news features, 500-2,000 words; essays on careers for writers, 1,000-3,000 words. Uses some sidebars. Also buys blog posts year round for The Writer's Notebook, 500-1,500 words, $100 per post.

Tip: "Keep in mind that 18,000 of our 35,000 readers are students or just-emerging writers."

WRITER'S DIGEST

10151 Carver Rd., Ste. 200, Cincinnati, OH 45242 | 513-531-2690, ext. 11483

wdsubmissions@fwmedia.com | *www.writersdigest.com*

Jessica Stravser, editor-in-chief

Description: Celebrates the writing life and what it means to be a writer in today's publishing environment. Magazine, eight times per year, 72 pages, circulation 110,000. Print subscription $19.96. Ads.

Submitting: Unsolicited freelance, 20%; assigned, 60%. Email query or manuscript in the message or as a Microsoft Word attachment. Responds in two to four months. Pays 30-50¢ per word on acceptance for first and electronic rights.

Guidelines: *www.writersdigest.com/submission-guidelines*; theme list: *www.writersdigest.com/advertise/editorialcalendar*

Sample: available at newsstands and through *www.writersdigestshop.com*. Manuscripts: "Inkwell," opinion pieces, 800-900 words and short how-to pieces, trends, humor, 300-600 words; "5-Minute Memoir," 600-word essay reflections on the writing life; author profiles, 800-2,000 words; articles on writing techniques, 1,000-2,400 words. Seasonal eight months ahead. Requires requested manuscript by email, copied into message. Kill fee 25%. Regularly uses sidebars.

Tip: "Although we welcome the work of new writers, we believe the established writer can better instruct our readers. Please include your publishing credentials related to your topic with your submission."

WRITERSWEEKLY.COM

200 2nd Avenue S. #526, St. Petersburg, FL 33710 | 305-768-0261
Angela@writersweekly.com | *www.writersweekly.com*
Angela Hoy, publisher

Description: Features new and updated markets and articles on selling the written word (making more money through writing), as well as information on publishing and self-publishing. Published by *BookLocker.com*, Inc. Free weekly digital newsletter. Circulation 25,000.

Submitting: Freelance: 10%. Buys one hundred four per year. Email query letter in body of the message; don't send manuscript until requested. Seasonal one month in advance. Responds in two days. Simultaneous OK. Pays $40-60 on acceptance and only via PayPal for onetime rights. Always pays kill fee.

Manuscripts: Freelance success stories, features containing lists of paying markets for writers by genre (including Christian), features on how to make more money writing. Length: 400 words for freelance success stories, 600 words for features.

Guidelines: *writersweekly.com/writersweekly-com-writers-guidelines*

Sample: on website

Tip: "*WritersWeekly* is a free publication. Please read our guidelines before querying."

WRITING CORNER

410-536-4610
editor@writingcorner.com | *writingcorner.com*

Description: As a readers' and writers' community, *WritingCorner.com* is comprised of input from both those who read and those who write (and those of you who do both). Website.

Submitting: Responds in two weeks; feel free to nudge after that. Send queries and manuscripts via email only. Accepts reprints. No payment for nonexclusive rights; regular contributors get free sidebar ads on the site.

Guidelines: *writingcorner.com/main-pages/submission-guidelines*

Manuscripts: Open to how-to articles on writing fiction and nonfiction, writing life, tips and tricks, basic and advance writing techniques, 600-900 words.

Tip: "We like articles that provide concrete, useful advice from those who have been in the trenches and made a successful journey with their writing."

PART 4

SPECIALTY MARKETS

10

DAILY DEVOTIONAL BOOKLETS AND WEBSITES

Note that most of these markets assign all manuscripts. If there is no information listed on getting an assignment, request a sample copy and writers guidelines if they are not on the website. Then write two or three sample devotionals to fit that particular format, and send them to the editor with a request for an assignment.

THE BRINK

114 Bush Rd., Nashville, TN 37217 | 800-877-7030, 615-361-1221
thebrink@randallhouse.com | *www.thebrinkonline.com*
David Jones, editor

Denomination: Free Will Baptist
Parent company: Randall House
Audience: college students and young adults
Type: quarterly print
Details: Devotions are by assignment only to coordinate with the curriculum. For feature articles, such as interviews, stories, and opinion pieces, email query with 100-200-word excerpt if available. Does not respond unless interested. Rights: all.

CHRISTIANDEVOTIONS.US

PO Box 6494, Kingsport, TN 37663
christiandevotionsministries@gmail.com | *www.ChristianDevotions.us*
Cindy Sproles, executive editor

Parent company: Christian Devotions Ministries

Audience: adults
Type: daily website
Details: Accepts freelance submissions. Length: 400 words. Payment: none. Rights: one-time. Bible version: author's choice, must be referenced.
Guidelines: *www.christiandevotions.us/writeforus*
Tip: Looking for "solid application and takeaway," as well as more males submitting.

DEAF DEVO (FORMERLY DAILY DEVOTIONS FOR THE DEAF)

21199 Greenview Rd., Council Bluffs, IA 51503 | 712-322-5493
JoKrueger@deafmissions.com | *www.deafmissions.com*
Jo Krueger, editor

Audience: deaf adults, teens
Type: print, every four months; also online and app
Details: Accepts freelance submissions. Length: 200-225 words. Payment: none. Rights: one-time. Bible version: Easy-to-Read.
Tip: "Write as if writing for an ESL audience."

DEVOKIDS

renee@devokids.com | *devokids.com*
Renee McCausey, executive editor

Parent company: Christian Devotions Ministries
Audience: kids ages 7-10
Type: website
Details: Takes freelance submissions. Length: 75-250 words. Email as an attached Word document. Payment: none. Rights: onetime.
Also accepts: submissions from kids
Guidelines: *devokids.com/write-for-us*

DEVOTIONS

www.standardlesson.com/standard-lesson-resources
See *The Quiet Hour* for details.

DEVOZINE

PO Box 340004, Nashville, TN 37203-0004 | 615-340-7252
devozine@upperroom.org | *devozine.org*
Sandy Miller, editor

Parent company: Upper Room Ministries
Audience: teens, ages 14-19

Type: bimonthly print

Details: Accepts freelance submissions. Themes and deadlines are posted on the website. Length: 150-250 words. Payment: $25 ($10-15 if part of a group). Weekend feature articles: 500-600 words; pays $100; query for an assignment.

Also accepts: poetry to 20 lines, submissions from teens

Guidelines: *devozine.upperroom.org/write-for-us/writers-guidelines*

FORWARD DAY BY DAY

412 Sycamore St., Cincinnati, OH 45202-4110 | 800-543-1813
editorial@forwardmovement.org | *www.forwardmovement.org*
Richelle Thompson, managing editor

Denomination: Episcopal

Audience: adults

Type: quarterly print, online, phone app, daily podcast and email

Details: Devotions are written on assignment. To get an assignment, send three sample meditations based on three of the following Bible verses: Psalm 139:21; Mark 8:31; Acts 4:12; Revelation 1:10. Likes author to complete an entire month's worth of devotions. Length: 210 words, including Scripture. Pays $300 for a month of devotions.

Guidelines: *www.forwardmovement.org/Pages/About/Writers-Guidelines.aspx*

Tip: "Forward Day by Day is not the place to score points on controversial topics. Occasionally, when the Scripture passage pertains to it, an author chooses to say something about such a topic. If you write about a hot-button issue, do so with humility and make certain your comment shows respect for persons who hold a different view."

FRUIT OF THE VINE

211 N. Meridian St., Ste. 101, Newberg, OR 97132 | 800-962-4014
emuhr@barclaypress.com | *www.barclaypress.com*
Eric Muhr, publisher

Parent company: Barclay Press

Audience: adults

Type: quarterly print

Details: Accepts freelance submissions. Must be Quaker by membership, association, or heritage. Length: 250 words. Payment: contributor copies and subscription. Rights: onetime. Bible version: NIV.

Guidelines: *tinyurl.com/y8vwx5gj*

Tip: "Efective devotionals usually contain examples or personal experiences to illustrate their themes. Such illustrations engage the reader and allow the work to be more persuasive. Devotionals often provide new insights on familiar ideas or passages or acquaint the reader with the unfamiliar. They are Bible-centered, challenging, and encouraging."

GOD'S WORD FOR TODAY

1445 N. Boonville Ave., Springfield, MO 65802 | 417-862-2781
RL-gwft@ag.org | *ag.org/top/devotional*
Dilla Dawson, editor

Denomination: Assemblies of God
Audience: adults
Type: quarterly print, online
Details: Request writers guidelines and sample assignment (unpaid). After samples are approved, writers will be added to the list for assignments. Length: 210 words. Payment: $25/devotion. Rights: all. Bible version: NIV.
Tip: "Writers will receive detailed guidelines upon inquiry."

KEYS FOR KIDS

PO Box 1001, Grand Rapids, MI 49501-1001 | 616-647-4500
editorial@keysforkids.org | *www.keysforkids.org*
Courtney Lasater, editor

Parent company: Keys for Kids Ministries
Audience: children ages 8-12, often used for family devotions
Type: quarterly print, daily online, phone app, radio
Details: Takes only freelance submissions. Payment: $30 on acceptance. Rights: all. Length: 350-375 words, including short fiction story. Seasonal four to five months ahead. Bible version: NKJV.
Guidelines: *www.keysforkids.org/WritersGuidelines*
Tip: "Don't be afraid of down-to-earth subjects kids face today. Divorce, abuse, pornography, racism, bullying, violence, substance abuse, and peer pressure can all be handled carefully and clearly."

LIGHT FROM THE WORD

PO Box 50434, Indianapolis, IN 46250-0434 | 317-774-7900
submissions@wesleyan.org | *www.wesleyan.org/wph*
Susan LeBaron, project communications manager

Denomination: Wesleyan
Audience: adults
Type: quarterly print, daily online
Details: Email a couple of sample devotions to fit the format and request an assignment. Write "Devotion Samples" in the subject line. Length: 225 words. Payment: $200 for seven devotions. Rights: all. Bible version: NIV '84.
Tip: Wesleyan writers only.

MUSTARD SEED MINISTRIES DEVOTIONALS

4854 W 350S, Berne, IN 46711 | 260-849-0549
msm.bob@live.com | *mustardseedministries.org*
Jan, editor

Audience: adults, teens
Type: weekly website
Details: Accepts freelance submissions through the website. See samples there. Length: 400 words. Payment: none. Accepts reprints.
Tip: "We accept all types of devotions. Each should relate to a personal story."

PATHWAYS TO GOD

2902 Enterprise Dr., Anderson, IN 46012 | 800-741-7721
editors@warnerpress.org | *www.warnerpress.org*
Karen Rhodes, editorial director of church and ministry resources

Denomination: Church of God
Audience: adults
Type: quarterly print
Details: Written on assignment only. To be considered as a writer, submit a sample devotional. Length: 140–150 words and should give readers living examples of what the Bible passage is about and how it can apply to life.
Guidelines: *www.warnerpress.org/submission-guidelines*

POCKETS

PO Box 340004, Nashville, TN 37203-0004 | 615-340-7252
pockets@upperroom.org | *pockets.upperroom.org*
Lynn W. Gilliam, editor

Parent company: Upper Room Ministries
Audience: children ages 6-12

Type: monthly print (except February)

Details: Primarily accepts unsolicited freelance manuscripts, only via mail. See the theme list and deadlines on the website. Payment on acceptance. Bible version: NRSV.

Types of manuscripts: Fiction and Scripture stories that can help children deal with real-life situations, 600-1,000 words, pays 14 cents/word. Poems, 16 lines maximum, pays $25 and up. Articles about children involved in environmental, community, and peace/justice issues, 400-1,000 words, pays 14 cents/word. Activities, puzzles, games, recipes: pays $25 and up.

Also accepts: submissions from children through age 12

Guidelines: *pockets.upperroom.org/write-for-us*

Tip: "We do not accept stories about talking animals or inanimate objects. Fictional characters and some elaboration may be included in Scripture stories, but the writer must remain faithful to the story."

THE QUIET HOUR

4050 Lee Vance Dr., Colorado Springs, CO 80918
thequiethour@davidccook.com | *www.davidccook.org*
Scott Stewart, editor

Parent company: David C. Cook

Audience: adults

Type: quarterly print

Details: By assignment only. North America postal address is necessary to receive contract and payment. Length: 200 words. Payment: $140 for seven devotionals. Rights: all. Bible version: NIV, KJV.

Tip: "Submit spec devotional on a key verse you select in a Scripture passage of your choice. Begin with anecdotal opening then transition to relevant biblical insight and encouragement for a life of faith rooted in the key verse."

REFLECTING GOD

PO Box 419527, Kansas City, MO 64141 | 816-931-1900
dcbrush@wordaction.com | *reflectinggod.com*
Duane Brush, editor

Denomination: Nazarene

Audience: adults

Type: quarterly print, online

Details: Send a couple of sample devotions to fit the format and request an assignment. Length: 180-200 words. Pays $115 for seven devotions.

Tip: "Our purpose is the pursuit to embrace holy living. We want to foster discussion about what it means to live a holy life in the 21st century."

THE SECRET PLACE

PO Box 851, Valley Forge, PA 19482-0851 | 800-458-3766
thesecretplace@abc-usa.org | *www.judsonpress.com*
Ingrid and Wayne Dvirnak, editors

Denomination: American Baptist
Audience: adults
Type: quarterly print, online
Details: Accepts freelance submissions; does not give assignments. Length: 150-200 words. Payment: $20 per published submission. Rights: first. Bible version: NRSV.
Also accepts: poems of 30 lines or fewer, $20 per poem
Tip: Use less-familiar Scriptures.

TAKE FIVE PLUS

1445 N. Boonville Ave., Springfield, MO 65802 | 417-862-2781
rl-take5plus@ag.org | *myhealthychurch.com*
Dilla Dawson, editor

Denomination: Assemblies of God
Audience: teens
Type: quarterly print
Details: Assignment only. Request writers guidelines and sample assignment (unpaid). After samples are approved, writers will be added to the list for assignments. Length: 210-235 words. Payment: $25 per devotion. Rights: all. Bible version: NIV.
Tip: "Writers will receive detailed guidelines upon inquiry."

THESE DAYS: DAILY DEVOTIONS FOR LIVING BY FAITH

100 Witherspoon St., Louisville, KY 40202 | 800-624-2412
beth@bethgaede.com | *www.ppcbooks.com/thesedays.asp*
Beth Gaede, editor

Denomination: Presbyterian Church (USA)
Audience: adults
Type: quarterly print
Details: Accepts freelance submissions. Length: 190 words. Payment:

$100 or $150 worth of books for seven devotions. Rights: first. Bible version: NRSV.

Tip: "Write thoughtful entries based on a Scripture passage, use gender-inclusive language for God and humanity, and include a brief closing prayer."

THE UPPER ROOM

1908 Grand Ave., Nashville, TN 37212 | 615-340-7252
ureditorial@upperroom.org | *upperroom.org*
Lindsay L. Gray, editorial director

Denomination: United Methodist
Audience: adults
Type: bimonthly print, daily online
Details: Accepts freelance submissions. Length: 300 words, which include everything on the printed page. Payment: $30. Rights: first, exclusive for one year. Bible versions: NIV, NRSV, CEB, KJV.
Guidelines: *submissions.upperroom.org/guidelines?locale=en*
Tip: "A strong devotional will include three main elements: 1. A personal story or experience. 2. A connection to Scripture. 3. A way for the reader to apply the message to his or her own life."

THE WORD IN SEASON

PO Box 1209, Minneapolis, MN 55440-4648 | 800-328-4648
rochelle@writenowcoach.com | *www.augsburgfortress.org*
Rochelle Melander, managing editor

Denomination: Evangelical Lutheran Church in America
Audience: adults
Type: quarterly print
Details: Assignment only. Request guidelines, and write trial devotions. Length: 200 words. Payment: $20 per devotion. Rights: all. Bible version: NRSV.
Tip: "Submit samples via guidelines. ELCA theological background is essential."

11

DRAMA

CHRISTIAN PUBLISHERS, LLC

PO Box 248, Cedar Rapids, Iowa 52406 | 844-841-6387
editor@christianpub.com | *www.christianpub.com*
Rhonda Wray, editor

Audiences: children, teens, adults

Details: Always looking for Christmas and Easter plays. Also publishes drama-related books, liturgies, and banners. Submit complete play, preferably through the website form or as an email attachment.

Types: full-length plays and musicals, one-act plays and musicals, dinner theater, children's programs and liturgies, liturgical dance programs, and banner liturgies

Guidelines: *www.christianpub.com/default.aspx?pg=ag*

Tip: "Please, be patient with response times. Although we try to respond within a short time, response times vary according to the time of the year. Just remember, we will give your script individual attention; and we don't want to rush the process."

CSS PUBLISHING GROUP, INC.

See entry in "**Book Publishers.**"

DOVE CHRISTIAN PUBLISHERS

See entry in "**Book Publishers.**"

DRAMA MINISTRY

2814 Azalea Pl., Nashville, TN 37204 | 866-859-7622
service@dramaministry.com | *www.dramaministry.com*
Vince Wilcox, general manager

Audiences: children, teens, adults

Details: Open to all topics, including seasonal/holidays. Email or mail script. Buys all rights.

Types: only short skits of 2-10 minutes, comedy, drama, monologue, readers theater

ELDRIDGE PUBLISHING CO., INC.

PO Box 4904, Lancaster, PA 17604 | 850-385-2463
newworks@histage.com | *www.95church.com*
Susan Shore, editor

Audiences: children, teens, adults

Details: Publishes fifteen to thirty scripts per year; receives three hundred submissions annually. Length: minimum 30 minutes. Submit complete script via email. Simultaneous OK. Responds in three months.

Types: full-length plays, one-act plays, compilations of skits, musicals, readers theater

Payment: royalty, no advance

Guidelines: *www.95church.com/Content/Files/95Church_guidelines.pdf*

Tip: Review the guidelines before submitting.

EMPOWERED PUBLICATIONS, INC.

529 County Road 31, Millry, AL 36558 | 251-754-9335
editor@empoweredpublicationsinc.com
www.empoweredpublicationsinc.com

Audiences: adult, young adult, children

Details: Must be conservative in nature and agree with our Statement of Faith. Email or mail proposal and estimated date of completion.

Submissions: holiday oriented or everyday occasion. Types: musicals, comedies, and dramas for both small and large casts.

GROUP PUBLISHING

See entry in "**Book Publishers**."

12

GREETING CARDS AND GIFTS

BLUE MOUNTAIN ARTS

Editorial Dept., PO Box 1007, Boulder, CO 80306 | 303-449-0536
editorial@sps.com | *www.sps.com*

Audience: adults

Products: general card publisher with some inspirational cards

Submissions: Looking for original, fresh, creative submissions on love, friendship, family, philosophies, and any other topic that one person might want to share with another. No rhyming poetry, overtly religious verse, one-liners, or humor. Submit by email (no attachments) or mail to Editorial Department. Responds in two to four months if interested. Holiday deadlines: Christmas and general holiday, July 15; Valentine's Day, September 12; Easter, November 8; Mother's Day, December 13; Father's Day, February 7.

Guidelines: *www.sps.com/help/writers_guidelines.html*

Payment: $300 per poem for worldwide, exclusive rights to publish it on a greeting card and other products; $50 per poem for one-time use in a book.

DESIGNER GREETINGS

11 Executive Ave., Edison, NJ 08817 | 732-662-6700
info@designergreetings.com | *www.designergreetings.com*

Audience: children, teens, adults

Products: general card company that does some religious cards for all occasions and holidays

Submissions: Rhyming verse and prose. Mail only, on index cards or full-size paper, to Editorial Department.

Guidelines: on the website under "Opportunities"

DICKSONS, INC.

709 B Ave E, Seymour, IN 47274 | 812-522-1308
submissions@dicksonsgifts.com | *www.dicksonsgifts.com*

Audience: adults
Products: figurines, crosses, wall decor, mugs, flags
Submissions: Two to eight lines, maximum sixteen, suitable for plaques, bookmarks, etc. Email submission. Responds in three months. Subjects can cover any gift-giving occasion and Christian, inspirational, and everyday social-expression topics. Phrases or acrostics of one or two lines for bumper stickers are also considered. Buys reprint rights.
Guidelines: *www.dicksonsgifts.com/t-contact.aspx*
Payment: royalty, negotiable
Tip: Looking for religious verses.

ELLIE CLAIRE

6100 Tower Cir., Ste. 210, Franklin, TN 37013 | 615-932-7600
marilynj@worthypublishing.com | *www.worthypublishing.com*
Marilyn Jansen, editorial director

Parent company: Worthy Publishing
Audience: adults
Products: gifts, journals, devotionals, gift books
Submissions: Email submissions. Also makes assignments. To be considered for an assignment, email letter, résumé, three full samples of devotional writing. Buys all rights.
Guidelines: by email
Payment: flat fee, royalty; $30-40 per devotion
Tips: "Please do not send unsolicited manuscripts or samples. Contact us first with an introduction and elevator pitch. If we are interested, we will ask for more. We operate in the gift market, and the writing will need to reflect that. We are not interested in Bible studies but in inspirational and encouraging devotions, funny stories with a spiritual component, and compilations from a Christian worldview."

GALLANT GREETINGS

5730 N. Tripp Ave., Chicago, IL 60646 | 800-621-4279, 847-671-6500
info@gallantgreetings.com | *gallantgreetings.com*

Audience: adults
Products: general card company with a religious line, "Seasons of Grace"

Submissions: Not accepting verse submissions at this time, but check the website for changes in this situation.

WARNER PRESS

2902 Enterprise Dr., Anderson, IN 46012 | 800-741-7721
editors@warnerpress.org | *www.warnerpress.org*
Karen Rhodes, editorial director of church and ministry resources

Denomination: Church of God
Audience: children, adults
Products: boxed everyday and Christmas cards
Submissions: Most accepted verses average four lines in length. Themes include birthday, anniversary, baby congratulations, sympathy, get well, kid's birthday and get well, thinking of you, friendship, Christmas, praying for you, encouragement. Use a conversational tone with no lofty poetic language, such as *thee, thou, art*. Responds in six to eight weeks. Email or mail with SASE. Buys all rights. Deadines: everyday, July 31; Christmas, October 1.
Guidelines: *www.warnerpress.org/submission-guidelines*

13

TRACTS

The following companies publish Gospel tracts but do not have writers guidelines. If you are interested in writing for them, email or phone to find out if they currently are looking for submissions. Also check your denominational publishing house to see if it publishes tracts.

CHRISTIAN LIGHT PUBLICATIONS

PO Box 1212, Harrisonburg, VA 22803-1212 | 800-776-0478
info@clp.org | *www.clp.org*

FELLOWSHIP TRACT LEAGUE

PO Box 164, Lebanon, Ohio 45036 | 513-494-1075
mail@fellowshiptractleague.org | *www.fellowshiptractleague.org*

GOOD NEWS PUBLISHERS

1300 Crescent St., Wheaton, IL 60187 | 630-682-4300
info@crossway.org | *www.crossway.org*

GOSPEL PUBLISHING HOUSE

1445 N. Boonville Ave., Springfield, MO 65802 | 800-641-4310
newproducts@gph.org | *gospelpublishing.com*

GOSPEL TRACT SOCIETY

PO Box 1118, Independence, MO 64051 | 816-461-6086
gospeltractsociety@gmail.com | *gospeltractsociety.org*

GRACE VISION PUBLISHERS

321-745-9966 (text only)
email through the website | *www.gracevision.com*

MOMENTS WITH THE BOOK
PO Box 322, Bedford, PA 15522 | 814-623-8737
email through the website | *mwtb.org*

TRACT ASSOCIATION OF FRIENDS
1501 Cherry St., Philadelphia, PA 19102
info@tractassociation.org | *www.tractassociation.org*

THE TRACT LEAGUE
2627 Elmridge Dr., Grand Rapids, MI 49534-1329 | 616-453-7695
info@tractleague.com | *tractleague.com*

14

BIBLE CURRICULUM

This list includes only the major, nondenominational curriculum publishers. If you are in a denominational church, also check its publishing house for curriculum products. Plus some organizations, like Awana Clubs International and Pioneer Clubs, also produce curriculum for their programs.

Since Bible curriculum is written on assignment only, you'll need to get samples for age groups you want to write for (from the company's website, large Christian bookstores, or your church) and study the formats and pieces. Look for editors' names on the copyright pages of teachers manuals, or call the publishing house for this information.

Then write query letters to specific editors. Tell why you're qualified to write curriculum for them, include a sample of curriculum you've written or other sample of your writing, and ask for a trial assignment. Since the need for writers varies widely, you may not get an assignment for a year or more.

Some of these companies also publish undated, elective curriculum books that are used in a variety of ministries. Plus some book publishers publish lines of Bible-study guides. (See "**Book Publishers**.") These are contracted like other books with a proposal and sample chapters.

A BEKA BOOKS

PO Box 17900, Pensacola, FL 32522-7900 | 877-356-9385
www.joyfullifesundayschool.com

Type: Sunday school
Imprint: Joyful Life

DAVID C . COOK

4050 Lee Vance Dr., Colorado Springs, CO 80918 | 800-708-5550
shop.davidccook.org

Types: Sunday school, vacation Bible school
Imprints: Accent, Action Bible, Bible-in-Life, David C. Cook, Echoes, Encounter, Gospel Light, HeartShaper, RIO, Scripture Press, Standard Lesson, Tru, and some denominational imprints

GROUP PUBLISHING

1515 Cascade Ave., Loveland, CO 80538 | 970-669-3836
PuorgBus@group.com | *www.group.com*

Types: Sunday school, vacation Bible school, children's worship
Imprints: Buzz, Dig In, FaithWeaver NOW, Grapple, Hands-On Bible, Play-n-Worship, Kids Own Worship
Guidelines: *grouppublishingps.zendesk.com/hc/en-us/articles/211878258-Submissions*

UNION GOSPEL PRESS

PO Box 6059, Cleveland, OH 44101 | 800-638-9988
editorial@uniongospelpress.com | *uniongospelpress.com*

Type: Sunday school
Guidelines: *uniongospelpress.com/index.php/prospective-writers*

URBAN MINISTRIES, INC.

1551 Regency Ct., Calumet City, IL 60409-5448 | 800-860-8642
urbanministries.com

Types: Sunday school, vacation Bible school

15

MISCELLANEOUS

These companies publish a variety of books and other products that fall into the specialty-markets category, such as puzzle books, game books, children's activity books, craft books, charts, church bulletins, and coloring books.

BARBOUR PUBLISHING

See entry in "**Book Publishers.**"

BROADSTREET PUBLISHING

See entry in "**Book Publishers.**"

CARSON-DELLOSA PUBLISHING GROUP

PO Box 35665, Greensboro, NC 27425-5665 | 800-321-0943
freelancesamples@carsondellosa.com | *www.carsondellosa.com*

Types: books with puzzles, activities, games, and children's worship bulletins; charts

Submissions: No unsolicited queries or manuscripts. To become an independent contractor, email or mail samples and a résumé. If you have samples from supplemental education materials, send those; however, they will accept all types of samples.

Guidelines: *www.carsondellosa.com/customer-service/freelance-opportunities*

CHRISTIAN FOCUS PUBLICATIONS

See entry in "**Book Publishers.**"

DAVID C . COOK

shop.davidccook.org
See entry in "**Book Publishers.**"

GROUP PUBLISHING

See entry in "**Book Publishers.**"

ROSE PUBLISHING

See entry in "**Book Publishers.**"

WARNER PRESS

2902 Enterprise Dr., Anderson, IN 46012 | 800-741-7721
editors@warnerpress.org | *www.warnerpress.org*
Karen Rhodes, editorial director of church and ministry resources

Denomination: Church of God

Church bulletins: Short devotionals that tie into a visual image and incorporate a Bible verse. Especially interested in material for holidays and special Sundays, such as Christmas, New Year's Day, Palm Sunday, Easter, Pentecost, and Communion. General themes are also welcome. Length: 250 words maximum. Deadline: April 30. Buys all rights. Payment varies.

Children's coloring and activity books: Most activity books focus on a Bible story or biblical theme, such as love and forgiveness. Ages range from preschool (ages 2-5) to upper elementary (ages 8-10). Include activities and puzzles in every upper-elementary book. Coloring-book manuscripts should present a picture idea and a portion of the story for each page. Deadlines: May 1 and October 1. Payment varies.

Guidelines: *www.warnerpress.org/submission-guidelines*

PART 5

SUPPORT FOR WRITERS

16

LITERARY AGENTS

Asking editors and other writers is a great way to find a reliable agent. You may also want to visit *www.sfwa.org/other-resources/for-authors/writer-beware/agents* for tips on avoiding questionable agents and choosing reputable ones.

The general market has an Association of Authors' Representatives (*www.aaronline.org*), also known as AAR. To be a member the agent must agree to a code of ethics. Their web site has a list of agents who don't charge fees, except for office expenses. The site also provides information on how to receive a list of approved agents. Some listings below indicate which agents belong to the AAR. Lack of such a designation, however, does not indicate the agent is unethical; most Christian agents are not members.

ALIVE LITERARY AGENCY

7680 Goddard St., Ste. 200, Colorado Springs, CO 80920

719-260-7080

submissions@aliveliterary.com | *www.aliveliterary.com*

Agents: Rick Christian, Bryan Norman, Lisa Jackson, Andrea Heinecke

Agency: Well-known in the industry. Established in 1989. Represents more than 125 clients. Member of Association of Authors' Representatives.

Types of books: adult novels, nonfiction, crossover, juvenile

New clients: Only taking proposals from authors who are personally referred by clients or close contacts of Alive. Contact by email. Responds in six to eight weeks to referrals only; may not respond to unsolicited submissions.

Commission: 15%

Fees: only extraordinary costs with client's preapproval

AMBASSADOR AGENCY

PO Box 50358, Nashville, TN 37205 | 615-370-4700
info@AmbassadorAgency.com | *www.AmbassadorAgency.com*

Agent: Wes Yoder, *wes@AmbassadorSpeakers.com*
Agency: Established in 1973. Represents twenty-five to thirty clients.
New clients: Open to unpublished book authors. Contact by email. Responds in four to six weeks.
Types of books: adult nonfiction and fiction, crossover books, no sci-fi or medical
Commission: 15%
Fees: none

BANNER SERVICES, LLC

PO Box 1828, Winter Park, CO 80482
mike@mikeloomis.co | *www.mikeloomis.co*

Agent: Mike Loomis
Agency: Established in 2009. Represents twelve clients.
Types of books: Christian nonfiction, business nonfiction, crossover
New clients: Open to new authors, specializing in unpublished book authors. Contact through the website with book synopsis and your website url. Responds in four weeks.
Commission: 15%
Fees: none for representation
Tip: Especially open to new/aspiring authors.

THE BINDERY

Colorado Springs, CO 80920
Info@thebinderyagency.com | *www.TheBinderyAgency.com*

Agent: Alexander Field
Agency: Established in 2017. Represents twenty-five clients.
Types of books: Christian living, spiritual formation, discipleship, theology, ministry and church leadership, and more
New clients: Open to writers who have not published a book, well-established book writers, self-published writers, and writers met at conferences. Initial contact: email, proposal, referral from current client. Accepts simultaneous submissions. Responds in eight to ten weeks.
Commission: 15%
Fees: none
Tip: "Platform is important, but your content is still king. Write a

great book, or book proposal, and build from there. Keep your query concise."

THE BLYTHE DANIEL AGENCY, INC.

PO Box 64197, Colorado Springs, CO 80962-4197 | 719-213-3427
submissions@theblythedanielagency.com | *www.theblythedanielagency.com*

Agent: Blythe Daniel, *blythe@theblythedanielagency.com*; Stephanie Alton, blog content manager, *stephanie@theblythedanielagency.com*

Agency: Established in 2005. Represents seventy clients. Sells to general market too.

Also does: publicity and blog campaigns; see listing in "Publicity and Marketing Services" chapter

Types of books: Christian life, spiritual growth, current events, inspirational/narrative nonfiction, business/leadership, church leadership, marriage, parenting, apologetics, social issues, women's issues, cooking, gift books, devotionals, children's

New clients: Open to unpublished book authors, previously published authors, self-published writers, writers meet at conferences, referrals from clients. Contact: email, referral from current client. Send proposal and three sample chapters. Accepts simultaneous submissions. Responds in two to three months.

Commission: 15%

Fees: none

Tip: "We are not acquiring fiction, poetry, or short stories. We are reviewing a limited number of Bible studies and devotionals that have a unique twist. Writers need to have a platform that spans a readership online. Tell me in a short pitch what your book is about, who the book is for, and how you are connected to the audience. I want to see how you are building your audience, even if it is small. Show me what you have built and what you have done, not what you are planning to do. I want to see that you have already started this process (i.e. gaining new subscribers, building your email list, social media, blogs). You need a distinguishable book hook that stands out from the same topic in other books. I need to see how you have developed your concept in a way that makes me say, 'I haven't heard anyone say it like that before.'"

BOOKS & SUCH LITERARY MANAGEMENT

52 Mission Cir., Ste. 122, PMB 170, Santa Rosa, CA 95409-5370
representation@booksandsuch.com | *www.booksandsuch.com*

Agents: Janet Kobobel Grant, Wendy Lawton, Rachelle Gardner, Rachel Kent, Cynthia Ruchti

Agency: Established in 1996. Represents 250 clients.

Types of books: adult fiction and nonfiction, some children's and YA. No poetry, academic books, or speculative adult fiction.

New clients: Open to writers who have not published a book, well-established book writers, and self-published writers. Contact by email with query first. Accepts simultaneous submissions. Responds in six to eight weeks if interested.

Commission: 15%

Fees: none

Tip: "Provide clear and compelling details about your project in your query. We read each query we receive and forward to the agent most likely to be interested in your project if it seems to be a good fit for our agency."

CHRISTIAN LITERARY AGENT

PO Box 428, Newburg, PA 17240 | 717-423-6621

keith@christianliteraryagent.com | *www.christianliteraryagent.com*

Agent: Keith Carroll

Agency: Established in 2010. Represents sixty-three clients.

Also does: writer coaching

Types of books: Christian, inspirational

Specialty: nonfiction

New clients: Open to new book authors, self-published writers, and writers who have a strong desire to break into the larger market. Initial contact: email, phone, website form, referral from current client. Responds in three to four weeks. Accepts simultaneous submissions.

Commission: 10%

Fees: $90 for admin costs

CREDO COMMUNICATIONS

3148 Plainfield Ave. N.E., Ste. 111, Grand Rapids, MI 49525

616-363-2686

connect@credocommunications.net | *www.credocommunications.net*

Agents: Timothy J. Beals, *tim@credocommunications.net*; Drew Chamberlin, *drew@credocommunicatons.net*; Karen Neumair, *karen@credocommunications.net*

Agency: Established in 2005. Represents seventy clients.

Also offers: editorial services for nonclients and coaching for self-published authors on design, typesetting, production, printing, marketing, sales, and distribution

Types of books: nonfiction, children's

New clients: By referral only from current client or publishing professional. Email proposal. Accepts simultaneous submissions. Responds in one month.

Commission: 15%

Fees: none

CURTIS BROWN, LTD.

10 Astor Pl., New York, NY 10003-6935| 212-473-5400
info@cbltd.com | *www.curtisbrown.com*

Agent: Laura Blake Peterson, *lbp@cbltd.com*

Agency: Member of Association of Authors' Representatives. General agency that handles some religious/inspirational books.

Types of books: fiction, nonfiction, children's

New clients: Query via email or mail with SASE. See the website for requirements with query. Responds in three to four weeks.

Fees: photocopying and some postage

D. C. JACOBSON & ASSOCIATES

PO Box 80945, Portland, OR 97280 | 503-850-4800
submissions@dcjacobson.com | *www.dcjacobson.com*

Agents: Don Jacobson, Jenni Burke, Tawny Johnson, Blair Jacobson

Agency: Established in 2006. Represents more than 100 clients. Don is the former owner of Multnomah Publishers.

Types of books: adult fiction and nonfiction, children's

New clients: Open to unpublished and self-published book authors. Email submissions and queries; no mail submissions. Responds in two months.

Commission: 15%

Fees: none

Tip: "Please review our submission guidelines at *dcjacobson.com/submissions*."

DANIEL LITERARY GROUP

601 Old Hickory Blvd. #56, Brentwood, TN 37027 | 615-730-8207
submissions@danielliterarygroup.com | *www.danielliterarygroup.com*

Agent: Greg Daniel, *greg@danielliterarygroup.com*

Agency: Established in 2007. Represents forty clients.

Types of books: nonfiction of all types
New clients: Open to new clients who have not published books. Contact by email; query first. Accepts simultaneous submissions. Responds in three to four weeks.
Commission: 15%
Fees: none
Tip: "Research the agency first before submitting, to be sure your project is appropriate for us."

FINE PRINT LITERARY MANAGEMENT

115 W. 29th St., 3rd Fl., New York, NY 10001 | 212-279-1282
peter@fineprintlit.com | *www.fineprintlit.com*

Agent: Peter Rubie
Agency: General agency that handles some spirituality books.
Types: adult fiction and nonfiction, some middle grade and YA fiction
New clients: Open to unpublished authors. Email query.
Commission: 15%

GARY D. FOSTER CONSULTING

733 Virginia Ave., Van Wert, OH 45891 | 419-238-4082
gary@garydfoster.com | *www.garydfoster.com*

Agent: Gary Foster
Agency: Established in 1989. Represents more than thirty clients.
Types of books: mostly adult nonfiction books, occasionally novels
New clients: Open to unpublished, well-established, and self-published authors. Email query or proposal. Accepts simultaneous submissions. Responds in three to ten days.
Commission: 15%
Fees: nominal initial fee
Tip: "No matter how excellent and timely an author's work, a strong platform is critical as well."

HARTLINE LITERARY AGENCY

123 Queenston Dr., Pittsburgh, PA 15235 | 412 -829-2483
jim@hartlineliterary.com | *www.hartlineliterary.com*

Agents: Jim Hart, *jim@hartlineliterary.com*; Joyce A. Hart, *joyce@hartlineliterary.com*; Cyle Young, *cyle@hartlineliterary.com*; Diana Flegal, *diana@hartlineliterary.com*; Linda Glaz, *linda@hartlineliterary.com*
Agency: Established in 1992. Represents 250 clients.

Types of books: Christian living, family, social issues, prayer, leadership, narrative nonfiction, romance, Amish, romantic suspense, thriller, suspense, women's fiction, speculative, sci-fi, YA, children's

New clients: Open to published authors, new authors, authors we meet at conferences. Initial contact: email, full proposal, referral from current client. Responds in four to six weeks.

Commission: 15%

Fees: none

Tips "Please look at our website before submitting. Guidelines are listed, along with detailed information about each agent. Be sure to include your biography and publishing history with your proposal. The author-agent relationship is a team effort. Working together we can make sure your manuscript gets the exposure and attention it deserves."

HIDDEN VALUE GROUP, LLC

27758 Santa Margarita Pkwy. #361, Mission Viejo, CA 92691
bookquery@hiddenvaluegroup.com | *www.HiddenValueGroup.com*

Agent: Nancy Jernigan, *njerigan@hiddenvaluegroup.com*

Agency: Established in 2001.

Also does: coaching

Types of books: family, marriage, parenting, fiction, inspirational, self-help, business, women's and men's issues

New clients: Open to previously published authors only, not including self-publishing. Mail or email proposal with two or three chapters. Responds in four to six weeks.

Commission: 15%

Fees: none

Tip: "Include how you will help support the marketing of your project. Include all social-media numbers; social-media platforms; radio, print, and TV marketing."

K J LITERARY SERVICES, LLC

1540 Margaret Ave., Grand Rapids, MI 49507 | 616-551-9797
kim@kjliteraryservices.com | *www.kjliteraryservices.com*

Agent: Kim Zeilstra

Agency: Established in 2006.

Also does: editing, proofreading, project management, permissions

New clients: Only taking new authors by referral at this time. Initial contact by email or phone.

Commission: 15%

KATHI J. PATON LITERARY AGENCY

PO Box 2236, Radio City Station, New York, NY 10101-2236
212-265-6586
KJPLitBiz@optonline.net | *www.PatonLiterary.com*

Agent: Kathi Paton
Agency: Established in 1987.
Also does: editing
Types of books: Christian life and issues
New clients: Email query only.
Commission: 15%

KIRKLAND MEDIA MANAGEMENT

PO Box 1539, Liberty, TX 77575 | 936-581-3944
admin@kirklandmediamanagment.com |
www.KirklandMediaManagement.com

Agent: Jessica Kirkland
Types of books: fiction, nonfiction, film contracts in the inspirational market; no children's, short stories, or poetry
New clients: Email query only. Guidelines on the web site.
Commission: 15%

THE KNIGHT AGENCY

232 W. Washington St., Madison, GA 30650 | 706 473-0994
pamela.harty@knightagency.net | *knightagency.net*

Agent: Pamela Harty
Agency: Established in 1996. Member of Association of Authors' Representatives. Agency represents 330 authors.
Types of books: Christian living
New clients: Open to writers who have not published a book, well-established book writers, and self-published writers. Initial contact by email. Responds in six weeks.
Commission: 15%
Fees: none
Tip: "Please visit our website for submission guidelines."

LITERARY MANAGEMENT GROUP, LLC

PO Box 41004, Nashville, TN 37204 | 615-812-4445
brucebarbour@literarymanagementgroup.com
www.literarymanagementgroup.com

Agent: Bruce R. Barbour
Agency: Established in 1996. Represents more than 100 clients.

Also does: book packaging, publishing consulting
Type of books: adult nonfiction
New clients: No unpublished authors. Email proposal. Accepts simultaneous submissions. Responds in three to four weeks.
Commission: 15%
Fees: none

MACGREGOR LITERARY, INC.

PO Box 1316, Manzanita, OR 97130 | 503-389-4803
chip@macgregorliterary.com | *www.MacGregorLiterary.com*

Agents: Chip MacGregor; Amanda Luedeke, *amanda@macgregorliterary.com*
Agency: Established in 2006. Member of Association of Authors' Representatives. Represents sixty clients.
Types of books: wide variety of nonfiction and select list of novelists
Specialty: memoir, Christian living
New clients: Open to writers with an established platform and a solid book idea. Initial contact: website form, referral from current client, query first. Accepts simultaneous submissions. Responds in one month.
Commission: 15%
Fees: none
Tip: "A well-written proposal and sample chapters is the best way to gain our attention. We're always looking for fresh ideas expressed through great writing, from authors with a proven platform."

MARK SWEENEY & ASSOCIATES

7900 Arlington Cir., Ste. 509, Naples, FL 34113 | 239-775-0044
sweeney2@comcast.net

Agents: Mark Sweeney, Janet Sweeney
Agency: Established in 2003. Represents seventy to eighty clients.
Types of books: nonfiction narrative, personal experience, apologetics, missional/biblical issues, leadership, cultural discussion, celebrity communicators, academic
Specialty: nonfiction narrative
New clients: Open to gifted communicators who are referrals from current clients. Contact by email. Query first. Accepts simultaneous submissions. Responds in one day.
Commission: 15%
Fees: none
Also does: publishing consulting

Tip: Looking for "authors seeking quality representation with relational emphasis."

NAPPALAND LITERARY AGENCY

446 E. 29th St. #1674, Loveland, CO 80539
literary@nappaland.com | *www.nappalandliterary.com*

Agent: Mike Nappa

Agency: Division of Nappaland Communications, Inc. Established in 1995. Represents twelve clients.

Types of books: literary fiction, suspense, YA fiction, literary nonfiction, history, leadership, family and parenting, pop culture, humor

New clients: Only if recommended by an existing Nappaland writer or editor. Query letter only by email. Accepts simultaneous submissions. Unsolicited submissions are automatically rejected unless sent during March 1—May 30. If interested in seeing more, he will contact you.

Commission: 15%

Fees: none

Tip: "Books by Nappaland authors must be relevant to modern American culture, to actual readers, and to the multitude of influences and concerns that define our current society."

NATASHA KERN LITERARY AGENCY, INC.

PO Box 1069, White Salmon, WA 98672
agent@natashakern.com | *www.natashakernliterary.com*

Agent: Natasha Kern

Agency: Established in 1987. Represents thirty-six religious clients.

New clients: Closed to queries from unpublished writers. Open to meeting with writers at conferences and accepting referrals from current clients and editors. Cannot read unsolicited queries or proposals.

SALLY APOKEDAK LITERARY AGENT

5252 Barrett Pkwy. #39, Marietta, GA 30064 | 678-744-7745
submissions@sally-apokedak.com | *sally-apokedak.com*

Agent: Sally Apokedak, *sally@sally-apokedak.com*

Agency: Previously with the Leslie H. Stobbe Literary Agency. Focuses on children and YA.

Also does: online courses, editing, consulting, critiquing, websites

Types of books: most interested in middle grade and YA

New clients: Open to writers whom she met at a conference, who have taken an online course from her, or who have been referred by a friend or current client. Contact with email query and proposal with full manuscript for fiction, first three chapters for nonfiction, or full picture book.

Commission: 15%

SERENDIPITY LITERARY AGENCY, LLC

1633 Broadway, New York, NY 10019
nadeen@serendipitylit.com | *www.serendipitylit.com*

Agent: Nadeen Gayle

Agency: Member of Association of Authors' Representatives. Established in 2000. General agency that handles some religious books.

Types of books: inspirational/religious nonfiction

New clients: Initial contact through website form. Accepts simultaneous submissions. Responds in four to six weeks.

Commission: 15%

Fees: none

THE SEYMOUR AGENCY

475 Miner Street Rd., Canton, NY 13617 | 239-398-8209
nicole@theseymouragency.com | *www.theseymouragency.com*

Agents: Nichole Resciniti; Julie Gwinn, *julie@theseymouragency.com*; Lizzie Poteet, *lizzie@theseymouragency.com*

Agency: Established in 1992. Member of Association of Authors' Representatives.

Types of books: inspirational, YA, middle grade, picture books, mysteries, thrillers, romance, science fiction, fantasy, women's fiction, literary fiction, historical fiction, speculative fiction, assorted nonfiction

New clients: Open to writers who have not published a book, well-established book writers, self-published writers, and writers agents meet at conferences. Contact by email with one-page query first or referral from current client. Responds in two weeks to queries, three months to proposals.

Commission: 15%

Fees: none

Tip: "Hone your craft. Take advantage of writers groups, critique partners, etc., to polish your manuscript into the best shape it can be."

SPENCERHILL ASSOCIATES

8131 Lakewood Main St. #205 Lakewood Ranch, FL 34202
941-907-3700
submissions@spencerhillassociates.com | *www.spencerhillassociates.com*

Agent: Karen Solem
Agency: Member of Association of Authors' Representatives. Established in 2001. General agent who represents fifteen to twenty-five clients with religious books.
Types of books: adult fiction and nonfiction
New clients: Initial contact by querying through website form or email. Responds in three months.
Commission: 15%

THE STEVE LAUBE AGENCY

24 W. Camelback Rd. A-635, Phoenix, AZ 85013 | 602-336-8910
info@stevelaube.com | *www.stevelaube.com*

Agents: Steve Laube, *krichards@stevelaube.com*; Tamela Hancock Murray, *ewilson@stevelaube.com*; Dan Balow, *vseem@stevelaube.com*; Bob Hostetler, *rgwright@stevelaube.com*
Agency: Established in 2004. Represents more than 250 clients.
Types of books: adult fiction in all subgenres and nonfiction of all types; see blog post by each agent for what he or she is looking for
New clients: Open to unpublished and published authors. Email proposal as attachment according to the guidelines on the website. Steve Laube also will take proposals by mail. Accepts simultaneous submissions. Responds in six to eight weeks.
Commission: 15%
Fees: none
Tip: "Since your book proposal is like a job application, you want to present yourself in the most professional manner possible. Your proposal will be a simple vehicle to convey your idea to us and, ultimately, to a publisher."

VAN DIEST LITERARY AGENCY

34947 S.E. Brooks Rd., Boring, OR 97009 | 503-676-8009
david@christianliteraryagency.com | *www.ChristianLiteraryAgency.com*

Agent: David Van Diest
Agency: Established in 2003. Represents twenty-five clients.
Types of books: nonfiction, select fiction, children's
New clients: Open to unpublished authors. Contact by email through the website. Responds in one month or not interessted.

Commission: 15%

Fees: none

Tip: "We believe the best books are yet to be written! We're not talking about 'new truth' revealed, but God's timeless truth delivered to a new audience, in a way that is fresh, understandable, and applicable to them and their lives."

WENDY SHERMAN ASSOCIATES, INC.

27 W. 24th St., Ste. 700B, New York, NY 10110 | 212-279-9027
submissions@wsherman.com | *www.wsherman.com*

Agents: Wendy Sherman, Cherise Fisher

Agency: General agency that handles some religious books. Established in 1999.

Types of books: adult spirituality and Christianity

New clients: Open to unpublished authors. Contact by email query only. Guidelines on the website.

Commission: 15%

Tip: "We have infinite respect for those writers who craft compelling query letters and follow our guidelines. Remember, there is an art to creating a truly sensational query letter!"

WHEELHOUSE LITERARY GROUP

Nashville, Tenn.
info@wheelhouseliterary.com | *www.wheelhouseliterarygroup.com*

Agent: Jonathan Clements

Agency: Established in 2010 after Jonathan worked five years with authors and brands for another agency.

Types of books: inspirational, historical, contemporary, military fiction; biography/memoir, sports, current events, pop culture

New clients: Email or send through the website form, following the requirements on the site. Responds in two months if interested in more information.

WILLIAM K . JENSEN LITERARY AGENCY

119 Bampton Ct., Eugene, OR 97404 | 541-688-1612
queries@wkjagency.com | *www.wkjagency.com*

Agent: William K. Jensen

Agency: Established in 2005. Represents forty clients.

Types of books: most types of Christian books, including Christian living, devotional, marriage, family life, apologetics, biography, gift books, cookbooks, prophecy, humor, health, inspirational, political, social issues, women's and men's issues, adult fiction; no science fiction, fantasy, or youth

New clients: Open to unpublished authors. Contact by email only; no attachments.. See the website for complete query details. Accepts simultaneous submissions. Responds in one month or not interested.

Commission: 15%

Fees: none

WINTERS & KING, INC.

2448 E. 81st St., Ste. 5900, Tulsa, OK 74137-4259 | 918-494-6868
dboyd@wintersking.com |
wintersking.com/practice-areas/publishing-agent-services

Agent: Thomas J. Winters

Agency: Established in 1983. Represents more than 100 clients. Part of a law firm.

Types of books: adult religious/inspirational novels and nonfiction for all ages, gift books, general-market with underlying Christian themes

New clients: Rarely open to unpublished authors; open to qualified new clients with a significant sales history and platform. Contact by phone or online form. Submit bio and proposal or outline with at least three chapter summaries; prefers full manuscript with description of platform available to help in promotion of the book.

Commission: 15%

Fees: none

WOLGEMUTH & ASSOCIATES

Aurora, CO | 407-909-9445
info@wolgemuthandassociates.com | *www.wolgemuthandassociates.com*

Agents: Robert Wolgemuth, Andrew Wolgemuth, Erik Wolgemuth, Austin Wilson

Agency: Established in 1992. Member of Association of Authors' Representatives.

Types of books: teen/YA and adult nonfiction

New clients: Only authors with at least one traditionally published book or by referral from current client or close contact. Query by email. Accepts simultaneous submissions.

Commission: 15%

Fees: none

WORDSERVE LITERARY GROUP

7061 S. University Blvd., Ste. 307, Centennial, CO 80122 | 303-471-6675
admin@wordserveliterary.com | *www.wordserveliterary.com*

Agents: Greg Johnson, *greg@wordserveliterary.com*; Sarah Joy Freese, *sarah@wordserveliterary.com*; Nick Harrison, *nick@wordserveliterary.com*; Keely Boeving, *keely@wordserveliterary.com*

Agency: Established in 2003. Represents 100 clients.

Types of books: Fiction and nonfiction, faith-based and general market, mostly adult, occasionally children's and YA. In fiction, we're interested in a broad spectrum of genres, including suspense, romance, women's, and Christian. In nonfiction we're looking at business, military, biography, health, self-help, memoir, and Christian topics.

New clients: Open to writers who have not published a book, well-established book writers, and self-published writers. Contact through website form. Responds in two months.

Commission: 15%

Fees: none

Tip: "Please review the submission guidelines on our website very carefully."

WORDWISE MEDIA SERVICES

4083 Avenue L, Ste. 255, Lancaster, CA 93536 | 661-382-8083
get.wisewords@gmail.com | *www.wordwisemedia.com/agency*

Agents: Steven Hutson, *steve@wordwisemedia.com*; David Fessenden; Michelle S. Lazurek

Agency: Established in 2011. Represents sixty clients, half with religious books. Member of Association of Authors' Representatives.

Types of books: novels and nonfiction for adults and children

New clients: Open to unpublished book authors. Prefers referrals or conference meets. For all submissions, use the query form on the website. For other inquiries, phone or email is OK; no postal mail. Accepts simultaneous submissions. Responds in one month; OK to nudge after then.

Commission: 15%

Fees: maybe for printing and postage at cost for a manuscript mailed to a publisher

Tip: "For all submissions, please follow the instructions on the website carefully. Specify the agent's name in the email subject line if you have a preference."

YATES & YATES

1551 N. Tustin Ave., Ste. 710, Santa Ana, CA 92705 | 714-480-4000
email@yates2.com | *www.yates2.com*

Agents: Sealy Yates, Matt Yates, Curtis Yates, Mike Salisbury
Agency: Established in 1989.
Types of books: adult nonfiction
New clients: No unpublished authors. Contact by email.
Commission: negotiable
Tip: "Our holistic approach combines agency representation, expert legal advice, marketing guidance, career coaching, creative counseling, and business-management consulting. We work with clients to focus their efforts, hone and sharpen their messages, obtain broad distribution, increase their influence, and build a lasting and successful career. In short, we help our clients make their ideas matter."

17

WRITERS CONFERENCES AND SEMINARS

ALABAMA

SOUTHERN CHRISTIAN WRITERS CONFERENCE

Tuscaloosa, Al | June
www.scwconference.com/SCWConference.com/Southern_Christian_Writers_Conference.html

Director: Joanne Sloan, 4195 Waldort Dr., Northport, AL 35473; 205-534-0595; *SCWC.writers@gmail.com*

Description: The SCWC is a two-day conference for beginners or experienced writers that focuses on several genres: nonfiction books, magazines, fiction, grammar, business aspects, legal aspects, etc.

Faculty includes: editors, agents, and publishers

Attendance: 160-200

ARIZONA

AMERICAN CHRISTIAN WRITERS MENTORING RETREAT

Phoenix, AZ | September 7-8 | *acwriters.com*

Director: Reg A. Forder, PO Box 110390, Nashville, TN 37222; 800-21-WRITE; *ACWriters@aol.com*

Description: Two-day intensive, hands-on work on a manuscript submitted in advance. Teachers include Dr. Dennis E. Hensley, Lin Johnson, and Jim Watkins.

Attendance: 6-30

CALIFORNIA

MOUNT HERMON CHRISTIAN WRITERS CONFERENCE

Mount Hermon, CA (near Santa Cruz) | March 23-27 (pre-conference clinics March 21-23) | *writers.mounthermon.org*

Director: Kathy Ide, *Kathy.Ide@MountHermon.org*

Description: Major morning tracks, small-group mentoring clinics, afternoon workshops, amazing keynote speakers, and one-on-one appointments with agents, editors, and best-selling authors, all in the beautiful California redwoods. Come for networking, divine connections, inspiration and encouragement, and the wonderful ecumenical Palm Sunday service.

Faculty includes: editors, agents, and publishers

Speakers: Liz Curtis Higgs and Allen Arnold

Special tracks: advanced writers, teens

Scholarships: partial

Attendance: 300-350

Contest: Promising Beginnings (one winner) and First Timer's Contest (ten winners): full scholarship, including meals and economy lodging

SAN DIEGO CHRISTIAN WRITERS' GUILD FALL CONFERENCE

San Diego, CA | October | *www.sandiegocwg.org*

Director: Jennie Gillespie, PO Box 270403, San Diego, CA 92198; 760-294-3269; *info@sandiegocwg.org*

Faculty includes: editors and agents

Scholarships: partial

Attendance: 200

SANTA BARBARA CHRISTIAN WRITERS CONFERENCE

Santa Barbara, CA | TBA | *www.cwgsb.com*

Director: Opal Mae Dailey, PO Box 40860, Santa Barbara, CA 93140; 805-252-9822; *info@cwgsb.com*

Description: In 20 years we have never heard an unhappy attendee. Come to our beautiful town.

Faculty includes: editors, agents, publishers

Scholarships: full

Attendance: 50-70

SoCAL CHRISTIAN WRITERS' CONFERENCE

CA | June | *www.SoCalCWC.com*

Director: Kathy Ide, *KathyIde@SoCalCWC.com*
Faculty includes: editors and agents
Special tracks: advanced writers, teens
Scholarships: full and partial
Attendance: 200

WEST COAST CHRISTIAN WRITERS CONFERENCE

Livermore, CA | February 17 | *www.westcoastchristianwriters.com*

Director: Susy Flory, 1660 Freisman Rd., Livermore, CA 94551; 510-854-1408; *info@westcoastchristianwriters.com*
Description: West Coast Christian Writers aims to equip and encourage writers of all levels in the craft and business of writing for publication through an annual conference offering quality instruction, industry updates, community, and personal inspiration.
Special track: one-day masterclass geared to intermediates and above
Faculty includes: editors, agents
Scholarships: partial
Attendance: 250
Contest: themed writing contest with cash prizes and scholarships

COLORADO

COLORADO CHRISTIAN WRITERS CONFERENCE

Estes Park, CO | May 16-19 | *colorado.writehisanswer.com*

Director: Marlene Bagnull, 951 Anders Rd., Lansdale, PA 19446; 484-991-8581; *mbagnull@aol.com*
Description: Sharpen your writing and marketing skills from your choice of eight continuing sessions and more than fifty workshops. Seven keynotes, four or more one-on-one 15-minute appointments.
Special track: teens
Faculty includes: editors, agents, and publishers
Scholarships: partial
Attendance: 200
Contest: For registered conferees. Entries based on the conference theme of "Write His Answer" from Habakkuk 2:2. Prose (maximum 500 words) or poetry by published and not-yet-

published authors. The winner in each of the four categories receives 50% off the registration fee for the following year. Entry fee $10.

WRITE IN THE SPRINGS

Colorado Springs, CO | April | *acfwcs.acfwcolorado.com*

Director: Mary Agius, PO Box 7862, Colorado Springs, CO 80933; 719-686-7761; *acfwcs.president@acfwcolorado.com*

Attendance: 40

WRITERS ON THE ROCK

Denver, CO | February 26 | *www.RedLetterBelievers.com*

Director: David Rupert, 14473 W. 3rd, Golden, CO 80401; 720-237-7487; *david@davidrupert.net*

Description: One of the largest and most exciting one-day gatherings of Christian writers in the US. We focus on motivation, inspiration, and encouragement of writers at all levels.

Faculty includes: editors, agents, and publishers

Attendance: 200

CONNECTICUT

reNEW RETREAT FOR NEW ENGLAND WRITING

West Hartford, CT | October 5-7 | *www.reNEWwriting.com*

Director: Lucinda Secrest McDowell, reNEW Writing, PO Box 290707, Wethersfield, CT 06129; *info@reNEWwriting.com*

Special track: speaking

Attendance: 75

DELAWARE

VINE & VESSELS CHRISTIAN WRITERS CONFERENCE

Georgetown, DE | October 20 | *www.vineandvessels.com*

Directors: Joyce Sessoms and Betty Ricks-Jarman, PO Box 1716, Seaford, DE 19973; 302-875-1650; *crownjewel777@comcast.net*

Description: "Connecting Pen to Purpose" features a keynote speaker, morning and afternoon workshops (six choices), continental breakfast, lunch, and book tables. This conference is particularly appropriate for beginners.

Speaker: Judith Reveal
Scholarships: partial
Attendance: 60

FLORIDA

ACFW CENTRAL FLORIDA SPRING SEMINAR

Orlando, FL | April | *www.cfacfw.org*

Director: Kristen Stieffe, 1655 Peel Ave., Orlando, FL 32806; 407-928-7801; *treasurer@cfacfw.com*
Description: Full-day seminar; changes yearly.
Attendance: 20

AMERICAN CHRISTIAN WRITERS MENTORING RETREAT

Orlando, FL | November 16-17 | *acwriters.com*

Director: Reg A. Forder, PO Box 110390, Nashville, TN 37222; 800-21-WRITE; *ACWriters@aol.com*
Description: Two-day intensive, hands-on work on a manuscript submitted in advance. Teachers include: Dr. Dennis E. Hensley, Lin Johnson, and Jim Watkins.
Attendance: 6-30

THE DEEP THINKERS RETREAT

Destin, FL | February 23-28 | *learnhowtowriteanovel.com/product/deep-thinkers-retreat-2018*

Director: Susan May Warren, 20 Wild Plum Dr., Grand Marais, MN 55604; *retreats@mybooktherapy.com*
Description: An in-depth brainstorming and writing coaching retreat.
Teachers: Susan May Warren and Rachel Hauck
Attendance: 20

EVANGELICAL PRESS ASSOCIATION ANNUAL CONVENTION

Orlando, FL | April 4-6 | *www.evangelicalpress.com/convention*

Director: Lamar Keener, Executive Director, PO Box 1787, Queen Creek, AZ 85142; 888-311-1731; *director@evangelicalpress.com*
Description: A Christian media conference for writers, editors, designers, digital media managers, and others involved in periodical publishing. Note: This conference changes location every year.

Special tracks: advanced writers, advanced editors
Faculty includes: editors
Attendance: 175
Contest: for members of the Evangelical Press Association, including freelance writers who enter articles or blog posts

FLORIDA CHRISTIAN WRITERS CONFERENCE

Leesburg, FL | February 21-25 | *www.FloridaCWC.net*

Director: Eva Marie Everson, PO Box 520224, Longwood, FL 32752; 407-615-4112; *FloridaCWC@aol.com*
Description: The theme for 2018 is Tell The Story . . . Expect the Unexpected. We offer approximately fifty faculty members from all across the Christian publishing industry—agents, editors, marketing experts, and freelance writers. We offer ten continuing classes, as well as nearly sixty one-hour workshops.
Special tracks: teens, pastors
Faculty includes: editors, agents, and publishers
Speaker: Tosca Lee
Scholarships: full, partial
Attendance: 250
Contest: *www.floridacwc.net/contestsyourchancetoshine*

GEORGIA

AMERICAN CHRISTIAN WRITERS MENTORING RETREAT

Atlanta, GA | July 6-7 | *acwriters.com*

Director: Reg A. Forder, PO Box 110390, Nashville, TN 37222; 800-21-WRITE; *ACWriters@aol.com*
Description: Two-day intensive, hands-on work on a manuscript submitted in advance. Teachers include: Dr. Dennis E. Hensley, Lin Johnson, and Jim Watkins.
Attendance: 6-30

ATLANTA CHRISTIAN WRITERS CONFERENCE

Atlanta, GA | August 24-26 | *www.ChristianAuthorsGuild.org*

Director: Cynthia L. Simmons, 6409 Bells Ferry Rd., Woodstock, GA 30189; 770-928-2795; *info@Christianauthorsguild.org*
Description: We critique manuscripts and have workshops.
Special track: Word Weavers Retreat
Faculty includes: editors

Scholarships: partial
Attendance: 25
Contest: GA Peach Contest for Word Weaver members

ILLINOIS

KARITOS ART AND WORSHIP CONFERENCE

Naperville, IL | July | *karitos.org*

Director: Bob Hay, 2650 Brookwood Way, Unit 217, Rolling Meadows, IL 60008; 847-925-8018; *roberthay@karitos.com*
Description: The mission of Karitos is to provide biblically based artistic and technical growth experiences to Christian artists, including writers.
Attendance: 150

WRITE-TO-PUBLISH CONFERENCE

Wheaton, IL (Chicago area) | June 13-16 | *www.writetopublish.com*

Director: Lin Johnson, 9118 W. Elmwood Dr., Ste. 1G, Niles, IL 60714-5820; 847-296-3964; *lin@writetopublish.com*
Description: Six to eight continuing tracks and thirty electives for beginning through advanced career writers. College credit through Taylor University.
Faculty includes: editors, agents, and publishers
Plenary speaker: Michelle Medlock Adams
Attendance: 150-175
Contest: Best New Writer and Writer of the Year awards, both for alumni who attend this year.

INDIANA

TAYLOR UNIVERSITY'S PROFESSIONAL WRITING CONFERENCE

Upland, IN | August 3-4 | *taylorsprofessionalwritersconference.wordpress.com*

Director: Linda Taylor, 236 W. Reade Ave., Upland, IN 46989; 765-998-5591; *taylorpwrconference@gmail.com*
Faculty includes: editors and agents
Special track: teens
Attendance: 150

KANSAS

CALLED TO WRITE

Pittsburg, KS | March | *calledtowriteconference.wordpress.com*

Director: Julane Hiebert, 350 Lake Rd., Council Grove, KS 66846; 785-561-0217; *julhiebert@gmail.com*

Scholarships: full and partial

Attendance: 70-75

Contest: For fiction, nonfiction, poetry, devotionals, children's fiction, and children's nonfiction.

KENTUCKY

KENTUCKY CHRISTIAN WRITERS CONFERENCE

Elizabethtown, KY | June 22-23 | *www.kychristianwriters.com*

Director: Mary Gaskins, PO Box 2719, Elizabethtown, KY 42702; 502-254-9520; *coordinator@kychristianwriters.com*

Description: Open-microphone Friday is one of our most popular features. Workshops are provided for both beginning and advanced authors; agents, editors, and publishers are on hand to answer your questions.

Special tracks: advanced writers, teens

Faculty includes: editors, publishers, agents

Speaker: H. Michael Brewer

Scholarships: partial

Attendance: 60

MICHIGAN

AMERICAN CHRISTIAN WRITERS MENTORING RETREAT

Grand Rapids, MI | June 8-9 | *acwriters.com*

Director: Reg A. Forder, PO Box 110390, Nashville, TN 37222; 800-21-WRITE; *ACWriters@aol.com*

Description: Two-day intensive, hands-on work on a manuscript submitted in advance. Teachers include: Dr. Dennis E. Hensley, Lin Johnson, and Jim Watkins.

Attendance: 6-30

BREATHE CHRISTIAN WRITERS CONFERENCE

Grand Rapids, MI | October 12-13 | *www.breatheconference.com*

Director: Ann Byle, 1765 3 Mile Rd. N.E., Grand Rapids, MI 49515; 616-389-4436; *breathewritersconference@gmail.com*

Description: A relaxed, information-filled, community-building conference for new and advanced writers of fiction, nonfiction and poetry. We offer thirty-six breakout sessions, one-on-ones, two plenary workshops, and two keynote events.

Speaker: Jocelyn Green

Faculty includes: editors, agents, and publishers

Scholarships: full and partial

Attendance: 140

MARANATHA CHRISTIAN WRITERS' CONFERENCE

Norton Shores, MI | September 27-29 | *www.maranathachristianwriters.com*

Director: Sherry Hoppen, 4759 Lake Harbor Rd., Norton Shores, MI 49441; 231-798-2161; *sherry@maranathachristianwriters.com*

Faculty includes: agents, editors, and publishers

Scholarships: partial

Attendance: 80

PENCON

Grand Rapids, MI | May 3-5 | *penconeditors.com*

Director: Jenne Acevedo, *pencon@christianeditor.com*

Description: PENCON is the only conference for editors in the Christian market. Note: This conference changes location every year.

Faculty includes: editors and publishers

Scholarships: full and partial

Attendance: 75

MINNESOTA

AMERICAN CHRISTIAN WRITERS MENTORING RETREAT

Minneapolis, MN | August 3-4 | *acwriters.com*

Director: Reg A. Forder, PO Box 110390, Nashville, TN 37222; 800-21-WRITE; *ACWriters@aol.com*

Description: Two-day intensive, hands-on work on a manuscript submitted in advance. Teachers include: Dr. Dennis E. Hensley, Lin Johnson, and Jim Watkins.

Attendance: 6-30

DEEP WOODS WRITING CAMP

Grand Marais, MN | June 16-23, Oct 13-20 |
learnhowtowriteanovel.com/product/deep-woods-writers-camp

Director: Susan May Warren, 20 Wild Plum Dr., Grand Marais, MN 55604; *susan@mybooktherapy.com*
Description: An intimate, deep dive into your writing with one-on-one coaching and focused writing time.
Special track: advanced writers
Speaker: Susan May Warren
Attendance: 10

MINNESOTA CHRISTIAN WRITERS GUILD SPRING SEMINAR

Minneapolis, MN | April 7
www.mnchristianwriters.com/2018-spring-seminar

Director: Stacy Monson; *stacy.monson@gmail.com*
Description: This annual seminar offers something for everyone—from novice to pro, from fiction writers to nonfiction writers.
Speaker: Cynthia Ruchti
Attendance: 30-40

MISSOURI

CHRISTIAN COMMUNICATORS CONFERENCE

Branson, MO | May 30—June 3 | *www.ChristianCommunicators.com*

Codirectors: Tammy Whitehurst, Sherry Poundstone, Lori Boruff; *contact@christiancommunicators.com*
Description: This one-of-a-kind conference educates, validates, and launches speakers to the next level. Beginner or seasoned speakers find value, clarity, and fresh ideas to apply and create successful speaking ministries.
Attendance: limited to 50

HEART OF AMERICA CHRISTIAN WRITERS NETWORK

Kansas City, MO | October | *www.hacwn.org*

Director: Jeanette Littleton, 3706 N.E. Shady Lane Dr., Gladstone, MO 64119; 816-459-8016; *hacwn@earthlink.net*
Faculty includes: editors, agents, and publishers
Attendance: 100
Contests: in most genres with $3 entry fee

NEBRASKA

WORDSOWERS CHRISTIAN WRITERS CONFERENCE

Omaha, NE | April 27-28 | *www.wordsowers.com*

Director: Jeanne Jacobson, 13002 S. 34th Cir., Bellevue, NE 68123; 402-933-1945; *jeanie@wordsowers.com*

Description: 2018 is Wordsowers' sixth conference and growing each year. We have both in-house editors, publishers, and agents, as well as those who Skype in.

Faculty includes: editors, publishers, and agents

Speaker: Ronie Kendig

Special tracks: advanced writers, teens

Scholarships: full and partial

Attendance: 85

NEVADA

REALM MAKERS

St. Louis, MO | July 19-21 | *www.realmmakers.com*

Director: Becky Minor, 939 N. Washington St., Pottstown, PA 19464; *info@faithandfantasyalliance.com*

Description: Realm Makers is for writers of faith who create science fiction, fantasy, and related subgenres. Note: This conference changes location every year.

Scholarships: full and partial, based on merit and needs

Faculty includes: agents and editors from both CBA and general markets

Attendance: 200+

Contest: for published books and book covers with cash awards

NEW MEXICO

CLASS WRITERS CONTREAT

Albuquerque, NM | November | *www.classeminars.org*

Director: Judy McLaughlin, CLASSeminars, PO Box 36551, Albuquerque, NM 87176; 702-882-0638; *classcontreat@gmail.com*

Faculty includes: editors, publishers

Scholarships: partial

Attendance: 50

THE CLASSEMINAR

Albuquerque, NM | *www.classeminars.org/events.html*

Director: Gerry Wakeland, CLASSeminars, PO Box 36551, Albuquerque, NM 87176; 702-882-0638; *classeminars@gmail.com*

Description: For anyone who wants to improve his or her communication skills for the spoken or written word, for professional or personal reasons.

Attendance: 75-100

NORTH CAROLINA

ASHEVILLE CHRISTIAN WRITERS CONFERENCE

Asheville, NC | February 16-18 | *www.ashevillechristianwritersconference.com*

Director: Cindy Sproles, PO Box 6494, Kingsport, TN 37663; *cindybootcamp@gmail.com*

Description: Held at the Cove, the Billy Graham Training Center, ACWC is a two-day, jam-packed conference. We provide training for those called to write and encourage first-time conferees into our conference. Our faculty is nationally known, and we cater to all levels of writing.

Special tracks: one-on-one mentoring, advanced writers

Faculty includes: editors, agents, publishers

Speakers: Bob Hostetler, Tim Shoemaker, Edie Melson

Scholarships: full, partial

Attendance: 125

Contest: Badge of Honor book contest is open to all conferees, and the winner has the opportunity for his or her book to be presented to the publication committee of Lighthouse Publishing of the Carolinas. (Publication is not promised.)

BLUE RIDGE "AUTUMN IN THE MOUNTAINS" NOVELIST RETREAT

Ridgecrest, NC | October 7-11 | *ridgecrestconferencecenter.org/event/novelist*

Director: Yvonne Lehman, 102 Corbett Ln., Black Mountain, NC 28711; 828-231-1963; *yvonnelehman3@gmail.com*

Description: Focus on writing craft, scripts, social media, and creativity.

Faculty includes: editors, agents, publishers

Attendance: 35-40

Contest: Golden Leaf Award for best proposal for an unpublished book

BLUE RIDGE MOUNTAINS CHRISTIAN WRITERS CONFERENCE

Black Mountain, NC | May 20-24 | *BlueRidgeConference.com*

Director: Edie Melson, 604 S. Almond Dr., Simpsonville, SC 29681; 864-373-4232; *Edie@ediemelson.com*

Special track: advanced writers

Faculty includes: editors, agents, publishers

Scholarships: partial

Attendance: 450

Contests: Selah, open to published writers (traditional and self-published); Director's Choice, open to former conferees who have a published book (traditional or self-published); Foundation Awards, open to unpublished attendees

MOUNTAINSIDE MARKETING CONFERENCE

Black Mountain, NC | January 12-15 | *www.MountainsideMarketingConference.com*

Director: Edie Melson, 604 S. Almond Dr., Simpsonville, SC 29681; 864-373-4232; *Edie@ediemelson.com*

Description: This is a hands-on marketing conference. Attendees will learn about social media, marketing, and branding.

Speakers: Edie Melson, DiAnn Mills

SHE SPEAKS

Concord, NC | July | *shespeaksconference.com*

Director: Lisa Allen, 630 Team Rd. #100, Matthews, NC 28105; 704-849-2270; *shespeaks@Proverbs31.org*

Description: Speaking and writing tracks.

Faculty includes: editors and agents

Attendance: 700

WRITING FOR YOUR LIFE

Raleigh, NC | May 9-10 | *writingforyourlife.com/conferences*

Director: Brian Allain, 139 Rt. 537, Colts Neck, NJ 07722; 732-371-6137; *brian@writingforyourlife.com*

Description: Writing for Your Life produces writing conferences featuring leading authors and industry experts presenting on various topics, generally in the areas of how to write, how to get published, and how to market. Our conferences, workshops, and retreats have a reputation of collegiality and lack of competitiveness among attendees. Come join us and enjoy the supportive environment.

Faculty includes: editors, agents, publishers
Special track: advanced writers
Attendance: 100-150

OHIO

NORTHWEST OHIO CHRISTIAN WRITERS

Holland, OH | October | *nwocw.org*

Director: Denise Shumway, 418 Danesmoor Rd., Holland, OH 43528; 419-345-6271; *denise.shumway@gmail.com*
Attendance: 35

OHIO CHRISTIAN WRITERS CONFERENCE

Cincinatti, OH | November 2-4 | *ohiochristianwriters.com*

Director: Cody Morehead, 735 Reading Rd., Mason, OH 45040; 937-207-3152; *cody@realpubzoo.com*
Description: Engaging and relevant, new conference.
Special track: advanced writers
Faculty includes: editors, agents, publishers
Speakers: Michelle Medlock Adams, Bob Hostetler, Edie Melson
Attendance: 100+
Contest: Almost an Author and Blue Seal Awards

OKLAHOMA

THE SUCCESSFUL WRITER CONFERENCE

Tulsa, OK | September | *thesuccessfulwriterconference.blogspot.com*

Director: Martha Curtis, Abiding Harvest United Methodist Church, 4407 S. Olive Ave., Broken Arrow, KY 74011; 918-855-8098; *marthajcurtis@yahoo.com*
Description: Our goal is to equip and encourage writers to follow their God-given dreams of setting words to paper. Whether writing for the religious or secular market; writing articles or novels; or writing news, features, devotionals, poetry, scripts, and essays, writers have a special calling to deliver well-crafted words to their readers.
Faculty includes: editors
Scholarships: full, partial
Attendance: 45

OREGON

OREGON CHRISTIAN WRITERS FALL CONFERENCE

Portland, OR | October 27 | *www.oregonchristianwriters.org*

Contact: Sue Miholer, Business Manager, 1075 Willow Lake Rd. N., Keizer, OR 97303; 503-393-3356; *business@oregonchristianwriters.org*

Speaker: Kathi Lipp

Attendance: 130

OREGON CHRISTIAN WRITERS SPRING CONFERENCE

Eugene, OR | May 19 | *www.oregonchristianwriters.org*

Contact: Sue Miholer, Business Manager, 1075 Willow Lake Rd. N., Keizer, OR 97303; 503-393-3356; *business@oregonchristianwriters.org*

Speaker: Terry Glaspey

Attendance: 130

OREGON CHRISTIAN WRITERS SUMMER COACHING CONFERENCE

Portland, OR | August 20-23 | *www.oregonchristianwriters.org*

Director: Lindy Jacobs, 60842 Taralon Pl., Bend, OR 97702; 541-408-6306; *lindyj@bendcable.com*

Description: Our conference gathers top national editors, agents, and award-winning authors in the field of Christian publishing to help writers take their writing to the next level and refresh their writing goals. The conference includes intensive coaching classes and workshops in multiple genres for both beginning and advanced levels, one-on-one meetings with editors and agents, manuscript reviews, free mentoring appointments, inspiring keynotes, and daily worship.

Special tracks: Five-hour preconference seminar with Donald Maass, advanced writers, YA

Faculty includes: editors, agents, publishers

Speakers: Robin Jones Gunn, Kim Meeder

Scholarships: partial

Attendance: 175-200

Contest: Cascade Writing Contest for several genres (published and unpublished) open to all from February 14 through March 31

OREGON CHRISTIAN WRITERS WINTER CONFERENCE

Salem, OR | February 24 | *www.oregonchristianwriters.org*

Contact: Sue Miholer, Business Manager, 1075 Willow Lake Rd. N.,

Keizer, OR 97303; 503-393-3356; *business@oregonchristianwriters.org*

Speaker: Ronie Kendig

Attendance: 130

PENNSYLVANIA

GREATER PHILADELPHIA CHRISTIAN WRITERS CONFERENCE

Lansdale, PA | July 26-28 | *philadelphia.writehisanswer.com*

Director: Marlene Bagnull, 951 Anders Rd., Lansdale, PA 19446; 484-991-8581; *mbagnull@aol.com*

Description: New location, lower price, same goal: "To encourage and equip you to write about a God who is real, who is reachable, and who changes lives." Six continuing sessions, thirty-six workshops, five keynotes, three or four early bird learning labs.

Special track: teens.

Faculty includes: editors, agents, and publishers

Scholarships: partial

Attendance: 220

Contest: For registered conferees. Entries based on the conference theme of "Write His Answer" from Habakkuk 2:2. Prose (maximum 500 words) or poetry by published and not-yet-published authors. The winner in each of the four categories receives 50% off the registration fee for the following year. Entry fee $10.

MONTROSE CHRISTIAN WRITERS CONFERENCE

Montrose, PA | July 22-27 | *www.montrosebible.org/OurEvents.aspx*

Director: Marsha Hubler, 1833 Dock Hill Rd., Middleburg, PA 17842; 570-837-0002; *marshahubler@wildblue.net*

Faculty includes: editors and agents

Special tracks: advanced writers and teens

Scholarships: partial, including Shirley Brinkerhoff Memorial Scholarship, a $150 grant toward tuition, given to a writer who's not yet secured a book contract but is actively striving to hone the craft of writing

Attendance: 100

ST. DAVIDS CHRISTIAN WRITERS' CONFERENCE

Grove City, PA | June 20-24 | *www.stdavidswriters.com/conferenc*

Director: Susan Lower, 717-372-3303, *inspireme@susanlower.com*
Faculty includes: editors and agents
Scholarships: full and partial
Attendance: 60
Contests: See detailed list on the website.

WRITING TO IMPACT LIVES

Lancaster, PA | February 9-10 | *www.munce.com*

Director: Marlene Bagnull, 484-991-8581; *mbagnull@aol.com*
Description: Opportunity for intermediate and advanced writers to learn from industry pros, with the option to stay for the February 11-13 Munce Christian Product Expo and meet retailers.
Faculty includes: editors
Special track: four-hour "Going Indie" learning lab with Sarah Bolme, director, CSPA
Attendance: 50 maximum

SOUTH CAROLINA

CAROLINA CHRISTIAN WRITERS CONFERENCE

Spartanburg, SC | March 9-10 | *www.fbs.org/writers*

Director: Linda Gilden, First Baptist Church, 250 E. Main St., Spartanburg, SC 29306; 864-583-7245; *linda@lindagilden.com*
Description: Bringing together writers of all levels to network, learn, and fellowship as they hone the craft of writing and learn new ways in which to reach the world. Panels, Lightning Learning, editor private appointments, genre group meetings, and more.
Faculty includes: editors, agents, publishers
Speaker: Todd Starnes
Scholarships: full
Attendance: 100

WRITE2IGNITE CONFERENCE FOR CHRISTIAN WRITERS OF LITERATURE FOR CHILDREN AND YOUNG ADULTS

Tigerville, SC | September 21-22 | *write2ignite.com*

Director: Deborah S. DeCiantis, 1201 Humbert Rd., Ware Shoals, SC 29692; 803-517-4143; *info.write2ignite@gmail.com*
Description: Annual conference focused on helping Christian writers (middle-school through adult) of work in any genre or market to communicate Christian worldview values to ages birth—young

adult. Offers keynote presenters and workshops plus consultations with faculty.

Faculty inludes: editors, agents, and publishers

Speakers: Jenny L. Cote, Tessa Emily Hall

Special track: teens

Scholarships: full

Attendance: 65-120

TENNESSEE

AMERICAN CHRISTIAN FICTION WRITERS (ACFW) CONFERENCE

Nashville, TN | September 20-23 | *www.acfw.com/conference*

Director: Robin Miller, PO Box 101066, Palm Bay, FL 32910-1066; *director@acfw.com*

Description: Continuing education sessions and workshop electives specifically geared for five levels of fiction writing experience from beginner to advanced.

Special track: advanced writers

Faculty includes: editors and agents

Scholarships: full scholarships

Attendance: 650

Contest: The Genesis Contest is for unpublished writers whose Christian fiction manuscript is completed. The Carol Awards honor the best of Christian fiction from the previous calendar year.

AMERICAN CHRISTIAN WRITERS MENTORING RETREAT

Nashville, TN | April 20-21 and October 12-13 | *acwriters.com*

Director: Reg A. Forder, PO Box 110390, Nashville, TN 37222; 800-21-WRITE; *ACWriters@aol.com*

Description: Two-day intensive, hands-on work on a manuscript submitted in advance. Teachers include: Dr. Dennis E. Hensley, Lin Johnson, and Jim Watkins.

Attendance: 6-30

MID-SOUTH CHRISTIAN WRITERS CONFERENCE

Collierville, TN | March 17 | *MidSouthChristianWriters.com*

Director: April Carpenter, PO Box 236, Nesbit, MS 38651; 901-378-0504; *midsouthchristianwriters@gmail.com*

Description: The MSCWC encourages beginning and experienced communicators to develop their writing talents for God's glory. All who enjoy writing are welcome.

Special track: Friday four-hour workshop on self-publishing

Faculty includes: editors

Speaker: Brandilyn Collins

Attendance: 100

WRITING FOR YOUR LIFE

Nashville, TN | February 6-8 | *writingforyourlife.com/conferences*

Director: Brian Allain, 139 Rt. 537, Colts Neck, NJ 07722; 732-371-6137; *brian@writingforyourlife.com*

Description: Writing for Your Life produces writing conferences featuring leading authors and industry experts presenting on various topics, generally in the areas of how to write, how to get published, and how to market. Our conferences, workshops, and retreats have a reputation of collegiality and lack of competitiveness among attendees. Come join us and enjoy the supportive environment.

Faculty includes: editors, agents, publishers

Special track: advanced writers

Attendance: 100-150

TEXAS

BAYOU CITY CHRISTIAN WRITERS CONFERENCE

Houston, TX | October 21 | *wotsacfw.blogspot.com*

Director: Kathrese McKee, 8765 Spring Cypress, Ste. L219, Spring, TX 77379; 281-787-6938; *wots.acfw@gmail.com*

Description: Bayou City Christian Writers Conference is the annual mini-conference sponsored by The Woodlands chapter of American Christian Fiction Writers (ACFW). The conference's purpose is to further the education of authors with topics about craft, marketing, and industry trends.

Attendance: 50

Contest: Storming the Short Story Contest awards are presented at the conference. The contest stories address an annual theme, and the winners are published in an anthology. The contest is a joint project of the Houston and The Woodlands chapters of ACFW. The contest accepts entries beginning in July.

TEXAS CHRISTIAN WRITERS CONFERENCE

Houston, TX | August | *www.centralhoustoniwa.com*

Director: Martha Rogers, 6038 Greenmont, Houston, TX 77092; 713-686-7209; *marthalrogers@sbcglobal.net*
Faculty includes: editors
Attendance: 60
Contests: Inspirational Writers Alive! Open Writing Competition

WASHINGTON

NORTHWEST CHRISTIAN WRITERS RENEWAL

Bellevue, WA | June 1-2 | *www.nwchristianwriters.org/Renewal2018*

Directors: Charles and Perry Harris, PO Box 2706, Woodinville, WA 98072; 206-250-6885; *renewal@nwchristianwriters.org*
Description: This conference is where writers, editors, and publishers can connect, network, and collaborate. Conferees will sharpen their skills, learn strategies, and form connections to boost their success on the writing journey.
Faculty includes: editors, agents, publishers
Keynote speaker: Rachel Hauck
Scholarships: full
Attendance: 130

CANADA

InSCRIBE CHRISTIAN WRITERS' FELLOWSHIP FALL CONFERENCE

Wetaskiwin, AB | September 20-22 | *inscribe.org/fall-conference*

Director: Ruth L. Snyder, PO Box 463, Glendon, AB T0A 1P0, Canada; 780-646-3068; *President@Inscribe.org*
Description: A party for the Christian writer's soul with workshops on writing, networking, worship, fun, and great food.
Special track: advanced writers
Faculty includes: editors, publishers
Speakers: Ann-Margret Hovsepian, Susan King
Scholarships: partial
Attendance: 75
Contest: Our fall contest details are available June 1st at *www.inscribe.org/contests.*

WRITE CANADA

Toronto, ON | June | *thewordguild.com*

Director: Andi M. Harris, The Word Guild, King George Rd., Ste. 226, 245, Brantford, ON N3R 7N7, Canada; *writecanada@thewordguild.com*

Description: Hosted by The Word Guild, an association of Christian Canadian writers and editors.

Special track: career writers

Faculty includes: editors and agents

Scholarships: partial

Attendance: 250

CONFERENCES THAT CHANGE LOCATIONS

The following conferences change locations every year but are listed with their 2018 locations:

AMERICAN CHRISTIAN FICTION WRITERS CONFERENCE

EVANGELICAL PRESS ASSOCIATION ANNUAL CONVENTION

PENCON

REALM MAKERS

18

WRITERS GROUPS

In addition to the groups listed here, check these websites for other groups in your area:

American Christian Writers chapters: *www.acwriters.com*
American Christian Fiction Writers chapters: *www.acfw.com*
Word Weavers International chapters: *www.Word-Weavers.com*

NATIONAL AND ONLINE

ACFW BEYOND THE BORDERS

www.facebook.com/groups/ACFWBeyondtheBorders

Contact: Iola Goulton, *iola@iolagoulton.com*
Members: 100
Affiliation: American Christian Fiction Writers

AMERICAN CHRISTIAN FICTION WRITERS

acfw.com

Contact: Robin Miller, executive director, PO Box 101066, Palm Bay, FL 32910; *director@acfw.com*
Services: Email loop, genre Facebook pages, online courses, critique groups, and local and regional chapters. Sponsors contests for published and unpublished writers and conducts the largest fiction conference annually.
Members: 2600+

CHRISTIAN AUTHORS NETWORK

ChristianAuthorsNetwork.com

Meetings: Online and at major writing-industry events, daily via private loop
Contact: Angela Breidenbach, *can_inc@yahoo.com*
Members: 125+

CHRISTIAN INDIE AUTHOR NETWORK

www.christianindieauthors.com

Meetings: 24/7 on Facebook and website
Contact: Mary C. Findley, 918-805-0669, *mjmcfindley@gmail.com*
Members: 400+

CHRISTIAN WOMEN WRITER'S GROUP

cwwriters.com

Meetings: weekly and monthly communications
Contact: Jen Gentry, 918-724-3996, *jennyokiern37@gmail.com*
Members: 100+
Affiliation: Christian Indie Author Network

INSPIRE CHRISTIAN WRITERS

www.inspirewriters.com

Meetings: regional and online critique groups
Contact: Robynne Miller, 530-217-8233, *inspiredirectors@gmail.com*
Members: 150
Affiliation: West Coast Christian Writers

JERRY JENKINS WRITERS GUILD

www.JerrysGuild.com

Contact: *WeCare@JerryJenkins.com*
Services: *New York Times* bestselling author Jerry Jenkins coaches subscribers online via Live Online Workshops (1 hour of training, 30 minutes of Q&A); Manuscript Repair & Rewrite sessions, in which he conducts a thorough revision of a member's first page; Master Classes (Jerry asks leading industry experts the questions you would ask); Office Hours, an extended monthly live Q&A session with Jerry; free access to Jumpstart Courses (fiction and nonfiction); all sessions recorded and archived for 24/7 member access.
Meetings: unscheduled pop-ups in major cities
Members: More than 2,000

PEN-SOULS

Meetings: online and email; monthly reminders are emailed to members to pray for one another and share urgent, personal prayer requests and publishing announcements
Contact: Janet Ann Collins, 530-272-4905, *jan@janetanncollins.com*
Members: 10-12

REALM MAKERS
www.realmmakers.com

Meetings: quarterly online
Contact: Rebecca Minor, *members@realmmakers.com*
Membership: 100
Membership fee: $40/year

WORD WEAVERS INTERNATIONAL, INC.
www.Word-Weavers.com

Contact: Eva Marie Everson, president, PO Box 520224, Longwood, FL 32708; 407-615-4112; *WordWeaversInternational@aol.com*
Services: Local chapters and Google Hangouts for manuscript critiquing. Sponsors the Florida Christian Writers Conference.
Members: 600
Membership fee: $45/year

WORD WEAVERS ONLINE GROUPS
www.Word-Weavers.com

Meetings: via Google Hangouts; times vary, two hours
Contact: Eva Marie Everson, 407-615-4112, *WordWeaversInternational@aol.com*
Members: 6 per "page," currently 14 pages
Affiliation: Word Weavers International

ALABAMA

FOLEY WORD WEAVERS

Meetings: Genesis Church, 3100 S. McKenzie, room A-7, Foley, AL; fourth Tuesday of the month, 7:00-9:00 p.m.
Contact: David Parks, *profparks@gmail.com*
Membership fee: $45/year
Affiliation: Word Weavers International

ARIZONA

CHANDLER WRITERS' GROUP
chandlerwriters.wordpress.com

Meetings: member's home, near Gilbert and Ocotillo Roads, Chandler, AZ; second Friday of the month, 9:00-11:30 a.m.

Contact: Jenne Acevedo, 480-510-0419, *jenneacevedo@cox.net*
Members: 10
Membership fee: none

CHRISTIAN WRITERS OF THE WEST

www.christianwritersofthewest.com

Meetings: Denny's, 4400 N. Scottsdale Rd., Scottsdale, AZ; last Saturday of the month, 1:00-3:00 p.m.
Contact: Brenda Poulos, 480-628-6728, *mtnst14@gmail.com*
Members: 30
Membership fee: $10/year
Affiliation: American Christian Fiction Writers

FOUNTAIN HILLS CHRISTIAN WRITERS' GROUP

Meetings: Fountain Hills Presbyterian Church, 13001 N. Fountain Hills Blvd., Fountain Hills, AZ; second Friday of the month, 9:00 a.m. to noon
Contact: Jewell Johnson, 480-836-8968, *tykeJ@juno.com*
Members: 12
Membership fee: $10/year
Affiliation: American Christian Writers

NORTHERN ARIZONA WORD WEAVERS

Meetings: Spirit of Joy Church, 330 Scenic Dr., Clarkdale, AZ; second Saturday of the month, 9:30-11:30 a.m.
Contact: Alice Klies, *alice.klies@gmail.com*
Members: 30
Membership fee: $45
Affiliation: Word Weavers International

ARKANSAS

ACFW ARKANSAS

www.facebook.com/ACFWAR

Meetings: Searcy Public Library, 113 E. Pleasure Ave., Searcy, AR; second Saturday of the month, 1:00 p.m.
Contact: Tara Johnson, 501-821-4976, *tara@tarajohnsonministries.com*
Members: 20
Affiliation: American Christian Fiction Writers

CALIFORNIA

ACFW ORANGE COUNTY

Meetings: location varies, Garden Grove, CA; second Thursday of the month, 6:30 p.m.
Contact: Deborah Marino, 714-873-5609, *deborahmarino7@gmail.com*
Members: 14
Affiliation: American Christian Fiction Writers

ACFW SAN FRANCISCO BAY AREA CHAPTER

www.meetup.com/ACFWSFBayArea

Meetings: Crosswalk Church, 445 S. Mary Ave., Sunnyvale, CA; third Saturday of odd months, 10 a.m. to noon
Contact: Katie Vorreiter, *acfwsfbayarea@gmail.com*
Members: 15
Affiliation: American Christian Fiction Writers

CIRCUIT WRITERS

Meetings: Grass Valley United Methodist Church, 236 S. Church St., Grass Valley, CA; first Tuesday of the month, 6:15 p.m.
Contact: Janet Ann Collins, 530-272-4905, *jan@janetanncollins.com*
Membership: 6

INSPIRE CASTRO VALLEY (CV) WRITERS GROUP

Meetings: 3 Crosses Church, 20600 John Dr., Castro Valley, CA; Mondays, 6:30-8:30 p.m. (email first)
Contact: Susy Flory, 510-828-5360, *susyflory@gmail.com*
Members: 15
Affiliation: Inspire Christian Writers

SAN DIEGO CHRISTIAN WRITERS' GUILD

www.sandiegocwg.org

Meetings: throughout San Diego county, CA; members-only Internet group
Contact: Jennie Gillespie, PO Box 270403, San Diego, CA 92198; 760-294-3269; *info@sandiegocwg.org*
Members: 200

COLORADO

ACFW COLORADO SPRINGS

www.acfwcs.acfwcolorado.com

Meetings: First Evangelical Free Church, 3022 W. Fontanero St., Colorado Springs, CO; generally first Saturday of the month
Contact: Mary Agius, 719-686-7761, *acfwcs.president@acfwcolorado.com*
Members: 45
Affiliation: American Christian Fiction Writers

ACFW COLORADO WESTERN SLOPE

www.westernslopeacfw.blogspot.com

Meetings: The Artful Cup, 3090 N. 12th St., Grand Junction, CO; fourth Saturday of the month, 10:00 a.m.
Contact: Niki Turner, *niki716@gmail.com*
Members: 9
Membership fee: $10/year
Affiliation: American Christian Fiction Writers

ACFW SOUTH DENVER

acfwsouthdenver.acfwcolorado.com

Meetings: Highlands Ranch Library, 9292 S. Ridgeline Blvd., Highlands Ranch, CO; see website for day and time
Contact: Caren Boddie, 720-331-9361, *hike5837@msn.com*
Members: 10
Affiliation: American Christian Fiction Writers

SPRINGS WRITERS

springswriters.wordpress.com

Meetings: Woodmen Valley Chapel, 250 E. Woodmen Rd., Colorado Springs, CO; second Tuesday of each month except July, August, and December, 6:00-8:00 p.m.
Contact: Scoti Springfield Domeij, 719-209-9066, *springswriters@gmail.com*
Members: 350

WRITERS ON THE ROCK, HIGHLANDS RANCH

www.facebook.com/groups/WritersOnTheRock

Meetings: Living Way Church, 345 E. Wildcat Reserve Pkwy., Littleton, CO; second Saturday of the month, 10:00 a.m.-2:00 p.m.

Contact: David Rupert, 720-237-7487, *info@writersontherock.com*
Members: 170

WRITERS ON THE ROCK, LAKEWOOD

www.writersontherock.com

Meetings: Green Mountain Recreation Center, 13198 W. Green Mountain Dr., Lakewood, CO; fourth Tuesday of the month, 7:00 p.m.
Contact: David Rupert, 720-237-7487, *info@writersontherock.com*
Members: 170

CONNECTICUT

WORD WEAVERS BERKSHIRES

wordweaversberkshires.org

Meetings: Sherman Church, 6 Church Rd., Sherman, CT 06784; third Saturday of the month, 9:00 a.m. to noon
Contact: Tara Alemany, *info@wordweaversberkshires.org*
Members: 15
Membership fee: $45/year
Affiliation: Word Weavers International

WORD WEAVERS SOUTH FAIRFIELD COUNTY

Meetings: Panera Bread, 2320 Black Rock Turnpike, Fairfield, CT; second Saturday of the month, 10:00 a.m. to noon
Contact: Tara Alemany, *info@wordweaversberkshires.org*
Membership fee: $45/year
Affiliation: Word Weavers International

DELAWARE

DELMARVA CHRISTIAN WRITERS' FELLOWSHIP

www.delmarvawriters.com

Meetings: Georgetown Presbyterian Church, Tunnell Hall, 203 N. Bedford St., Georgetown, DE; third Saturday of the month, 9:00 a.m. to noon
Contact: Candy Abbott, 302-856-6649, *info@delmarvawriters.com*
Members: 20+
Membership fee: none

KINGDOM WRITERS FELLOWSHIP

Meetings: Atlanta Road Alliance Church, 22625 Atlanta Rd., Seaford, DE; second Thursday of the month, 6:15-8:30 p.m.
Contact: Eva Maddox, 302-628-4594, *evacmaddox@outlook.com*
Members: 10
Affiliation: Delmarva Christian Writers' Fellowship

VINE AND VESSELS CHRISTIAN WRITERS FELLOWSHIP

www.vineandvessels.com

Meetings: Seaford Library, 600 N. Market St., Seaford, DE; fourth Saturday of the month, 10 a.m. to noon
Contact: Joyce Sessoms, 302-382-9904, *crownjewel777@comcast.net*; or Betty Ricks-Jarman, 302-448-5939
Members: 10-12
Affiliation: Delmarva Christian Writers' Fellowship

FLORIDA

ACFW CENTRAL FLORIDA CHAPTER

www.cfacfw.org

Meetings: Grace Covenant Presbyterian Church, 1655 Peel Ave., Orlando, FL; third Saturday of the month, January—October, noon to 2 p.m.
Contact: Kristen Stieffel, 407-928-7801, *treasurer@cfacfw.com*
Members: 15
Affiliation: American Christian Fiction Writers

BRANDON CHRISTIAN WRITERS

brandonchristianwriters.wordpress.com

Meetings: St. Andres United Methodist Church, 3315 Bryan Rd., Brandon, FL; fourth Thursday of the month, January—October, 7:00-9:00 p.m.
Contact: Kat Heckenbach, *info@brandonchristianwriters.com*
Members: 20
Membership fee: $20
Affiliation: American Christian Writers

CALLAHAN CREATIVE WRITING WORKSHOP

www.callahanwriters.blogspot.com

Meetings: Callahan Branch Library, 450077 State Road 200, Ste. 15, Callahan, FL; selected Tuesdays, 6:15-8:00 p.m.

Contact: Nancy Lee Bethea, 904-403-4360, *nancyleebethea@gmail.com*
Members: 40-50
Affiliation: American Christian Fiction Writers

NORTH JAX WORD WEAVERS

Meetings: North Jacksonville Baptist Church, 8531 N. Main St., Jacksonville, FL; second Saturday of the month, 10 a.m. to 1:00 p.m.
Contact: Richard New, *loco7mo@yahoo.com*
Members: 4
Membership fee: $45/year adults, $35/year teens
Affiliation: Word Weavers International

SOUTH FLORIDA WORD WEAVERS

Meetings: Hartman Household, 1729 N.W. 36 Ct., Oakland Park, FL; second Saturday of the month, 9:30 a.m.
Contact: Patricia Hartman, *patricia@patriciahartman.com*
Members: 15
Membership fee: $45/year
Affiliation: Word Weavers International

SPACE COAST WORD WEAVERS

Meetings: Brevard County Public Libraries, 308 Forrest Ave., Cocoa, FL; second Sunday of the month, 2:00-4:30 p.m.
Contact: Dylyce P. Clarke, *1royaldy@gmail.com*
Members: 12
Membership fee: $45/year
Affiliation: Word Weavers International

SUNCOAST CHRISTIAN WRITERS GROUP

Meetings: Panera Bread, Largo Mall, 10500 Ulmerton Rd., Largo, FL; third Thursday of the month, 10 a.m.
Contact: Elaine Creasman, 727-251-3756, *emcreasman@aol.com*
Members: 15

VOLUSIA WORD WEAVERS

Meetings: Faith Church Fellowship Hall, 4700 S. Clyde Morris Blvd., Port Orange, FL; first Monday of the month, 7:00 p.m.
Contact: Patricia Keough-Wilson, *keoughwilson_239@msn.com*
Members: 20
Membership fee: $45/year
Affiliation: Word Weavers International

WORD WEAVERS DESTIN

Meetings: Village Baptist Church, bldg. 8, 101 Matthew Dr., Destin, FL; second Saturday of the month, 9:30 a.m.
Contact: Chris Manion, *Writeaway@me.com*
Members: 6
Membership fee: $45/year
Affiliation: Word Weavers International

WORD WEAVERS GAINESVILLE FLORIDA

Meetings: alternating member homes, Gainesville, FL; fourth Sunday of the month, 2:00-4:00 p.m.
Contact: John Brewer, *aplbytes@gmail.com*
Members: 5-10
Membership fee: $45/year
Affiliation: Word Weavers International

WORD WEAVERS LAKE COUNTY

Meetings: Calvary Chapel, 1601 W. Main St., Leesburg, FL; second Saturday of the month, 10 a.m.
Contact: C. Kevin Thompson, *ckevinthompson@gmail.com*
Members: 7
Membership fee: $45/year
Affiliation: Word Weavers International

WORD WEAVERS OCALA CHAPTER

Meetings: Marion County Public Library, Ocala, 2720 E. Silver Springs Blvd., Ocala, FL; third Sunday of the month, 1:30-4:00 p.m.
Contact: Delores Kight, *Delores@FHRX.net*
Members: 10+
Membership fee: $45/year
Affiliation: Word Weavers International

WORD WEAVERS OF CLAY COUNTY

Meetings: Fleming Island, FL; third Saturday of the month, 10:00 a.m.
Contact: Shari McGriff, *Shari.McGriff@gmail.com*
Members: 7
Membership fee: $45/year
Affiliation: Word Weavers International

WORD WEAVERS OF THE TREASURE COAST

Meetings: First Church of God, 1105 58th Ave., Vero Beach, FL; first Saturday of the month or second Saturday if the first falls on a major holiday, 9:30 a.m.
Contact: Loretta Beasley, *ruhischild2@bellsouth.net*
Members: 17
Membership fee: $45/year
Affiliation: Word Weavers International

WORD WEAVERS ORLANDO

www.facebook.com/wordweaversorlando

Meetings: Calvary Chapel, 5015 Goddard Ave., Orlando, FL; second Saturday of the month, 9:45 a.m.
Contact: Rick Whitted, *Rick@rawhitted.com*
Members: 40-45
Membership fee: $45/year
Affiliation: Word Weavers International

WORD WEAVERS TAMPA

Meetings: Jan Powell, 1901 S. Village Ave., Tampa, FL; first Saturday of the month, 9:30 a.m. to noon
Contact: Donna Mumma, *WriteMore@Verizon.net*
Members: 22
Membership fee: $45/year
Affiliation: Word Weavers International

GEORGIA

ACFW NORTH GEORGIA

www.acfwnga.com

Meetings: Buford First United Methodist Church, 285 E. Main St., Buford, GA; fourth Tuesday of each month, 7:00-9:00 p.m.
Contact: Kristi Ann Hunter, *acfwnga@gmail.com*
Members: 20
Affiliation: American Christian Fiction Writers

CHRISTIAN AUTHORS GUILD, INC.

www.christianauthorsguild.org

Meetings: Prayer & Praise Christian Fellowship, 6409 Bells Ferry Rd., Woodstock, GA; first Monday of the month, 7:00 p.m.

Contact: M. L. Anderson, *info@christianauthorsguild.org*
Members: 50
Membership fee: $30/year

WORD WEAVERS GREATER ATLANTA

Meetings: 4541 Vendome Pl. N.E., Roswell, GA; first Saturday of the month, 9:00-11:30 a.m.
Contact: Dana Turpin, *alboc@bellsouth.net*
Membership fee: $45/year
Affiliation: Word Weavers International

WORD WEAVERS WOODSTOCK

Meetings: Prayer & Praise Christian Fellowship, 6409 Bells Ferry Rd., Woodstock, GA; third Monday of the month, 7:00 p.m.
Contact: Jennifer Henn, *JenniferHennWriter@gmail.com*
Members: 15
Membership fee: $45/year
Affiliation: Word Weavers International

ILLINOIS

ACFW CHICAGO CHAPTER

www.acfwchicago.com

Meetings: Schaumburg Public Library, 130 S. Roselle Rd., Schaumburg, IL; second Friday of every month
Contact: Lara Helmling, 815-979-8614, *Lara@larahelmling.com*
Members: 20
Affiliation: American Christian Fiction Writers

AURORA ILLINOIS WORD WEAVERS

Meetings: email for location; second Saturday of each month, 1:00-3:00 p.m.
Contact: Cindy Huff, *cindyhuff11@gmail.com*
Members: 7
Membership fee: $45/year
Affiliation: Word Weavers International

WORD WEAVERS LAND OF LINCOLN

Meetings: Lincoln Christian University, 100 Campus View Dr., Lincoln, IL; second Saturday of every month, 10:00 a.m.
Contact: April Godsil, *godsil@springnet1.com*

Members: 9
Membership fee: $45/year
Affiliation: Word Weavers International

WORD WEAVERS O'FALLON

www.scribesofpraise.org

Meetings: First Baptist Church O'Fallon, 1111 E. Hwy. 50, O'Fallon, IL; second Saturday of each month, 1:00-2:00 p.m.
Contact: Tammika Jones, *tmdjones1@gmail.com*
Members: 4
Membership fee: $45/year
Affiliation: Word Weavers International

WORD WEAVERS ON THE BORDER

Meetings: email for location; fourth Wednesday of the month, 7:00-8:30 p.m.
Contact: Kathleen Helgesen, *KathleenHelgesen@gmail.com*
Members: 7
Membership fee: $45/year
Affiliation: Word Weavers International

INDIANA

ACFW INDIANA CHAPTER

www.hoosierink.blogspot.com

Meetings: various places in Indiana, quarterly
Contact: Karla Akins, 260-578-1775, *acfwindianachapter@gmail.com*
Members: 50
Affiliation: American Christian Fiction Writers

BLUFFTON CHRISTIAN WRITING CLUB

Facebook group: Bluffton IN Christian Writing Group

Meetings: River Terrace Retirement Community, 400 Caylor Blvd., Bluffton, IN; third Monday of the month, 6:30-8:30 p.m.
Contact: Kayleen Reusser, *kjreusser@adamswell.com*
Members: 12
Membership fee: none

FORT WAYNE CHRISTIAN WRITING CLUB

Meetings: Waynedale Public Library, 2200 Lower Huntington Rd.,

Fort Wayne, IN; fourth Tuesday of the month, 6:00-8:00 p.m.
Contact: Kayleen Reusser, *kjreusser@adamswells.com*
Members: 10

HEARTLAND CHRISTIAN WRITERS

www.facebook.com/Heartland-Christian-Writers-Community-181346731973054

Meetings: Mount Pleasant Christian Church's Community Life Center, 381 N. Bluff Rd., Greenwood, IN; third Monday of every month, 9:30 a.m. and 6:30 p.m.
Contact: Michele Israel Harper, 317-550-9755, *MicheleIsraelHarper@gmail.com*
Members: 45+

KANSAS

ACFW KANSAS CITY WEST

www.facebook.com/ACFWKansasCityWestChapter

Meetings: Bonner Springs City Library, 201 N. Nettleton Ave., Bonner Springs, KS; second Saturday of every month, 1:00-3:00 p.m.; optional critique group, 3:30-5:00 p.m.
Contact: Susan Hollaway, *acfwkcwest@gmail.com*
Members: 10-15
Affiliation: American Christian Fiction Writers

LOUISIANA

WORD WEAVERS LAFAYETTE

Meetings: Lafayette Parish South Regional Library, 6101 Johnston St., Lafayette, LA; second Saturday of the month, 12:30-2:30 p.m.
Contact: John Boudreaux, *Goofus12000@hotmail.com*
Membership fee: $45/year
Affiliation: American Christian Fiction Writers

MARYLAND

MOUNTAIN CHRISTIAN CHURCH WRITERS' GROUP

MountainCC.org/WritersGroup

Meetings: New Life Center, Room 118/120, 1824 Mountain Rd., Bel

Air, MD; Sundays, 2:30-4:30 p.m.
Contact: Mary Bach, 410-877-1824 ext. 131, *marybach@mountainchristian.org*
Members: 20+

MICHIGAN

WORD WEAVERS WEST MICHIGAN–GRANDVILLE

Meetings: Russ' Restaurant, 4440 Chicago Dr., S.W., Grandville, MI; first and third Tuesdays, 6:30-8:30 p.m.
Contact: Kathy Bruins, *author@kathybruins.com*
Members: 5
Membership fee: $45/year
Affiliation: Word Weavers International

WORD WEAVERS WEST MICHIGAN–HOLLAND

Meetings: City on a Hill, 100 Pine St., Zeeland, MI; first and third Tuesdays of the month, 12:30-2:30 p.m.
Contact: Kathy Bruins, *author@kathybruins.com*
Members: 10
Membership fee: $45/year
Affiliation: Word Weavers International

WORD WEAVERS WEST MICHIGAN–MUSKEGON

Meetings: Norton Shores Public Library, 705 Seminole Rd., Norton Shores, MI; first and third Tuesdays, 5:45-7:45 p.m.
Contact: Kathy Bruins, *author@kathybruins.com*
Members: 10
Membership fee: $45/year
Affiliation: Word Weavers International

WORD WEAVERS WEST MICHIGAN–NORTH GRAND RAPIDS

Meetings: York Creek Community Center, 3999 Alpenhorn N.W., Walker, MI; first and third Tuesday of the month, 6:30-8:30 p.m.
Contact: Kathy Bruins, *author@kathybruins.com*
Membership fee: $45/year
Affiliation: Word Weavers International

MINNESOTA

ACFW MINNESOTA N.I.C.E.

www.acfwminnesotanice.com

Meetings: Trinity Baptist Church, 2220 Edgerton St., Maplewood, MN; usually fourth Sunday of the month, 6:00-8:00 p.m.
Contact: Gabrielle Meyer, *acfw.mn_nice@yahoo.com*
Members: 25
Affiliation: American Christian Fiction Writers

MINNESOTA CHRISTIAN WRITERS GUILD

www.mnchristianwriters.com

Meetings: Oak Knoll Lutheran Church, 600 Hopkins Crossroad, Minnetonka, MN; second Monday of the month, September—May, 7:00-8:30 p.m.
Contact: Beverly Snyder, *info@mnchristianwriters.com*
Membership fee: $50/year

MISSOURI

HEART OF AMERICA CHRISTIAN WRITERS NETWORK

www.hacwn.org

Meetings: Greater Kansas City area; monthly informational meetings, biweekly critique groups
Contact: Jeanette Littleton, 816-459-8016, *HACWN@earthlink.net*
Members: 150

HEARTLAND CHRISTIAN COLLEGE WRITERS GUILD

www.facebook.com/groups/663817230321189

Meetings: Solid Rock Café, 6512 Shelby Rd., Bethel, MO; first Monday of the month, 6:30 p.m.
Contact: Kathy Nickerson, *Kathy@kathynick.com*
Members: 20
Membership fee: none

OZARKS CHAPTER OF AMERICAN CHRISTIAN WRITERS

www.OzarksACW.org

Meetings: University Heights Baptist Church, 1010 S. National,

Springfield, MO; second Saturday September—May, 10:00 a.m.-2:00 p.m.

Contact: Dr. Jeanetta Chrystie, 417-832-8409, *OzarksACW@yahoo.com*

Members: 50

Membership fee: $20, $30 family, $10 subscription only

Affiliation: American Christian Writers

NEBRASKA

MY THOUGHTS EXACTLY

mythoughtsexactlywriters.wordpress.com

Meetings: place varies, Fremont, NE; time varies

Contact: Cheryl, 402-727-6508, *Cheryl@seekingbalancebycheryl.com*

Members: 6

NEW JERSEY

NORTH JERSEY CHRISTIAN WRITERS GROUP

www.njcwg.blogspot.com

Meetings: Cornerstone Christian Church, 495 Wyckoff Ave., Wyckoff, NJ; usually first Saturday of each month, 10:00 a.m. to noon

Contact: Barbara Higby, *njcwgroup@gmail.com*

Members: 12

NEW YORK

SOUTHERN TIER CHRISTIAN WRITERS

Meetings: Olean First Baptist Church, 133 S. Union St., Olean, NY; first and third Mondays, April—October, 7:00 p.m.; first Monday only November—March, 6:00 p.m.

Contact: Deb Wuethrich, 716-379-8702, *deborahmarcein@gmail.com*

Members: 9

Affiliation: American Christian Writers

WORD WEAVERS WESTERN NEW YORK

Meetings: email for place; third Thursday of every month, 6:30-9:00 p.m.

Contact: Janet Erikson, *janericks@aol.com*

Membership fee: $45/year
Affiliation: Word Weavers International

NORTH AND SOUTH DAKOTA

ACFW DAKOTAS

www.facebook.com/groups/ACFWDakotas

Meetings: location, day of week, and frequency varies by region
Contact: Shannon McNear, 843-327-0583, *sdmcnear@gmail.com*
Members: 15
Affiliation: American Christian Fiction Writers

NORTH CAROLINA

CHARLOTTE WORD WEAVERS

Meetings: Carmel Presbyterian Church, Ligon Hall, 2048 Carmel Rd., Charlotte, NC; third Saturday of the month, 2:00-4:00 p.m.
Contact: Kim Dent, *Kimberlyjamesdent@gmail.com*
Members: 20
Membership fee: $45/year
Affiliation: Word Weavers International

WILMINGTON WORD WEAVERS

Meetings: Live Oak Church, 740 S. College Rd., Wilmington, NC; first Monday of the month, 7:00 p.m.
Contact: Erika Rizkallah, *ELRizkallah@gmail.com*
Members: 20
Membership fee: $45/year
Affiliation: Word Weavers International

OHIO

ACFW OHIO

www.facebook.com/groups/220166801456380

Meetings: Etna United Methodist Church, 500 Pike St., Etna, OH; first Saturday of the month, noon to 3:00 p.m.
Contact: Tamera Lynn Kraft, 330-733-8007, *tkrafty@sbcglobal.net*
Membership: 20
Affiliation: American Christian Fiction Writers

BEING A HAPPY HEALTHY HOLY WOMAN

www.facebook.com/HappyHealthyHolyWoman

Meetings: Abundant Season Anointed Ministries International, 643 Troy St., Dayton, OH; conference call monthly, annual meeting
Contact: Dr. J. Robinson, 937-275-3770, *happyhealthyholy@live.com*
Members: 1100
Membership fee: none

DAYTON CHRISTIAN SCRIBES

Meetings: Kettering Seventh-Day Adventist Church, 3939 Stonebridge Rd., Kettering, OH; second Thursday of the month, 7:00-9:00 p.m.
Contact: Lois Pecce, 937-433-6470, *daytonchristianscribes@gmail.com*
Members: 35
Affiliations: Dayton Christian Writers Guild, Middletown Area Christian Writers

DAYTON CHRISTIAN WRITERS GUILD

www.facebook.com/ChristianAuthorToles

Meetings: Corinthian Baptist Church, 700 S. James McGhee Blvd. Dayton, OH; second Saturday of the month, 2:00 p.m.
Contact: Tina Tole, through Facebook page

MIDDLETOWN AREA CHRISTIAN WRITERS (MAC WRITERS)

www.facebook.com/MACwriters

Meetings: Healing Word Assembly of God, 5303 S. Dixie Hwy., Middleton, OH; third Tuesday of each month, 7:00-8:30 p.m.
Contact: Donna J. Shepherd, 513-423-1627, *donna.shepherd@gmail.com*
Members: 25
Membership fee: $30/year, $5/meeting

NORTHWEST OHIO CHRISTIAN WRITERS

www.nwocw.org

Meetings: St. Mark's Lutheran Church, 315 S. College, Bowling Green, OH; fourth Friday of January, March, May, July, and September, 11:00 a.m.
Contact: Shelley R. Lee, 419-308-3615, *shellyrlee@gmail.com*
Members: 25
Membership fee: $20
Affiliation: American Christian Writers

WORD WEAVERS NORTHEAST OHIO

Meetings: First Church of the Brethren, 122 E. 3rd St., Ashland, OH; first Thursday of each month, 6:30 p.m.
Contact: Tina Hunt/Shellie Arnold, *neohwordweavers@gmail.com*
Members: 8
Membership fee: $45/year
Affiliation: Word Weavers International

OKLAHOMA

FELLOWSHIP OF CHRISTIAN WRITERS

fellowshipofchristianwriters.org

Meetings: Kirk of the Hills Presbyterian Church, 4102 E. 61st, Tulsa, OK; second Tuesday of month, 7:00 p.m.
Contact: Martha Curtis, 918-855-0809, *marthajcurtis@yahoo.com*
Members: 50
Membership fee: $35

OKLAHOMA CHRISTIAN FICTION WRITERS

okcchristianfictionwriters.blogspot.com

Meetings: Henderson Hills Baptist Church, 1200 E. I-35 Frontage Rd., Edmond, OK; third Saturday of each month, 1:00-3:00 p.m.
Contact: J. J. Johnson, 405-615-9594, *ocfwchapter@gmail.com*
Members: 35
Affiliation: American Christian Fiction Writers

WORDWRIGHTS

www.wordwrights-okc.com

Meetings: Catholic Pastoral Center, Room B13, 7501 N.W. Expressway, Oklahoma City, OK; second Saturday of the month, 10:00 a.m. to noon
Contact: Milton Smith, *hiswordmatters@yahoo.com*
Members: 30

OREGON

OREGON CHRISTIAN WRITERS

www.oregonchristianwriters.org

Meetings: Portland, OR metro area, three all-day Saturday conferences, summer coaching conference

Contact: *president@oregonchristianwriters.com*, 503-393-3356
Membership fee: $60/year, $75 couples, $35 students and seniors

WORD WEAVERS PORTLAND EAST

Meetings: Panera Bread, 1017 N.W. Civic Dr., Gresham, OR; second Saturday of every month, 10:00 a.m.
Contact: Tere Belcher, *talkin_tere@yahoo.com*
Members: 10
Membership fee: $45/year
Affiliation: Word Weavers International

WORDWRIGHTS

Meetings: Gresham/east Multnomah County, OR; two times a month, Thursday afternoons
Contact: Susan Thogerson Maas, 503-663-7834, *susan.maas@frontiercom*
Members: 5

PENNSYLVANIA

ACFW PENNSYLVANIA STATE CHAPTER

acfwpennsylvania.com

Meetings: online, fourth Tuesday of the month, 7:30 p.m.
Contact: Donna L. H. Smith, 717-201-2675, *dlhswriter@windstream.net*
Members: 35
Affiliation: American Christian Fiction Writers

CHRISTIAN WRITERS GUILD

Meetings: Perkin's Restaurant, 505 Galleria Dr., Johnstown, PA; last Tuesday of each month except July and December, 1:00 p.m.
Contact: Betty Rosian, 814-255-4351, *wordsforall@hotmail.com*
Members: 12

GREATER PHILLY CHRISTIAN WRITERS FELLOWSHIP

www.writehisanswer.com/cwfsmorningcritiquegroup

Meetings: Marlene Bagnull's home, 951 Anders Rd., Lansdale, PA; monthly, usually the third Thursday, 10 a.m.-12:30 p.m.
Contact: Marlene Bagnull, 484-991-8581, *mbagnull@aol.com*
Members: 10
Membershiip fee: none

JOHNSTOWN AREA CHRISTIAN WRITERS GUILD

Meetings: Perkins Restaurant, 505 Galleria Dr., Richland, PA; last Tuesday of each month except December
Contact: Betty Rosian, 814-255-4351, *wordsforall@hotmail.com*
Members: 12
Membership fee: $10/year

LANCASTER CHRISTIAN WRITERS

lancasterchristianwriterstoday.Blogspot.com

Meetings: Lancaster Alliance Church, 210 Pitney Rd., Lancaster, PA; third Saturday of the month, 9:30 a.m. to noon
Contact: Jeanette Windle, *jeanette@jeanettewindle.com*
Affiliation: American Christian Writers

LANSDALE, PA WOMEN'S CRITIQUE GROUP

www.writehisanswer.com/cwfseveningcritiquegroup

Meetings: Marlene Bagnull's home, 951 Anders Rd., Lansdale, PA; every other Thursday, 7:30-10:00 p.m.
Contact: Marlene Bagnull, 484-991-8581, *mbagnull@aol.com*
Members: 12
Membership fee: none

SOUTH CAROLINA

SOUTH CAROLINA CHAPTER OF ACFW

scwritersacfw.blogspot.com

Meetings: North Anderson Baptist Church, 2308 N. Main St., Anderson, SC; usually fourth Saturday of the month except July and December, November is third Saturday, 2:00-5:00 p.m.
Contact: Elva Martin, 864-226-7024, *elvacmartin@gmail.com*
Members: 20+
Affiliation: American Christian Fiction Writers

WORD WEAVERS LEXINGTON CHAPTER

www.LexingtonWordWeavers.com

Meetings: Riverbend Community Church, 1015 Corley Mill Rd., Lexington, SC; second Monday of every month, 6:45-9:00 p.m.
Contact: Jean Wilund, *info@lexingtonwordweavers.com*
Members: 33
Membership fee: $45/year
Affiliation: Word Weavers International

WORD WEAVERS SUMMERVILLE

Meetings: Summerville Presbyterian Church, 407 S. Laurel St., Summerville, SC; first Monday of each month, 7:00 p.m.
Contact: Jeannine Brummett, *Summerville.lady@yahoo.com*
Members: 9
Membership fee: $45/year
Affiliation: Word Weavers International

WRITING 4 HIM

Meetings: Christian Supply, 1600 Reidville Rd., Spartanburg, SC 29301; second Thursday of the month, 9:45 a.m.
Contact: Linda Gilden, *linda@lindagilden.com*
Members: 75
Membership fee: none

TENNESSEE

ACFW MEMPHIS

Meetings: Compassion Church, 3505 S. Houston Levee, Germantown, TN; third Saturday of the month except December, 10 a.m. to noon
Contact: Loretta Eidson, *Loretta@LorettaEidson.com*
Members: 15
Affiliation: American Christian Fiction Writers

CHATTANOOGA WORD WEAVERS

Meetings: McKee Library, Southern Adventist University, 4881 Taylor Cir., Collegedale, TN; second Thursday of the month, 7:00-9:00 p.m.
Contact: Roberta Fish, *robertamfish@gmail.com*
Members: 12
Membership fee: $45/year
Affiliation: Word Weavers International

MIDDLE TENNESSEE ACFW

Meetings: Woodmont Baptist Church, 2100 Woodmont Blvd., Nashville, TN; first Saturday of every month, 10 a.m. to noon
Contact: Julie Gwinn, 615-957-3443, *julie@theseymouragency.com*
Members: 25
Affiliation: American Christian Fiction Writers

WORD WEAVERS NASHVILLE

Meetings: Metro Baptist Church, Fellowship Hall, 322 E Cedar St., Goodlettsville, TN; 6:00–8:00 p.m.
Contact: Callie Daruk, *DarukC@Gmail.com*
Membership fee: $45/year
Affiliation: Word Weavers International

TEXAS

ACFW CENTRAL TEXAS CHAPTER

www.centexacfw.com

Meetings: Georgetown Public Library, 402 W. 8th St., Georgetown, TX; second Saturday of the month, 9:30-11:30 a.m.
Contact: Joy Nord, 512-626-7304, *glyndajoynord@yahoo.com*
Members: 20
Affiliation: American Christian Fiction Writers

ACFW DFW CHAPTER (AKA READY WRITERS)

www.dfwreadywriters.blogspot.com

Meetings: Arlington Community Church, 1715 W. Randol Mill Rd., Arlington, TX; second Saturday of every month, 10:00 a.m.
Contact: J. A. Marx, 972-841-4477, *embattledspirit@jamarx.net*
Members: 25-30
Affiliation: American Christian Fiction Writers

ACFW HOUSTON

www.houstonchristianauthors.com

Meetings: 16806 Glenshannon Dr., Houston, TX; second Saturday of the month, 2:00 p.m.
Contact: Lisa Godfrees, *houstonchristianauthors@gmail.com*
Members: 10
Membership fee: $10
Affiliation: American Christian Fiction Writers

ACFW, THE WOODLANDS
(FORMERLY WRITERS ON THE STORM)

wotsacfw.blogspot.com

Meetings: Lupe Tortilla, 19437 Interstate 45, Shenandoah, TX; third Saturday of every month except October and December, 11:00 a.m.-1:00 p.m.

Contact: Kathrese McKee, *wots.acfw@gmail.com*
Members: 30
Membership fee: $30/year
Affiliation: American Christian Fiction Writers

ALAMO CITY CHRISTIAN FICTION WRITERS

Meetings: La Madeleine, 722 N.W. Loop 410, San Antonio, TX; second Saturday of the month, 10 a.m. to noon
Contact: Allison Pittman, 210-241-7257 (text preferred)
Members: 15
Affiliation: American Christian Fiction Writers

CENTRAL HOUSTON INSPIRATIONAL WRITERS ALIVE!

www.centralhoustoniwa.com

Meetings: Houston's First Baptist Church, 7474 Katy Fwy. (I-10), Houston, TX; second Thursday of each month except July, August, and December, 7:00 p.m.
Contact: Dana Battista, 832-315-8430, *loveeternal@comcast.net*
Members: 22

CROSS REFERENCE WRITERS

sites.google.com/site/crossreferencewriters

Meetings: Aldersgate United Methodist Church, 2201 Earl Rudder Fwy. S., College Station, TX; first Thursday of the month, 7:00-8:30 p.m.
Contact: Tammy Hensel, 979-204-0674, *CrossRefWriters@yahoo.com*
Members: 10

ROCKWALL CHRISTIAN WRITERS GROUP

rcwg.blogspot.com

Meetings: Lake Pointe Church, 701 E. I-30, Rockwall, TX; second Monday of each month, 7:00 p.m.
Contact: Darren Sapp, 214-477-4039, *darrenlsapp@gmail.com*
Members: 40

STORY HELP GROUPS

www.storyhelpgroups.org

Meetings: various locations in Dallas/Fort Worth, TX area; check the website
Contact: Frank Ball, *frank.ball@storyhelpgroups.org*
Members: 250

WRITERS LIFE GROUP

Meetings: Lakewood Church, 3700 Southwest Freeway, Houston, TX; second and fourth Fridays of each month, 7:00-8:30 p.m.
Contact: Melanie Stiles, 832-259-9576, *melstiles@aol.com*
Members: 125

VIRGINIA

CAPITAL CHRISTIAN WRITERS

capitalchristianwriters.org

Meetings: Truro Episcopal Church, Gunnell House, 10520 Main St., Fairfax, VA; second Monday of odd months
Contact: Betsy Dill, 703-803-9447, *ccwriters@gmail.com*
Members: 25

JOYWRITERS

www.facebook.com/JoyWriters-An-American-Christian-Writers-Chapter-146894242070595

Meetings: Galax, VA area
Contact: Vie Herlocker, 276-237-7574, *vherlock@yahoo.com*
Members: 7
Affiliation: American Christian Writers

RICHMOND WORD WEAVERS

Meetings: Mount Vernon Baptist Church, 11220 Nuckols Rd., Glen Allen, VA; second Tuesday of each month, 7:30 p.m.
Contact: Mary Beth Dahl, *mbdahl@marybethdahl.org*
Members: 7
Membership fee: $45/year
Affiliation: Word Weavers International

WORD WEAVERS WILLIAMSBURG

Meetings: James City County Library, 7770 Croaker Rd., Williamsburg, VA; second Monday of the month, 5:30-8:00 p.m.
Contact: Lauren Kraft, *oneilvt@gmail.com*
Members: 2
Membership fee: $45/year
Affiliation: Word Weavers International

WASHINGTON

CHRISTIAN SCRIBES

Meetings: SonBridge, 1200 S.E. 12th St., College Place, WA; second and fourth Tuesday of each month, 3:00 p.m.
Contact: Helen Heavirland, 541-938-3838, *hlh@bmi.net*
Members: 5

VANCOUVER CHRISTIAN WRITERS

Meetings: Vancouver, WA
Contact: Jon Drury, 510-909-0848, *jondrury2@yahoo.com*
Members: 5-7

WALLA WALLA CHRISTIAN WRITERS

Meetings: SonBridge, 1200 S.E. 12th St., College Place, WA; first and third Tuesday of each month, 3:00 p.m.
Contact: Helen Heavirland, 541-938-3838, *hlh@bmi.net*
Members: 5

WISCONSIN

ACFW WISCONSIN SOUTHEAST

www.facebook.com/wiseacfw

Meetings: Wisconsin Lutheran College, 8800 W. Bluemound Rd., Milwaukee, WI; first Thursday of the month 6:30-8:30 p.m.
Contact: Susan M. Baganz, 920-539-9311, *silygoos@gmail.com*
Members: 25
Affiliation: American Christian Fiction Writers

PENS OF PRAISE CHRISTIAN WRITERS

Meetings: Faith Church, 2201 42nd St., Manitowoc, WI; third Monday of every month, 6:30-8:30 p.m.
Contact: Becky McLafferty, 920-758-9196, *rebeccamclafferty@gmail.com* or Sue Kinney, 920-242-3631, *susanmarlenekinney@gmail.com*
Members: 8-12

WESTERN WISCONSIN CHRISTIAN WRITERS GUILD

www.wwcwg.com

Meetings: Bethesda Lutheran Church, 123 W. Hamilton, Eau Claire, WI; second Tuesday of each month, 7:00 p.m.

Contact: Sheila Wilkinson, 715-839-1207, *wwcwg.info@gmail.com*
Members: 20

WORD AND PEN CHRISTIAN WRITERS CLUB

wordandpenchristianwriters.wordpress.com

Meetings: St. Thomas Episcopal Church, 226 Washington St., Menasha, WI; second Monday of the month except December, 7:00-9:00 p.m.
Contact: Chris Stratton, 920-739-0752, *gcefsi@new.rr.com*
Members: 14
Membership fee: $10/year

CANADA

MANITOBA CHRISTIAN WRITERS ASSOCIATION

Meetings: Bleak House, 1637 Main St., Winnipeg, MB; Saturdays once a month, 1:30-4:00 p.m.
Contact: Frieda Martens, 204-256-3642, *friedamartens1910@gmail.com*
Membership: 16
Membership fee: $25/year, $3 visitors
Affiliation: InScribe Christian Writers' Fellowship

THE WORD GUILD

www.thewordguild.com

Contact: Ruth Thorogood, executive director, 245 King George Rd., Ste. 226, Brantford, ON N3R 7N7, Canada; 800-969-9010; *info@thewordguild.com*
Services: Regional writers chapters across Canada. Sponsors the annual Write Canada conference in Toronto and contests and awards for Canadian Christian writers.
Members: 325

19

EDITORIAL SERVICES

Entries in this chapter are for information only, not an endorsement of editing skills. Before hiring a freelance editor, ask for references if they are not posted on the website; and contact two or three to help determine if this editor is a good fit for you. You may also want to pay for an edit of a few pages or one chapter before hiring someone to edit your complete manuscript.

A LITTLE RED INK | BETHANY KACZMAREK

Jarrettsville, MD | 443-608-4013
editor@bethanykaczmarek.com | *www.bethanykaczmarek.com*

Contact: email
Services: manuscript evaluation, substantive editing/rewriting, copyediting, proofreading
Types of manuscripts: short stories, novels, adult, teen/YA
Charges: hourly rate
Credentials/experience: An ACFW Editor of the Year finalist (2015), Bethany enjoys working with both traditional and indie authors. Several of her clients are award-winning and best-selling authors, though she does work with aspiring authors as well. She has edited for speculative fiction publishing houses Enclave Publishing and Brimstone Fiction.

A LITTLE RED INK | ERYNNE NEWMAN

Travelers Rest, SC | 919-229-1357
ALittleRedInk@gmail.com | *www.ALittleRedInk.com*

Contact: email, website form
Services: manuscript evaluation, substantive editing/rewriting, copyediting, proofreading
Types of manuscripts: short stories, novels, book proposals, adult, teen/YA
Charges: hourly rate

Credentials/experience: Rita Award-winning editor with five years of experience.

A WAY WITH WORDS WRITING AND EDITORIAL SERVICES | RENEE GRAY-WILBURN

Colorado Springs, CO | 719-271-7076
waywords@earthlink.net

Contact: email

Services: substantive editing/rewriting, copyediting, proofreading, ghostwriting, coauthoring, write website text, create small group Bible study guides, write curriculum lesson plans, write discussion questions for books, write from transcriptions, write children's books and other material, résumé design and writing

Types of manuscripts: articles, nonfiction books, devotionals, short stories, novels, curriculum, gift books, technical material, adult, teen/YA, picture books, easy readers, middle grade

Charges: hourly rate

Credentials/experience: More than twenty years of freelance writing and editing. Wrote five children's books for Capstone Press; extensive curriculum writing for David C. Cook and Group Publishing; wrote children's articles/activities and parenting articles for Focus on the Family; developed online study guides for Wallbuilders; extensive copyediting and proofreading for NavPress (including the Remix Message Bible), David C. Cook, WaterBrook, and major international ministries, as well as numerous independent authors.

AB WRITING SERVICES LLC | ANN BYLE

3149 Boyes Ave. N.E., Grand Rapids, MI 49525 | 616-389-4436
annbyle@gmail.com | *www.annbylewriter.com*

Contact: email

Services: manuscript evaluation, copyediting, proofreading, ghostwriting, coauthoring, book-contract evaluation, brochures, newsletters, website text, discussion questions for books, back-cover copy, writing coach

Types of manuscripts: articles, nonfiction books, devotionals, novels, query letters, book proposals, adult

Charges: flat fee

Credentials/experience: Ann is a former newspaper copyeditor and newsletter editor, as well as a former literary agent. She is currently a full-time freelance writer for national and local publications, coauthor of a nonfiction book, and author of *Christian Publishing 101*. She has thousands of articles to her credit; has interviewed hundreds of authors, publishing professionals, and others; written back-cover copy and press releases; and is cofounder of the Breathe Christian Writers Conference.

ABOVE THE PAGES | PAM LAGOMARSINO

Coulterville, CA | 209-878-0245
abovethepages@gmail.com | *www.abovethepages.com*

Contact: email
Services: manuscript evaluation, substantive editing/rewriting, copyediting, proofreading, create small group/Bible study guides, write discussion questions for books
Types of manuscripts: articles, nonfiction books, devotionals, short stories, curriculum, gift books, adult, teen/YA, picture books, easy readers, middle grade, homeschool and children's ministry materials
Charges: flat fee, word rate
Credentials/experience: AA in English communication; two years of editing experience for Christian nonfiction books, devotionals, sermons, workbooks, homeschool curriculum, and children's materials; certificates in Essential Skills for Editing nonfiction and editing children's books from The Christian PEN; certificate for Keys to Effective Editing from Sandhills Community College.

ACADEMIC EDITOR | NATALIE NYQUIST

Chicago, IL
nyquist.n.m@gmail.com | *natalienyquist.com*

Contact: email
Services: copyediting, proofreading, manuscript evaluation, substantive editing/rewriting, ghostwriting, coauthoring, small group/Bible study guides, curriculum lesson plans, discussion questions for books, PowerPoint presentations, writing coach, back-cover copy, citations and bibliographies, consulting
Types of manuscripts: nonfiction books, devotionals, novels, short stories, academic, book proposals, Bible studies, gift books, adult, teens/YA, picture books, easy readers, middle grade, textbooks, dissertations, theses, one sheets
Charges: flat fee, hourly rate, custom

Credentials/experience: Five years of experience proofreading and editing for traditional publishing houses, twelve years of experience working with private clients. Four hundred fifty book projects completed for publishing houses. Clients include Gilead Publishing, HarperCollins Hudson Bible, Kirkus, Moody, P&R, Thomas Nelson, W Publishing, Zondervan. I've worked with award-winning and *New York Times* bestselling authors and projects. I specialize in academic content and love citations and bibliographies. I also work with a few private clients per year and teach courses through the PEN Institute. Portfolio of projects on my website. LinkedIn: *www.linkedin.com/in/natalienyquist.*

ACEVEDO WORD SOLUTIONS LLC | JENNE ACEVEDO

Chandler, AZ | 480-510-0419
jenneacevedo@gmail.com | *www.jenneacevedo.com*

Contact: email
Services: substantive editing/rewriting, copyediting, proofreading, coauthoring, create newsletters, write website text, create small group/Bible study guides, write discussion questions for books, writing coach
Types of manuscripts: articles, nonfiction books, devotionals, query letters, book proposals, curriculum, gift books, adult, teen/YA, picture books, easy readers, middle grade
Charges: hourly rate, word rate
Credentials/experience: Co-owner of Christian Editor Network LLC; director of The Christian PEN: Proofreaders and Editors Network; director of PENCON; member of the Christian Editor Connection; founder and director of the Chandler Writers' Group since 2011.

ACW CRITIQUE SERVICE | REG A. FORDER

PO Box 110390, Nashville, TN 37222 | 800-21-WRITE
ACWriters@aol.com | *www.ACWriters.com*

Contact: email
Services: manuscript evaluation, substantive editing/rewriting, copyediting, proofreading
Types of manuscripts: articles, nonfiction books, devotionals, poetry, short stories, novels, query letters, book proposals, curriculum, scripts, gift books, technical material, adult, teen/YA, picture books, easy readers, middle grade
Charges: flat fee, hourly rate, page rate, word rate

Credentials/experience: Established for 35 years. Staff of experienced editors.

ADIRONDACK EDITING | SUSAN UTTENDORFSKY

adirondackediting@gmail.com | *www.adirondackediting.com*

Contact: email

Services: manuscript evaluation, substantive editing/rewriting, copyediting, proofreading, ghostwriting, writing coach

Types of manuscripts: nonfiction books, short stories, novels, book proposals, adult, teen/YA, picture books, easy readers, middle grade

Charges: word rate

Credentials/experience: As of May 2017, we've edited more than two hundred ninety fiction and nonfiction books for customers in more than twenty-four countries, covering one hundred twenty-six genres/categories—with a 60% repeat customer rate.

AM EDITING AND FREELANCE WRITING | ANGELA MCCLAIN

125 Mariner Dr., Kings Mountain, NC 28086 | 980-295-3364

ameditting35@gmail.com | *www.ameditting.webs.com*

Contact: email

Services: copyediting, proofreading, ghostwriting, create brochures, create newsletters, website text, small group/Bible study guides, writing coach

Types of manuscripts: nonfiction books, devotionals, poetry, short stories, novels, gift books, teen/YA

Charges: page rate

Credentials/experience: I have many years of experience for editing.

AMBASSADOR COMMUNICATIONS | CLAIRE HUTCHINSON

Sun City West, AZ | 812-390-7907

claire@clairehutchinson.net | *www.ambassadorcommunications.biz*

Contact: email

Services: manuscript evaluation, substantive editing/rewriting, copyediting, proofreading, ghostwriting, coauthoring, write website text, create small group/Bible study guides, write curriculum lesson plans, write discussion questions for books, create PowerPoint presentations, writing coach

Types of manuscripts: articles, nonfiction books, devotionals, poetry,

short stories, novels, query letters, scripts, gift books, adult, teen/YA, picture books, easy readers, middle grade
Charges: flat rate, page rate
Credentials/experience: BA, MA, two screenwriting certificates from UCLA.

AMI EDITING | ANNETTE IRBY

Tacoma, WA | 206-234-7780
editor@AMIediting.com | *www.AMIediting.com*

Contact: email
Services: manuscript evaluation, substantive editing/rewriting, copyediting, proofreading, critiquing
Types of manuscripts: short stories, novels
Charges: hourly rate
Credentials/experience: Annette spent five years working in acquisitions with a CBA publisher. She has more than thirteen years of experience editing in the CBA marketplace and has worked with several well-known authors and publishers. She's an author and an active book reviewer. See her website for testimonials.

AMY BOEKE'S EDITING SERVICE | AMY BOEKE

3149 Sandy Hollow Rd., Rockford, IL 61109
abboeke@gmail.com | *alight2readby.wordpress.com*

Contact: email
Services: substantive editing/rewriting, copyediting, proofreading, ghostwriting, create brochures, create newsletters, write website text, create small group/Bible study guides, write curriculum lesson plans, write discussion questions for books, create PowerPoint presentations, writing coach, back-cover copy
Types of manuscripts: articles, nonfiction books, devotionals, short stories, novels, query letters, book proposals, curriculum, Bible studies, gift books, adult, teen/YA
Charges: hourly rate
Credentials/experience: BA English studies, Taylor University; MAT secondary English education, Rockford College. Eight years of experience freelance editing/writing.

AMY DROWN

Kalispell, MT | 719-244-1743
editing@amydrown.com | *www.amydrown.com/editing*

Contact: email
Services: manuscript evaluation, substantive editing/rewriting, copyediting, proofreading
Types of manuscripts: novels, adult, teen/YA, back-cover copy, pitch sheets
Charges: flat fee, word rate
Credentials/experience: Internationally recognized freelance editor specializing in inspirational fiction writing and editing since 2009. I contract with publishers, as well as directly with authors, both published and prepublished, and offer highly competitive rates.

ANDI L. GREGORY

AndiLGregory@outlook.com | *www.AndiLGregory.com*

Contact: email
Services: copyediting, proofreading
Types of manuscripts: short stories, novels, query letters, book proposals, teen/YA, middle grade
Charges: word rate
Credentials/experience: I have published reviews for *Christian Book Previews*, *The Aboite Independent*, and *Church Libraries* and devotions for *The Secret Place*, *The Aboite Independent*, and *Fire Bible for Kids Devotional*. I graduated from Taylor University with a BA in professional writing and have attended multiple writers conferences. I have also done an editing internship with Lighthouse Publishing of the Carolinas and a newsletter-focused internship with Kathy Ide Book Services.

ANDREA MERRELL

60 McKinney Rd., Travelers Rest, SC 29690 | 864-616-5889
AndreaMerrell7@gmail.com | *www.AndreaMerrell.com, www.TheWriteEditing.com*

Contact: email, website form
Services: manuscript evaluation, substantive editing/rewriting, copyediting, proofreading, writing coach, website coach, back-cover copy
Types of manuscripts: articles, nonfiction books, devotionals, short stories, novels, adult, teen/YA
Charges: hourly rate
Credentials/experience: Professional freelance editor. Associate editor with LPC Books and Christian Devotions Ministries. Member of The Christian PEN: Proofreaders and Editors Network.

ANDY SCHEER EDITORIAL SERVICES

5074 Plumstead Dr., Colorado Springs, CO 80920 | 719-282-3729
Andy@AndyScheer.com | *AndyScheer.com*

Contact: email
Services: manuscript evaluations and critiques, copyediting, substantive editing/rewriting, back-cover copy and makeovers
Types of manuscripts: novels, nonfiction books, short stories, book proposals, one-sheets, adult, teen/YA
Charges: page rate; per project for critiques, back-cover copy, and one sheets
Credentials/experience: More than thirty years of experience in Christian writing, editing, and publishing. Former editor-in-chief of Jerry B. Jenkins Christian Writers Guild. Has served as a judge for national fiction and nonfiction contests and edited fiction and nonfiction for *New York Times* best-selling authors.

ANN KROEKER

Westfield, IN | 317-763-0002
ann@annkroeker.com | *annkroeker.com*

Contact: email
Service: writing coach
Types of manuscripts: articles, nonfiction books, devotionals, poetry, short stories, query letters, book proposals, gift books, adult
Charges: flat fee, hourly rate
Credentials/experience: Coaching offered as a package of services at a monthly rate; for occasional, one-time coaching needs I charge an hourly rate. When a client requests extensive editorial services that exceed the scope of the coaching package, I quote a flat rate per project.

ARMOR OF HOPE WRITING SERVICES | DENISE WALKER

Covington, GA | 678-656-8930
dwalker@armorofhopewritingservices.com |
www.armorofhopewritingservices.com

Contact: email
Services: copyediting, proofreading, ghostwriting, coauthoring, write curriculum lesson plans, write discussion questions for books, create PowerPoint presentations
Types of manuscripts: nonfiction books, devotionals, short stories, novels, curriculum, teen/YA, picture books, easy readers, middle grade

Charges: fees are on the website

Credentials/experience: Freelance proofreader (children's books and Christian manuscripts), middle-school language arts teacher for twelve years.

ASPIRE EDITING SERVICES | CHRISTY DISTLER

Warminster, PA | 267-231-6723
christy@aspireeditingservices.com | *www.aspireeditingservices.com*

Contact: email

Services: manuscript evaluation, substantive editing/rewriting, copyediting, proofreading

Types of manuscripts: nonfiction books, devotionals, poetry, short stories, novels, adult, picture books, easy readers

Charges: word rate

Credentials/experience: Educated at Temple University and University of California–Berkeley. Thirteen years of editorial experience, both as an employee and a freelancer. Currently works mostly for publishing houses but accepts freelance work as scheduling allows.

AUTHOR SUPPORT SERVICES | RUSSELL SHERRAD

Carmichael, CA | 916-967-7251
russellsherrard@reagan.com | *www.sherrardsebookresellers.com/WordPress/author-support-services-the-authors-place-to-get-help*

Contact: email

Services: manuscript evaluation, substantive editing/rewriting, copyediting, proofreading, blog administration, free services

Types of manuscripts: articles, nonfiction books, devotionals, short stories, novels, teen/YA, picture books, easy readers, middle grade

Charges: flat fee

Credentials/experience: Writing and editing e-books since 2009, freelance services for multiple number of clients.

BA WRITING SOLUTIONS LLC | BLAKE ATWOOD

PO Box 836662, Dallas, TX 75083-6662 | 469-844-7660
blake@editfor.me | *www.blakeatwood.com*

Contact: website form

Services: manuscript evaluation, substantive editing/rewriting, copyediting, ghostwriting, coauthoring, book-contract evaluation, create small group/Bible study guides, write discussion questions for books

Types of manuscripts: articles, nonfiction books, devotionals, query letters, book proposals, Bible studies

Charges: word rate

Credentials/experience: Blake is a full-time editor, author, and ghostwriter. He has written two books, including *Don't Fear the Reaper: Why Every Author Needs an Editor*; ghostwritten five books; cowritten three; and edited dozens more. He is a monthly columnist for *TheWriteLife.com*, is coleader of the Dallas-area chapter of the Nonfiction Authors Association, and belongs to the Editorial Freelancers Association and the Christian Proofreaders and Editors Network. After obtaining his BA in English from Southwestern University, Blake was a proofreader for the Texas Senate, a Director of Communications for a large church, a law-firm copywriter, and an editor for an online startup. Since launching his business in 2014, Blake has helped more than sixty authors get their polished words into the world, both through self-publishing and traditional publishing routes.

BARBARA KOIS

1007 Cherry St., Wheaton, IL 60187 | 630-532-2941
barbara.kois@gmail.com | *www.barbarakois.com*

Contact: email

Services: manuscript evaluation, substantive editing/rewriting, copyediting, proofreading, ghostwriting, coauthoring, write website text, newsletters, write discussion questions for books, PowerPoint presentations, writing coach, back-cover copy

Types of manuscripts: articles, nonfiction books, devotionals, poetry, short stories, novels, Bible studies, gift books, adult, teen/YA

Charges: custom

Credentials/experience: Barbara is a writer, editor, author coach, and speaker for writers conferences. She has written or cowritten eight books. She has published more than six hundred articles in the *Chicago Tribune,* as well as articles in a variety of magazines. She has edited hundreds of books for authors, spanning many topics. She is a regular contributor to technology and other corporate websites and serves as a corporate communications consultant.

BODY AND SOUL PUBLISHING, LLC | SHELLEY HITZ

PO Box 6542, Colorado Springs, CO | 719-445-6558
shelley@shelleyhitz.com | *www.shelleyhitz.com*

Contact: email

Services: author coach
Types of manuscripts: nonfiction books
Charges: monthly or yearly fee
Credentials/experience: Author of more than forty books and owner of *AuthorAudienceAcademy.com* where I help authors get their first drafts out of their heads and onto paper in record time. I teach self-publishing and book marketing.

BOOKOX | THOMAS WOMACK

165 S. Timber Creek Dr., Sisters, OR 97759 | 541-788-6503
Thomas@BookOx.com | *www.BookOx.com*

Contact: email
Services: manuscript evaluation, substantive editing/rewriting, copyediting, proofreading, ghostwriting, coauthoring, create small group/Bible study guides, write discussion questions for books, writing coach, indexing
Types of manuscripts: nonfiction books, devotionals, short stories, novels, book proposals, Bible studies, gift books, picture books, easy readers, middle grade, business, leadership
Charges: flat fee, hourly rate, word rate
Credentials/experience: Four decades of full-time book editing.

BREAKOUT EDITING | DORI HARRELL

Yakima, WA | 509-910-2220
doriharrell@gmail.com | *www.doriharrell.wix.com/breakoutediting*

Contact: email
Services: substantive editing/rewriting, copyediting, proofreading, write website text
Types of manuscripts: articles, nonfiction books, devotionals, short stories, novels, query letters, adult, teen/YA, picture books, middle grade
Charges: word rate
Credentials/experience: Dori is a multiple award-winning writer. She freelance edits full-time and has edited more than a hundred novels and nonfiction books. As an editor, she releases more than twenty-five books annually.

BRIANNA STORM HILVETY

brianna@theliterarycrusader.com | *theliterarycrusader.com*

Contact: email, website form
Services: copyediting, proofreading

Types of manuscripts: articles, nonfiction books, short stories, novels, adult, teen/YA

Charges: word rate

Credentials/experience: I'm a silver member of The Christian PEN, an associate editor for Castle Gate Press, and the copy editor for *KingdomPen.org*.

BUTTERFIELD EDITORIAL SERVICES | DEBRA L. BUTTERFIELD

4810 Gene Field Rd. #2, St. Joseph, MO 64506 | 816-752-2171
deb@debralbutterfield.com | *DebraLButterfield.com*

Contact: website form

Services: manuscript evaluation, substantive editing/rewriting, copyediting, proofreading, writing coach

Types of manuscripts: articles, nonfiction books, devotionals, short stories, novels, query letters, book proposals, adult

Charges: hourly rate

Credentials/experience: Seven years of experience as a reelance editor, three years as editor for a traditional publisher.

byBRENDA STUDIO | BRENDA WILBEE

4631 Quinn Ct., #202, Bellingham, WA 98226
Brenda@BrendaWilbee.com | *www.BrendaWilbee.com*

Contact: email

Services: manuscript evaluation, substantive editing/rewriting, copyediting, create brochures, create newsletters, small group/Bible study guides, PowerPoint presentation, book packaging

Types of manuscripts: articles, nonfiction books, devotionals, novels, Bible studies, gift books, memoirs, adult

Charges: flat fee, hourly rate, custom; edit first chapters for free, determine time involved, and charge a flat rate

Credentials/experience: BA in creative writing, MA in professional writing, degree in graphic design. Seven combined years teaching composition at Western Washington University and two community colleges. Community ed instructor five years at the University of Washington, teaching fiction, nonfiction, and romance writing. Written ten books (more than 700,000 books sold), one hundred plus devotionals, two hundred plus articles. Graphic designer for fifteen years, working with professionals in private practice and authors wanting sell sheets, bookmarks, brochures, and posters.

C. S. LAKIN, AUTHOR, EDITOR, WRITING COACH

335 Casa Loma Rd., Morgan Hill, CA 95037 | 530-200-5466
cslakin@gmail.com | *www.livewritethrive.com*

Contact: email

Services: manuscript evaluation, substantive editing/rewriting, copyediting, proofreading, ghostwriting, coauthoring, website text, small group/Bible study guides, curriculum lesson plans, discussion questions for books, writing coach, back-cover copy, specializing in fiction and nonfiction manuscripts critiques

Types of manuscripts: articles, nonfiction books, devotionals, poetry, short stories, novels, query letters, book proposals, gift books, curriculum, Bible studies, gift books, adult, teen/YA, picture books, easy readers, middle grade, scene or chapter outlines

Charges: hourly rate, page rate

Credentials/experience: Best-selling author of more than thirty fiction and nonfiction titles, C. S. Lakin has clients in six continents and works with beginning to established authors. She does more than two hundred manuscript critiques a year and has a deep understanding of novel structure across genres. She offers online video courses at *cslakin.teachable.com* and teaches workshops and retreats all over the US. Her award-winning blog, *Live Write Thrive*, has helped thousands of writers hone their craft, get marketing advice, and find encouragement for the writing journey. She offers all editing services, from proofreading to content editing to ghostwriting and has an eight-book writing-craft series, The Writer's Toolbox.

CANOPY EDITING SERVICES | LINDA W. YEZAK

Nacogdoches, TX | 936-568-0565
linda.yezak@lwyezak.com | *lindayezak.com*

Contact: email

Services: manuscript evaluation, substantive editing/rewriting, copyediting, ghostwriting, coauthoring

Types of manuscripts: short stories, novels, adult, teen/YA, creative nonfiction

Charges: hourly rate

Credentials/experience: Ten years of experience. Content editor for two small publishers; editorial assistant for a literary agent; copy editor for an online magazine. Silver member of The Christian PEN; additional courses in editing fiction and author mentoring.

CARLA ROSSI EDITORIAL SERVICES | CARLA ROSSI

The Woodlands, TX
carla@carlarossi.com | *www.carlarossi.com*

Contact: email

Services: manuscript evaluation, substantive editing/rewriting, copyediting, writing coach, specializing in content editing of romance fiction

Types of manuscripts: short stories, novels, adult

Charges: word rate

Credentials/experience: Freelance editor for two years. Traditionally published since 2008. Independently published since 2014. Silver member of The Christian PEN. Member of Romance Writers of America and serve on the board of my local chapter.

CHRISTIAN COMMUNICATOR MANUSCRIPT CRITIQUE SERVICE | SUSAN TITUS OSBORN

3133 Puente St., Fullerton, CA 92835 | 714-313-8651
susanosb@aol.com | *www.christiancommunicator.com*

Contact: email, phone

Services: manuscript evaluation, substantive editing/rewriting, copyediting, proofreading, ghostwriting, book-contract evaluation, write website text, create small group/Bible study guides, write curriculum lesson plans, write discussion questions for books, writing coach

Types of manuscripts: articles, nonfiction books, devotionals, poetry, short stories, novels, query letters, book proposals, curriculum, scripts, gift books, technical material, adult, teen/YA, picture books, easy readers, middle grade

Charges: flat fee, hourly rate, page rate, word rate

Credentials/experience: Have a staff of fourteen editors with more than thirty years of experience. Recommended by Evangelical Christian Publishers Association and a number of publishing houses and agents.

CHRISTIAN EDITOR CONNECTION | CHRISTI MCGUIRE

Lakewood Ranch, FL | 941-201-8964
Coordinator@ChristianEditor.com | *www.ChristianEditor.com*

Contact: email

Services: manuscript evaluation, substantive editing/rewriting, copyediting, proofreading, ghostwriting, coauthoring, writing coach

Types of manuscripts: articles, nonfiction books, devotionals, poetry, short stories, novels, query letters, book proposals, curriculum, scripts, gift books, technical material, adult, teen/YA, picture books, easy readers, middle grade

Charges: flat fee, hourly rate, page rate, word rate

Credentials/experience: The Christian Editor Connection began in 2007 as a matchmaking service to connect authors, publishers, and agents with qualified, established, professional editorial freelancers who meet their specific needs.

THE CHRISTIAN PEN: PROOFREADERS AND EDITORS NETWORK | JENNE ACEVEDO

480-510-0419
jenne@christianeditor.com | *www.thechristianpen.com*

Contact: website form

Service: membership network for Christian editors

Charges: annual membership fee

Description: The Christian PEN is dedicated to equipping aspiring and established freelance editors with education, networking, and community. We offer three levels of membership: bronze, silver, and gold. Our members range from no experience to highly-experienced professionals.

CHRISTIANMANUSCRIPTSUBMISSIONS.COM | CINDY CARTER

5801 S. McClintock Dr., Ste. 104, Tempe, AZ 85201 | 408-966-3998
ccarter@ecpa.org | *www.ChristianManuscriptSubmissions.com*

Contact: website form

Service: online manuscript-submission service

Types of manuscripts: book proposals for all kinds of books and all ages

Charges: $98 for six months

Description: Managed by the Evangelical Christian Publishers Association (ECPA).

CM CREATIVE CONSULTING, LLC | CHRISTI MCGUIRE

Lakewood Ranch, FL | 941-201-8964
Christi@ChristiMcGuire.com | *www.ChristiMcGuire.com*

Contact: email

Services: manuscript evaluation, substantive editing/rewriting, copyediting, proofreading

Types of manuscripts: nonfiction books, devotionals, query letters, book proposals, curriculum, adult

Charges: hourly rate, word rate

Credentials/experience: Christi, freelance editor, writer, and consultant, has been in the Christian publishing industry for sixteen years. Currently, her primary focus is partnering with authors in the creative process to polish their nonfiction book manuscripts and help them navigate the path to publishing. She is on the teaching faculty for PENCON, the only convention for Christian editors in the industry. Christi is a co-owner of the Christian Editor Network, LLC; the director for the Christian Editor Connection; and the director of The PEN Institute, an online educational institute for Christian editors, as well as a member of the Editorial Freelance Association.

COLLABORATIVE EDITORIAL SOLUTIONS | ANDREW BUSS

Tuscan, AZ
info@collaborativeeditorial.com | *collaborativeeditorial.com*

Contact: email

Services: copyediting, proofreading

Types of manuscripts: articles, nonfiction books, adult, academic

Charges: hourly rate, page rate

Credentials/experience: Member of the Editorial Freelancers Association, the Society of Biblical Literature, and the Society for Scholarly Publishing.

COMMUNICATION ASSOCIATES | KEN WALKER

729 Ninth Ave. #331, Huntington, WV 25701 | 304-525-3343
kenwalker33@gmail.com | *www.KenWalkerWriter.com*

Contact: email

Services: manuscript evaluation, substantive editing/rewriting, copyediting, ghostwriting, coauthoring, small group/Bible study guides, write discussion questions for books

Types of manuscripts: articles, nonfiction books, devotionals, Bible studies, adult

Charges: custom based on project

Credentials/experience: Ghosted or edited more than fifty books, written more than four thousand bylined articles.

CORNERSTONE-INK EDITING | VIE HERLOCKER

Fancy Gap, VA | 276-237-7574
vherlock@yahoo.com | *www.cornerstone-ink.com*

Contact: email

Services: manuscript evaluation, substantive editing/rewriting, copyediting

Types of manuscripts: articles, nonfiction books, devotionals, short stories, novels, query letters, book proposals, adult, teen/YA, middle grade

Charges: hourly rate

Credentials/experience: Member of The Christian PEN: Proofreaders and Editors Network. Certified through Christian Editors Connection. Editor for a small publisher since 2008.

THE CORPORATE PEN | CATHY STREINER

Orange Park, FL | 904-527-8117

Cathy@thecorporatepen.com | *www.thecorporatepen.com*

Contact: email

Services: substantive editing/rewriting, copyediting, proofreading, ghostwriting, coauthoring, create brochures, create newsletters, write website text, create small group/Bible study guides, write discussion questions for books, writing coach

Types of manuscripts: articles, nonfiction books, devotionals, short stories, novels, scripts, gift books, technical material, adult, teen/YA

Charges: flat fee, page rate, word rate, hourly rate with a maximum amount

Credentials/experience: Extensive experience with the written word. Cathy began making her living as a writer prior to 1990, and in 2001 established her own company. She self-published a Christian novel in 2009 under a pseudonym and enjoys using her writing and editing skills to help other Christians.

CREATIVE ENTERPRISES STUDIO | MARY HOLLINGSWORTH

Bedford, TX | 817-312-7393

ACreativeShop@aol.com | *CreativeEnterprisesStudio.com*

Contact: email

Services: manuscript evaluation, substantive editing/rewriting, copyediting, proofreading, ghostwriting, coauthoring, write website text, write discussion questions for books

Types of manuscripts: nonfiction books, devotionals, short stories, novels, book proposals, curriculum, gift books, adult, teen/YA, picture books, easy readers, middle grade

Charges: rates vary according to the work required, estimates provided

Credentials/experience: CES is a publishing services company, hosting more than 150 top Christian publishing freelancers. We work with large, traditional Christian publishers on books by best-selling authors. We also produce custom, first-class books on a turnkey basis for independent authors, ministries, churches, and companies.

CREST PUBLISHER SERVICES | EDWARD BOLME

PO Box 481022, Charlotte, NC 28269 | 704-995-6739
info@crestpub.com | *www.crestpub.com*

Contact: email

Services: copyediting, proofreading, write website text

Types of manuscripts: nonfiction books, short stories, novels, book proposals, technical material, adult, teen/YA

Charges: flat fee, hourly rate, word rate

Credentials/experience: Published author with more than twenty years of experience.

CREWS AND COULTER EDITORIAL SERVICES | JANET CREWS AND KAY COULTER

713 Gila Trl. (Janet) or 806 Hopi Trl. (Kay), Temple, TX 76504
254-314-2600 or 254-778-6490
janetkcrews@gmail.com | *bkcoulter@sbcglobal.net* | *www.crewscoultereditorialservices.com*

Contact: email

Services: manuscript evaluation, substantive editing/rewriting, copyediting, proofreading, ghostwriting, coauthoring, create brochures, create newsletters, create PowerPoint presentations, writing coach

Types of manuscripts: nonfiction books, devotionals, short stories, novels, query letters, book proposals, curriculum, gift books, adult, teen/YA, middle grade

Charges: hourly rate

Credentials/experience: Janet and Kay have a combined thirty-six years of experience as editors. Kay is also a published author. Both are members of The Christian PEN and Christian Editor Connection and have worked for several publishers as contract editors, as well as freelance editors with individuals. Kay is experienced in ghostwriting and working with non-native English speakers. Both have experience in editing academic papers.

CROSS & DOT EDITORIAL SERVICES | KATIE VORREITER

San Jose, CA | 408-812-3562
Katie@CrossAndDot.net | *www.CrossAndDot.net*

Contact: email

Services: copyediting, proofreading

Types of manuscripts: articles, nonfiction books, devotionals, short stories, novels, curriculum, gift books, technical material, adult, teen/YA, middle grade

Charges: flat rate

Credentials/experience: Certificate in professional sequence in editing, U.C. Berkeley; MA in international management; BA in English and Spanish.

CYPRESS WIND | RACHEL HILLS

Mooresville, IN | 317-443-0019
emRachel@CypressWind.com | *www.CypressWind.com*

Contact: email

Services: substantive editing/rewriting, copyediting, proofreading, writing coach, web page and blog copyediting

Types of manuscripts: articles, nonfiction books, short stories, novels, adult, teen/YA

Charges: rates based on the project

Credentials/experience: I have sixteen years of experience editing for academics and various certifications and training in editing and writing.

DR. DENNIS E . HENSLEY

6824 Kanata Ct., Fort Wayne, IN 46815-6388 | 260-485-9891
Dnhensley@hotmail.com | *www.dochensley.com*

Contact: email

Services: manuscript evaluation, substantive editing/rewriting, copyediting, proofreading, ghostwriting, writing coach, columns, interviews

Types of manuscripts: articles, nonfiction books, devotionals, poetry, short stories, novels, query letters, book proposals, academic, adult, teen/YA

Charges: page rate

Credentials/experience: Dr. Hensley holds four degrees in communication, including a Ph.D. in English. He is the author of ten published novels and more than fifty published nonfiction books. He has written more than thirty-five hundred articles, devotions, testimonies, interviews, and columns for hundreds of newspapers and magazines. He is an annual judge for two industry awards. He is a professor of communication at Taylor University.

DIANA BRANDMEYER

O'Fallon, IL | 314-690-3616
diana@dianabrandmeyer.com | *www.dianabrandmeyer.com*

Contact: email
Services: substantive editing/rewriting, writing coach
Types of manuscripts: short stories, novels, adult, teen/YA
Charges: word rate
Credentials/experience: CBA best-selling author, member of American Christian Fiction Writers, editing more than ten years, member of The Christian PEN.

DONE WRITE EDITORIAL SERVICES | MARILYN A. ANDERSON

127 Sycamore Dr., Louisville, KY 40223 | 502-244-0751
shelle12@aol.com | *www.TheChristianPEN.com*

Contact: email
Services: manuscript evaluation, copyediting, proofreading
Types of manuscripts: articles, nonfiction books, devotionals, poetry, short stories, novels, curriculum, technical material, adult, picture books, easy readers, middle grade, doctoral dissertations, and theses
Charges: hourly rate
Credentials/experience: I am qualified by an MA in English and a BA in English and the humanities from the University of Louisville. I taught English grammar and literature for four years and have tutored ESL students for twelve years. I worked as a writer, editor, and proofreader of educational curriculum, as well as in the energy, utility, and benefits industries for about eighteen years. To date, I have edited fifty-four books, a workbook, thirty-three doctoral dissertations, and a master's thesis, along with innumerable business projects. I have written a company history in three different formats and a glossary of utility terms. I conduct editing and proofreading services for both publishing houses and independent authors. I am a charter and gold member of The Christian PEN: Proofreaders and Editors Network and a member of the Christian Editor Connection.

EAGLE EYE EDITS | TOM THREADGILL

Bells, TN | 731-501-0479
tom@eagleeyeedits.com | *www.EagleEyeEdits.com*

Contact: email
Services: manuscript evaluation, substantive editing/rewriting, copyediting, proofreading, writing coach
Types of manuscripts: novels
Charges: word rate
Credentials/experience: Tom has several years of experience as both an editor and author. Ongoing training ensures the latest industry standards are applied. His editing style leans heavily toward teaching new authors, with developmental editing and mentoring his specialty.

ECHO CREATIVE MEDIA | BRENDA NOEL

Smyrna, TN | 615-223-0754
bnoel@thewordeditor.com

Contact: email
Services: substantive editing/rewriting, copyediting, proofreading, ghostwriting, write website text, create small group/Bible study guides, write curriculum lesson plans, write discussion questions for books
Types of manuscripts: articles, nonfiction books, devotionals, short stories, book proposals, curriculum, gift books, adult, teen/YA, picture books, easy readers
Charges: flat fee, hourly rate
Credentials/experience: Fifteen years of experience in the Christian publishing industry.

EDIT RESOURCE, LLC | ERIC AND ELISA STANDFORD

19265 Lincoln Green Ln., Monument, CO 80132 | 719-290-0757
info@editresource.com | *www.editresource.com*

Contact: website form
Services: manuscript evaluation, substantive editing/rewriting, copyediting, proofreading, ghostwriting, coauthoring, create small group/Bible study guides, curriculum lesson plans, write discussion questions for books, writing coach, back-cover copy
Types of manuscripts: nonfiction books, devotionals, novels, query letters, book proposals, curriculum, Bible studies, adult, teen/YA
Charges: flat fee, hourly rate

Credentials/experience: Eric and Elisa have a combined forty plus years of editorial experience, both as in-house employees and as independent service providers, and are well-recognized members of the Christian publishing community. They also represent other top indie editors; see the "Team" page on the website.

EDITING BY LUCY | LUCY CRABTREE

Lawrence, KS | 913-543-1782
editingbylucy@gmail.com | *editingbylucy.com*

Contact: email
Services: copyediting, proofreading
Types of manuscripts: articles, nonfiction books, short stories, novels, query letters, book proposals, adult
Charges: word rate
Credentials/experience: Polished writer and editor with nine years of professional experience in the publishing industry (seven years) and educational settings (two years). Well-versed in Microsoft Office and Adobe Creative Suite. Familiarity with Associated Press, American Psychological Association, and *Chicago Manual* style books. Experience with Drupal, WordPress, and Blogger.

EDITING GALLERY LLC | CAROL CRAIG

2622 Willona Dr., Eugene, OR 97408 | 541-735-1834
kf7orchid@gmail.com | *www.editinggallery.com*

Contact: email
Services: manuscript evaluation, substantive editing/rewriting, coauthoring, writing coach, back-cover copy, developmental editing
Types of manuscripts: novels, query letters, book proposals, adult, teen/YA, picture books, easy readers, middle grade
Charges: hourly rate
Credentials/experience: English major at the University of Oregon. I have studied novel craft for twenty years, have edited for fifteen years, and have a long list of published authors. For a partial list see my website.

eDITMORE EDITORIAL SERVICES | TAMMY DITMORE

501-I S. Reino Rd. #194, Newbury Park, CA 91320 | 805-630-6809
tammy@editmore.com | *www.editmore.com*

Contact: email
Services: manuscript evaluation, substantive editing/rewriting,

copyediting, proofreading, website text, small group/Bible study guides, write discussion questions for books, create PowerPoint presentations

Types of manuscripts: articles, nonfiction books, devotionals, curriculum, Bible studies, gift books, adult, teen/YA, academic

Charges: custom

Credentials/experience: A specialist in nonfiction, I offer consultations, critiques, developmental editing, copyediting, and proofreading services. I work closely with authors, publishers, editors, organizations, and businesses. My specialties include Christian and spiritual material, academic authors and publishers, personal histories and current events, and publications on aging and Alzheimer's disease. I am familiar with Chicago, APA, MLA, SBL, and AP styles.

EDITOR FOR YOU | MELANIE RIGNEY

4201 Wilson Blvd. #110328, Arlington, VA 22203
editor@editorforyou.com | *www.editorforyou.com*

Contact: email

Services: manuscript evaluation

Types of manuscripts: nonfiction books, devotionals, short stories, novels, query letters, book proposals, adult

Charges: flat fee

Credentials/experience: More than 30 years as an editor and writer, including time as editor of *Writer's Digest* magazine and acquisitions/editing experience with *Writer's Digest* books, Macmillan Computer Publishing, Thomson Financial Publishing. Please see my website for more details.

EDITOR WORLD, LLC | PATTI FISHER

Newport, VA | 614-500-3348
info@editorworld.com | *www.editorworld.com*

Contact: email

Services: copyediting, proofreading

Types of manuscripts: articles, nonfiction books, devotionals, poetry, short stories, novels, query letters, book proposals, curriculum, scripts, gift books, technical material, adult, teen/YA, picture books, easy readers, middle grade

Charges: word rate

Credentials/experience: See website. Credentials of each editor are listed in individual profiles, along with client ratings.

ELAINA RAMSEY

Alexandria, VA | 703-403-3424
elainabueno@gmail.com

Contact: email
Services: substantive editing/rewriting, copyediting, proofreading, write website text, create small group/Bible study guides, write curriculum lesson plans, write discussion questions for books
Types of manuscripts: articles, devotionals, curriculum, scripts
Charges: hourly rate
Credentials/experience: As a former editor of *Sojourners* magazine, I am experienced in editing religious and social-justice content from across the theological and political spectrum. Trained in Associated Press style. I am adept at developing discussion guides, toolkits, and preaching resources. MTS degree and solid experience leading campaigns. I specialize in faith-based media, messaging, and advocacy for racial justice and women's empowerment.

ELIZABETH EASTER

Choctaw, CA | 405-259-9625
FictionEditingService@yahoo.com | *penworthypress.com*

Contact: email
Services: manuscript evaluation, substantive editing/rewriting, copyediting, proofreading, writing coach
Types of manuscripts: devotionals, poetry, short stories, novels, query letters, book proposals, adult, teen/YA
Charges: flat fee, hourly rate, page rate, word rate
Credentials/experience: Twenty years as a freelance proofreader and editor; three years as a proofreader or an associate editor with small presses; many years as a writer (under a pseudonym) who has been edited. My job is not to make your story mine but to hunker down inside your story, get to know it, and help you tell it to the best of your ability.

ELOQUENT EDITS, LLC | DENISE ROEPER

Port Orange, FL | 386-299-8814
denise.eloquentedits@gmail.com | *www.eloquentedits.com*

Contact: email
Services: copyediting, proofreading
Types of manuscripts: nonfiction books, short stories, novels, teen/YA, middle grade

Charges: word rate, also review a document and provide an estimate

Credentials/experience: I have edited and proofread print matter ranging from brochures, business print, website content to fiction manuscripts. Specialties are editing fiction, motivational, and spiritual print. Accepting projects that require a short turnaround time.

FACETS EDITORIAL SERVICES | DEBORAH CHRISTENSEN

PO Box 354, Addison, IL 60107 | 630-830-5787
dcfacets@earthlink.net | *www.Plowingthefields.wordpress.com*

Contact: email, phone

Services: substantive editing/rewriting, copyediting, proofreading, write website text, writing coach

Types of manuscripts: articles, nonfiction books, devotionals, short stories, novels, curriculum, adult, teen/YA

Charges: hourly rate

Credentials/experience: I served as the editor and writer for Christian Service Brigade (CSB Ministries) for eighteen years and for Lighthouse Christian Products for eleven years. I mentored writers with the Jerry B. Jenkins Christian Writers Guild. I am proficient with Associated Press style, *Chicago Manual of Style*, and *The Christian Writer's Manual of Style*.

FAITH EDITORIAL SERVICES | REBECCA FAITH

Novelty, OH | 216-906-0205
rebecca@faitheditorial.com | *www.faitheditorial.com*

Contact: email

Services: substantive editing/rewriting, copyediting, proofreading, create newsletters, create small group/Bible study guides, write discussion questions for books, transcription

Types of manuscripts: articles, nonfiction books, technical material, adult, teen/YA, sermons

Charges: hourly rate, word rate

Credentials/experience: I was the managing editor for a Christian nonprofit newsletter for six years. I currently copyedit, proofread, and write content for a global Christian ministry that includes material for the website, study guides, and sermon synopses and outlines. In addition, I currently edit technical, peer-reviewed papers for journal publications and manage and train a team of copy editors.

FAITHFULLY WRITE EDITING | DAWN KINZER

25914 188th Ave. S.E., Covington, WA 98042 | 206-235-2663
dawnkinzer@comcast.net | *www.faithfullywriteediting.com*

Contact: email

Services: manuscript evaluation, substantive editing/rewriting, copyediting, proofreading

Types of manuscripts: articles, nonfiction books, devotionals, short stories, novels, adult, teen/YA

Charges: flat fee, page rate

Credentials/experience: Dawn launched Faithfully Write Editing in 2010. Since then, she has edited for First Steps Publishing, FutureWord Publishing, and writers pursuing publication. Her own published work includes short stories, devotions, numerous articles, and a historical romance series. Serving as a judge for contests that award excellence in Christian fiction has given her additional opportunities to serve the writing community. She is a member of the Northwest Christian Writers Association and the American Christian Fiction Writers, as well as The Christian PEN and the Christian Editor Connection—both nationwide professional networks for Christian freelance editors.

FAITHWORKS EDITORIAL & WRITING, INC. | NANETTE THORSEN SNIPES

PO Box 1596, Buford, GA 30518 | 770-945-3093
nsnipes@bellsouth.net | *www.faithworkseditorial.com*

Contact: email, website form

Services: manuscript evaluation, copyediting, proofreading, brochures, create newsletters, website text, work-for-hire projects

Types of manuscripts: articles, nonfiction books, devotionals, poetry, short stories, query letters, gift books, adult, picture books, easy readers, middle grade, memoirs, business

Charges: hourly rate, page rate

Credentials/experience: Member: The Christian PEN (Proofreaders & Editors Network), Christian Editor Connection, Christian Editor Network. Proofreader for corporate newsletters, thirteen years. Published writer for more than twenty-five years. Published hundreds of articles in magazines and stories in more than sixty compilation books, including Guideposts, B&H, Regal, and Integrity. Twelve years of editorial experience in both adult and children's short fiction and books, memoirs, short stories, devotions, articles, business. Rates are generally by page but, under specific circumstances, by the hour. Editorial clients have published with such houses as Zondervan, Tyndale, and Revell.

THE FINAL TOUCH PROOFREADING & EDITING | HEIDI MANN

Ely, MN | 701-866-4299

mann.heidi@gmail.com | *www.FinalTouchProofreadingAndEditing.com*

Contact: email

Services: copyediting, proofreading

Types of manuscripts: articles, nonfiction books, devotionals, novels, curriculum, adult, teen/YA, picture books, easy readers, middle grade, Bible studies

Charges: flat rate, hourly rate

Credentials/experience: Fourteen years of experience as a seminary-trained Lutheran pastor; excellent understanding of writing mechanics and style, honed through years of higher education and professional use; freelance editor since 2007 serving authors, publishers, and other entities; have completed multiple educational courses to enhance my knowledge and skills; passionate about writing that intersects with Christian faith. Member of The Christian PEN.

FINDLEY FAMILY VIDEO PUBLICATIONS | MARY C. FINDLEY

Tulsa, OK | 918-805-0669

mjmcfindley@gmail.com | *www.elkjerkyforthesoul.wordpress.com*

Contact: email

Services: copyediting, proofreading, create brochures, create newsletters, write website text, create small group/Bible study guides, write curriculum lesson plans, write discussion questions for books, create PowerPoint presentations

Types of manuscripts: articles, nonfiction books, devotionals, poetry, short stories, novels, curriculum, technical material, adult, teen/YA, picture books, easy readers, middle grade

Charges: word rate

Credentials/experience: Former editor at Bob Jones University Press; proofreader/copy editor for American Advertising Distributors' promotional literature from coupon to book-length; copy editor for many indie authors, fiction and nonfiction, most genres, via online contact. References available on request.

FINESSE WRITING & EDITING SERVICE | DEB PORTER

PO Box 12, St Clair, NSW, Australia, 2759 | +61 412 530 765
finessewriting.com.au

Contact: email, phone
Services: manuscript evaluation, substantive editing/rewriting, writing coach
Types: nonfiction books, devotionals, short stories, novels, adult, teen/YA
Charges: page rate
Credentials/experience: As an editor and writing coach for more than thirteen years, working with *FaithWriters.com*, and as a publisher for the past three years, I have helped countless people hone their writing skills.

FISTBUMP MEDIA, LLC | DAN KING

Sarasota, FL | 941-780-4179
dan@fistbumpmedia.com | *fistbumpmedia.com*

Contact: email
Services: manuscript evaluation, proofreading, write website text
Types of manuscripts: nonfiction books, devotionals, short stories, novels, teen/YA
Charges: flat rate, word rate
Credentials/experience: Fistbump Media provides self-publishing support services in addition to blog/website hosting and design, email subscriber management, and social-media services. We support experienced and first-time writers and leverage the power of self-publishing. References and portfolio are on the website.

THE FOREWORD COLLECTIVE, LLC | MOLLY KEMPF HODGIN, NICOLE CORSE LEVINE

1726 Charity Dr., Brentwood, TN 37027
info@theforewordcollective.com | *www.theforewordcollective.com*

Contact: email, website form
Services: manuscript evaluation, substantive editing/rewriting, copyediting, proofreading, ghostwriting, coauthoring, brochures, newsletters, website text, PowerPoint presentations, writing coach, back-cover copy
Types of manuscripts: articles, nonfiction books, devotionals, novels, query letters, book proposals, gift books, adult, teens/YA, picture books, easy readers, middle grade
Charges: custom rate

Credentials/experience: "We employ a wide variety of creative professionals on a per-project basis, including editors, copyeditors, designers, writers, photographers, marketers, and public-relations pros. We have more than thirty years of publishing experience between us, and we want to put that experience to work for you. Molly was most recently the associate publisher for the specialty division of HarperCollins Christian Publishing, handling gift and children's books. Nicole was most recently the editorial director at InSight Publishing.

FRANKFORT WRITERS CENTER | CHARITY SINGLETON CRAIG

358 N. Jackson St., Ste. B, Frankfort, IN 46041 | 317-446-1818
charity@frankfortwriterscenter.com | *www.frankfortwriterscenter.com*

Contact: email
Services: manuscript evaluation, substantive editing/rewriting, copyediting, create brochures, create newsletters, write website text, writing coach
Types of manuscripts: articles, nonfiction books, devotionals, short stories, novels, query letters, book proposals, adult
Charges: combination of hourly and word rate
Credentials/experience: Bachelor's degree in communications; more than twenty years of experience with writing and editing; author of *On Being a Writer: 12 Simple Habits for a Writing Life That Lasts*; frequent workshop leader.

FREELANCE WRITING & EDITING SERVICES | ROBIN SCHMITT

Rockford, MI | 616-350-0576
schmitt.freelancer@sbcglobal.net | *robinschmitt.com*

Contact: email, phone
Services: manuscript evaluation, substantive editing/rewriting, copyediting, ghostwriting, coauthoring, brochures, newsletters, website text, small group/Bible study guides, curriculum lesson plans, discussion questions for books, PowerPoint presentations, writing coach, back-cover copy
Types of manuscripts: articles, nonfiction books, devotionals, short stories, novels, curriculum, Bible studies, scripts, gift books, adult, teens/YA, picture books, easy readers, middle grade
Charges: flat fee, hourly rate, page rate, word rate
Credentials/experience: More than 20 years of experience as a writer

and editor in Christian publishing. I've edited many books, both fiction and nonfiction, for adults, teens, and children. In every project I take on, I always strive for the highest standard of excellence.

FRENCH AND ENGLISH COMMUNICATION SERVICES | DIANE GOULLARD

3104 E. Camelback Rd. #124, Phoenix, AZ 85016-4502 | 602-870-1000
RequestFAECS2008@cox.net | *www.FrenchAndEnglish.com*

Contact: email, phone, website form, mail
Services: copyediting, proofreading, coauthoring, brochures, website text, small group/Bible studies, discussion questions for books; French to English and English to French proofreading, translating
Types of manuscripts: articles, nonfiction books, devotionals, poetry, short stories, novels, query letters, book proposals, curriculum, Bible studies, scripts, gift books, technical material, adult, teens/YA, picture books, easy readers, middle grade, technical, scientific, lyrics
Charges: flat fee, hourly rate, page rate, word rate, custom
Credentials/experience: Visit my website for bio, references, and experience.

GALADRIEL GRACE

admin@galadrielgrace.com | *galadrielgrace.com*

Contact: email, website form, social media
Services: substantive editing/rewriting, copyediting, proofreading, create brochures, create newsletters, write website text, create small group/Bible study guides, write curriculum lesson plans, write discussion questions for books, query letters
Types of manuscripts: short stories, novels, query letters, curriculum, Bible studies, teen/YA
Charges: flat rate, page rate, word rate, custom
Credentials/experience: Member of the Christian PEN; several years of experience teaching English and language; writing and editing children's books, curriculum, query letters, website content, newsletters, and content for promotional marketing materials.

GINGER KOLBABA

Elgin, IL | 847-366-6547
ginger@gingerkolbaba.com | *www.gingerkolbaba.com*

Contact: email

Services: manuscript evaluation, substantive editing/rewriting, copyediting, proofreading, ghostwriting, coauthoring, create small group/Bible study guides, write discussion questions for books, writing coach

Types of manuscripts: articles, nonfiction books, devotionals, novels, novels, query letters, book proposals, adult, teen/YA

Charges: hourly rate for editing, flat rate for writing

Credentials/experience: More than twenty years in the industry. Former editor of *Today's Christian Woman* and *Marriage Partnership* magazines and *Kyria.com*, all national, award-winning publications of Christianity Today International. Written or contributed to more than thirty books and five hundred articles, both in print and online. Clients include many publishing houses and best- selling authors.

HANEMAN EDITORIAL | NATALIE HANEMAN

Franklin, TN | 615-712-4430

nathanemann@gmail.com | *www.nataliehanemannediting.com*

Contact: email

Services: manuscript evaluation, substantive editing/rewriting, copyediting

Types of manuscripts: nonfiction books, novels, book proposals, adult, teen/YA, middle grade

Charges: flat fee

Credentials/experience: Eleven years in-house at publishing houses, eight of those at Thomas Nelson in the fiction division under the tutelage of Allen Arnold. Since 2012, I've been freelance editing fiction and nonfiction (substantive and line), as well as helping authors get their synopses ready to submit to agents. I've edited more than three hundred manuscripts and particularly love working with newer authors or authors who are unsure if they should publish traditionally or indie. Certified by the Christian Editors Connection.

HAYHURST EDITORIAL LLC | SARAH HAYHURST

505 Middleton Pl., Grayson, GA 30017 | 715-548-1514

sarah@sarahhayhurst.com | *www.sarahhayhurst.com*

Contact: email

Services: copyediting, proofreading, newsletters, website text, small group/Bible study guides

Types of manuscripts: articles, nonfiction books, devotionals, curriculum, Bible study guides, adult

Charges: word rate

Credentials/experience: Gold-level member of the Christian Editors Connection.

HENRY MCLAUGHLIN

Saginaw, TX

henry@henrymclaughlin.org | *www.henrymclaughlin.org*

Contact: email

Services: manuscript evaluation, substantive editing/rewriting, copyediting, ghostwriting, coauthoring, create PowerPoint presentations, writing coach

Types of manuscripts: nonfiction books, short stories, novels, adult

Charges: flat fee, hourly rate, page rate

Credentials/experience: I have been a full-time writer since 2010. My first novel won the Operation First Novel contest. I have published both traditionally and independently, as well as in magazines and anthologies. I have coached and edited eleven authors in both fiction and nonfiction. I have worked extensively with writers groups, coaching and teaching the craft of writing. I have also taught the craft at conferences, workshops, seminars, and webinars.

HESTERMAN CREATIVE | DR. VICKI HESTERMAN

PO Box 6788, San Diego, CA 92166

vhes@icloud.com

Contact: email

Services: manuscript evaluation, substantive editing/rewriting, copyediting, proofreading, coauthoring, create newsletters, write website text, create small group/Bible study guides, writing coach

Types of manuscripts: articles, nonfiction books, devotionals, novels, query letters, book proposals, gift books, adult, teen/YA

Charges: industry-standard hourly rate based on word count and work needed; binding quote given with sample chapters and synopsis

Credentials/experience: Thirty years of experience in the field, both Christian and secular: newspaper photojournalist, publishing-house book editor, university writing professor, book collaborator, and writing coach.

HONEST EDITING SERVICES | BILL LELAND

Bend, OR
bill@writersedgeservice.com | *www.honestediting.com*

Contact: email, website form

Services: Honest Editing offers three specific editorial services for Christian manuscripts. (1) We can create professional proposals for enhancing your presentation to publishers; (2) We can do a full evaluation of a manuscript that identifies both strengths and weaknesses in a manuscript and points the author in the right direction to improve the manuscript/writing style; (3) We can perform a full edit, page by page, of an entire manuscript. All these are done by professional editors for a flat fee as outlined at our website.

Types of manuscripts: nonfiction books, devotionals, novels, book proposals, Bible studies, gift books, adult, teen/YA

Charges: flat fee

HONEYCOMB HOUSE PUBLISHING LLC | DAVID E . FESSENDEN

315 3rd St., Ste. 1, New Cumberland, PA 17070 | 215-767-9600
dave@fessendens.net | *www.davefessenden.com*

Contact: email

Services: manuscript evaluation, substantive editing/rewriting, copyediting, proofreading, coauthoring, book-contract evaluation, write website text, create small group/Bible study guides, write curriculum lesson plans, write discussion questions for books, writing coach, back-cover copy

Types of manuscripts: articles, nonfiction books, devotionals, short stories, novels, query letters, book proposals, curriculum, Bible studies, gift books, technical material, academic, adult, teen/YA

Charges: flat fee, word rate

Credentials/experience: Twenty-five years of professional experience in Christian publishing, writing, and editing.

INKSNATCHER | SALLY HANAN

Austin, TX | 512-351-5869
inkmeister@inksnatcher.com | *www.inksnatcher.com*

Contact: email, text

Services: substantive editing/rewriting, copyediting, proofreading, ghostwriting, coauthoring, write website text, write discussion questions for books

Types of manuscripts: articles, nonfiction books, short stories, novels, curriculum, gift books, adult, teen/YA, easy readers, middle grade

Charges: flat rate, hourly rate, word rate

Credentials/experience: Established in 2007, Inksnatcher has edited books and written copy for Bobby Conner, Shawn Bolz, Jon Hamill, and Dennis Cramer, among many others.

INSPIRATION FOR WRITERS, INC. | SANDY TRITT

1527 18th St., Parkersburg, WV 26101 | 304-428-1218
IFWeditors@gmail.com | *www.InspirationForWriters.com*

Contact: email, phone

Services: manuscript evaluation, substantive editing/rewriting, copyediting, proofreading, ghostwriting, write curriculum lesson plans, write discussion questions for books, writing coach, consulting

Types of manuscripts: nonfiction books, devotionals, short stories, novels, query letters, book proposals, curriculum, scripts, gift books, adult, teen/YA, middle grade

Charges: flat fee, word rate

Credentials/experience: We are one of the oldest and most respected editing/writing companies on the Internet today. All our editors-writers are published authors with years of editing experience who've been specially trained to edit according to our high standards.

JAMES WATKINS

jim@jameswatkins.com | *jameswatkins.com*

Contact: email

Services: manuscript evaluation, substantive editing/rewriting, copyediting, ghostwriting, coauthoring, write website text, write discussion questions for books, writing coach

Types of manuscripts: articles, nonfiction books, devotionals, book proposals, adult

Charges: page rate

Credentials/experience: Award-winning editor (four Evangelical Press Awards), developed the editing course at Taylor University, served as an editor and editorial director at Wesleyan Publishing House for more than twenty years, and is the author of twenty books and more than 2,000 articles.

JAMIE CHAVEZ

Murfreesboro, TN
jamie.chavez@gmail.com | *www.jamiechavez.com*

Contact: email

Services: manuscript evaluation, substantive editing/rewriting, copyediting, coauthoring, write website text, write discussion questions for books

Types of manuscripts: articles, nonfiction books, novels, book proposals, curriculum, gift books, adult, teen/YA, picture books, easy readers, middle grade

Charges: flat fee

Credentials/experience: Eleven years with Thomas Nelson Publishers and twelve years as a freelance editor. See website for more complete bio.

JANIS WHIPPLE

9608 Regiment Ct., Land O Lakes, FL 34638 | 954-579-8545
janiswhipple@gmail.com

Contact: email

Services: manuscript evaluation, substantive editing/rewriting, copyediting, proofreading, coauthoring, create brochures, create small group/Bible study guides, write discussion questions for books, writing coach

Types of manuscripts: articles, nonfiction books, devotionals, query letters, book proposals, curriculum, gift books, adult, teen/YA

Charges: hourly rate, sometimes do fee projects

Credentials/experience: Thirty years of editing, ten years as an in-house editor with B&H Publishers in acquisitions and managing editing, fifteen years as a freelance editor and writing coach.

JEANETTE GARDNER LITTLETON, PUBLICATION SERVICES

3706 N.E. Shady Lane Dr., Gladstone, MO 64119-1958 | 816-459-8016
jeanettedl@earthlink.net | *www.linkedin.com/in/jeanette-littleton-b1b790101*

Contact: email

Services: manuscript evaluation, substantive editing/rewriting, copyediting, proofreading, book-contract evaluation, create brochures, create newsletters, write website text, create small group/Bible study guides, write curriculum lesson plans, write discussion questions for books, back-cover copy, indexing

Types of manuscripts: articles, nonfiction books, devotionals, short stories, novels, query letters, book proposals, curriculum, Bible studies, gift books, technical material, adult, teen/YA

Charges: flat fee, hourly rate, page rate

Credentials/experience: I've been a full-time editor and writer for thirty years for a variety of publishers. I've written five thousand articles and edited thousands of articles and dozens of books. Please see my profile at LinkedIn.

JEANETTE HANSCOME

San Ramon, CA
jeanettehanscome@gmail.com | *jeanettehanscome.com*

Contact: email, website form

Services: manuscript evaluation, substantive editing/rewriting, copyediting, ghostwriting, coauthoring, write website text, write discussion questions for books, writing coach, back-cover copy, brochures, newsletters

Types of manuscripts: articles, nonfiction books, devotionals, short stories, novels, query letters, book proposals, gift books, adult, teen/YA, middle grade, blog posts

Charges: hourly rate

Credentials/experience: I am the author of five books and hundreds of published articles, devotions, and stories, who teaches and critiques at writers conference. My experience includes twenty-two years as a writer and fifteen years as a freelance editor.

JEFF PEPPLE

15317 Laurel Ridge, Leo, IN 46765 | 260-627-7347
jhpepple@hotmail.com

Contact: email, phone

Services: manuscript evaluation, substantive editing/rewriting, copyediting, proofreading, write website text

Types of manuscripts: articles, nonfiction books, devotionals, short stories, novels, curriculum, scripts, gift books, technical material, adult, teen/YA, easy readers, middle grade

Charges: flat fee, hourly rate, page rate, word rate

Credentials/experience: BA in professional writing, Taylor University.

JENNIFER EDWARDS WRITING & EDITING | JENNIFER EDWARDS

Loomis, CA | 916-768-4207
mail.jennifer.edwards@gmail.com | *www.jedwardsediting.net*

Contact: email
Services: manuscript evaluation, substantive editing/rewriting, copyediting, proofreading, write website text, create small group/ Bible study guides, write curriculum lesson plans, write discussion questions for books, create PowerPoint presentations
Types of manuscripts: articles, nonfiction books, devotionals, curriculum, scripts, gift books, technical material
Charges: flat fee
Credentials/experience: Master's degree in biblical and theological studies from Western Seminary; gold member of the Christian Editor Network. Managing editor of the publishing arm of Principles To Live By (PTLB, *ptlb.com*). I also manage the marketing processes for PTLB, promoting their consultants, events, and book launches, including website, blog, email campaigns, social-media elements, and donor relations.

JHWRITING+ | NICOLE HAYES

Randleman, NC | 410-709-8549
jhwritingplus@yahoo.com | *www.jhwritingplus.com*

Contact: email
Services: manuscript evaluation, substantive editing/rewriting, copyediting, proofreading, ghostwriting, coauthoring, write website text, create small group/Bible study guides, write curriculum lesson plans, write discussion questions for books, writing coach
Types of manuscripts: articles, nonfiction books, devotionals, poetry, short stories, novels, curriculum, gift books, technical material, adult, teen/YA
Charges: flat rate, word rate
Credentials/experience: Bachelor's degree in English; PhD in education. Although I do most writing, editing, and proofreading projects, my niche is creative nonfiction (engaging, dramatic, factual prose). I have been writing and editing for more than twenty-five years.

JK PAYLEITNER & ASSOCIATES | JAY PAYLEITNER

629 N. Tyler Rd., Saint Charles, IL 60174 | 630-377-7899
jaypayleitner@me.com | *www.jaypayleitner.com*

Contact: email

Services: ghostwriting, coauthoring, brochures, website text, back-cover copy

Types of manuscripts: nonfiction books, devotionals, scripts, gift books

Charges: flat fee

Credentials/experience: Author of twenty plus books with Harvest House, Bethany, Cook, Broadstreet, Worthy, Tyndale, and Howard with sales of more than a half-million books. Scripted and produced five thousand plus hours of radio for Josh McDowell, Prison Fellowship, Bible League, Voice of the Martyrs, Today's Father, etc. Wrote and produced scores of print ads for airlines, retailers, manufacturers, and publishers, including the first ad for the book *Left Behind*.

JLC EDITING SERVICES | JODY COLLINS

1403 Newport Ct. S.E., Renton, WA 98058 | 425-260-0948
heyjode70@yahoo.com | *www.jodyleecollins.com*

Contact: email

Services: manuscript evaluation, copyediting, proofreading, create small group/Bible study guides, write curriculum lesson plans, writing coach, big-picture edit of your message/vision

Types of manuscripts: articles, nonfiction books, devotionals, book proposals, curriculum, picture books, easy readers

Charges: hourly rate, page rate, word rate

Credentials/experience: BA in liberal studies, English major. Teaching credential, 1991. Post-graduate work included courses in writer's workshop and teaching writing. More than twenty-five years of experience writing and editing. Blog content editor/ coordinator for Faith & Culture Writer's Community.

JOY MEDIA | JULIE-ALLYSON IERON

Park Ridge, IL
joy@joymediaservices.com | *www.joymediaservices.com*

Contact: email

Services: manuscript evaluation, substantive editing/rewriting, copyediting, ghostwriting, coauthoring, write website text, create small group/Bible study guides, write discussion questions for books, writing coach

Types of manuscripts: articles, nonfiction books, devotionals, book proposals, gift books, adult

Charges: hourly rate

Credentials/experience: Master's degree in journalism and more than twenty-five years of experience in Christian publishing, writing, editing, and public relations. Specializes in Christian living, Bible study, and business/ministry promotions. Coaches first-time authors.

KATHY IDE BOOK SERVICES | KATHY IDE

Kathy@KathyIde.com | www.KathyIde.com

Contact: email

Services: manuscript evaluation, copyediting, proofreading, ghostwriting, coauthoring, create small group/Bible study guides, writing coach

Types of manuscripts: articles, nonfiction books, devotionals, short stories, novels, query letters, book proposals, Bible studies, scripts, gift books, adult, teen/YA

Charges: hourly rate

Credentials/experience: Kathy is the author of *Proofreading Secrets of Best-Selling Authors* and the editor-compiler of the Fiction Lover's Devotional series. She has ghostwritten ten nonfiction books and a series of five novels. Kathy has been a professional freelance editor since 1998, offering a full range of editorial services for aspiring writers, established authors, and book publishers. She speaks at writers conferences across the country and is the director of the Mount Hermon Christian Writers Conference and the SoCal Christian Writers' Conference. Kathy is a co-owner of the Christian Editor Network, parent company to The Christian PEN: Proofreaders and Editors Network, the Christian Editor Connection, the PEN Institute, and PENCON.

KATHY TYERS GILLIN

Bozeman, MT

kathytyers@yahoo.com | www.kathytyers.com

Contact: email

Services: substantive editing/rewriting, copyediting, proofreading, writing coach

Types of manuscripts: articles, nonfiction books, novels, adult, teen/YA

Charges: hourly rate

Credentials/experience: *New York Times* best-selling author of ten science-fiction novels and three nonfiction books, including *Writing Deep Viewpoint: Invite Your Readers Into the Story*. Experience editing multiple fiction genres and nonfiction from scholarly theological works to family history. Thirty years writing experience. MA in Christianity and the arts, Regent College, Canada.

KATIE PHILLIPS CREATIVE SERVICES | KATIE PHILLIPS

2727 N. Amidon, Wichita, KS 67204 | 316-293-9202
morford.katie@gmail.com | *www.storyforhisglory.com*

Contact: email

Services: manuscript evaluation, substantive editing/rewriting, brochures, newsletters, website text, writing coach, back-cover copy, author-branding coaching

Types of manuscripts: articles, short stories, novels, book proposals, scripts, adult, teen/YA, soft speculative fiction

Charges: flat fee, word rate, custom

Credentials/experience: Katie brings ten plus years of experience in journalism, communications, fiction writing, and marketing to her editing business. She is a 2017 Advanced Writers and Speakers Association (AWSA) Golden Scroll Fiction Editor of the Year finalist and has received accolades from industry leaders Steve Barclift (editor, Kregel) and Jeff Gerke (editor, author). She is a silver member of The Christian PEN and has completed the Christian Writers Guild Apprenticeship and Journeyman mentorship courses under literary agent Les Stobbe and author DiAnn Mills. Katie is also a cofounder and managing editor at indie publisher Crosshair Press.

KEELY BOEVING EDITORIAL | KEELY BOEVING

Denver, CO | 303-916-7498
keely.boeving@gmail.com | *www.keelyboeving.com*

Contact: email

Services: manuscript evaluation, substantive editing/rewriting, copyediting, ghostwriting, coauthoring

Types of manuscripts: nonfiction books, novels, query letters, book proposals, adult, teen/YA, middle grade

Charges: hourly rate

Credentials/experience: Experienced editor and copy editor, formerly worked in editorial for Oxford University Press. Have worked with independent clients, literary agencies, and publishers as a freelancer for the past several years.

KELLY KAGAMAS TOMKIES

Bexley, OH | 614-270-0185
kellytomkies@gmail.com | *users.wowway.com/~kakwrite/About.html*

Contact: email

Services: substantive editing/rewriting, copyediting, proofreading, ghostwriting, writing coach

Types of manuscripts: articles, nonfiction books, devotionals, short stories, novels, query letters, book proposals, adult, teen/YA, picture books, easy readers, middle grade

Charges: flat fee

Credentials/experience: I have nearly twenty years of editorial experience, including authoring seven books for different publishers, contributing chapters to two National Geographic books, serving as editor of three major business magazines, and years of experience writing and editing for publishers and individual authors. My client list includes HarperCollins, John Wiley & Sons, McGraw-Hill, Kirkus Editorial, Fountainhead Press, Barbour Books, Vantage Press, and Gadfly, LLC, as well as individual authors who wish to find publishers or self-publish.

KIM PETERSON

1114 Buxton Dr., Knoxville, TN 37922 | 865-693-9363
peterskus@yahoo.com | *naturewalkwithgod.wordpress.com*

Contact: email

Services: manuscript evaluation, substantive editing/rewriting, copyediting, proofreading, create brochures, create newsletters, write website text, create small group/Bible study guides, write curriculum lesson plans, write discussion questions for books, create PowerPoint presentations, writing coach, back-cover copy, virtual assistant

Types of manuscripts: articles, nonfiction books, devotionals, poetry, short stories, novels, query letters, book proposals, curriculum, academic, Bible studies, gift books, technical material, adult, teen/YA, blog posts

Charges: hourly rate

Credentials/experience: MA in print communication. Taught college-level writing for twenty-five years. Agent's fiction reader for ten years.

KRISTEN STIEFFEL

4532 Commander Dr., Apt. 2122, Orlando, FL 32822 | 407-928-7801
kristen@kristenstieffel.com | *www.kristenstieffel.com*

Contact: email
Services: manuscript evaluation, substantive editing/rewriting, copyediting, proofreading, ghostwriting, coauthoring, writing coach
Types of manuscripts: nonfiction books, novels
Charges: custom
Credentials/experience: I have been a freelancer for seventeen years and was a newspaper page designer and copyeditor for ten years. I've been trained in developmental editing and copyediting by the Editorial Freelancers Association and in the special requirements of fiction editing by the Christian Proofreader and Editor Network. I've edited dozens of books in multiple genres, but my specialty is science fiction and fantasy; I am a published author in these genres.

LEE WARREN COMMUNICATIONS | LEE WARREN

Omaha, NE | 402-740-5795
leewarrenjr@outlook.com | *www.leewarren.info/editing*

Contact: email
Services: copyediting, proofreading
Types of manuscripts: nonfiction books, devotionals, novels
Charges: word rate
Credentials/experience: Lee Warren has copyedited for three publishing houses, one manuscript critique service, and a Christian newspaper. He's also copyedited and proofread dozens of manuscripts through his own service; testimonials available on the website.

LES STOBBE, COACH AND WRITER

300 Doubleday Rd., Tryon, NC 28782 | 828-808-7127
lhstobbe123@gmail.com | *www.stobbeliterary.com*

Contact: email
Services: substantive editing/rewriting, ghostwriting, coauthoring, book-contract evaluation, writing coach, back-cover copy
Types of manuscripts: nonfiction books, devotionals, book proposals, curriculum, Bible studies, adult
Charges: flat fee, custom
Credentials/experience: Magazine editor, book editor, curriculum

editor, writer of small-group studies, title-creation specialist, ghostwriter for national clients, writer coach and agent, international lecturer on writing, journalist in residence at Gordon College. I deliver assignments on time.

LESLIE L. MCKEE EDITING | LESLIE L. MCKEE

lmckeeediting@gmail.com | *lmckeeediting.wixsite.com/lmckeeediting*

Contact: email

Services: substantive editing/rewriting, copyediting, proofreading, write discussion questions for books

Types of manuscripts: nonfiction books, devotionals, poetry, short stories, novels, adult, teen/YA, picture books, easy readers, middle grade

Charges: word rate, per-project rate

Credentials/experience: Freelance editor with various large and small publishing houses since 2012, working with traditionally published and self-published authors. Member of The Christian PEN and American Christian Fiction Writers. See website for details on services offered, as well as testimonials.

LESLIE SANTAMARIA

1024 Walnut Creek Cove, Winter Springs, FL 32708 | 407-497-5365

leslie@lesliesantamaria.com | *www.lesliesantamaria.com*

Contact: email

Services: manuscript evaluation, copyediting, proofreading, newsletters, website text, curriculum lesson plans, discussion questions for books, writing coach, back-cover copy

Types of manuscripts: query letters; book proposals; curriculum; children's nonfiction, curriculum, and short stories

Charges: custom, flat fee for critiques, $35/hour for coaching

Credentials/experience: Published author, journalist, and book reviewer with more than twenty-five years of book and magazine editing experience and a BA in English. Specializes in the children's market.

LIBBY GONTARZ WORD SERVICES | LIBBY GONTARZ

Apache Junction, AZ | 480-278-4848

libbygontarz@gmail.com | *www.libbygontarz.com*

Contact: email

Services: substantive editing/rewriting, copyediting, proofreading, write website text

Types of manuscripts: articles, nonfiction books, curriculum, adult, middle grade

Charges: flat fee, hourly rate, sample edit and quote available

Credentials/experience: Following a successful career teaching at the fourth grade and middle school levels, Libby moved into corporate training, working with school districts across the United States to improve student test scores. Subsequently, she has written and edited educational materials for instruction and assessment of student learning at the elementary, junior-high, and high-school levels. Libby has also worked for a weekly newspaper, writing and coordinating articles on local businesses and politics, penning a weekly column and editing the community and business sections. Libby especially enjoys helping writers of Christian nonfiction and personal memoir to bring their dreams of independent publication to reality. Member of The Christian PEN.

LIGHTHOUSE EDITING | DR. LON ACKELSON

13326 Community Rd. #11, Poway, CA 92064 | 858-748-9258
Isaiah68la@sbcglobal.net | *lighthouseedit.com*

Contact: website form

Services: manuscript evaluation, substantive editing/rewriting, copyediting, proofreading, ghostwriting, coauthoring, back-cover copy

Types of manuscripts: articles, nonfiction books, devotionals, query letters, book proposals, curriculum, Bible studies, adult

Charges: flat fee, hourly rate, page rate

Credentials/experience: A professional editor for thirty-three years and a published writer for forty years.

LIGHTNING EDITING SERVICES | DENISE LOOCK

Waynesville, NC | 908-868-5854
denise@lightningeditingservices.com | *www.lightningeditingservices.com*

Contact: email

Services: manuscript evaluation, substantive editing/rewriting, copyediting, proofreading, create newsletters, create small group/ Bible study guides, write discussion questions for books, create PowerPoint presentations

Types of manuscripts: articles, nonfiction books, devotionals, gift books, teen/YA, middle grade

Charges: flat fee, hourly rate

Credentials/experience: Associate editor for Lighthouse Publishing of the Carolinas (five years); high-school English teacher and college instructor (twenty-nine years); editor of *The Journey Christian Newspaper* (three years); author of two devotional books.

LINDSAY A. FRANKLIN

Escondido, CA | 858-243-8134
Lindsay@LindsayAFranklin.com | *lindsayafranklin.com*

Contact: email
Services: manuscript evaluation, substantive editing/rewriting, copyediting, proofreading, ghostwriting, coauthoring, writing coach
Types of manuscripts: nonfiction books, short stories, novels, adult, teen/YA, picture books, easy readers, middle grade
Charges: hourly rate, word rate
Credentials/experience: Award-winning, published author; member of The Christian PEN.

LINE UPON LINE | LYNNE TAGAWA

San Antonio, TX | 210-544-4397
lbtagawa@gmail.com |*www.lynnetagawa.com*

Contact: email
Services: copyediting, proofreading
Types of manuscripts: articles, nonfiction books, short stories, novels, curriculum, scripts, adult, teen/YA, middle grade; specializing in theological, historical, and science/medicine
Charges: word rate
Credentials/experience: Copy editor with Chapel Library of Pensacola; high-school writing instructor; silver member of The Christian PEN; author of *Sam Houston's Republic*; member of American Christian Fiction Writers.

LISA BARTELT

Lancaster, PA | 717-673-7236
lmbartelt@gmail.com | *lisabartelt.com*

Contact: email
Services: copyediting, proofreading, coauthoring, create newsletters, write website text
Types of manuscripts: articles, nonfiction books, devotionals, novels, query letters
Charges: hourly rate
Credentials/experience: Eight years of writing and editing for daily

newspapers; member of American Christian Fiction Writers and The Christian PEN; published articles in *Thriving Family*, *Prayer Connect*, and *The Upper Room*; wrote curriculum for Group Publishing.

LOGOS WORD DESIGNS, LLC | LINDA NATHAN

PO Box 735, Maple Falls, WA 98266-0735 | 360-599-3429
lindalogosword.com | *www.logosword.com*

Contact: email

Services: manuscript evaluation, substantive editing/rewriting, copyediting, proofreading, ghostwriting, write website text, write discussion questions for books

Types of manuscripts: articles, nonfiction books, devotionals, short stories, novels, query letters, book proposals, gift books, technical material, adult, teen/YA, apologetics, academic, law, journalism, interviews, reviews, business, the arts, health/social sciences, education, history, and marketing communications

Charges: word rate

Credentials/experience: Linda has operated Logos Word Designs since 1992. She has more than thirty years of experience as an independent freelance writer, editor, and publishing consultant, working with authors and institutions on a wide range of projects. She has ten years of experience in most areas of the legal field as a paralegal, legal secretary, and notary public. She has also edited nearly a hundred college textbooks and helped numerous authors achieve publication. Member of Northwest Independent Editors Guild, Editorial Freelancers Association, American Christian Fiction Writers. Certified with Christian Editor Connection.

LOUISE M . GOUGE

Kissimmee, FL | 407-694-5765
Louisemgouge@aol.com | *www.blog.Louisemgouge.com*

Contact: email

Services: copyediting

Types of manuscripts: devotionals, short stories, novels, query letters, book proposals

Charges: word rate

Credentials/experience: College English professor; multipublished, award-winning author of twenty-three novels.

LUCIE WINBORNE

Longwood, FL | 321-439-7743
lwinborne704@gmail.com | *www.bluetypewriter.com*

Contact: email

Services: copyediting, proofreading

Types of manuscripts: articles, nonfiction books, devotionals, poetry, short stories, novels, query letters, book proposals, curriculum, scripts, gift books, adult, teen/YA, easy readers, middle grade, blog posts

Charges: hourly rate

Credentials/experience: Member of The Christian PEN and Editorial Freelancers Association. Copy editor for Global Hope Network International and Ask God Today Ministries. Proofreader for Lighthouse Publishing of the Carolinas. Experience in proofreading and copyediting fiction, nonfiction, educational, and business documents. Demonstrated adherence to deadlines and excellent communication skills.

MARCY WEYDEMULLER

San Francisco, CA | 925-876-4860
marcy@sowinglightseeds.com | *www.marcyweydemuller.com*

Contact: email

Services: manuscript evaluation, substantive editing/rewriting, create small group/Bible study guides, write curriculum lesson plans, write discussion questions for books, writing coach

Types of manuscripts: articles, nonfiction books, devotionals, short stories, novels, curriculum, adult, teen/YA, picture books, easy readers, middle grade

Charges: hourly rate

Credentials/experience: I have worked on more than forty published novels, and four of the authors I work with have published three or more series. My current edits have included historical fiction, historical Christmas novella, YA contemporary, middle-readers both historical and contemporary, suspense-mystery, woman's romance, and memoir. I have more than twenty-five years of experience writing, mentoring, and teaching, both in fiction and nonfiction, including Bible studies and college composition. I have completed a BA in history and sociology and an MFA in writing, with a special focus on fantasy, poetry, and children's literature.

MARK MY WORD EDITORIAL SERVICES, LLC | VICKI ADANG

Indianapolis, IN | 317-549-5176
vadang@outlook.com | *www.mmwllc.net*

Contact: email
Services: manuscript evaluation, substantive editing/rewriting, copyediting, proofreading
Types of manuscripts: articles, nonfiction books, adult, teen/YA, easy readers, middle grade
Charges: hourly rate
Credentials/experience: I have more than twenty years of editorial experience, ranging from Christian fiction (*The Hungering Dark* by Stephen Clark) to reference works (*Comparative Religion For Dummies*) to creative nonfiction (*Busy and Blessed: 10 Simple Steps for Parents Seeking Peace*).

MARTI PIEPER

Mount Dora, FL | 352-409-3136
marti@martipieper.com | *www.martipieper.com*

Contact: email
Services: manuscript evaluation, substantive editing/rewriting, copyediting, proofreading, ghostwriting, coauthoring, write website text, create small group/Bible study guides, write curriculum lesson plans, write discussion questions for books, writing coach
Types of manuscripts: articles, nonfiction books, devotionals, poetry, query letters, book proposals, curriculum, adult, teen/YA
Charges: flat fee, hourly rate
Credentials/experience: BS in education, MDiv in communications. Fifteen years professional writing and editorial experience, including magazine editing and freelance editing for publishers. Have ghostwritten eight traditionally published nonfiction books, one a best-seller.

MENTOR ME CAREER NETWORK | CHERYL ROGERS

Tampa, FL | 863-288-0802
cheryl@mentormecareernetwork.com | *www.mentormecareernetwork.com*

Contact: email
Services: manuscript evaluation, substantive editing/rewriting, copyediting, proofreading, ghostwriting, coauthoring, create brochures, create newsletters, write website text, create small group/Bible study guides, writing coach

Types of manuscripts: articles, nonfiction books, adult, teen/YA, middle grade
Charges: flat rate, hourly rate, word rate
Credentials/experience: BA in journalism and sociology; more than five years of book editing/freelancing; one year of newspaper copyediting; eleven years of newspaper reporting; four years of desktop design, including brochures, booklets, and flyers.

MICHELLE BURFORD EDITORIAL SERVICES, LLC | MICHELLE BURFORD

New York, NY | 646-883-5122
Michelle@MichelleBurford.com | *www.MichelleBurford.com*

Contact: email
Services: ghostwriting
Types of manuscripts: nonfiction books
Charges: flat fee
Credentials/experience: Number 1 *New York Times* best-selling ghostwriter (celebrity memoir); founding senior editor of *O, The Oprah Magazine;* Harvard-trained journalist.

MONICA SHARMAN EDITING | MONICA SHARMAN

Colorado Springs, CO | 719-373-6042
monicasharman@yahoo.com | *www.monicasharman.wordpress.com/monica-sharman-editing*

Contact: email
Services: copyediting, proofreading
Types of manuscripts: articles, nonfiction books, devotionals, poetry, short stories, curriculum, gift books, technical material, adult, teen/YA, picture books, easy readers, middle grade
Charges: flat fee, hourly fee
Credentials/experience: Certified with Christian Editor Connection. Monica has worked with both traditional publishers and self-publishing authors. Previous projects include Bible studies, devotionals, Christian nonfiction, fiction, poetry, blog content, and business website content. Monica is known for her technical accuracy, sharp eye, and light touch preserving the author's voice. See her website for previous clients and more information.

MWORDS | MARLENE MCCURLEY

Milcreek, WA | 425-243-4660
mwordsedit@gmail.com | *www.mwords.net*

Contact: email
Services: manuscript evaluation, substantive editing/rewriting, copyediting, proofreading
Types of manuscripts: articles, nonfiction books, devotionals, short stories, novels, gift books, adult, teen/YA, picture books, easy readers, middle grade
Charges: word rate
Credentials/experience: Editing credential from the Graham School at the University of Chicago. Member of Northwest Independent Editors Guild, Editorial Freelancers Association, The Christian PEN, and Northwest Christian Writers Association (NCWA). Volunteer for the Alzheimer's Association and NCWA. Fifteen years of experience in multiple genres.

NEXT INDEX SERVICES | JESSICA MCCURDY CROOKS

6703 N.W. 7th Ave., KIN 2614, Miami, FL 33126-6007 | 876-354-4084
Jessica@JessicaCrooks.com | *www.next-index.com*

Contact: email
Services: copyediting, proofreading, website text, indexing
Types of manuscripts: articles, nonfiction books, devotionals, novels, adult, teen/YA, middle grade
Charges: flat fee, hourly rate, page rate, word rate
Credentials/experience: MA. My training as a librarian and records manager gives me an eye for detail and finding information. I also know how readers tend to search for information, a skill that helps me arrive at keywords and phrases for the indexes I write. I have more than twenty years of indexing experience.

NOBLE CREATIVE, LLC | SCOTT NOBLE

PO Box 131402, St. Paul, MN 55113 | 651-494-4169
snoble@noblecreative.com | *www.noblecreative.com*

Contact: email
Services: manuscript evaluation, substantive editing/rewriting, copyediting, proofreading, ghostwriting, write website text, create small group/Bible study guides, writing coach
Types of manuscripts: articles, nonfiction books, devotionals, query letters, book proposals, curriculum, adult

Charges: flat fee

Credentials/experience: Nearly twenty years of experience as an award-winning journalist, writer, editor, and proofreader. More than 1,000 published articles, many of them prompting radio and television appearances. Won several awards from Evangelical Press Association. Worked with dozens of published authors and other public figures, as well as first-time authors and small businesses. Have a BA and MS from St. Cloud State University and an MA from Bethel Seminary.

NOVEL IMPROVEMENT EDITING SERVICES | JEANNE MARIE LEACH

Hudson, CO | 303-536-4241

jeanne@novelimprovement.com | *novelimprovement.com*

Contact: email

Services: manuscript evaluation, substantive editing/rewriting, copyediting, proofreading, writing coach, speaking on fiction topics

Types of manuscripts: short stories, novels, query letters, book proposals, adult, teen/YA

Charges: flat fee, page rate

Credentials/experience: Past coordinator and current gold member of The Christian PEN: Proofreaders and Editors Network; member of Christian Editor Network; and member of American Christian Fiction Writers, where she received the 2012 Member Service Award. She teaches four online courses on editing fiction (thirty-two weeks) per year to editors and authors through the PEN Institute and has mentored more than a dozen authors who have gone on to win numerous awards in the writing industry. She speaks on writing and editing fiction at conferences and Christian writers organizations.

OASHEIM EDITING SERVICES | CATHY OASHEIM

Chantilly, VA | 720-373-9486

admin@cathyoasheim.com | *www.cathyoasheim.com*

Contact: email

Services: substantive editing/rewriting, copyediting, proofreading, create newsletters, write website text, create small group/Bible study guides, write curriculum lesson plans, write discussion questions for books, create PowerPoint presentations

Types of manuscripts: articles, nonfiction books, devotionals, short stories, novels, query letters, gift books, technical material, adult, teen/YA, picture books, easy readers, middle grade

Charges: flat fee, hourly rate, page rate, word rate

Credentials/experience: Copy editor providing substantial editing services for Christian fiction and nonfiction, military stories, oral history, and academia using American Psychological Association, MLA, Associated Press, and *The Christian Writer's Manual* style guides. More than twelve years of technical writing experience, more than four years working with a Christian independent publishing company. Constant Contact and Mail Chimp, devotionals, newsletters, book covers, e-book formatting, I can do. Christian, former telecom engineer (technical), degree in applied psychology (APA), mediator (contracts), and Navy veteran (oral history).

ODD SOCK PROOFREADING & COPYEDITING | STEVE MATHISEN

Aberdeen, WA | 206-660-8431

scmathisen98037@hotmail.com | *oddsock.me*

Contact: email

Services: substantive editing/rewriting, copyediting, proofreading

Types of manuscripts: nonfiction books, short stories, novels, adult, teen/YA, middle grade

Charges: page rate

Credentials/experience: I am a silver member of The Christian PEN: Proofreaders and Editors Network. Several of the books I have worked on have gone on to be quite successful and have won awards. See the list of books on the "Covers & Testimonials" page on my website.

OUR WRITTEN LIVES | RACHAEL HARTMAN

Universal City, TX | 318-319-6893

publisher@owlofhope.com | *www.OurWrittenLives.com*

Contact: email

Services: manuscript evaluation, substantive editing/rewriting, copyediting, proofreading, ghostwriting, coauthoring, book-contract evaluation, create small group/Bible study guides, write curriculum lesson plans, write discussion questions for books, writing coach

Types of manuscripts: articles, nonfiction books, devotionals, curriculum

Charges: hourly rate

Credentials/experience: Member of Christian Small Publisher Association. MS in human services, specialization in counseling; BA in liberal studies with a minor in writing; and certified life coach. Ten years in the writing and publishing industry; established Our Written Lives in 2013; author of three books.

PAMELA GOSSIAUX

Whitmore Lake, MI | 734-846-0112
pam@pamelagossiaux.com | *www.PamelaGossiaux.com*

Contact: email

Services: manuscript evaluation, substantive editing/rewriting, copyediting, proofreading, write website text, write discussion questions for books

Types of manuscripts: articles, nonfiction books, devotionals, short stories, novels, query letters, book proposals, gift books, adult, teen/YA, picture books, easy readers, middle grade

Charges: flat fee, hourly rate

Credentials/experience: Published author, twenty-five years of journalism experience, writing workshop teacher, dual BA degrees in creative writing and English language and literature. I have worked with writers in many genres, both fiction and nonfiction, including best-sellers.

PEGGYSUE WELLS

3419 E. 1000 North, Roanoke, IN 46783 | 260-433-2817
peggysuewells@gmail.com | *www.PeggySueWells.com*

Contact: email, website form

Services: manuscript evaluation, substantive editing/rewriting, copyediting, proofreading, ghostwriting, coauthoring, brochures, newsletters, write website text, create small group/bible study guides, write curriculum lesson plans, write discussion questions for books, writing coach, back-cover copy

Types of manuscripts: articles, nonfiction books, devotionals, short stories, novels, query letters, book proposals, curriculum, Bible studies, scripts, gift books, technical material, adult, teen/YA

Charges: hourly rate

Credentials/experience: PeggySue is the author of twenty-five traditionally published books, including a couple of best-sellers and an audio finalist. She writes and edits fiction and nonfiction.

PERFECT WORD EDITING SERVICES | LINDA HARRIS

5785 Cedar Creek View #101, Colorado Springs, CO 80915 | 719-464-5189
lharris@perfectwordediting.com | *www.perfectwordediting.com*

Contact: email, website form
Services: substantive editing/rewriting, copyediting, proofreading, create brochures, newsletters, create small group/Bible study guides, write curriculum lesson plans, write discussion questions for books, back-cover copy
Types of manuscripts: articles, nonfiction books, devotionals, query letters, book proposals, curriculum, Bible studies, academic, adult, picture books, easy readers, middle grade
Charges: page rate, word rate
Credentials/experience: More than thirty-five years of experience in editing and writing. Member of The Christian PEN and The Christian Editor Connection. Instructor of Editing Children's Books class for The PEN Institute, speaker at PENCON conference. Specializing in children's book editing.

PICKY, PICKY INK | SUE MIHOLER

1075 Willow Lake Rd. N., Keizer, OR 97303 | 503-393-3356
suemihler@comcast.net

Contact: email
Services: copyediting, brochures, newsletters, website text, small group/Bible study guides, back-cover copy
Types of manuscripts: articles, nonfiction books, devotionals, Bible studies, gift books
Charges: hourly rate
Credentials/experience: I have edited more than sixty full-length books since 1998 for publishers and individuals.

PLOT & PROSE | MARY KEANE

Park Ridge, IL | 773-691-7477
info@plotandprose.com | *www.plotandprose.com*

Contact: email
Services: substantive editing/rewriting, copyediting, proofreading
Types of manuscripts: short stories, novels, adult, teen/YA, easy readers, middle grade
Charges: word rate
Credentials/experience: Completed Fiction Editing 1, 2, 3 from

The Christian PEN. Writer and indie author. Specializing in independent authors, debut authors, e-book publishing.

PRATHER INK LITERARY SERVICES | VICKI PRATHER

Raymond, MS | 601-573-4295
pratherINK@gmail.com | *pratherink.wordpress.com*

Contact: email
Services: copyediting, proofreading, coauthoring
Types of manuscripts: nonfiction books, devotionals, poetry, short stories, novels, gift books, adult, teen/YA, picture books, middle grade
Charges: hourly rate, word rate
Credentials/experience: The Christian PEN silver member.

PROFESSIONAL PUBLISHING SERVICES | CHRISTY CALLAHAN

PO Box 461, Waycross, GA 31502 | 912-809-9062
professionalpublishingservices@gmail.com | *www.ChristyCallahan.com*

Contact: email
Services: manuscript evaluation, substantive editing/rewriting, copyediting, proofreading, newsletters, website text, small group/Bible study guides, curriculum lesson plans, discussion questions for books, writing coach
Types of manuscripts: nonfiction books, devotionals, short stories, novels, curriculum, Bible studies, gift books, technical material, academic, adult, teen/YA
Charges: flat fee, hourly rate, custom
Credentials/experience: Christy graduated Phi Beta Kappa from Carnegie Mellon University and then earned her MA in Intercultural Studies from Fuller Seminary. A gold member of The Christian PEN: Proofreaders and Editors Network and certified by the Christian Editor Connection (CEC), she was selected as a judge for the 2016 CEC Excellence in Editing Award in the category of nonfiction. Christy has taken the following courses with The Christian PEN: Editing Fiction I & II and Advanced Fiction Editing. She also completed the 40-hour Foundational Course (Christian track) with the Institute for Life Coach Training.

PWC EDITING | PAUL W. CONANT

527 Bayshore Pl., Dallas, TX 75217-7755 | 214-289-3397
pwcediting@gmail.com | *www.pwc-editing.com*

Contact: email
Services: copyediting, proofreading, brochures, newsletters, website text
Types of manuscripts: articles, nonfiction books, devotionals, short stories, novels, query letters, book proposals, Bible studies, technical material, adult, teens/YA, middle grade, academic
Charges: hourly rates; prefers a 2,000-word sample in order to make the most appropriate estimate for a manuscript
Credentials/experience: Member of Christian Editors Connection, The Christian PEN, and *Thumbtack.com*. Fifteen years of experience with dissertations, twenty-two years with magazines, twenty years with books. Has worked with new or ESL writers, as well as publishers.

RALENE BURKE

Vine Grove, KY | 270-823-3874
raleneburke@gmail.com | *www.raleneburke.com*

Contact: email
Services: manuscript evaluation, substantive editing/rewriting, copyediting, proofreading, writing coach
Types of manuscripts: articles, nonfiction books, devotionals, short stories, novels, adult, teen/YA
Charges: hourly rate, page rate
Credentials/experience: Numerous novels, short stories, and articles edited for clients, a couple who have been up for awards. Ralene has taken classes through The Christian PEN and the University of California—San Diego to sharpen her editing skills. Member of The Christian PEN, American Christian Fiction Writers, and Realm Makers.

REBECCA LUELLA MILLER

rluellam@yahoo.com | *rewriterewordrework.wordpress.com*

Contact: email
Services: manuscript evaluation, substantive editing/rewriting, copyediting, proofreading, writing coach
Types of manuscripts: articles, nonfiction books, devotionals, short stories, novels, query letters, book proposals, technical material, adult, teen/YA

Charges: flat fee, page rate, word rate

Credentials/experience: Rebecca has worked as a freelance editor for fifteen years, editing books by such authors as Bryan Davis and Jill Williamson and working with AMG Publishers on other projects. Previously she taught English at the middle-school and high-school levels. She has a BA in English from Westmont College.

REBECCA LYLES

Boise, ID | 208-562-1592
beckylyles@beckylyles.com | *www.beckylyles.com*

Contact: email

Services: manuscript evaluation, substantive editing/rewriting, copyediting, proofreading, writing coach

Types of manuscripts: articles, nonfiction books, devotionals, short stories, novels, query letters, book proposals, adult, teen/YA

Charges: hourly rate, page rate

Credentials/experience: Rebecca is a multipublished author who has edited fiction and nonfiction for more than fifteen years, including brochures, white papers, newsletters, educational material, and Bible studies on the nonfiction side and short stories, children's books, and award-winning novels on the fiction side.

RED QUILL EDITING | JUDITH ROBL

PO Box 802, Lyons, KS 67554
jrlight620@yahoo.com | *www.judithrobl.com*

Contact: email, website form

Services: copyediting, proofreading, brochures, website text, writing coach, back-cover copy

Types of manuscripts: articles, nonfiction books, devotionals, short stories, novels, book proposals, Bible studies, gift books, adult

Charges: negotiated rate based on ten-page evaluation of manuscript

Credentials/experience: Former English teacher, published by Harvest House, first reader for Sheaf House, private clientele since 2001.

REFINE SERVICES | KATE MOTAUNG KATE

refineservices.com | *www.refineservices.com*

Contact: email

Services: copyediting, proofreading, newsletters, write website text, writing coach

Types of manuscripts: articles, nonfiction books, devotionals, Bible studies

Charges: custom fee
Credentials/experience: See website for experience and testimonials.

REVISIONS BY RACHEL, LLC | RACHEL E. NEWMAN

Owasso, OK | 918-207-2833
Editor@RevisionsbyRachel.com | *www.RevisionsbyRachel.com*

Contact: email
Services: manuscript evaluation, substantive editing/rewriting, copyediting, proofreading, indexing
Types of manuscripts: nonfiction books, novels, query letters, book proposals, curriculum, adult, teen/YA, picture books, easy readers, middle grade, speculative fiction
Charges: word rate
Credentials/experience: Rachel holds a BS in paralegal studies from Northeastern State University in Oklahoma. She graduated summa cum laude in 2006 and was awarded the Certified Paralegal designation by the National Association of Legal Assistants. Certified with Christian Editor Connection. She is a gold member of The Christian PEN: Proofreaders and Editors Network, is an established freelance editor with Christian Editor Connection, is an instructor with The PEN Institute, serves as a judge for the Excellence in Editing Award, and has served as faculty for PENCON, the only conference for editors in the Christian market.

ROBIN'S RED PEN | ROBIN PATCHEN

1808 Thunderbird Blvd., Edmond, OK 73013 | 405-816-4867
robin@robinpatchen.com | *robinpatchen.com/editing*

Contact: email
Services: manuscript evaluation, substantive editing/rewriting, copyediting, writing coach
Types of manuscripts: nonfiction books, short stories, novels, adult, teen/YA
Charges: page rate
Credentials/experience: Robin is one of the authors of *5 Editors Tackle the 12 Fatal Flaws of Fiction Writing*, an in-depth guide to self-editing. She is a multipublished, award-winning author and freelance editor specializing in Christian fiction. As a general editor with Lighthouse Publishing of the Carolina's Smitten line and a freelance copyeditor for Serenade Press, she has the privilege of working with exceptionally talented romance and historical romance authors. Patchen loves mentoring new authors and

helping established authors polish their books. She enjoys reading and editing almost every clean YA and adult genre. For more information, visit her website.

SALISBURY ALEXANDER COMMUNICATIONS | KIRT G. SALISBURY

2130 Sunset Dr., Ste. 104, Vista, CA 92081 | 760-212-2872
kirtwrites81@icloud.com

Contact: email
Services: ghostwriting, brochures, newsletters, website text, back-cover copy
Types of manuscripts: technical material, articles, devotionals, query letters, response letters, nonfiction books
Charges: flat fee
Credentials/experience: Has written advertising and promotional materials for high-tech scientific equipment, Christian and biomedical magazines, and biomedical newsletters. Ghostwritten for more than twenty-four major Christian ministries for their partner communications, premium books, fundraising appeals, and response letters.

SALLY E . STUART

15935 S.W. Greens Way, Tigard, OR 97224 | 503-642-9844
stuartcwmg@aol.com

Contact: email, phone
Services: manuscript evaluation, book-contract evaluation
Types of manuscripts: articles, nonfiction books, novels, book proposals
Charges: $40 per hour for critiques, $45 per hour for phone/personal consultations
Credentials/experience: Author of thirty-eight books, including twenty-seven editions of *The Christian Writers Market Guide* and her latest, *The Writing World Defined: A to Z*. More than forty-five years of experience as a writer, teacher, and marketing expert.

SARAH HAMAKER

4207 Collier Rd., Fairfax, VA 22030 | 703-691-1676
shamaker@verizon.net | *sarahhamakerfiction.com*

Contact: email
Services: copyediting, proofreading, ghostwriting, write website text
Types of manuscripts: articles, nonfiction books, novels, query letters, book proposals, adult

Charges: flat fee, hourly rate

Credentials/experience: I'm a professional freelance writer and editor with more than twenty years of editorial and book-editing experience. I've worked as a project manager/ghostwriter on numerous projects, including books and articles. I work to ensure we're a good fit before proceeding and love helping writers polish their work.

SCRIVEN COMMUNICATIONS | KATHIE SCRIVEN

22 Ridge Rd. #220, Greenbelt, MD 20770 | 240-542-4602
KathieScriven@yahoo.com | *www.linkedin.com/in/kathie-scriven-46981037*

Contact: email, phone

Services: manuscript evaluation, substantive editing/rewriting, copyediting, proofreading

Types of manuscripts: articles, short stories, nonfiction books, book proposals, query letters, website text, back-cover copy, adult

Charges: hourly rate

Credentials/experience: I have edited more than seventy-five Christian nonfiction books and more than a hundred shorter projects, including booklets, biographical sketches, press releases, and grant applications. Former editor of four Christian publications and freelance writer for several Christian and general-market publications. Bachelor's degree in mass communication with a concentration in journalism from Towson University. I'm happy to email a document that describes my credentials and experience in more detail.

SEACOAST SYNERGY | PATRICIA WATKINS

Imperial Beach, CA | 970-308-3188
SeacoastSynergy@outlook.com | *www.seacoastsynergysd.com*

Contact: email

Services: proofreading, write discussion questions for books

Types of manuscripts: articles, nonfiction books, short stories, novels, adult, teen/YA, picture books, easy readers, middle grade

Charges: flat fee, page rate

Credentials/experience: Patricia is a published author and educator with extensive experience proofreading fiction and nonfiction. She enjoys creating thought-provoking discussion questions for both genres. During her eight years as a literacy instructor for gifted students, she edited, compiled, and produced a yearly student literary magazine. She is a member of the San Diego Christian Writers Guild.

SHERRY CHAMBLEE

Sun Valley, CA | 818-767-8765
chambleeservices@gmail.com | *www.offscript.weebly.com*

Contact: email
Services: copyediting, proofreading
Types of manuscripts: articles, nonfiction books, devotionals, poetry, short stories, novels, gift books, technical material, adult, teen/YA, picture books, easy readers, middle grade
Charges: word rate
Credentials/experience: I am a freelance editor, working directly with authors for the past four years. I have edited both fiction and nonfiction, including works ranging from illustrated children's picture books and middle-grade chapter books to young-adult and adult Christian fiction.

SHERYL MADDEN

Seattle, WA | 206-919-2203
madden58sheryl@gmail.com | *www.sheryl-madden.com*

Contact: email
Services: copyediting, proofreading, brochures, newsletters, website text, small group/Bible study guides, discussion questions for books, back-cover copy
Types of manuscripts: articles, nonfiction books, devotionals, short stories, novels, Bible studies, adult
Charges: page rate
Credentials/experience: Certificate in professional editing, freelancing since 2015.

SHIRL'S EDITING SERVICES | SHIRL THOMAS

9379 Tanager Ave., Fountain Valley, CA 92708 | 714-968-5726
shirlth@verizon.net

Contact: email, phone
Services: manuscript evaluation, substantive editing/rewriting, copyediting, proofreading, ghostwriting, coauthoring, writing coach
Types of manuscripts: articles, nonfiction books, devotionals, poetry, short stories, novels, query letters, book proposals, scripts, gift books, technical material, adult

Charges: hourly rate

Credentials/experience: Professional writer since 1973 and editor since 1994. Complete résumé available.

SIGHTHOUND EDITORIAL SERVICES | MEGAN LEE

Herndon, VA | 703-229-2369
sighthoundeditorial@gmail.com | *www.meganwhitsonlee.net/editing*

Contact: email

Services: manuscript evaluation, substantive editing/rewriting, copyediting, proofreading, write discussion questions for books, writing coach

Types of manuscripts: novels, adult, teen/YA

Charges: flat fee, hourly rate, page rate, word rate

Credentials/experience: I'm a published author with an MFA in creative writing from George Mason University. As an editor with Pelican Book Group, I evaluate manuscripts for acquisition and work closely with authors and other editors to ensure manuscripts meet their potential throughout the publication process. Additionally, I've taught English to high school and college students for the past fifteen years.

smWORDWORKS | SUSAN G. MATHIS

945 Rangely Dr., Colorado Springs, CO 80921 | 719-331-9352
mathiswordworks@gmail.com | *www.SusanGMathis.com*

Contact: email

Services: manuscript evaluation, copyediting, proofreading. coauthoring, writing coach

Types of manuscripts: articles, nonfiction books, novels

Charges: word rate

Credentials/experience: Susan is the founding editor of *Thriving Family* magazine and the former editor or editorial director of twelve Focus on the Family publications, including *Focus on the Family* magazine and *Focus on Your Child* newsletters. Susan is also the author of five books, including two nonfiction, two picture books, and one novel.

SO IT IS WRITTEN LLC | TENITA JOHNSON

Rochester, MI | 313-999-6942
info@soitiswritten.net | *www.soitiswritten.net*

Contact: emails

Services: copyediting, proofreading, ghostwriting, write website text, writing coach

Types of manuscripts: articles, nonfiction books, devotionals, poetry, short stories, novels, adult, teen/YA, picture books, easy readers, middle grade

Charges: page rate

Credentials/experience: More than sixteen years of writing and editing experience in all forms of media, including newspapers, magazines, and manuscripts.

STARCHER DESIGNS | KARA D. STARCHER

PO Box 93, Chloe, WV 25235 | 330-705-3399
info@starcherdesigns.com | *www.starcherdesigns.com*

Contact: email

Services: manuscript evaluation, substantive editing, copyediting, proofreading, ghostwriting, coauthoring, create small group/Bible study guides, write curriculum lesson plans, write discussion questions for books, writing coach, back-cover copy

Types of manuscripts: nonfiction books, devotionals, short stories, novels, curriculum, Bible studies, gift books, adult

Charges: word rate

Credentials/experience: BA in publishing with minor in English, more than fifteen years as an editor.

STEEPLE VIEW COACHING | ANDREA BOESHAAR

PO Box 33, Newberg, WI 53060 | 414-708-8930
AuthorAndreaBoeshaar@gmail.com | *www.AndreaBoeshaar.com*

Contact: email

Services: manuscript evaluation, substantive editing/rewriting, writing coach

Types of manuscripts: short stories, novels, teen/YA

Charges: page rate

Credentials/experience: Author of more than thirty books, certified Christian life coach.

STICKS AND STONES | JAMIE CALLOWAY-HANAUER

Annapolis, MD | 510-972-3285
snsedits@gmail.com | *www.snsedits.com*

Contact: email

Services: manuscript evaluation, substantive editing/rewriting, copyediting, proofreading, ghostwriting, coauthoring, book-contract evaluation, write website text, create small group/Bible study guides, write curriculum lesson plans, write discussion questions for books, writing coach

Types of manuscripts: articles, nonfiction books, devotionals, poetry, short stories, novels, query letters, book proposals, curriculum, adult, teen/YA, easy readers, middle grade

Charges: flat fee

Credentials/experience: Jamie has eighteen years of experience in the editing field. Previously a full-time public interest attorney who also edited part-time, she is now the owner-operator of Sticks and Stones, where she specializes in academic, legal, and faith-based fiction and nonfiction for adults and teens; ghostwriting; and proposal and query review and development.

SUE'S SIMPLE SNIPPETS | SUE A. FAIRCHILD

Watsontown, PA | 570-939-0318

sueafairchild74@gmail.com | *suessimplesnippets.wordpress.com*

Contact: email, website form

Services: substantive editing/rewriting, copyediting, proofreading, discussion questions for books, writing coach, back-cover copy

Types of manuscripts: articles, nonfiction books, devotionals, short stories, novels, query letters, book proposals, Bible studies, gift books, adult, teen/YA, middle grade

Charges: hourly rate, word rate

Credentials/experience: Gold member editor for Christian Editor Network, blog coordinator for The Christian PEN and St. Davids Christian Writers' Association, local newspaper correspondent, and published devotional and YA author. Specializing in full developmental editing for devotionals, full-length novels (YA, fantasy, romance, women's contemporary), articles, and short stories.

SUPERIOR EDITING SERVICE | JAN ACKERSON

611 S. Elm, Three Oaks, MI 49128 | 269-756-9912

jan_ackerson@yahoo.com | *www.superioreditingservice.com*

Contact: email

Services: substantive editing/rewriting, copyediting, writing coach

Types of manuscripts: poetry, short stories, novels, gift books, adult, teen/YA, picture books, easy readers, middle grade

Charges: word rate

Credentials/experience: Seven years editing (both freelance and for

Breath of Fresh Air Press), author of *Stolen Postcards*, short stories in multiple anthologies.

TANDEM SERVICES | JENNIFER VANDER KLIPP

PO Box 492, Belmont, MI 49306 | 414-465-2567
hello@tandemservicesjvk.com | *www.tandemservicesjvk.com*

Contact: email
Services: manuscript evaluation, substantive editing/rewriting, copyediting, proofreading, ghostwriting, coauthoring, create small group/Bible study guides, writing coach
Types of manuscripts: articles, nonfiction books, devotionals, short stories, novels, query letters, book proposals, gift books, adult, teen/YA, picture books, easy readers, middle grade
Charges: flat rate, hourly fee, word rate, specific to each project
Credentials/experience: Tandem Services brings together a group of industry professionals with more than twenty years of experience in business, marketing, and publishing to help writers navigate the world of publishing, indie or traditional. Our staff includes experienced, in-house editors at Big Five publishers, as well as published authors. Our services include complex project management, writing and editing, marketing, and graphic design. Our clients include Our Daily Bread Ministries, Credo Communications, Zondervan, HarperCollins Christian Publishing, Barbour Publishing, and Concordia, as well as many individual authors.

TISHA MARTIN EDITORIAL | TISHA MARTIN

1615 2350th St., Atlanta, IL 61723 | 850-583-7051
tmartinwrites@gmail.com | *www.tishamwrites.com*

Contact: phone
Services: manuscript evaluation, substantive editing/rewriting, copyediting, proofreading, ghostwriting, coauthoring, brochures, newsletters, website text, write curriculum lesson plans, write discussion questions for books, create PowerPoint presentations, writing coach, formatting
Types of manuscripts: articles, nonfiction books, devotionals, short stories, novels, curriculum, Bible studies, gift books, technical material, adult, teen/YA, middle grade, academic
Charges: flat fee, hourly rate, page rate, word rate
Credentials/experience: With a BA in professional writing and an MS in English education, I have been tutoring since 2010 and

editing since 2014. As a detailed editor and proofreader, my intent is to encourage you in building a successful editor/author/reader relationship. I've worked with beginning, indie or self-published, best-selling, and traditionally published authors, professional editing agencies, large corporations, and publishing houses. And you—if you're interested. I specialize in clean fiction, educational, technical, and nonfiction pieces; project-management assistance; and social-media and writing coaching. In addition to being an editor, I'm a silver member of The Christian PEN, an avid member of American Christian Fiction Writers, and assistant director of PENCON, an editing conference. Offers a sample edit. Visit my website for more information.

TLC GRAPHICS | TAMARA DEVER

Austin, TX | 512-669-5744
tamara@tlcgraphics.com | *www.TLCGraphics.com*

Contact: email
Services: substantive editing/rewriting, copyediting, proofreading, ghostwriting, coauthoring, indexing
Types of manuscripts: nonfiction books, devotionals, novels, gift books, adult, teen/YA, picture books, easy readers, middle grade, homeschool and children's ministry materials
Charges: flat fee based on individual project
Credentials/experience: Award-winning design firm and author guidance with more than twenty-five years of publishing experience. Small, caring team working with you, taking your raw manuscript through editorial, design, and printing to provide a beautiful and salable book you'll be proud to represent. Services are à la carte with design contract.

TUPPANCE ENTERPRISES | JAMES PENCE

PO Box 99, Greenville, TX 75403 | 469-730-6478
james@pence.com | *jamespence.com*

Contact: email
Services: manuscript evaluation, substantive editing/rewriting, copyediting, proofreading, coauthoring, writing coach
Types of manuscripts: articles, nonfiction books, devotionals, short stories, novels, query letters, book proposals, curriculum, Bible studies, technical material, adult, teen/YA, academic
Charges: word rate
Credentials/experience: I've been writing professionally since 2000

and have been published by Osborne/McGraw-Hill, Tyndale, Kregel, Baker, Mountainview Books, and Thomas Nelson (ghostwriting). My published works include textbooks, how-to books, novels, Christian living, and memoir.

TURN THE PAGE WRITER CRITIQUES | CINDY THOMSON

Pataskala, OH | 614-354-3904
cindyswriting@gmail.com | *cindyswriting.com/hire-me*

Contact: email
Services: manuscript evaluation, proofreading, critiques
Types of manuscripts: articles, novels
Charges: page rate, word rate
Credentials/experience: Traditionally published author of eight books, past mentor for the Jerry B. Jenkins Christian Writers Guild, mentor for local high-school students.

THE VERSATILE PEN | CHRISTY PHILLIPPE

8816 S. 73rd East Ave., Tulsa, OK 74133 | 918-284-7635
christy6871@aol.com | *www.theversatilepen.com*

Contact: email
Services: manuscript evaluation, substantive editing/rewriting, copyediting, proofreading, create brochures, create newsletters, write website text, create small group/Bible study guides, write curriculum lesson plans, write discussion questions for books
Types of manuscripts: articles, nonfiction books, devotionals, short stories, novels, curriculum, gift books, adult, teen/YA
Charges: hourly rate, word rate
Credentials/experience: More than twenty years of experience as managing editor, senior editor, and editorial director of various publishing companies and as the owner of The Versatile Pen.

WHALIN & ASSOCIATES | W. TERRY WHALIN

Highlands Ranch, CO 80126 | 720-708-4953
terry@terrywhalin.com | *thewritinglife.ws*

Contact: email
Services: substantive editing/rewriting, ghostwriting, coauthoring, create small group/Bible study guides, write discussion questions for books
Types of manuscripts: nonfiction books, devotionals, book proposals, gift books, adult
Charges: flat fee

Credentials/experience: Terry has written more than sixty books for traditional publishers, including one book that has sold more than 100,000 copies. He has written for more than fifty publications and worked in acquisitions at three publishing houses.

WORD MARKER EDITS | KATHRESE MCKEE

8765 Spring Cypress, Ste. L219, Spring, TX 77379 | 281-787-6938
kmckee@kathresemckee.com | *www.wordmarkeredits.com*

Contact: email
Services: manuscript evaluation, substantive editing/rewriting, copyediting, proofreading, ghostwriting
Types of manuscripts: short stories, novels, adult, teen/YA, middle grade
Charges: hourly rate, page rate, word rate
Credentials/experience: Kathrese is an editor, fiction author, former middle-school reading and ESL teacher, speaker, and blogger. She specializes in editing speculative fiction written from a Christian worldview but is also available to edit other genres and fiction for the general market. She is a silver member of The Christian PEN: Proofreaders and Editors Network.

WORDMELON, INC. | MARGOT STARBUCK

Durham, NC | 919-321-5440
wordmelon@gmail.com | *www.wordmelon.com*

Contact: email
Services: manuscript evaluation, substantive editing/rewriting, ghostwriting, coauthoring, create small group/Bible study guides
Types of manuscripts: articles, nonfiction books, devotionals, query letters, book proposals
Charges: flat fee
Credentials/experience: Margot has an MDiv from Princeton Theological Seminary and a bachelor's degree from Westmont College. She is the author, coauthor, and collaborator on seven books and ghostwriter on others. She has lent her touch to more than fifty major publishing projects. Visit her website to see endorsements and a current CV.

WORDS FOR WRITERS | GINNY L. YTTRUP

Granite Bay, CA | 916-276-7359
email through website | *www.wordsforwriters.net*

Contact: email

Services: manuscript evaluation, substantive editing/rewriting, proofreading, writing coach

Types of manuscripts: articles, nonfiction books, devotionals, short stories, novels, query letters, book proposals, adult, teen/YA

Charges: hourly rate, page rate

Credentials/experience: Ginny is an award-winning novelist and trained life coach who combines her skills when coaching writers and evaluating manuscripts. She works with beginning and published writers of both fiction and nonfiction.

WRITE BY LISA | LISA THOMPSON

Litchfield Park, AZ | 623-258-5258
writebylisa@gmail.com | *www.writebylisa.com*

Contact: email

Services: manuscript evaluation, substantive editing/rewriting, copyediting, proofreading, ghostwriting, coauthoring, create newsletters, write website text, create small group/Bible study guides, write curriculum lesson plans, write discussion questions for books, writing coach

Types of manuscripts: articles, nonfiction books, devotionals, short stories, novels, query letters, book proposals, curriculum, gift books, adult, teen/YA, middle grade

Charges: word rate

Credentials/experience: I have a BA in elementary education with a minor in English. I have been writing and editing full-time since 2009 and have satisfied clients all over the world, many of whom return for additional business and refer other clients to me.

THE WRITE EDITOR | ERIN K. BROWN

Corvallis, MT | 406-239-5590
thewriteeditor@gmail.com | *www.writeeditor.net*

Contact: email

Services: manuscript evaluation, substantive editing/rewriting, copyediting, proofreading, write discussion questions for books

Types of manuscripts: articles, nonfiction books, devotionals, short stories, novels, query letters, book proposals, curriculum, gift books, adult, teen/YA, middle grade

Charges: flat fee, hourly rate, word rate, page rate

Credentials/experience: Erin is a full-time, professional freelance editor, proofreader, and writer (since 2001). Her editing specialty is nonfiction works, including self-help, how-to, devotionals,

Bible studies, biography, memoir, history, apologetics, leadership, ministry, family, health and wellness, inspiration, personal growth, relationships, success, and homeschool. Erin's formal training in editorial practices and procedures, ten years in Christian retailing, twenty-six years in education, and more than ten years as a judge for a national fiction award affords her a wide knowledge and experience base that she brings to her editing. She combines her love of editing and teaching through The Pen Institute, teaching nonfiction editing skills to other professional editors.

WRITE HIS ANSWER MINISTRIES | MARLENE BAGNULL

951 Anders Rd., Lansdale, PA 19446 | 484-991-8581
mbagnull@aol.com | *writehisanswer.com*

Contact: email, phone
Services: manuscript evaluation, copyediting, proofreading
Types of manuscripts: articles, nonfiction books, devotionals, short stories, novels, adult
Charges: flat fee, hourly rate
Credentials/experience: More than thirty years of experience in publishing, leading critique groups, and directing writers conferences; author of nine books and more than a thousand sales to Christian periodicals; editor, typesetter, and publisher of ten Ampelos Press books.

WRITE NOW EDITING | KARIN BEERY

Elk Rapids, MI | 231-350-0226
email through website | *writenowedits.com*

Contact: email
Services: manuscript evaluation, substantive editing/rewriting, proofreading, ghostwriting, write website text, writing coach
Types of manuscripts: short stories, novels, query letters, book proposals, adult, teen/YA
Charges: flat fee for copy work, per word for novel editing
Credentials/experience: Christian Editor Connection certified substantive fiction editor, The Christian PEN: Proofreaders and Editors Network gold member, American Christian Fiction Writers Association, American Christian Writers Association, American Writers and Artists Inc., trained copywriter.

WRITE NOW SERVICES | KAREN APPOLD

Lehigh Valley, PA | 610-351-5400
kappold@msn.com | *www.WriteNowServices.com*

Contact: email
Services: copyediting, proofreading, newsletters, write website text
Types of manuscripts: articles, devotionals, curriculum, Bible studies
Charges: custom
Credentials/experience: BA in English from Penn State University.

WRITE PATHWAY EDITORIAL SERVICES | ANN KNOWLES

Wilmington, NC | 910-231-9520
annknowles03@aol.com | *www.WritePathway.com*

Contact: email
Services: copyediting, proofreading, ghostwriting, coauthoring, writing coach, transcription, Spanish translation
Types of manuscripts: articles, nonfiction books, devotionals, poetry, short stories, novels, query letters, book proposals, curriculum, gift books, adult, teen/YA, picture books, easy readers, middle grade
Charges: project cost
Credentials/experience: Retired educator, MA in education, certified ESL and Spanish; ESL training consultant for public schools and community colleges. I joined The Christian PEN: Proofreaders and Editors Network in 2005 and started Write Pathway in 2007. I have taken numerous courses from The Christian PEN, American Christian Fiction Writers, Write Integrity Press, and Christian Writers International. Presenter at writers conferences.

WRITE WAY COPYEDITING LLC | DIANA SCHRAMER

Sun Prairie, WI | 608-837-8091
diana@writewaycopyediting.com | *www.writewaycopyediting.com*

Contact: email, phone
Services: manuscript evaluation, substantive editing/rewriting, copyediting
Types of manuscripts: articles, nonfiction books, devotionals, short stories, novels, gift books, adult, teen/YA, picture books, easy readers, middle grade
Charges: hourly rate
Credentials/experience: I have been a full-time, freelance copy editor for six years. I have edited 170 book-length manuscripts, fiction, nonfiction, and creative nonfiction, ranging from 15,000 words to more than 100,000, and have evaluated more than eight hundred fifty manuscripts for editorial recommendation. References on request.

WRITER'S EDGE SERVICE | BILL LELAND

Wheaton, IL
info@writersedgeservice.com | *www.writersedgeservice.com*

Contact: email

Services: Professional editors with many years of experience in working with major Christian publishers evaluate, screen, and expose potential books to traditional Christian publishing companies.

Types of manuscripts: books, all kinds except poetry, and all ages

Charges: $99

Description: For more than twenty years, it has been a method of effective communication between writers and major traditional Christian publishers. Because most traditional publishers no longer accept unsolicited manuscripts, new or relatively unknown writers have little chance to be seen by a traditional publisher unless they have a credible literary agent. Writer's Edge Service, in full cooperation with more than seventy-five traditional, royalty-based Christian publishers, gives writers another option. The acquisition editors of these companies view relevant manuscripts that make the cut at Writer's Edge because they know they have been carefully screened and evaluated before being passed to them for consideration. Over the years, hundreds of authors have been successfully published because of Writer's Edge Service.

THE WRITER'S FRIEND | DONNA CLARK GOODRICH

Mesa, AZ | 480-962-6694
dgood648@aol.com | *www.thewritersfriend.net*

Contact: email

Services: copyediting, proofreading

Types of manuscripts: articles, nonfiction books, devotionals, short stories, novels, query letters, book proposals, gift books, adult, teen/YA, picture books, easy readers, middle grade

Charges: hourly rate, page rate

Credentials/experience: More than fifty years editing and proofreading for publishers and writers.

WRITER'S RELIEF, INC. | RONNIE L. SMITH

Wood Ridge, NJ | 866-405-3003
info@wrelief.com | *www.writersrelief.com*

Contact: email, phone

Services: proofreading, creative writing submissions
Types of manuscripts: poetry, short stories, novels, query letters, book proposals
Charges: flat fee, page rate, word rate
Credentials/experience: Helping authors reach their publishing goals since 1994. Writer's Relief, Self-Publishing Relief, and Web Design Relief offer a complete array of services to facilitate every step of an author's path to publishing—from making targeted submissions to traditional publishing markets, to offering self-publishing guidance and marketing support, to building author websites.

WRITER'S TABLET, LLC | TERRI WHITMIRE

4371 Roswell Rd #315, Marietta, GA 30062 | 770-648-4101
Writerstablet@gmail.com | *www.Writerstablet.org, www.FunCreativeWriting.com*

Contact: email
Services: manuscript evaluation, substantive editing/rewriting, copyediting, proofreading, coauthoring, create brochures, create newsletters, write website text, create small group/Bible study guides, write curriculum lesson plans, write discussion questions for books, create PowerPoint presentations, writing coach
Types of manuscripts: articles, nonfiction books, devotionals, poetry, short stories, novels, curriculum, adult, teen/YA, picture books, easy readers, middle grade
Charges: flat fee
Credentials/experience: Certification in children's literature, BS in computer science, literary assistant to a New York agency, communications degree, published authors. We have assisted numerous clients in website content, website design, developmental editing, manuscript critique, copyediting, manuscript formatting, Kindle publishing, self-publishing, and various other business writing requests. Our talented team also serves as writing coaches to young writers through our business *www.funcreativewriting.com.*

WRITTEN BY A PRO | SHARLA TAYLOR

Richmond Hill, GA | 912-656-6857
rittenbyapro@msn.com | *www.writtenbyapro.com*

Contact: email
Services: manuscript evaluation, substantive editing/rewriting, copyediting, proofreading, ghostwriting, coauthoring, write

website text, create small group/Bible study guides, write curriculum lesson plans, write discussion questions for books, create PowerPoint presentations, writing coach, résumé/CV writer, LinkedIn profile writer, job-search strategist, and facilitator of an online Bible study for job seekers

Types of manuscripts: articles, nonfiction books, devotionals, short stories, novels, query letters, book proposals, curriculum, scripts, gift books, adult, teen/YA, middle grade

Charges: flat fee, hourly rate, word rate, service options and prices for job seekers on website

Credentials/experience: Certified professional résumé writer; certified career enlightenment LinkedIn writer; experienced job-search strategist with more than twenty years in the careers industry; leads a free online Bible study for job seekers based on the Theology of Work project (*www.theologyofwork.org*). Sharla has developed thousands of résumés for business leaders, executives, career-changers, people reentering the workforce, and recent college graduates.

YO PRODUCTIONS, LLC | YOLONDA TONETTE SANDERS

PO Box 32329, Columbus, OH 43232 | 614-452-4920
info_4u@yoproductions.net | *www.yoproductions.net*

Contact: email, phone, website form

Services: manuscript evaluation, substantive editing/rewriting, copyediting, proofreading, ghostwriting, coauthoring, brochures, newsletters, create small group/Bible study guides, write curriculum lesson plans, write discussion questions for books, create PowerPoint presentations, writing coach, back-cover copy

Types of manuscripts: articles, nonfiction books, devotionals, poetry, short stories, novels, query letters, book proposals, curriculum, Bible studies, scripts, technical material, adult, teen/YA, academic

Charges: flat fee, hourly rate, word rate, custom

Credentials/experience: More than thirteen years of professional editing and writing experience, editor and writer for a national publication.

YOUR TIME TO WRITE | MARY BUSHA

Ocala, FL | 517-416-0133
yourtimetowrite@gmail.com

Contact: email

Services: manuscript evaluation, copyediting, proofreading, writing coach

Types of manuscripts: nonfiction books, devotionals, book proposals, gift books
Charges: hourly rate, page rate
Credentials/experience: More than thirty-five years in publishing, including newspapers, magazines, and books. Works with author from book idea to publication and all steps in between. Full résumé available on request. First one-hour consultation at no charge.

YOUR VOICE, ONLY BETTER! | SHARMAN J. MONROE

3431 S. Dakota Ave. N.E., Washington, DC 20018 | 240-353-8000
myjourneytome@gmail.com | *www.myjourneytome-thediscovery.com*

Contact: email
Services: substantive editing/rewriting, copyediting, proofreading, small group/Bible study guides
Types of manuscripts: nonfiction books, devotionals, novels, gift books, adult, teens/YA
Charges: hourly or flat rate, custom
Credentials/experience: More than twenty-five years of experience in writing, editing, and proofreading. Editor of more than fifteen books—nonfiction, fiction, and different genres—over the past two years. Member of The Christian PEN. Published author of *The PLAN: A Way to Success.*

INTERNATIONAL

AIMEE REID

Hamilton, ON, Canada | 905-317-9234
areid@aimeereid.com | *www.aimeereid.com*

Contact: email
Services: manuscript evaluation, substantive editing/rewriting, create small group/Bible study guides, write curriculum lesson plans, write discussion questions for books
Types of manuscripts: articles, nonfiction books, devotionals, curriculum, adult, teen/YA, picture books, easy readers, middle grade
Charges: hourly rate
Credentials/experience: Developmental and stylistic editing for all audience ages.

AOTEAROA EDITORIAL SERVICES | VENNESSA NG

PO Box 228, Oamaru, New Zealand 9444 | +6-422-434-6995
editor@aotearoaeditorial.com | *www.aotearoaeditorial.com*

Contact: email
Services: manuscript evaluation, substantive editing/rewriting, copyediting, proofreading, writing coach
Types of manuscripts: short stories, novels, adult
Charges: page rate
Credentials/experience: Fourteen years of experience working with Christian fiction authors. Member of The Christian PEN.

CELTICFROG EDITING | ALEX MCGILVERY

Flin Flon, MB, Canada | 204-271-2066
thecelticfrog@gmail.com | *celticfrogediting.com*

Contact: email, comment on website
Services: manuscript evaluation, writing coach, character and plot arcs, tone, voice, writing quality, technical
Types of manuscripts: articles, nonfiction books, devotionals, short stories, novels, adult, teen/YA, middle grade
Charges: flat fee, hourly rate; free, no-obligation test edit of the first 5,000 words of a book for new clients
Credentials/experience: I've been a writer and book reviewer for more than thirty years, a content editor for the past three years. I've edited more than forty books, many of which have hit bestseller status on Amazon. See the website for the titles of published books I've worked on.

CHRISTIAN EDITING SERVICES | IOLA GOULTON

Tauranga, New Zealand
igoulton@christianediting.co.nz | *www.christianediting.co.nz*

Contact: email
Services: manuscript evaluation, substantive editing/rewriting, copyediting, proofreading
Types of manuscripts: novels, adult, teen/YA
Charges: hourly rate
Credentials/experience: Iola is a member of The Christian PEN: Proofreaders and Editors Network, American Christian Fiction Writers, Romance Writers of New Zealand, and Omega Writers. She has completed fiction editing courses with The Christian PEN, as well as a range of courses through Lawson Writers Academy and

American Christian Fiction Writers, and won the 2016 Genesis Award for novella.

EDIPPEN & QUILL | CALEB AJINOMOH

Lagos, Nigeria 100278 | +234-703-941-1298

femmefatalelit.fiction2016@gmail.com | *edippe.skynova.io*

Contact: email

Services: substantive editing/rewriting, copyediting, ghostwriting

Types of manuscripts: nonfiction books, short stories, novels, adult, picture books

Charges: page rate

Credentials/experience: With more than four years working the editorial desk at West Africa's foremost tabloid (*The Sun Newspaper*) and copyediting for *Mustard Magazine*, Africa's biggest Christian music magazine, I set out to begin my own business two years ago. I have worked with one Harvard Law undergraduate and a local rapper for their nonfiction projects. Currently a member of The Christian PEN and looking for ambitious, genre-defying authors to work with.

EXTRA INK EDITS | MEGAN EASLEY-WALSH

Ireland but American editor

www.Megan@ExtraInkEdits.com | *www.ExtraInkEdits.com*

Contact: email

Services: manuscript evaluation, copyediting, proofreading, writing coach, back-cover copy

Types of manuscripts: nonfiction books, devotionals, short stories, novels, query letters, Bible studies, gift books, adult, teen/YA

Charges: flat fee, page rate

Credentials/experience: More than nine years of experience as a writing consultant and editor, best-selling author, former college writing teacher.

NEXT LEVEL EDITING AND TRANSCRIPTION | DARLENE OAKLEY

248 Oakdale Ave., St. Catharines, ON, Canada L2P 2K6 | 289-696-2382

nextleveleditingandt@gmail.com | *nextleveleditingandtranscription.com*

Contact: email

Services: manuscript evaluation, substantive editing/rewriting, copyediting, proofreading, social-media strategy consulting and development

Types of manuscripts: articles, nonfiction books, devotionals, short stories, novels, Bible studies, adult, teen/YA

Charges: word rate, custom

Credentials/experience: More than fifteen years of editing experience (including publishing house), forty-five edited titles (including two of my own), social-media strategy development specifically for authors.

NITPICKING WITH A PURPOSE | MARSHA MALCOLM

Savanna-la-mar, Westmoreland, Jamaica | 876-823-2092
purposefulnitpicker@gmail.com | *www.nitpickingwithapurpose.com*

Contact: email

Services: copyediting, proofreading

Types of manuscripts: short stories, novels, picture books, easy readers, middle grade

Charges: word rate

Credentials/experience: Expert rating certification in Keys to Editing.

SPLASHDOWN BOOKS | GRACE BRIDGES

Glenfield, Auckland, NZ 0629 | +6-422-472-2301
gracebridges1@gmail.com | *www.gracebridges.kiwi*

Contact: email

Services: manuscript evaluation, substantive editing/rewriting, copyediting, proofreading; accepting only those manuscripts that are already in good condition, with an appropriate corresponding discount

Types of manuscripts: novels, adult, teen/YA, picture books, easy readers, middle grade, speculative genre

Charges: word rate

Credentials/experience: Ten years in publishing and editing; signed off on the final quality of more than forty books published under my label, with over a dozen professionally recognized. Based in New Zealand, I specialize in science fiction and fantasy and in making American concepts internationally understandable.

VINEMARC COMMUNICATIONS | MARCIA LAYCOCK

PO Box 637, Blackfalds, AB, Canada T0M 0J0 | 403-885-9828
vinemarc@telus.net | *www.marcialeelaycock.com*

Contact: email

Services: manuscript evaluation, copyediting, proofreading

Types of manuscripts: articles, nonfiction books, devotionals, poetry, short stories, novels, gift books, adult, teen/YA

Charges: flat fee

Credentials/experience: Marcia has been publishing for almost thirty years. Her work has been endorsed by Janette Oke, Phil Callaway, and Sigmund Brouwer. She has won many awards for her writing and taught writing courses at conferences and online.

20

PUBLICITY AND MARKETING SERVICES

THE ADAMS GROUP | GINA ADAMS

6688 Nolensville Rd., Ste. 108-149, Brentwood, TN 37027
888-253-3620
email thourgh website | *www.adamsprgroup.com*

Contact: email, phone
Services: social-media book campaigns and management, press kit, branding, radio and TV interviews, media coaching, video production, press releases, blogger book tours
Books: Christian fiction, nonfiction, children's books
Charges: flat rate
Credentials/experience: BS in business and marketing. In the Christian marketplace for nearly three decades. Membership in National Religious Broadcasters and Evangelical Press Association.

AUTHOR SUPPORT SERVICES | RUSSELL SHERRARD

Carmichael, CA | 916-967-7251
russellsherrard@reagan.com | *www.sherrardsebookresellers.com/WordPress/author-support-services-the-authors-place-to-get-help*

Contact: email
Services: Twitter and Facebook marketing, submitting URL to search engines
Books: Christian e-books, fiction, nonfiction
Charges: flat fee
Credentials/experience: Writing and editing since 2009; currently providing freelance services for multiple clients.

THE BLYTHE DANIEL AGENCY, INC . | BLYTHE DANIEL

PO Box 64197, Colorado Springs, CO 80962-4197 | 719-213-3427
email through website | *www.theblythedanielagency.com*

Other publicist: Stephanie Alton, *stephanie@theblythedanielagency.com*, blog content manager
Contact: email
Services: range of publicity campaigns utilizing broadcast and print media and the internet, including blogs, websites, online magazines, TV and radio interviews, and book reviews
Books: primarily adult and young-adult nonfiction
Charges: customized by campaign
Credentials/experience: "We have personal relationships with hundreds of media outlets that we have developed over the last 20 years in the business. Through our relationships, understanding of the changing media landscape, and careful selection of content we promote, we are able to provide our clients more opportunities to bring recognition to their book(s)." Blythe worked five years as the publicity director and two years as the marketing director for Thomas Nelson.

CHRISTIAN SMALL PUBLISHERS ASSOCIATION | SARAH BOLME

PO Box 481022, Charlotte, NC 28269 | 704-277-7194
cspa@christianpublishers.net | *www.christianpublishers.net*

Contact: email
Services: information and tools for success in publishing and marketing, including representation at trade shows, cooperative marketing, book review program, and educational seminars
Books: Christian
Charges: flat fee
Credentials/experience: "CSPA has been representing, strengthening, and promoting small publishers and independently published authors in the Christian marketplace since 2004."

EABOOKS PUBLISHING | CHERI COWELL

Oviedo, FL | 407-712-3431
Cheri@eabookspublishing.com | *www.eabookspublishing.com*

Contact: email
Services: marketing coaching that includes branding, website and blog, and social media
Books: fiction, nonfiction, children's
Charges: flat fee
Credentials/experience: "Traditionally published author who now

owns a self-publishing company that also offers this coaching service because it is what I wish I had: one-on-one coaching."

ENLIVEN YOUR TRIBE | BRIAN ALLAIN

brian@enlivenyourtribe.com | *enlivenyourtribe.com*

Contact: email

Services: platform development, strategic marketing, social-media marketing, consulting

Books: all kinds

Charges: flat fee

Credentials/experience: "Have supported several Christian writers, including Frederick Buechner, Kathleen Norris, Diana Butler Bass, Leslie Leyland Fields, Marcus Borg, and others.

LITFUSE PUBLICITY GROUP | AMY LATHROP

903-874-8363

amy@litfusegroup.com | *www.litfusegroup.com*

Other publicists: Audra Jennings, *audra@litfusegroup.com*; Caitlin Wilson, *caitlin@litfusegroup.com*

Contact: email

Services: publicity, blog tours, online events, social-media management and consulting, launch teams, and author-assist services

Books: fiction and nonfiction

Charges: custom packages

Credentials/experience: Clients have included Thomas Nelson, Zondervan, Tyndale, WaterBrook Multnomah, Kregel, Abingdon, and many other Christian publishers.

MCCLURE/MUNTSINGER PUBLIC RELATIONS | PAMELA MCCLURE AND JANA MUNTSINGER

PO Box 804, Franklin, TN 37065 | 615-595-8321

info@mmpublicrelations.com | *www.mmpublicrelations.com*

Contact: email

Services: customized publicity campaigns, including radio, TV, internet, and social media

Books: any book they like

Charges: customized by campaign

Credentials/experience: "After more than 40 combined years of book publicity, we have long and strong relationships with dozens of editors, writers, and producers. We specialize in knowing how to place religious books in Christian and general-market media, traditional outlets, and online."

MEDIA CONNECT | SHARON FARNELL

301 E. 57th St., New York, NY 10022 | 212-593-6337
farnells@plannedtvarts.com | *www.media-connect.com*

Contact: email
Services: full-service book publicity firm with TV and radio campaigns, print, online, book tours, etc.
Books: Christian and general market, primarily nonfiction but also children's and some fiction
Charges: custom rate
Credentials/experience: "Since joining the company in 1997, Sharon has been instrumental in helping faith-based authors and publishers reach both the Christian and mainstream audience. She has successfully placed her clients in a variety of top media outlets."

SERVE LITERARY & MEDIA | JASON JONES

2255 Memorial Blvd. #12238, Murfreesboro, TN 37129 | 615-258-5581
jason@serverliterary.com | *serveliterary.com*

Other publicists: Judy McDonough, *judy@serveliterary.com*; Jandra Sutton, *jandra@serveliterary.com*
Contact: email, website form
Services: book publicity, author representation/consultation, digital marketing
Specialties: Christian living, culture, and faith books
Charges: custom rates
Credentials/experience: Prior to Jason's joining the PR by the Book team in 2013 and the launch of SERVE Literary & Media, he spent five years with Thomas Nelson/Harper Collins Christian Publishing. There, he led campaigns for eleven *New York Times* best-selling titles and managed some of the industry's most successful authors. With nearly twenty years of experience in public relations, Jason's prepublishing career includes directing the efforts of one of Memphis, Tennessee's most widely-respected agencies, Sossaman + Associates, and six years in professional baseball, where he managed the media/public relations department of the Memphis Redbirds.

SIDE DOOR COMMUNICATIONS | DEBBIE LYKINS

224-234-6699
email through website | *www.sidedoorcom.net*

Contact: email

Services: media relations, working with both Christian and traditional media, as well as online media and bloggers

Books: "We focus primarily on Christian nonfiction titles and the occasional novel. We look for well-written, well-edited books on topics that we believe will be of interest to the media. We also consider the author's credentials on the subject. No self-published novels."

Charges: custom fee

Credentials/experience: More than two decades of experience in marketing, public relations, and communications, with more than fifteen years in Christian book publicity. Authors represented have been featured in numerous media outlets.

VERITAS COMMUNICATIONS | DON S. OTIS

PO Box 1505, Sandpoint, ID 83864 | 719-275-7775
don@veritasincorporated.com | *www.veritasincorporated.com*

Contact: email

Services: booking for radio and television shows, news services, and select print sources; media materials; training in how authors can best present themselves or their books

Specialty: training, writing releases that get results, public speaking

Books: primarily nonfiction (Christian or conservative), some selected fiction; topics vary from marriage and family, finances, men's or women's issues, cultural trends, biblical sexuality, health, apologetics, leadership; selective on prophecy and theology titles

Charges: flat fee

Credentials/experience: "More than 25 years serving as a publicist and working with more than 1,000 authors, dozens of publishers, and scheduling 30,000 interviews. Published author of five books, former producer and radio host, cofounder of the Voice of Hope Radio Network."

WILDFIRE MARKETING | ROB EAGAR

3625 Chartwell Dr., Suwanee, GA 30024 | 770-887-1462
Rob@StartaWildfire.com | *www.StartaWildfire.com*

Contact: phone

Services: book marketing, book-launch services, author-platform growth, author-income growth, The *New York* Times bestseller insights
Specialty: book marketing
Books: all nonfiction and fiction
Charges: flat fee
Credentials/experience: "I've coached over 450 authors at all levels and helped books hit *The New York Times* bestseller list three different ways, including new fiction, new nonfiction, and backlist nonfiction. My clients have produced 11 *New York Times* bestsellers. I wrote the bible of book marketing, *Sell Your Book Like Wildfire*."

21

LEGAL AND **ACCOUNTING SERVICES**

CHRIS MORRIS CPA, LLC | CHRIS MORRIS

Surprise, AZ | 623-451-8182

cmorris@chrismorriscpa.com | *chrismorriscpa.com/cwmg*

Contact: website form

Services: accounting, taxes, business consulting, royalty calculations, sales-tax calculations

Charges: flat fee, hourly rate

Credentials/experience: "I specialize in working with authors, editors, and creative entrepreneurs, providing the perfect degree of support, so you build your business. As a CPA, of course I can do your taxes for you. But I can also help you at every stage of your business."

22

CONTESTS

A listing here does not guarantee endorsement of the contest. For guidelines on evaluating contests, go to *www.sfwa.org/other-resources/for-authors/writer-beware/contests.*

Note: Dates may not be accurate since many sponsors had not posted their 2018 dates before press time.

CHILDREN AND TEENS

CORETTA SCOTT KING BOOK AWARD

www.ala.org/awardsgrants/awards/24/apply

Sponsored by Coretta Scott King Task Force, American Library Association. Annual award for children's books published the previous year by African-American authors and/or illustrators. Books must promote an understanding and appreciation of the "American Dream" and fit one of these categories: preschool to grade 4, grades 5–8, grades 9–12.

Deadline: December 1
Prize: $1,000 and plaque

FIRST EDITION CHILDREN'S BOOK WRITING CONTEST

firsteditionproject.com/childrens-book-contest.html

Sponsored by Southwest Human Development in Arizona, dedicated to early childhood development. Manuscripts appropriate for children from birth to five years old, 600 words or fewer, original, and not previously published in any form or currently under consideration by another publisher. Retellings of traditional stories, such as fairy tales, will be considered, as long as the manuscript is unique and in the writer's own words.

Deadline: October 15

Entry fee: starts at $50 and varies with submission date
Prizes: publication with $1,000 advance, 8% royalty, and author copies

POCKETS FICTION-WRITING CONTEST

www.pockets.upperroom.org/write-for-us

Must be unpublished and not historical or biblical fiction. Previous winners not eligible. Length: 800-1,000 words. Send to Pockets Fiction Contest, Lynn W. Gilliam, Editor, PO Box 340004, Nashville TN 37203-0004. Designate "Fiction Contest" on outside of envelope. Send SASE for return and response.

Deadline: submit between March 1 and August 15
Prize: $500 and publication in *Pockets*

SOCIETY OF CHILDREN'S BOOK WRITERS AND ILLUSTRATORS

www.scbwi.org/awards/grants/for-authors

Sponsors a variety of contests, scholarships, and grants.

Deadline: varies by contest
Prizes: ten awards for published authors and five for unpublished authors, plus grants for emerging voices and student writers

FICTION

ALLIANCE AWARD

www.realmmakers.com

Sponsored by The Faith and Fantasy Alliance to give readers their say in what speculative fiction novels they enjoyed most in the preceding year. Only readers may nominate books in this contest. Books may be traditionally published or self-published.

Deadline: submit between January 1 and 20
Entry fee: none
Prize: certificate of recognition

AMERICAN CHRISTIAN FICTION WRITERS CONTESTS

www.acfw.com/contests

Genesis Contest for unpublished Christian fiction writers in a number of categories/genres. First Impressions award for unpublished writers. Carol Awards for best Christian fiction published the previous year.

Deadline: varies by contest
Entry fee: varies by category and membership

BARD FICTION PRIZE

www.bard.edu/bfp

Sponsored by Bard College. Awarded to a promising, emerging young writer of fiction, 39 years or younger and an American citizen. Entries must be previously published.

Deadline: June 15
Entry fee: none
Prize: $30,000 and appointment as writer-in-residence for one semester at Bard College, Annandale-on-Hudson, New York

BOSTON REVIEW SHORT STORY CONTEST

www.bostonreview.net/contests

Previously unpublished short stories no longer than 5,000 words.

Deadline: October 1
Entry fee: $20
Prize: $1,500 plus publication

BULWER-LYTTON FICTION CONTEST

www.bulwer-lytton.com

Sponsored by San Jose State University English Department. For the worst opening line to a novel. Each submission must be a single sentence; multiple entries allowed. Entries will be judged by categories: general, detective, western, science fiction, romance, etc. Overall winners, as well as category winners.

Deadline: June 30

FLANNERY O'CONNOR AWARD FOR SHORT FICTION

www.ugapress.org/index.php/series/FOC

Sponsored by University of Georgia Press. For collections of short fiction. Length: 40,000–75,000 words. Contestants must be residents of North America.

Deadline: submit between April 1 and May 31
Entry fee: $30
Prize: $1,000 plus publication under royalty book contract

GLIMMER TRAIN PRESS FICTION CONTESTS

www.glimmertrain.com/pages/writing_guidelines.php

Categories: short story for new writers, very short fiction, fiction open, family matters, and standard. See the website for definitions of each category. Emerging writers are welcome in all categories. Short Story Award for New

Writers is exclusively open to writers whose fiction has not appeared, nor is scheduled to appear, in any print publication with a circulation greater than 5,000.

Deadline: varies according to category

Entry fee: $2 processing fee per manuscript

Prizes: first place, $700-$3,000 plus publication in *Glimmer Train Stories*

GRACE PALEY PRIZE FOR SHORT FICTION

www.awpwriter.org/contests/awp_award_series_overview

Sponsored by Association of Writers and Writing Programs. Short-story collections. May contain stories previously published in periodicals. Length: 150-300 pages.

Deadline: submit between January 1 and February 28

Entry fee: $25

Prize: $5,000 and publication

JACK DYER FICTION PRIZE

craborchardreview.siu.edu/submissions-annual-lit.html

Sponsored by Southern Illinois University Department of English. Annual competition in poetry, short story (6,000 words), and literary nonfiction (6,500 words) on a theme.

Deadline: March 21 to May 31 (may vary)

Entry fee: $12

Prizes: $1,250 each and publication in *Crab Orchard Review*

JAMES JONES FIRST NOVEL CONTEST

www.wilkes.edu/pages/1159.asp

Sponsored by Wilkes University. For a first novel or novel-in-progress by a US writer who has not published a novel. Submit a two-page outline and the first fifty pages of an unpublished novel.

Deadline: March 15

Entry fee: $30

Prizes: first place, $10,000; two runners-up, $1,000 each. A selection from the winning work is published in *Provincetown Arts*

KATHERINE ANNE PORTER PRIZE IN SHORT FICTION

untpress.unt.edu/submitting-katherine-anne-porter-prize-short-fiction

Sponsored by University of North Texas Press. Quality unpublished fiction by emerging writers of contemporary literature. Can be a combination of short-shorts, short stories, and novellas from 100 to 200 pages (27,500-50,000 words). Material should be previously unpublished in book form.

Deadline: submit between May 1 and June 30

Entry fee: $25

Prize: $1,000 and publication by UNT Press

NATIONAL WRITERS ASSOCIATION NOVEL-WRITING CONTEST

www.nationalwriters.shoppingcartsplus.com/f/Novel_Form4.pdf

To encourage development of creative skills and recognize and reward outstanding ability in the area of novel writing. Any genre or category of novel manuscript may be entered. Only unpublished works in the English language. Maximum length: 100,000 words. Must be submitted via USPS.

Deadline: postmarked by April 1

Entry fee: $35

Prizes: first place, $500 and possible representation; second place, $250; third place, $150; fourth through tenth places, book of the winner's choice; honorable mentions, certificate

NATIONAL WRITERS ASSOCIATION SHORT-STORY CONTEST

www.nationalwriters.shoppingcartsplus.com/f/Short_Story_Contest1.pdf

Any genre of story. Length: 5,000 words maximum. Submit only unpublished works in the English language via mail.

Deadline: postmarked by July 1

Entry fee: $15

Prizes: first place, $250; second place, $100; third place, $50; fourth through tenth places, recognition

REALM MAKERS AWARDS

www.realmmakers.com

Sponsored by The Faith and Fantasy Alliance. Realm Makers Genre Awards in these categories: debut, science fiction, fantasy, young adult, supernatural/paranormal, and horror/other (for those who don't feel other categories accurately characterize their speculative work). Realm Award recognizes the most excellent speculative novel written by a Christian author in the previous calendar year. Length: 60,000 words minimum; 50,000 words minimum for young adult. Parable Award for Excellence in Cover Design is awarded to the best overall cover for a speculative novel written by a Christian author.

Deadline: submit between January 1 and 20
Entry fee: $35
Prizes: cash

SERENA MCDONALD KENNEDY AWARD

www.snakenationpress.org/submission-guidelines

Sponsored by Snake Nation Press. Novellas up to 50,000 words or short-story collections up to 200 pages, published or unpublished.

Deadline: August 31
Entry fee: $25
Prize: $1,000 and publication

SILVER QUILL SOCIETY BEST SHORT FICTION CONTEST

www.thestorytellermagazine.com/contests

Sponsored by *The Storyteller Anthology/Magazine*. Open genre contest but must be about family in some way and suitable for a family magazine. Length: 3,000 words maximum. Can enter multiple stories with separate entry fee for each one.

Deadline: September 25
Entry fee: $5
Prizes: first place, $50; second place, $25; third place, $15; honorable mention, $10

TOBIAS WOLFF AWARD FOR FICTION

www.bhreview.org/contest-submissions-guidelines

Sponsored by Western Washington University's *Bellingham Review*. Length: 6,000 words maximum.

Deadline: submit between December 1 and March 15
Entry fee: $20
Prize: $1,000 plus publication

NONFICTION

ANNIE DILLARD AWARD IN CREATIVE NONFICTION

bhreview.org/contest-submissions-guidelines

Sponsored by Western Washington University's *Bellingham Review*. Unpublished essays on any subject. Length: 6,000 words maximum.

Deadline: submit between December 1 and March 15
Entry fee: $20 for first submission, $10 each additional one
Prize: $1,000

AWP PRIZE FOR CREATIVE NONFICTION

www.awpwriter.org/contests

Sponsored by Association of Writers and Writing Programs. Open to published and unpublished authors. Book collection of nonfiction manuscripts. Length: 150–300 pages.

Deadline: submit between January 1 and February 28
Entry fee: $15 for members, $30 for nonmembers
Prize: $2,500 and publication with the University of Georgia Press

THE BECHTEL PRIZE

www.twc.org/publications/bechtel-prize

Sponsored by Teachers & Writers Collaborative. For unpublished essays that explore themes related to creative writing, arts education, and/or the imagination. Length: 3,500 words maximum.

Deadline: December 16
Entry fee: $20
Prize: $1,000 and publication

EVENT NON-FICTION CONTEST

www.eventmagazine.ca/contest-nf

Unpublished creative nonfiction. Length: 5,000 words maximum.

Deadline: October 15
Entry fee: $34.95, includes a one-year subscription to *EVENT*
Prizes: first place, $1,500; second place, $1,000; third place, $500 plus publication

GRAYWOLF PRESS NONFICTION PRIZE

www.graywolfpress.org/resources/submission-and-contest-guidelines

For the best literary nonfiction book manuscript in progress by a US resident not yet established in this genre. Literary nonfiction includes memoir, biography, and history.

Deadline: varies, currently listed as January
Entry fee: none
Prize: $12,000 advance and publication of finished book

GUIDEPOSTS WRITERS WORKSHOP CONTEST

www.guideposts.org/enter-the-guideposts-writers-workshop-contest

Contest is held in even years with a mid-June deadline. Submit an original, unpublished, true, first-person story (your own or ghostwritten for another person) in 2,000 words or fewer about an experience that changed your life. Show how faith made a difference. Twelve winners will attend an all-expenses-paid, weeklong writers workshop in Rye, New York, to learn about inspirational storytelling and writing for Guideposts publications.

JOHN GUYON LITERARY NONFICTION

craborchardreview.siu.edu/submissions-annual-lit.html

Sponsored by Southern Illinois University Department of English. Annual competition. Literary nonfiction, 6,500 words.

Deadline: mid-March to May 31 (may vary)
Entry fee: $12
Prize: $1,250 and publication in *Crab Orchard Review*

NEW LETTERS PRIZE FOR NONFICTION

www.newletters.org/writers-wanted/writing-contests

For unpublished essays. Length: 8,000 words maximum.

Deadline: May 18
Entry fee: $20 for first entry, $15 per additional entry
Prize: $1,500 and magazine subscription

RICHARD J . MARGOLIS AWARD

award.margolis.com

Sponsored by Blue Mountain Center. Given annually to a promising young journalist or essayist whose work combines warmth, humor, wisdom, and concern with social justice. Submit at least two examples of published or unpublished work and a short biographical note, including a description of current and anticipated work. Length: 30 pages maximum.

Deadline: July 1
Prize: $5,000 plus a one-month residency at the Blue Mountain Center in Blue Mountain Lake, New York

PLAYS, SCRIPTS, SCREENPLAYS

ACADEMY NICHOLL FELLOWSHIPS IN SCREENWRITING

www.oscars.org/nicholl/about

International contest open to any writer who has not optioned or sold a treatment, teleplay, or screenplay for more than $25,000. May submit up to three scripts.

Deadline: submit between March 7 and May 2
Entry fee: $45-85, depending on submission date
Prizes: up to five $35,000 fellowships; recipients will be expected to

complete at least one original feature-film screenplay during the fellowship year

AMERICAN ZOETROPE SCREENPLAY CONTEST

www.zoetrope.com/contests

To find and promote new and innovative voices in cinema. For screenplays and television pilots. No entrant may have earned more than $5,000 as a screenwriter for theatrical films or television or for the sale of, or sale of an option to, any original story, treatment, screenplay, or teleplay. Prizes, fellowships, awards, and other contest winnings are not considered earnings and are excluded from this rule. Length: film scripts, 70-130 pages; one-hour television pilot scripts, 45-65 pages; half-hour television scripts, 22-34 pages.

Deadline: September 19
Entry fee: $35-$50, depending on submission date
Prizes: first place, $5,000, plus consideration for film option and development; ten finalists will also get this consideration

AUSTIN FILM FESTIVAL SCREENWRITERS COMPETITION

austinfilmfestival.com/submit

Offers a number of contest categories, including narrative feature, narrative short, documentary feature, documentary short for screenplays, screenplay, teleplay, and scripted digital competition.

Deadline: varies by type
Entry fee: $35-70, varies by type and submission date
Prizes: $1,000-$5,000

KAIROS PRIZE FOR SPIRITUALLY UPLIFTING SCREENPLAYS

www.kairosprize.com

Sponsored by Movieguide. For feature-length screenplays. Judges consider not only a script's entertainment value and craftsmanship, but also whether it is uplifting, inspirational, and spiritual and if it teaches lessons in ethics and morality. Length: 87-130 pages; will accept scripts up to 150 pages (not counting the title page) for an additional $20.

Deadline: October
Entry fee: varies, depending on submission date
Prizes: $15,000 each for first-time and professional screenwriters

MILDRED AND ALBERT PANOWSKI PLAYWRITING COMPETITION

www.nmu.edu/forestrobertstheatre/playwritingcompetition

Sponsored by Forest Roberts Theatre, Northern Michigan University. Unpublished, unproduced, full-length plays. Award to encourage and stimulate artistic growth among educational and professional playwrights. Provides students and faculty members the opportunity to mount and produce an original work on the university stage.

Deadline: submit between June 1 and December 1

Prize: $2,000, a summer workshop, a fully mounted production, and transportation to Marquette, Michigan

MOONDANCE INTERNATIONAL FILM FESTIVAL COMPETITION

www.moondancefilmfestival.com

Offers a variety of awards for films, screenplays, librettos, and features that raise awareness about social issues.

Deadline: May 30

Entry fees: $50–100

Prize: promotion to film companies for possible option

SCRIPTAPALOOZA SCREENPLAY COMPETITION

www.scriptapalooza.com/competition/awards.php

Any screenplay from any genre considered; must be the original work of the author (multiple authorship acceptable). Shorts competition: screenplays fewer than 40 pages.

Deadline: submit between January 5 to April 30

Entry fee: varies by submission date

Prizes: first place, $10,000; each genre winner, $500 (action, adventure, comedy, drama, family, science fiction, thriller/ horror, historical), plus access to more than 50 producers through Scriptapalooza's network

SCRIPTAPALOOZA TV COMPETITION

www.scriptapaloozatv.com/competition

Scripts for television pilots, one-hour dramas, reality shows, and half-hour sitcoms. Length: pilots, 30-60 pages; one-hour program, 50-60 pages; reality show, one- to five-page treatment; half-hour sitcom, 25-35 pages.

Deadline: submit October 2-16

Entry fee: $45-50, varies with deadline

Prizes in each category: first place, $500; second place, $200; third place, $100, plus access to more than 50 producers through Scriptapalooza's network

POETRY

49TH PARALLEL POETRY AWARD

bhreview.org/contest-submissions-guidelines

Sponsored by Western Washington University's *Bellingham Review*. Up to three poems in any style or on any subject.

Deadline: submit between December 1 and March 15
Entry fee: $20; international entries, $30
Prize: $1,000 and publication

ANHINGA-ROBERT DANA PRIZE FOR POETRY

www.anhingapress.org/anhinga-robert-dana-prize

Sponsored by Anhinga Press. For poets submitting a manuscript of original poems in English. Length: 48–80 pages.

Deadline: February 15 to May 30
Entry fee: $28 per manuscript
Prize: $2,000, a reading tour, and publication by Anhinga Press

BALTIMORE REVIEW POETRY CONTEST

baltimorereview.submittable.com/submit

All styles and forms of poetry, directed toward an announced theme. Maximum of three entries.

Deadline: November 30
Entry fee: $10
Prizes: $100-500 and publication

BARBARA MANDIGO KELLY PEACE POETRY AWARDS

www.peacecontests.org/#poetry

Sponsored by Nuclear Age Peace Foundation. Awards to encourage poets to explore and illuminate positive visions of peace and the human spirit. Poems must be original, unpublished, and in English. May submit up to three poems for one entry fee.

Deadline: July 1
Entry fee: adults, $15; youth ages 13-18, $5; none for ages 12 and under
Prizes: adult winner, $1,000; youth winner, $200; ages 12 and under, $200

BLUE MOUNTAIN ARTS POETRY CARD CONTEST

www.sps.com/poetry

Biannual contest. Original poems. May be rhymed or unrhymed, although unrhymed is preferred. Poems also considered for greeting cards or anthologies. Original creations in English only. No limit to number of entries.

Deadlines: June 30 and December 31
Entry fee: none
Prizes: $350, $200, $100

BOSTON REVIEW ANNUAL POETRY CONTEST

www.bostonreview.net./contests

Submit up to five unpublished poems in English; no more than ten pages total. Submit manuscripts in duplicate with cover note.

Deadline: June 1
Entry fee: $20, includes a subscription to *Boston Review*
Prize: $1,500 plus publication

CAVE CANEM POETRY PRIZE

cavecanempoets.org/prizes/cave-canem-poetry-prize

Sponsored by Cave Canem Foundation. Supports the work of black poets of African descent with excellent manuscripts and who have not found a publisher for their first book. Offered every other year. Length: 48-75 pages.

Deadline: varies, with a spring season date
Entry fee: $15
Prize: $1,000 plus publication by a national press and copies of the book, with a feature reading in New York City

THE COMSTOCK REVIEW CHAPBOOK CONTEST

comstockreview.org/comstock-writers-group-chapbook

Submissions must be unpublished as a collection, but individual poems may have been published previously in journals. Length: 25-34 pages. Poems may run longer than one page.

Deadline: submit between August 1 and October 31
Entry fee: $30
Prize: $1,000 plus publication and author copies

FLO GAULT STUDENT POETRY PRIZE

www.sarabandebooks.org/flo-gault

Sponsored by Sarabande Books. For full-time Kentucky undergraduate students. Submit up to three poems.

Deadline: submit September 1—November 15
Prize: $500 and publication

HOLLIS SUMMERS POETRY PRIZE

www.ohioswallow.com/poetry_prize

Sponsored by Ohio University Press. For an unpublished collection of original poems written in English, 60–95 pages. Open to both those who have not published a book-length collection and to those who have.

Deadline: December 1
Entry fee: $30
Prize: $1,000 plus publication in book form by Ohio University Press

THE JAMES LAUGHLIN AWARD

www.poets.org/academy-american-poets/james-laughlin-award-guidelines

Sponsored by Academy of American Poets. To recognize a second full-length print book of original poetry by a US citizen, permanent resident, or person who has DACA/TPS status, forthcoming within the next calendar year. Author must have published one book of poetry in English in a standard edition (48 pages or more) in the United States; publication of chapbooks (less than 48 pages) does not disqualify. Length: 48-100 pages.

Prize: $5,000 plus publication

KATE TUFTS DISCOVERY AWARD

www.cgu.edu/tufts

Sponsored by Claremont Graduate University. Award presented annually for a first poetry volume published in the preceding year by a poet of genuine promise.

Deadline: June 30
Prize: $10,000

KINGSLEY TUFTS POETRY AWARD

www.cgu.edu/pages/6422.asp

Sponsored by Claremont Graduate University. Presented annually for a published book of poetry by a midcareer poet to both honor the poet and provide the resources that allow artists to continue working toward the pinnacle of their craft.

Deadline: June 30
Prize: $100,000

MURIEL CRAFT BAILEY MEMORIAL POETRY AWARD

comstockreview.org/annual-contest

Sponsored by *The Comstock Review*. Unpublished poems up to 40 lines. No limit on number of submissions.

Deadline: submit between April 1 and July 15
Entry fee: postal: $5 per poem for up to five poems; online: $27.50 for five poems
Prizes: first place, $1,000; second place, $250; third place, $100

NEW LETTERS PRIZE FOR POETRY

www.newletters.org/writers-wanted/writing-contests

A single poetry entry may contain up to six poems, and the poems need not be related.

Deadline: May 18
Entry fee: $20 first entry, $15 for every subsequent entry; if entering online, add a $5 service charge to entry fee; includes a one-year subscription to *New Letters*
Prize: $1,500 for best group of three to six poems

PHILIP LEVINE PRIZE FOR POETRY

www.fresnostate.edu/artshum/english/levineprize

Sponsored by California State University Department of English. An annual book contest for original English, previously unpublished, full-length poetry manuscripts. Length: 48-80 pages with no more than one poem per page.

Deadline: submit between July 1 and September 30
Entry fee: $25
Prize: $2,000 and publication by Anhinga Press

POETRY SOCIETY OF VIRGINIA POETRY CONTESTS

poetrysocietyofvirginia.org

More than twenty-five categories for adults and students. Form and length limit of entries vary according to the categories. All entries must be unpublished, original, and not scheduled for publication before the winners of the competition are announced.

Deadline: submit between November 1 and January 19
Entry fee: $5 per poem for nonmembers
Prizes: $100, $50, $30, $20, varying according to specific competition

RICHARD PETERSON POETRY PRIZE

craborchardreview.siu.edu/submissions-annual-lit.html

Sponsored by *Crab Orchard Review*, Southern Illinois University, Carbondale Department of English, on an announced theme. Unpublished poems by a United States citizen, permanent resident, or person who has DACA/TPS status. Length: five pages maximum. Limit three entries.

Deadline: submit between August 30 and October 31 (may vary)
Entry fee: $12
Prize: $1,250 and publication online

SLIPSTREAM ANNUAL POETRY CHAPBOOK COMPETITION

www.slipstreampress.org/contest.html

Sponsored by Slipstream Press. Entries may be any style, format, or theme. Length: 40 pages maximum.

Deadline: December 1
Entry fee: $20
Prize: $1,000 plus fifty published copies of chapbook

SOUL-MAKING KEATS LITERARY COMPETITION: JANICE FARRELL POETRY PRIZE

soulmakingcontest.us/guidelines-rules/

Sponsored by National League of American Pen Women. Three poems per entry. One poem per page, one-page poems only. Free verse, blank verse, and prose poems.

Deadline: November 30
Entry fee: $5 per entry
Prizes: first place, $100; second place, $50; third place, $25

SUMMERTIME BLUES POETRY CONTEST

www.thestorytellermagazine.com

Sponsored by *The Storyteller* magazine. Poems may be rhyming or nonrhyming and should be about summer, although this topic isn't mandatory. Length: 40 lines maximum. Multiple entries accepted.

Deadline: postmarked by August 31
Entry fee: $5 per three poems
Prizes: first place, $25 plus publication; second place, $15; third place, $10

TOI DERRICOTTE & CORNELIUS EADY CHAPBOOK PRIZE

cavecanempoets.org/prizes/toi-derricotte-cornelius-eady-chapbook-prize

Sponsored by Cave Canem Foundation. Dedicated to the discovery of exceptional chapbook-length manuscripts by black poets. Presented in collaboration with the O, Miami Poetry Festival and The Center for the Humanities at the CUNY Graduate Center.

Deadline: September 30
Entry Fee: $12
Prize: $500, publication, ten copies of the chapbook, a four-day writer residency, and a feature reading

TOM HOWARD/MARGARET REID POETRY CONTEST

winningwriters.com/our-contests/tom-howard-margaret-reid-poetry-contest

Sponsored by Winning Writers. Poetry in any style or genre. Length: 250 lines maximum.

Deadline: submit between April 15 and September 30
Entry fee: $12 per poem
Prizes: Tom Howard Prize, $1,500 for poem in any style or genre; Margaret Reid Prize, $1,500 for poem that rhymes or has a traditional style; $100 each for ten honorable mentions in any style

UTMOST NOVICE CHRISTIAN POETRY CONTEST

www.utmostchristianwriters.com/poetry-contest/poetry-contest-rules.php

Sponsored by Utmost Christian Writers Foundation. Unpublished poems may be rhymed or free verse, up to 60 lines. Need not be religious in content. Maximum of five entries.

Deadline: February 28
Entry fee: $20 per poem
Prizes: $1,000, $500, $300, $200; ten honorable mentions, $100; best rhyming poem, $300; honorable mention rhyming poem, $200

VIOLET REED HAAS PRIZE FOR POETRY

www.snakenationpress.org/submission-guidelines

Sponsored by Snake Nation Press. Length: 75-100 page manuscript. Previously published eligible.

Deadline: August 31
Entry fee: $25
Prize: $1,000 plus publication

WERGLE FLOMP HUMOR POETRY CONTEST

winningwriters.com/our-contests/wergle-flomp-humor-poetry-contest-free

Sponsored by Winning Writers. Submit one published or unpublished humor poem up to 250 lines.

Deadline: April 1
Entry fee: none
Prizes: first place, $1,000; second place, $250; ten honorable mentions, $100; plus the top twelve entries will be published online

MULTIPLE GENRES

ATHANATOS CHRISTIAN MINISTRIES NOVEL AND NONFICTION CONTEST

www.christianwritingcontest.com

A contest to develop a genre of fiction that might be called "literary apologetics," the use of fiction and story to communicate the gospel and the worldview associated with it. Length: 40,000–90,000 words.

Deadline: March 1
Entry fee: $90-100
Prizes: first place, $2,500 and possible book contract; two runner-up awards, $1,000 and possible book contract

BLUE RIDGE CONFERENCE WRITING CONTEST

www.blueridgeconference.com/contest-info

Sponsors three book contests for fiction or nonfiction: Foundation Awards, Director's Choice, and The Selahs. Look for details about guidelines, deadlines, and entry fees on the website after January 1.

CHRISTIAN INDIE AWARDS

www.christianaward.com

This award is designed to promote and bring recognition to quality Christian books by small publishers and independently published authors. Books must be printed in English, for sale in the United States, and promote the Christian faith. Publishers and authors may nominate titles for the award, and Christian readers vote to determine the winners.

Deadline: November 15
Entry fee: $45

COLUMBIA JOURNAL CONTESTS

columbiajournal.org/submit/winter-contest

Fiction and nonfiction, 5,000 words maximum; poetry, five pages maximum.

Deadline: December 1
Entry fee: $15 per submission
Prizes: $500 plus publication in each category

EDITOR'S REPRINT AWARDS

www.sequestrum.org/editors-reprint-award-fiction-and-nonfiction
www.sequestrum.org/editors-reprint-award-poetry

Sponsored by *Sequestrum* journal. Contest open to previously published manuscripts in prose (fiction and creative nonfiction up to 12,000 words) and poetry (up to 50 lines).

Deadline: April 30
Entry fee: $15
Prizes: first prize awarded in both categories, $200 and publication; runners-up, $25 and publication

ERIC HOFFER BOOK AWARD

www.hofferaward.com

Eighteen categories for books from small, academic, and micro presses, including self-published, e-books, and older books. The prose category is for creative fiction and nonfiction fewer than 10,000 words.

Deadline: January 21
Entry fee: varies by category
Prizes: $2,000 grand prize, other prizes awarded in categories

THE EUPLE RINEY MEMORIAL AWARD

www.thestorytellermagazine.com

Sponsored by *The Storyteller*. Open-genre contest but must be about family—good or bad. Can be fiction or nonfiction (indicate which). Length: 3,000 words maximum. No pornography, graphic anything, New Age, or children's stories will be accepted.

Deadline: June 30
Entry fee: $5
Prizes: first place, $50; second place, $25; third place, $15; honorable mention, $10. Plus an editor's choice award.

EVANGELICAL PRESS ASSOCIATION CONTEST

www.evangelicalpress.com/contest

Higher Goals awards in a variety of categories for periodical manuscripts published in the previous year. Although most submissions are made by publication staff members, associate EPA members may also submit their articles.

Deadline: early January

Entry fee: $50

INSCRIBE CHRISTIAN WRITERS' FELLOWSHIP CONTEST

inscribe.org/contests

Sponsors contests for InScribe members: Fall Contest, Winter Contest, Word Challenge, FellowScript Contests, Barnabas Award, Janette Oke Award, Post Conference Contest.

Deadline, entry fees, awards: vary with each contest

INSPIRATIONAL WRITERS ALIVE! OPEN WRITING COMPETITION

www.centralhoustoniwa.com

Categories: article, poetry, short story for young adults/adults, short story for children/teens, devotional, book proposal for nonfiction and fiction, drama. Limit of two entries in each category. Members receive discounts on entry fees. Awards presented to winners at the Texas Christian Writers' Conference each fall.

Deadline: submit between January 1 and May 15

Entry fee: $5–$15, depending on category and membership status

Prizes: first place, $30; second place, $20; third place, $15

NARRATIVE MAGAZINE CONTESTS

www.narrativemagazine.com/submit-your-work

Biannual contests in a variety of categories, including short stories, essays, memoirs, poetry, and literary nonfiction. Entries must be previously unpublished. Length: varies by category.

Deadline: varies

Entry fee: varies

Prizes: vary by category

NARRATIVE MAGAZINE 30 BELOW CONTEST

www.narrativemagazine.com/node/345528

For writers ages 18-30. Fiction, nonfiction, poetry (up to five poems), essays, memoirs. Length: 15,000 words maximum. Restrictions on previously published works.

Deadline: November 19
Entry fee: $25 per entry
Prizes: $1,500, $750, $300, plus ten finalists will receive $100 each

NATIONAL WRITERS ASSOCIATION CONTESTS

www.nationalwriters.com/page/page/2734945.htm

Sponsors six contests: nonfiction, novel, young writers, poetry, short short, and David Raffelock Award for Publishing Excellence.

Deadline: varies by contest
Entry fee: varies by contest
Prizes: vary by contest

NEW LETTERS AWARDS FOR WRITERS

www.newletters.org/writers-wanted/writing-contests

Sponsored by University of Missouri—Kansas City. Entries accepted in these categories: poetry, essay, short-story.

Deadline: May 18
Entry fee: $20 for first entry; $15/additional entry
Prize: $1,500 for the best in each category

NEW MILLENNIUM AWARDS

submit.newmillenniumwritings.org

Sponsored by New Millennium Writings. Fiction and nonfiction: 6,000 words maximum. Flash fiction (short-short story): 1,000 words maximum. Poetry: three poems to five pages total. No restrictions as to style or subject matter.

Deadline: November 30
Entry fees: $20, $45 for three entries, $72 for five entries
Prizes: $1,000 plus publication for each category

OREGON CHRISTIAN WRITERS CASCADE AWARDS

oregonchristianwriters.org

Contests for novels; nonfiction books; memoir; young adult/middle grade fiction and nonfiction books; poetry; children's chapter and picture books; articles, columns, and blog posts; short stories/flash fiction; and devotionals. Separate divisions for published and unpublished authors.

Deadline: submit between February 14 and March 31
Entry fees: $30-35 for members, $40-45 for nonmembers; awards presented at the summer conference in Portland, Oregon

PROMISING BEGINNINGS CHRISTIAN WRITERS' CONTEST

www.KathyIde.com

This contest is open to both published and unpublished writers. Submit the first five pages of an unpublished or self-published book manuscript, fiction or nonfiction (any genre except poetry), for YA or adult readership (no children's). Must follow the formatting guidelines on the Promising Beginnings blog at *www.KathyIde.com*. Submissions will be judged on whether the quality of the writing shows promise.

Deadline: November 30
Entry fee: none
Prize: full scholarship to Mount Hermon Christian Writers Conference (including meals and economy lodging) or to SoCalChristian Writers' Conference (including meals, dorm lodging, and travel reimbursement)

SOUL-MAKING KEATS LITERARY COMPETITION

www.soulmakingcontest.us

Sponsored by National League of American Pen Women, Nob Hill, San Francisco Branch. Categories include flash fiction, short story, memoir vignette, humor, novel excerpt, intercultural essay, creative nonfiction, religious essay, young-adult poetry, and young-adult prose.

Deadline: November 30
Entry fee: $5
Prizes in each category: first place, $100; second place, $50; third place, $25

TENNESSEE WILLIAMS/NEW ORLEANS LITERARY FESTIVAL

tennesseewilliams.net/contests

Tennessee Williams gained some early recognition by entering a writing contest. The festival that bears his name now sponsors writing contests in poetry, fiction, very short fiction, and one-act playwriting.

Deadline, entry fee, prizes: vary according to genre

WILLIAM FAULKNER–WILLIAM WISDOM CREATIVE WRITING COMPETITION

wordsandmusic.org/william-faulkner-wisdom-competition/competition-guidelines

Sponsored by The Pirate's Alley Faulkner Society, Inc. Seven categories: novel, novella, book-length narrative fiction, novel-in-progress, short story, essay, poetry, and short story by a high-school student. For previously unpublished work only.

Deadline: submit between January 1 and May 15
Entry fee: varies by category
Prizes: $250-7,500, depending on category

THE WORD GUILD CHRISTIAN WRITING AWARDS

thewordguild.com/contests

The Word Awards recognize the best work published in the previous year in thirty-five categories of writing, including novels, nonfiction books, articles, columns, poems, song lyrics, scripts, and screenplays. Fresh Ink Student Writers Contest for never-before-published student writers. In the Beginning for unpublished novice and emerging writers. The Grace Irwin Prize for Canadian writers who are Christians; recognizes the best book published in the previous year. The Leslie K. Tarr Award celebrates a major career contribution to Christian writing and publishing in Canada. The Partnership Award recognizes an individual or organization that has shown exceptional support and encouragement for Canadian writers and editors who are Christians.

Deadline, entry fees, prizes: vary according to the award and its guidelines

WRITER'S DIGEST COMPETITIONS

www.writersdigest.com/writers-digest-competitions

Every other month, *Writer's Digest* presents a creative challenge for fun and prizes, providing a short, open-ended prompt for short-story submissions based on that prompt. Winner receives publication in *Writer's Digest*. Also sponsors annual contests for feature articles, short stories (multiple genres), poetry, personal essays, and self-published books (categories vary).

Deadline, entry fees: vary according to contest
Prizes for annual contest: first place, $1,000; second place, $500; and more places for each contest; grand prize, $5,000

THE WRITERS' UNION OF CANADA AWARDS & COMPETITIONS

www.writersunion.ca/awards

Short Prose Competition for Developing Writers for fiction or nonfiction by an author who has not yet published a book. Length: 2,500 words maximum. Danuta Gleed Literary Award for the best first collection of short fiction.

Deadlines: Short Prose, March 1; Danuta, January 31
Entry fee: $29
Prizes: Short Prose, $2,500; Danuta, $10,000, plus two finalist awards for $500 each

WRITERS-EDITORS NETWORK ANNUAL INTERNATIONAL WRITING COMPETITION

www.writers-editors.com/Writers/Contests/Contest_Guidelines/contest_guidelines.htm

Nonfiction and fiction: 4,000 words maximum; children's literature (story, fiction-book chapter, poem, magazine article, or nonfiction-book chapter targeted to a specific age group): 4,000 words maximum. Poetry may be traditional or free verse. All entries must be unpublished or self-published and not accepted for publication by a traditional publisher at the time they are entered in the contest.

Deadline: March 15
Entry fees: poetry, $5 for members, $10 for nonmembers; prose: $10 for members, $20 for nonmembers
Prizes: $150, $100, $75, plus one-year membership in Writers-Editors Network

RESOURCES FOR CONTESTS

These websites are sources for announcements about other contests.

DAILY WRITING TIPS

www.dailywritingtips.com/25-writing-competitions

FREELANCE WRITING

www.freelancewriting.com/writingcontests.php

FUNDS FOR WRITERS

fundsforwriters.com/contests

NEW PAGES

www.newpages.com/classifieds/big-list-of-writing-contests

POETS & WRITERS

www.pw.org/grants

TETHERED BY LETTERS
tetheredbyletters.com/resources/contest-list

THE WRITE LIFE
thewritelife.com/27-free-writing-contests

THE WRITER
www.writermag.com/writing-resources/contests

DENOMINATIONAL PUBLISHERS

ANGLICAN
The Anglican Journal

ASSEMBLIES OF GOD
Enrichment
God's Word for Today
Live
My Healthy Church
Take Five Plus

BAPTIST
B&H Publishing
The Brink
CommonCall
Earthen Vessel Publishing
Facts & Trends
HomeLife
Judson Press
Mature Living
On Mission
Point
Parenting Teens
ParentLife
Randall House Publications
The Secret Place
Triple J Publishing, LLC
Word&Way

BRETHREN
BMH Books
GraceConnect
In Part

CATHOLIC
Acta Publications
America
American Catholic Press
The Arlington Catholic Herald
Ave Maria Press
Catholic Book Publishing Corp.
Catholic Digest
Catholic New York
Catholic Sentinel
Celebrate Life
Christ Our Hope
Columbia
Commonweal
Eureka Street
Franciscan Media
Image Books
Leaves
Liguorian
Liturgical Press
Loyola Press
Our Sunday Visitor Newsweekly

Paraclete Press
Parish Liturgy
Pauline Books & Media
Paulist Press
Prairie Messenger
Resurrection Press
Scepter Publishers
St. Anthony Messenger
Saint Catherine of Siena Press
St. Mary's Messenger
U.S. Catholic

CHARISMATIC

See Pentecostal.

CHRISTIAN CHURCH/ CHURCH OF CHRIST

Christian Standard
College Press Publishing

CHURCH OF GOD

Bible Advocate
The Church Herald & Holiness Banner
The Gem
Gems of Truth
Now What?
Pathways to God
Pentecostal Messenger
Warner Press

EPISCOPAL

Forward Day by Day
Forward Movement
The Living Church

EVANGELICAL COVENANT

The Covenant Companion

EVANGELICAL FREE

EFCA Today

LUTHERAN

Canada Lutheran
The Canadian Lutheran
Concordia Publishing House
Fortress Press
Langmarc Publishing
The Lutheran Digest
Lutheran Forum
The Lutheran Journal
Lutheran Witness
Northwestern Publishing House
Sparkhouse Family
The Word in Season

MENNONITE

Canadian Mennonite
The Messenger
Purpose

MESSIANIC

The Messianic Times

METHODIST

Abingdon Press
Christian Living in the Mature Years
Good News
Light + Life Magazine
Methodist History
Pockets
The Upper Room
Weavings

NAZARENE

Beacon Hill Press
Holiness Today
Reflecting God
Standard

OPEN BIBLE

Message of the Open Bible

ORTHODOX
Ancient Faith Publishing

PENTECOSTAL/CHARISMATIC
Charisma
Empowered Publications, Inc.
Harrison House Publishers
Ministry Today
Whitaker House

PRESBYTERIAN
byFaith
Presbyterians Today
These Days
Westminster/John Knox Press

QUAKER/FRIENDS
Friends Journal
Friends United Press

REFORMED
Christian Courier
Faith Alive Christian Resources
P&R Publishing
Perspectives

SALVATION ARMY
Faith & Friends
New Frontier Chronicle
SAConnects
War Cry
Young Salvationist

SEVENTH-DAY ADVENTIST
Guide
Insight
Ministry
Our Little Friend
Pacific Press
Primary Treasure
Vibrant Life

UNITED CHURCH OF CANADA
United Church Observer

WESLEYAN
Light from the Word

GLOSSARY

Advance: Money a publisher pays to an author up front, against future royalties. The amount varies greatly from publisher to publisher and is often paid in two or three installments (on signing the contract, on delivery of the manuscript, and on publication).

All rights: An outright sale of your manuscript. The author has no further control over any subsidiary rights.

Anecdote: A short, poignant, real-life story, usually used to illustrate a single thought. It need not be humorous.

Assignment: When an editor asks a writer to create a specific manuscript for an agreed-on price.

As-told-to story: A true story you write as a first-person account about someone else.

Audience: The people who are expected to be reading your manuscript, in terms of age, life experience, knowledge of and interest level in the story or subject. Publishers want to be sure a writer understands their assumed audience well.

Audiobooks: Spoken-word books available on compact disc, MP3 file, or streaming via the internet.

Backlist: A publisher's previously published books that are still in print a year or more after publication.

Bar code: Identification code and price on the back of a book, read by a scanner at checkout counters.

Bible versions:

AMP—*Amplified Bible*
ASV—*American Standard Version*
CEB—*Common English Bible*

CEV—*Contemporary English Version*
CSB—*Christian Standard Bible*
ESV—*English Standard Version*
GNB—*Good News Bible*
GWB—*God's Word Bible*
HCSB—*Holman Christian Standard* Bible
ICB—*International Children's Bible*
KJV—*King James Version*
MEV—*Modern English Version*
MSG—*The Message*
NAB—*New American Bible*
NABRE—*New American Bible Revised Edition*
NASB—*New American Standard Bible*
NEB—*New English Bible*
NET—*New English Translation*
NIrV—*New International Reader's Version*
NIV—*New International Version*
NJB—*New Jerusalem Bible*
NKJV—*New King James Version*
NLT—*New Living Translation*
NRSV—*New Revised Standard Version*
RSV—*Revised Standard Version*
TEV—*Today's English Translation* (aka *Good News Bible*)
TLB—*The Living Bible*
TNIV—*Today's New International Version*

Bio: Brief information about the author.

Bluelines: The last printer's proofs used to catch errors before a book or periodical is printed. May be physical pages or digital proofs in PDF format.

Book proposal: Submission of a book idea to an agent or editor. It usually includes a hook, summary and purpose of the book, target market, uniqueness of the book compared to similar ones in the marketplace, chapter-by-chapter summaries or plot synopsis, marketing and promotion information, your credentials, and delivery date, plus one to three sample chapters, including the first one.

Byline: Author's name printed below the title of a story, article, etc.

Camera-ready copy: The text and artwork for a book that are ready for the press.

Chapbook: A small book or pamphlet containing poetry, religious readings, etc.

Circulation: The number of copies sold or distributed of each issue of a periodical.

Clips: Copies of articles you have had published in newspapers or magazines.

Column: A regularly appearing feature, section, or department in a periodical with the same heading. It's written by the same person or a different freelancer each time.

Concept statement: A 50- to 150-word summary of your proposed book.

Contributing editor: A freelance writer who has a regular column or writes regularly for the periodical.

Contributor's copy: Copy of an issue of a periodical sent to an author whose work appears in it.

Copyright: Legal protection of an author's work. A manuscript is automatically copyrighted in your name when you produce it. You don't need to register it with the Copyright Office unless you are self-publishing a book or other publication.

Cover letter: A letter that accompanies some manuscript submissions. Usually it's needed only if you have to tell the editor something specific, to give your credentials for writing a manuscript of a technical nature, or to remind the editor that the manuscript was requested or expected. Often used as the introduction to a book proposal. Rarely used for an article submission; query letters are used instead.

Credits, list of: A listing of your previously published works.

Critique: An evaluation of a manuscript.

Defamation: A written or spoken injury to the reputation of a living person or organization. If what is said is true, it cannot be defamatory.

Derivative work: A work derived from another work, such as a condensation or abridgment. Contact the copyright owner for permission before doing the abridgment, and be prepared to pay that owner a fee or royalty.

Devotional: A short manuscript based on a Scripture verse or passage that shares a personal spiritual discovery, inspires to worship, challenges to commitment or action, or encourages.

Editorial guidelines: See "Writers guidelines."

Endorsements: Flattering comments about a book, usually printed on the back cover or in promotional material.

Essay: A short composition expressing the author's opinion on a specific subject.

Evangelical: A person who believes that one receives God's forgiveness for sins through Jesus Christ and believes the Bible is the authoritative word of God. This is a broad definition for a label with broad application.

Exegesis: Interpretation of a Scripture passage.

Feature article: In-depth coverage of a subject, usually focusing on a person, an event, a process, an organization, a movement, a trend, or an issue. It's written to explain, encourage, help, analyze, challenge, motivate, warn, or entertain, as well as to inform.

Filler: A short item used to "fill" a page of a periodical. It could be a joke, anecdote, light verse, short humor, puzzle, game, etc.

First rights: An editor buys the right to publish a manuscript that has never been published and to do so only once.

Foreign rights: Selling or giving permission to translate or reprint published material in another country.

Foreword: Opening remarks in a book to introduce the book and its author.

Freelance: Supplied by freelance writers.

Freelancer or freelance writer: A writer who is not on salary but sells his or her material to a number of different publishers.

Galley proof: A typeset copy of a book used to detect and correct errors before printing.

General market: Non-Christian market, sometimes called secular market.

Genre: Refers to a type or classification, as in fiction or poetry. For instance, westerns, romances, and mysteries are fiction genres.

Glossy: A photo with a shiny, rather than matte, finish. Also, a publication printed on such paper.

Go-ahead: When a publisher tells you to write or submit your article.

Hard copy: A printed manuscript, as opposed to one sent via email.

Holiday/seasonal: A manuscript that has to do with a specific holiday or season. This material must reach the editor the stated number of months prior to the holiday or season.

Honorarium: A small flat fee, as opposed to paying a set amount per word.

Humor: The amusing or comical aspects of life that add warmth and color to an article or story.

Independent book publisher: A book publisher who charges authors to publish their books or buy a certain number of copies, as opposed to a royalty house that pays authors. Some independent publishers also pay a royalty. Sometimes called a subsidy, vanity, or custom publisher.

Interdenominational: Distributed to a number of different denominations.

ISBN: International Standard Book Number, an identification code needed for every version of a book.

Journal: A periodical presenting information in a particular area, often for an academic or educated audience.

Kill fee: A fee paid for a completed article done on assignment that is subsequently not published. The amount is usually 25–50% of the original payment.

Libel: To defame someone by an opinion or a misquote that puts his or her reputation in jeopardy.

Little/Literary: Small-circulation periodicals whose focus is providing a forum for the literary writer, rather than on making money. Often they do not pay or pay in copies.

Mainstream fiction: Other than genre fiction (such as romance, mystery, or fantasy). Stories of people and their conflicts handled on a deeper level.

Mass market: Books intended for a wide, general market, produced in a smaller format, usually with smaller type and sold at a lower price. The expectation is that their sales will be higher.

Ms: Abbreviation for manuscript.

Mss: Abbreviation for more than one manuscript.

Multiple submissions: Submitting more than one manuscript at a time to the same publisher, usually reserved for poetry, greeting cards, or fillers, not articles. Also see "Simultaneous submissions."

NASR: Abbreviation for North American serial rights. Permission for a periodical targeting readers in the US and Canada to publish a piece.

New-adult fiction: A developing fiction genre with protagonists ages 18-25. In the general market, these novels often explore sexual themes considered too "adult" for the YA or teen market. They tend to be marketed to older teen readers.

Nondenominational: Not associated with a particular denomination.

Novella: A short novel, usually 20,000–35,000 words. The length varies from publisher to publisher.

On acceptance: Publisher pays a writer at the time the manuscript is accepted for publication.

On assignment: Writing a manuscript at the specific request of an editor.

On publication: Publisher pays a writer when his or her manuscript is published.

On speculation/spec: Writing something for an editor with the agreement that the editor will buy it only if he or she likes it.

Onetime rights: Selling the right to publish a manuscript one time to more than one periodical, primarily to nonoverlapping audiences, such as different denominations.

Over the transom: Unsolicited manuscripts sent to a book editor. Comes from the old "transom" which was a window above the door in office buildings. Manuscripts could be pushed "over the transom" into the locked office.

Overrun: The extra copies of a book printed during the initial print run.

Pen name/pseudonym: A name other than your legal name used on a manuscript to protect your identity or that of people included or when you wish to remain anonymous. Put the pen name in the byline under the title and your real name with your contact information.

Periodical: A magazine, newsletter, or newspaper.

Permissions: Asking permission to use text or art from a copyrighted source.

Personal experience: An account based on a real-life experience.

Personality profile: A feature article that highlights a specific person's life or accomplishments.

Plagiarism: Stealing and using the ideas or writing of someone else as your own, either as is or rewriting slightly to make them sound like your own.

POD/Print-on-demand: A printing process where books are printed one at a time or in small numbers instead of in quantity. The production cost per book is higher, but no warehousing is necessary.

POV: Point-of-view. A fiction term that describes the perspective of the one telling the story, such as first person or third person.

Press kit: A compilation of promotional materials for a book or author, used to publicize a book.

Public domain: Work for which copyright protection has expired. Copyright laws vary from country to country; but in the US, works published before 1923 have entered the public domain.

Query letter: A letter sent to an editor about an article or book you propose to write and asking if he or she is interested in seeing it.

Reprint rights: Selling the right to reprint an article that has already been published. You must have sold only first or onetime rights originally and wait until it has been published the first time.

Response time: The number of weeks or months it takes an editor to get back to you about a query, proposal, or manuscript you sent.

Review copies: Books given to reviewers or buyers for bookstore chains and online sellers.

Royalty: The percentage an author is paid by a publisher on the sale of each copy of a book.

SASE: Self-addressed, stamped envelope. Always send it with a hard-copy manuscript or query letter.

SASP: Self-addressed, stamped postcard. May be sent with a hard-copy manuscript to be returned by the editor to indicate it arrived safely.

Satire: Ridicule that aims at reform.

Second serial rights: See "Reprint rights."

Secular market: An outdated term for the non-Christian publishing market.

Serial: Refers to publication in a periodical, such as first serial rights.

Sidebar: A short feature that accompanies an article and either elaborates on the human interest side of the story or gives additional information on the topic. It is often set apart by appearing within a box or border.

Simultaneous submissions: Sending the same manuscript to more than one editor at the same time. Usually this is done with nonoverlapping periodical markets, such as denominational publications or newspapers in different cities, or when you are writing on a timely subject. Most periodical editors don't accept simultaneous submissions, but they are the norm in the book market. Be sure to state in a cover letter that it is a simultaneous submission.

Slander: The verbal act of defamation.

Slanting: Writing an article to meet the needs of a particular market.

Slush pile: The stack of unsolicited manuscripts that arrive at an editor's desk or email inbox.

Staff-written material: Manuscripts written by the members of a magazine staff.

Subsidy publisher: See "Independent book publisher."

Subsidiary rights: All the rights, other than book rights, included in a book contract, such as translations, audiobooks, book clubs, and movies.

Synopsis: A brief summary of a work, ranging from one paragraph to several pages.

Tabloid: A newspaper-format publication about half the size of a regular newspaper.

Take-home paper: A small periodical given to Sunday-school students, children through adults. These mini-magazines are published with the curriculum.

Think piece: A magazine article that has an intellectual, philosophical, or provocative approach to a subject.

Trade magazine: A magazine whose audience is in a particular business.

Unsolicited manuscript: A manuscript an editor did not specifically ask to see.

Vanity publisher: See "Independent book publisher."

Vignette: A short, descriptive literary sketch of a brief scene or incident.

Vita: An outline of one's personal history and experience.

Work-for-hire: A manuscript you create for an agreed payment and give the publisher full ownership and control of it. You must sign a contract for this agreement to be legal.

Writers guidelines: Information provided by an editor that gives specific guidance for writing for the publication or publishing house. If the information is not offered online, email or send an SASE with your request for printed guidelines.

INDEX

B

C

D

E

F

M

N

O

P

R

S

T

U

V

W